THE THINGS WE MEAN

The Things We Mean

Stephen Schiffer

CLARENDON PRESS · OXFORD

OXFORD
UNIVERSITY PRESS

Great Clarendon Street, Oxford OX2 6DP

Oxford University Press is a department of the University of Oxford.
It furthers the University's objective of excellence in research, scholarship,
and education by publishing worldwide in

Oxford New York

Auckland Bangkok Buenos Aires Cape Town Chennai
Dar es Salaam Delhi Hong Kong Istanbul Karachi Kolkata
Kuala Lumpur Madrid Melbourne Mexico City Mumbai Nairobi
São Paulo Shanghai Taipei Tokyo Toronto

Oxford is a registered trade mark of Oxford University Press
in the UK and in certain other countries

Published in the United States
by Oxford University Press Inc., New York

British Library Cataloguing in Publication Data

Data available

Library of Congress Cataloging in Publication Data

Data available

ISBN 0–19–824108–9 (hbk.)
ISBN 0–19–925776–0 (pbk.)

1 3 5 7 9 10 8 6 4 2

Typeset by Newgen Imaging Systems (P) Ltd., Chennai, India
Printed in Great Britain
on acid-free paper by
Biddles Ltd., Guildford & King's Lynn

For Joe

ACKNOWLEDGEMENTS

So many people, over so many years, have helped to determine the views expressed in this book that I can't possibly attempt to thank them here. Among those who have directly influenced this book, either by their comments on parts of it or by conversations with me about the views expressed in it, I would like especially to thank the following: an anonymous reader for Oxford University Press; David Barnett; Dorit Bar-On; Ned Block; Paul Boghossian; Ray Buchanan; David Chalmers; Cian Dorr; James Dreier; David Enoch; Kit Fine; Salvatore Florio; Lizzie Fricker; Paul Horwich; Janine Jones; Andreas Kemmerling; Nikola Kompa; Saul Kripke; Wolfgang Künne; Michael Lynch; Gary Ostertag; Adam Pautz; Chris Peacocke; Adrian Piper; Tobias Rosefeldt; Ian Rumfitt; Josh Schechter; Bartoz Wieckowski; and Tim Williamson. My greatest debt is to Hartry Field. Many of my views were forged or refined in my countless debates and discussions with him, and several of his comments on parts of earlier drafts of this book either suggested specific improvements or exposed mistakes. Most of all, I must thank Michele Crow and Joe Schiffer for the fun I had with them when I wasn't writing this book.

S.S.

CONTENTS

CONTENTS

Introduction

Do there exist such things as the things we mean? If so, then those things are also the things we believe, and the things in terms of which we must understand not only the meanings of linguistic expressions, but their references and truth-values as well. If such entities as the things we mean and believe exist, an account of their nature must be the most foundational concern in what philosophers call *the theory of content*, whose concern is the nature of linguistic and mental representation.

In this book I argue that there do exist such things as the things we mean and believe, and I aim to give an account both of their nature and of how that nature affects certain foundational issues in the theory of content which turn on the nature of content. The book may be viewed as dividing into two main parts. The first part consists of Chapters 1 and 2, and it articulates and partially motivates the positive theory of propositional content this book has to offer (the entire book provides a more complete case for the theory).

In Chapter 1, 'The Face-Value Theory', a prima facie case is made for the face-value theory of belief reports of the form 'A believes that S': that theory of the logical form of those reports which must be defeated if it's not to be accepted. According to this theory, reports of the form in question say that A stands in the belief relation to the proposition that S. This theory leaves open the question of the nature of the propositions to which that-clauses refer. The debate about this further question among face-value theorists tends to presuppose the *compositionality hypothesis* that (nearly enough) the referent of a that-clause token is determined by its structure and the referents its component expressions have in that token. Virtually all face-value theorists who accept the compositionality hypothesis hold that the proposition to which a that-clause refers is, in a sense spelled out in the text, a structured proposition whose components are the referents the expressions in the that-clause have in that that-clause. This seems warranted, for the only conception of unstructured propositions that coheres with the compositionality hypothesis individuates propositions by their possible-worlds truth conditions, and this has the unfortunate consequence that one believes every necessarily true proposition if one believes any, since there is just one such proposition to begin with—namely, the one individuated by the set of all possible worlds.

The big debate among face-value theorists of structured propositions is about the nature of the propositional building blocks, the basic components of the structured propositions to which that-clauses refer. Russellians (as I call them) hold that propositional building blocks are the objects and properties our beliefs are about, whereas Fregeans (as I call them) hold that they aren't those things but rather things we might call *concepts*, or *modes of presentation*, of those objects and properties, it being a question open to debate among Fregeans how exactly these further things are to be understood. Both positions, however, confront serious problems, and the close of the chapter leaves us wondering whether there might not be a plausible account of propositions which coheres with the denial of the compositionality hypothesis.

In Chapter 2, 'Pleonastic Propositions', I present a theory of propositions that complements the face-value theory but doesn't entail the compositionality hypothesis. What is more, the theory enjoys a positive motivation that is independent of the travails of familiar accounts of propositions. Pleonastic propositions are but one kind of pleonastic entity. Pleonastic entities are entities whose existence is secured by *something-from-nothing transformations*, these being conceptually valid inferences that take one from a statement in which no reference is made to a thing of a certain kind to a statement in which there is a reference to a thing of that kind. For example, the property of being a dog is a pleonastic entity. From the statement

> Lassie is a dog,

whose only singular term is 'Lassie', we can validly infer its pleonastic equivalent

> Lassie has the property of being a dog,

which contains the new singular term 'the property of being dog', whose referent is the property of being a dog. It's because something-from-nothing transformations often take one from a statement to a pleonastic equivalent of that statement that I call the entities these transformations introduce *pleonastic* entities. In spelling this out and giving the notion of a pleonastic entity a more rigorous and precise explication, I begin with fictional entities, since they provide a kind of pleonastic entity whose members clearly exemplify certain key attributes I wish to ascribe to all pleonastic entities. The discussion of fictional entities leads to an official definition of pleonastic entities in terms of the notion of one theory's being a conservative extension of another, and the account in these terms is used to show how our knowledge of something-from-nothing entailments (e.g. if Lassie is a dog, then Lassie has the property of being a dog) is a priori conceptual knowledge, thus explaining how we're able to have knowledge and reliable beliefs about these sorts of entity.

The propositions to which that-clauses refer, and thus the propositions comprising the ranges of our propositional-attitude relations, are pleonastic entities (whence 'pleonastic propositions'), but there is more to their nature than can be discerned merely from the something-from-nothing transformations into which they enter. What is especially important for the theory of content are the ways in which the relation between that-clauses and the propositions to which they refer is different from the usual relation between singular terms and their referents. Especially important in this regard is the way in which contextually determined criteria for truth-evaluating belief reports both determine and individuate the propositions to which the that-clauses in those reports refer. An important upshot of this extended discussion is that it enables us to conceptualize pleonastic propositions as both fine-grained *and* unstructured.

Chapters 3 to 8 comprise the second part of the book, wherein the theory of pleonastic propositions is brought to bear on certain issues in the theory of content.

Chapter 3, 'Meanings and Knowledge of Meaning', has as its overarching question 'Are there such *things* as the meanings of expressions and, if so, what is their nature?', but it approaches this question obliquely via the question 'What is it to know what an expression means?' My answer to the knowledge-of-meaning question is given in terms of being in a state that plays a certain role in the information processing that occurs when one understands an utterance, and this answer, together with the dialectic leading up to it, suggests that there are no such things as expression meanings, since, if there were, knowledge of meaning would be something other than what it actually is. There is, however, less to this impressive-sounding result than meets the eye, since things I call *characters** (in homage to David Kaplan's characters, which I argue can't play the role of expression meanings), and which I explain in terms of constraints on pleonastic propositions, can be construed as meanings, since something has meaning just in case it has a character*, and two expressions, in the same or different languages, have the same meaning just in case they have the same character*. This leads to a critical discussion of 'two-dimensional semantics', especially as practised by David Chalmers and Frank Jackson.

Chapter 4, 'Having Meaning', continues the discussion of Chapter 3 by asking what relation must obtain between an expression and a character* in order for the latter to be the character* of the former. This question soon becomes the actual-language-relation question 'What relation must obtain between a person and a language, conceived as a certain kind of abstract entity, in order for that language to be that person's public-language idiolect?' I offer an answer in terms of the preceding chapter's language-processing account of knowledge of meaning, and this answer segues into the language-of-thought-relation question 'What relation must obtain between a person and a language in order for that language to be that person's *lingua mentis*?' I offer an answer that in turn leads to questions, which I do my best to answer, about various kinds of compositional semantics and about the nature of the supervenience of the intentional on the non-intentional, and how best to explain, or at least demystify, it.

Chapter 5, 'Vagueness and Indeterminacy', takes on a topic of paramount importance to the theory of content and to logic. We don't yet know the correct semantics and logic for vague language, and since just about every expression is to some extent vague, this means we don't yet know the correct semantics and logic for natural language. A theory of vagueness must lie at the heart of any complete theory of meaning. This chapter offers a theory of vagueness, and of indeterminacy generally, since the indeterminacy of vague borderline propositions is, as we see in the two subsequent chapters, only one source of indeterminacy, albeit the most prevalent.

Vagueness is a philosophical problem because of the problems it engenders, and all these problems have their source in the infamous sorites paradox: a person with $50 million is rich, and a person with only 3¢ isn't, but you can't remove a person from the ranks of the rich by removing 1¢ from her fortune, which means that, for any n, if a person with n is rich, then so is a person with $n - 1$¢. The paradox is that these three individually plausible claims appear to be mutually incompatible. Now, vagueness is the possibility of borderline cases, and the crux of any resolution of the sorites will be based on what it has to say about what it is to be a borderline case. According to the view I propose, vagueness is neither a semantic nor an epistemological notion, but rather a *psychological* notion. There are, I claim, two kinds of partial belief: *standard partial belief*, the familiar kind which (to a first approximation) is normatively governed by the axioms of classical probability theory and which can therefore be identified, under suitable idealization, with subjective probability, and what I call *vagueness-related partial belief*, which is not normatively governed by the probability calculus and can't under any idealization be identified with subjective probability. To regard something as a borderline case of a property is to have some inclination to judge it to have the property, and some inclination to judge it not to have the property, when it's clear that nothing can be forthcoming to resolve the matter for one (all relevant facts are already in). In this case, one may v-believe the thing to have the property to degree .5, and v-believe it not to have the property to degree .5, and the possibility of a state of affairs like that, under ideal epistemic conditions for judging the proposition in question, is what makes the thing a borderline case of the property. Indeterminacy generally, and not just the indeterminacy of borderline vague propositions, is also explicated in terms of vagueness-related partial belief. Much of the chapter is devoted to spelling this out, and to saying something about how the two kinds of partial belief interact, how degrees of complex vagueness-related partial beliefs are determined, and how classical logic and semantics are affected (both bivalence and the law of excluded middle turn out to be indeterminate on my account).

The account of vagueness in terms of vagueness-related partial belief is brought to bear on the sorites paradox, and here I advert to a distinction I introduced elsewhere between happy- and unhappy-face solutions to paradoxes.[1] A paradox is a set of apparently incompatible propositions each one of which enjoys some plausibility when viewed on its own. A happy-face solution to a paradox would do two things: it would identify the odd guy(s) out—that is, it would tell us that the paradox-generating propositions weren't really incompatible or else it would identify the ones that weren't true, and then it would explain away their spurious appearance so that we were never taken

---

[1] Schiffer (1995–6).

in by them again. I believe few of the classical philosophical paradoxes have happy-face solutions, and I argue the same is true of the sorites paradox. An unhappy-face 'solution' is simply an explanation of why the paradox can't have a happy-face solution, and this explanation will appeal to an irresolvable tension in the underived conceptual role of the concept, or concepts, generating the paradox. Now, an unhappy-face solution can be weak (mildly unhappy) or strong (very unhappy). A weak unhappy-face solution shows that a paradox-free concept can be fashioned to do the work we expected from the paradox-generating concept, whereas a strong unhappy-face solution shows that no such paradox-free variant is possible. I argue that the sorites can in a sense have only a strong unhappy-face solution, but then this turns out not to be such a calamitous thing.

Both the notion of vagueness-related partial belief and the explication of vagueness and indeterminacy in terms of it are available to a theorist who doesn't share my conception of pleonastic entities, but, as I see things, the notion of pleonastic properties plays a crucial role in the motivation for the account of vagueness and indeterminacy in terms of vagueness-related partial belief. For the notion of pleonastic properties enables us to see how it is that a kind of partial belief can be *constitutive* of a property's having indeterminate application, as opposed to merely *tracking* the indeterminate application of a property whose nature is wholly independent of our conceptual practices.

Chapters 6 and 7 apply my psychological account of indeterminacy to two long-standing problems in the theory of meaning—normative, and especially moral, discourse and conditionals. As these two chapters make clear, I see both problems as sub-problems of the problem of indeterminacy. In Chapter 6, 'Moral Realism and Indeterminacy', I argue that cognitivism is true—'Eating animals is wrong' has the same sort of meaning as 'Eating animals is a source of protein'—but that no substantive moral propositions are determinately true (the proposition that it's morally wrong to do what one morally ought not to do isn't 'substantive'). Cognitivism is cheaply obtained, given the doctrine of pleonastic propositions. The indeterminacy of moral propositions is argued for in two stages. In the first stage I argue on epistemological grounds, without any appeal to my account of indeterminacy, that there are no determinate moral truths, and in the second stage I argue to the same conclusion on the basis of my account of indeterminacy. Then I try to say what it is about our moral concepts that precludes moral propositions from being determinately true, and I discuss the bearing of my argument on other kinds of evaluative discourse, especially evaluative epistemological discourse, such as the notion of justified belief.

Chapter 7, 'Conditionals and Indeterminacy', begins by pointing out that, given the doctrine of pleonastic propositions, there can be no doubt about there being conditional propositions in exactly the same sense as there are any other propositions, and that some of these propositions are determinately true, others determinately false. At the same time, conditionals are a philosophical problem largely because of forceful arguments to show that there are no conditional propositions. I reply to these arguments by bringing my account of indeterminacy to bear on them, and it turns out that, while a conditional proposition may be determinately true or determinately false, most of the ones of interest to us are indeterminate. As with the indeterminacy of moral propositions, many indeterminate conditional propositions provide a unique kind of indeterminacy which has nothing to do with the indeterminacy of borderline propositions.

The chapter begins with the problem posed by indicative conditionals (e.g. 'If Oswald didn't kill Kennedy, then someone else did'), this problem being the fact that there are arguments both for and against the existence of indicative-conditional propositions. The problem is resolved by appeal to my account of indeterminacy and its attendant account of pleonastic propositions, and I venture to say what the conditions are for an indicative-conditional proposition's being determinately true or determinately false. But my resolution generates its own little paradox, in that the way we form our partial beliefs in indicative-conditional propositions isn't what their truth conditions predict. I offer a sort of unhappy-face solution to this paradox, one that makes an important concession to non-cognitivist accounts of indicative-conditional sentences according to which 'If A, then C' expresses not belief in the indicative-conditional proposition that if A, then C ($A \rightarrow C$, for short) but rather conditional belief in C, given A.

Just as there are indicative-conditional propositions, so there are counterfactual-conditional propositions (e.g. the proposition expressed by 'If Oswald hadn't killed Kennedy, someone else would have'), and they have the same conditions for being determinately true or determinately false as indicative-conditional propositions. Nevertheless, there are important dependencies, in both directions, between indicative- and counterfactual-conditional propositions. If one forms a partial belief in the indicative-conditional proposition $A \rightarrow C$ when one is uncertain about A, one's degree of belief in $A \rightarrow C$ = one's conditional subjective probability of C, given A, but if one knows A to be false, the degree to which one believes $A \rightarrow C$ = the degree to which one believes the counterfactual-conditional proposition that if A had been the case, then C would have been the case ($A \square \rightarrow C$, for short). At the same time, the degree to which one believes $A \square \rightarrow C$ when that proposition isn't determinately true or determinately false = the degree to which one supposes one would believe $A \rightarrow C$ in a contextually relevant scenario in which one was uncertain about A.

Chapter 8, 'Why Pleonastic Propositions? Content in Information and Explanation', concludes the book by asking what pleonastic propositions do for us, how we would be worse off if we didn't make use of them. Pleonastic propositions play two important, and importantly related, roles. First, we use pleonastic propositions both to exploit the beliefs of others as a source of information about the world and to exploit the world as a source of information about the beliefs and desires of others. Secondly, we use them to explain the behaviour of ourselves and others. The ability of pleonastic propositions to play their source-of-information role is explained in terms of their providing a systematic way of correlating the brain states that subserve our beliefs with external states of affairs and of their enabling the belief properties that embed them to index functional roles of underlying brain states in a way that yields the reliability generalizations we rely on in exploiting head–world connections as sources of information. The next big question is whether other things—in particular non-pleonastic propositions or linguistic entities of some kind—might play the source-of-information role as well as pleonastic propositions do. I argue that no other kind of proposition can do as well as pleonastic propositions, because no other kind of proposition is as fine-grained as they are, and the more fine-grained a proposition is, the better it is at capturing functional differences that enable a better exploitation of head–world reliability correlations. As for whether sentential entities can do better, I argue that problems having to do with irreducible indexicality make them a virtual non-starter. Because of the way the explanatory role of pleonastic propositions depends on its source-of-information role, the upshot is that pleonastic propositions are best at what they do.

The rest of Chapter 8 is about the nature of propositional-attitude explanations and the role of propositions in them. The default position is that propositional-attitude properties (believing that it's raining, wanting not to get wet) play a *causal-explanatory* role—although it's not altogether clear what that is supposed to mean. Whatever it means, many philosophers have doubted that it's possible for propositional-attitude properties to play such a role. Two sections of the chapter are devoted to a critical survey of the reasons philosophers have had for this scepticism and of their positive views of what is going in common-sense propositional-attitude because-statements ('Al left the house because he thought his mother-in-law was coming to visit'), if they're not used to give correct causal explanations. None of the views discussed do better than fall short of what they claim to do. The issue about the causal-explanatory role of propositional-attitude notions is murky because the notion of causal explanation is murky, but the murkiness can be bypassed, and the book ends on a conciliatory note. The bottom line about content in explanation, I suggest, is that the explanatory role of propositional-attitude notions is their use in correct because-statements, and it's possible to account for the value of propositional-attitude because-statements by appeal to features of them no one would dispute. I end the book by saying that we need pleonastic propositions and that in this book I've tried to give a theory both of what they are in themselves and of their place in nature, language, and thought.

Although I'm only a few pages into this work, excuses are in order. My last book, *Remnants of Meaning*,[2] which was a refutation of my first book, *Meaning*,[3] concluded with the 'no-theory theory of meaning', the claim that there could be no correct positive theory of meaning. Now I'm introducing a third book whose offering is a positive theory of meaning. What kind of chutzpah is this? Only a mild kind, actually. This book is, at least in spirit, more of a sequel to *Remnants of Meaning* than an apostasy of it, although it presupposes no acquaintance with that book. Much of this book deals with questions not broached in the earlier work, and where I have changed my mind, I say why.

---

[2] Schiffer (1987a).   [3] Schiffer (1972).

1

The Face-Value Theory

1.1 INTRODUCTION

A major theme of this book will be that all notions of linguistic and mental content are ultimately to be explained in terms of the things we mean and believe, and that these fundamental units of content are propositions of a certain kind, which, for reasons that will emerge, I call *pleonastic propositions*. My initial way of motivating pleonastic propositions will be via a theory of belief reports which appears at face value to be correct; it's the default theory that must be defeated if it's not to be accepted. I think the theory is right. The face-value theory constrains, but provides no complete account of, the nature of the propositions we believe, and any completion of the theory will leave behind its face-value status. That's where pleonastic propositions first come in.

In Section 1.2 I state the face-value theory and motivate its default status. Its having this status doesn't preclude its being defeated, but the full defence of the theory can't be made available until the theory is conjoined with a theory of the nature of the propositions we believe. Most proponents of the face-value theory accept a certain compositionality assumption that constrains them to opt for propositions that are 'structured' in a sense to be explained. This is explained in 1.3. The issue of structured propositions creates a contest between (what I'll call) Russellian propositions and Fregean propositions. This is explained in 1.4, and a number of problems are raised for each option. Section 1.5 discusses ways in which Russellians and Fregeans might respond to those problems, and 1.6 asks where in logical space we might go next.

1.2 THE THEORY AND ITS PRIMA FACIE STATUS

The face-value theory is about belief reports of the form

(1) *A* believes that *S*

and holds that reports of that form are true just in case the referent of the '*A*' term stands in the belief relation to the proposition to which the 'that *S*' term refers. The face-value plausibility of this theory is made plain in the following way.

The part which implies that (1) consists of a two-place transitive verb flanked by slots for two singular argument terms gets its default status by way of being the most straightforward way of accounting for the validity of inferences like these:

> Harold believes that there is life on Venus, and so does Fiona.
> So, there is something that they both believe—to wit, that there is life on Venus.

> Harold believes everything that Fiona says.
> Fiona says that there is life on Venus.
> So, Harold believes that there is life on Venus.

> Harold believes that there is life on Venus.
> That there is life on Venus is Fiona's theory.
> So, Harold believes Fiona's theory.

> Harold believes that there is life on Venus.
> That there is life on Venus is implausible.
> So, Harold believes something implausible—to wit, that there is life on Venus.

These inferences appear to be formally valid, and the most straightforward way of accounting for that formal validity is to represent them, respectively, as having the following logical forms:[1]

> *Fab* & *Fcb*
> ∴ ∃*x*(*Fax* & *Fcx*)

---

[1] In what follows I represent 'Fiona's theory' as a logical singular term, rather than as a Russellian definite description; but nothing turns on this. The validity of the arguments would also be captured if that-clauses were represented as Russellian definite descriptions whose denotations were propositions. Although for present purposes I can allow a reading of 'singular term' which tolerates definite descriptions *à la* Russell, I consider the idea to be a non-starter as applied to that-clauses (see Schiffer forthcoming). It clearly won't do to say that 'Harold believes that there is life on Venus' means that Harold believes the proposition

$\forall x(Fax \rightarrow Gbx)$
Fac
∴ *Gbc*

Fab
$b = d$
∴ *Fad*

Fab
Gb
∴ $\exists x(Gx \& Fax)$.

These are the forms the inferences enjoy if, but only if, that part of the face-value theory is correct which holds that (1) is composed of a two-place transitive verb flanked by slots for two singular argument terms.

Another, though less powerful, way of motivating the same part of the face-value theory is via the following two steps. First, inferences like the displayed examples make a prima facie case for taking that-clauses to be singular terms. Secondly, given that 'A' and 'that S' in (1) hold places for singular terms, and given that the only other word in (1) is 'believes', it would take a very strong motivation, not yet supplied, to treat 'believes' as there functioning as anything other than a two-place predicate, so that instances of (1) are true just in case the referent of the 'A' term stands in the belief relation—the relation expressed in (1) by 'believes'—to the referent of the 'that S' term.[2]

expressed by 'There is life on Venus', since, among other problems, one can't know that Harold believes that there is life on Venus without knowing what Harold believes, the content of his belief, whereas someone—e.g. a monolingual speaker of Hungarian—could know that Harold believes the proposition expressed by 'There is life on Venus' without having any idea of what Harold believes, and any description that got around that problem—say, 'the proposition which ascribes to Venus, thought of in such-and-such way, the property of sustaining life, thought of in such-and-such way'—would, among other problems, require belief reporters to be sophisticated theorists about the referents of that-clauses.

[2] I am not alone in remarking on the face-value status of the part of the face-value thesis whose motivation I have just been explaining. Thus Tyler Burge: 'The most elementary point about the semantics of sentences about propositional attitudes is that such sentences have the form of a *relational* propositional-attitude predicate with singular argument places for at least a subject (e.g. a person) and something believed (thought, desired, intended, said). This latter ... is, with some qualification, the semantical value of the grammatical object of the propositional-attitude verb' (1980). Thus George Bealer: 'There is very strong logical and linguistic evidence for the following tenets. (1) "Say", "mean", "believe", "is possible", and so forth often function as predicates, and "that"-clauses function as singular terms in companion sentences (e.g., "I believe that A" ...)' (2002; in context it's clear that he means that 'believes' often functions as a binary predicate). Even Donald

The remaining part of the face-value theory, which says propositions are the referents of that-clauses in utterances of form (1), gets its prima facie status in the following way. Consider

Ramona believes that eating carrots improves eyesight.

If, as the face-value theory has it, 'that eating carrots improves eyesight' is a singular term, then, obviously, its referent is *that eating carrots improves eyesight*, and, it would seem, we can straight away say the following things about this thing, *that eating carrots improves eyesight*, which is the referent of the that-clause singular term:

- *That eating carrots improves eyesight is abstract*: it has no spatial location, nor anything else that can make it a physical object.
- It is *mind- and language-independent* in two senses. First, its existence is independent of the existence of thinkers or speakers. *That eating carrots improves eyesight* wasn't brought into existence by anything anyone said or thought. Secondly, *that eating carrots improves eyesight* can be expressed by a sentence of just about any natural language but itself belongs to no language.
- It has a *truth condition*: *that eating carrots improves eyesight* is true iff eating carrots improves eyesight.
- It has its truth condition *essentially*: it is a *necessary truth* that *that eating carrots improves eyesight* is true iff eating carrots improves eyesight. The contrast here is with sentences. The *sentence* 'Eating carrots improves eyesight' is also true iff eating carrots improves eyesight, but that is a *contingent* truth that would have been otherwise had English speakers used 'carrots' the way they now use 'bicycles'.
- It has its truth condition *absolutely*, i.e. without relativization to anything. The contrast is again with sentences. The sentence 'Eating carrots improves eyesight' has its truth condition only *in English* or *among us*. There might be another language or population of speakers in which it means that camels snore; but *that eating carrots improves eyesight* has its truth condition everywhere and everywhen.

From all this we may conclude, by an obvious generalization, that things believed are what philosophers nowadays call *propositions*: abstract, mind- and language-independent entities that have truth conditions, and have their truth conditions both essentially and absolutely.

Davidson—somewhat surprisingly given his (1984*a*)—writes: 'There is … no plausible alternative to taking belief sentences as relational, and therefore no alternative to taking the [that-clause in a belief sentence] as a singular term which, by referring to an appropriate entity, specifies the relevant belief' (2001*a*: 57–8).

Such is the prima facie motivation for the face-value theory. We can't properly assess it before we're told what account of propositions is to complement it.

1.3 COMPOSITIONALITY AND STRUCTURED VERSUS UNSTRUCTURED PROPOSITIONS

The face-value theory leaves plenty of room for those who accept it to disagree about the further nature of the propositions we believe, and the fate of the face-value theory depends on how this further issue is resolved. One issue is whether the propositions to which that-clauses refer are, in a certain technical sense, *structured* or *unstructured*. To say that a proposition is structured is to say that it is individuated wholly in terms of certain items as related in a certain way, where those items, as related in that way, determine a truth condition for the proposition. These items that determine the identity of a given proposition are said to be *constituents* of that structured proposition, and these constituents may themselves be propositions, or propositions containing other propositions, or propositions containing other propositions containing other propositions, and so on; but every proposition is ultimately built up from items that are not propositions, and these basic components are called *propositional building blocks*. Basic structured propositions are made up wholly of these building blocks, and all other structured propositions are derived by repeated applications of certain recursive rules. Theorists of structured propositions, as we'll presently see, can and do differ on the nature of these building blocks, and thus on the nature of the structured propositions to which that-clauses refer. But a structured proposition of any nature may be represented as an ordered pair of the form

$$\langle\langle x_1,\ldots,x_n\rangle, X^n\rangle^3$$

where there is a function f such that $\langle\langle x_1,\ldots,x_n\rangle, X^n\rangle$ is true iff there is an n-ary relation R^n and items $y_1,\ldots,y_n$ such that $f(X^n) = R^n, f(x_1) = y_1,\ldots,f(x_n) = y_n$, and $\langle y_1,\ldots,y_n\rangle$ instantiates R^n.[4] Nothing prevents f

---

[3] When $n = 1$, it is customary to write $\langle x, X\rangle$ rather than $\langle\langle x\rangle, X\rangle$.

[4] Unary relations are properties. Also, falsity conditions are a little more complicated, and I'll get to them in the next section.

from being the identity function, and that is what it is for those structured propositions I'll call *Russellian propositions* (after Bertrand Russell, of course). So, merely by way of illustration, the Russellian propositions

- that Fido is a dog
- that Fido loves Fi Fi
- that Fido loves Fi Fi and Fi Fi loves Fido
- that there are tigers

may be represented respectively as

- $\langle$Fido, doghood$\rangle$
- $\langle\langle$Fido, Fi Fi$\rangle$, the love relation$\rangle$
- $\langle\langle\langle$Fido, Fi Fi$\rangle$, the love relation$\rangle$, $\langle\langle$Fi Fi, Fido$\rangle$, the love relation$\rangle\rangle$, the conjunction relation$\rangle$
- $\langle$the property of being a tiger, the property of being instantiated$\rangle$.[5]

Even though Russellians often speak of their propositions as *being* ordered pairs, it is important to think of ordered pairs of the form $\langle\langle x_1,\ldots,x_n\rangle, X^n\rangle$ as *representing*, rather than being, structured propositions. Otherwise one will be stuck with having to decide—if, say, one is a Russellian—whether the proposition that Fido is a dog is identical to $\langle$Fido, doghood$\rangle$ or to $\langle$doghood, Fido$\rangle$, or whether it is indeterminate to which of the two it is identical.[6] Better to think of structured propositions as *sui generis* abstract entities individuated in terms of their 'constituents' as related to one another in a certain way rather than attempt to reduce them to some sort of set-theoretic entity. In the next section we'll see that, for all intents and purposes, the rivalry among theorists of structured propositions is played out between theorists of Russellian propositions and theorists of what I'll call *Fregean* propositions (after Gottlob Frege, of course).

*Un*structured propositions are propositions that are not structured; they are not individuated by propositional building blocks as related in a certain way. How plausible is it that that-clauses refer to unstructured propositions? That all depends on the fate of what I'll call the *compositionality hypothesis* (CH), which is usually a shared

---

[5] *Vide* Soames (1989).

[6] Compare Benacerraf (1965) for a similar question that arises with respect to the identification of numbers with sets.

presupposition among those who debate whether the referents of that-clauses are structured or unstructured propositions.

To a first approximation, CH holds that the referent of a that-clause token is determined by its structure and the referents its component expressions have in that token.[7] This is a first approximation because it needs to be qualified in order to deal with implicit references sometimes made in the utterance of a that-clause, such as the implicit reference to a place made in the that-clause in 'Henrietta believes that it's raining'. CH, then, is better put by saying that the referent of a that-clause token is determined by its structure and the referents of its component expressions together with whatever implicit references are made in the utterance of the that-clause. This is still rough, but it is good enough for what follows, and we can understand the issue about structured versus unstructured propositions relative to CH in the following way.

First, let's say that an expression has a *primary* reference in a that-clause if it has reference in the that-clause, and its referent doesn't function to help determine the referent of some other expression in the that-clause. Thus, in the that-clause in 'Ralph believes that that guy standing next to Betty is a pickpocket', 'that guy standing next to Betty' has a primary reference, but 'Betty' doesn't. We may now say that, given CH, a that-clause token τ refers to a *structured* proposition just in case a necessary condition for any other that-clause token τ' to refer to the same proposition is that exactly the same primary references are made in the utterance of τ' as are made in the utterance of τ. This is because if CH holds and a that-clause token refers to a structured proposition, then the components of that proposition will be the referents determined by the primary references made in the utterance of the token. Thus, a proposition is *un*structured, given CH, just in case it is possible for two that-clause tokens to refer to it even though different primary references are made in their utterances. For example, if, as Robert Stalnaker holds,[8] propositions are individuated by their possible-worlds truth conditions, then the that-clauses in 'George believes that every dog is a dog' and 'George believes that $7 + 5 = 12$' will refer to the same proposition, since both are true in every possible world.

---

[7] I would have said 'syntax' instead of 'structure' if syntax always mirrored logical form.

[8] See e.g. Stalnaker (1984).

There is reason to doubt that both CH is true and that-clauses refer to unstructured propositions. For it would seem that the *only* way of individuating unstructured propositions given CH is in the Stalnaker way, which entails that there is only one necessarily true proposition and that, consequently, your child knows every mathematical truth just by virtue of knowing that every dog is a dog. Stalnaker has gone to some lengths to explain away the counter-intuitiveness of such consequences. There is some question whether he has succeeded.

If, however, the propositions we believe are unstructured *and CH fails to hold*, then we are not constrained to individuate propositions by their possible-worlds truth conditions, and no Stalnakerian counter-intuitive consequences need ensue. Those unpalatable consequences require its being the case *both* that that-clauses refer to unstructured propositions *and* that CH is true. There are two ways to endorse unstructured propositions: relative to CH, and relative to the denial of CH. It is only the theorist of unstructured propositions *who accepts CH* who must individuate propositions by their possible-worlds truth conditions. Perhaps (he says coyly) a theorist of unstructured propositions who denies CH can individuate propositions as finely as anyone, if not more finely. There will be more on this later.

1.4 STRUCTURED PROPOSITIONS: RUSSELLIANS VERSUS FREGEANS

Virtually every propositionalist accepts CH and rejects unstructured propositions. Among theorists of structured propositions the big contest, for all intents and purposes, is between the Russellian conception of structured propositions and the Fregean conception of them.

Russellian propositions are structured entities whose basic components, or propositional building blocks, are the objects and properties our beliefs are about. As we already know, a typical Russellian would hold that the that-clause in 'Alice believes that Bob loves Carol' refers to a proposition that may be represented as the ordered pair ⟨⟨Bob, Carol⟩, the love relation⟩.[9] For the Russellian, every proposition may

---

[9] The 'typical' Russellian is one who takes names and (at least) other one-word singular terms to be 'directly referential'—i.e. to contribute their referents to the propositions expressed by sentences containing them. The typical Russellian is a Russellian before she

be taken to be an ordered pair of the form $\langle\langle x_1,\ldots,x_n\rangle, R^n\rangle$, where $\langle x_1,\ldots,x_n\rangle$ is an n-ary sequence of things of any ontological category and R^n is an n-ary relation (properties are one-place relations), and we noticed in the preceding section how this plays out with respect to various examples. For any possible world w, $\langle\langle x_1,\ldots,x_n\rangle, R^n\rangle$ is true in w iff $\langle x_1,\ldots,x_n\rangle$ instantiates R^n in w, false in w otherwise.[10]

The Fregean position is best thought of as a reaction to certain problems encountered by the Russellian position. Think of the Fregean as a theorist who began as a Russellian, encountered problems with her position, and then developed Fregeanism as the antidote to those problems.[11] Three problems motivated the switch.

One problem was the problem of 'empty names'. According to the Russellian, the referent of 'George Eliot' in

(2) Ralph believes that George Eliot was a man

is George Eliot, and the proposition to which (2)'s that-clause refers is the 'singular proposition'

⟨George Eliot, the property of being a man⟩.

Suppose, however, that it transpires that there never was such a person as George Eliot, that *Middlemarch* and the other novels displaying that name as the name of its author were in fact written by a committee. Then it would seem that the Russellian would have to say that (2)'s that-clause fails to refer to anything, since it contains a term that fails to refer to anything, and that therefore (2) would have no truth-evaluable content. At the same time, however, it seems intuitively that

(3) Ralph believes that George Eliot was a man, but in fact there was no such person; a committee wrote all the novels

---

encounters problems with her being a Russellian. The point of the qualification is that even general propositions are Russellian for the Russellian—composed of the objects and properties they're about—so when, for example, Russell argued that names are disguised definite descriptions, he wasn't ceasing to be a Russellian. Unless I explicitly indicate otherwise, however, I shall pretty much mean 'typical Russellian' by 'Russellian'.

[10] Perhaps this is slightly tendentious. A possible Russellian position may refuse to assign the 'singular proposition' that Pavarotti sings a truth-value in possible worlds in which Pavarotti does not exist. Nothing in the context of the present discussion turns on this.

[11] In the beginning of (1892), Frege in effect tells us that he held a version of the Russellian theory but gave it up because of its difficulty in accounting for the difference in 'cognitive content' between sentences of the form '$a = a$' and those of the form '$a = b$'.

might well be true if there were no such person as George Eliot. But it can't be that (3) but not (2) would be true should George Eliot not exist.

A second problem manifests itself in examples like the following:

(4) Ralph rationally believes that George Eliot adored groundhogs and Mary Ann Evans did not adore woodchucks.

(5) Ralph rationally believes that George Eliot adored groundhogs and George Eliot did not adore groundhogs.

Intuitively, (5) can't be true, but (4) can easily be true. All it would take would be for Ralph not to be aware either that George Eliot was Mary Ann Evans or that the property of being a groundhog is the property of being a woodchuck. Yet, and this was the problem, the Russellian who also accepts the face-value theory must evidently hold that (4) and (5) can't differ in truth-value, since they differ only in their that-clauses and both that-clauses refer to the same Russellian proposition. Notice that the same problem can arise even without a difference of terms. Lois Lane can't express a rational belief when, pointing to a single photograph of Superman, she utters 'I believe that he flies and he doesn't fly', but that utterance can express a rational belief if her first utterance of 'he' is accompanied by her indicating a photo of Superman in a caped spandex outfit while her second utterance of 'he' is accompanied by her indicating a photo of him in his mild-mannered-reporter guise.

A third problem was similar to, but significantly different from, the second problem, and came to light with an example like

(6) Ralph believes that George Eliot adored groundhogs but doesn't believe that Mary Ann Evans adored woodchucks.

It seems obvious that (6) might be true, notwithstanding that George Eliot = Mary Ann Evans and the property of being a groundhog = the property of being a woodchuck. But the Russellian must hold that both that-clauses in (6) refer to the same Russellian proposition, and that therefore, assuming the face-value theory, (6) is not only false, but necessarily false. The problem is not restricted to names. For example, after an accident that caused her to suffer amnesia, Claudia Schiffer (no relation) may say both

I don't believe that I'm German

and

I believe that she's German

where, intuitively, both reports are true, and where the that-clause occurrences of both 'I' and 'she' refer to her (in uttering 'she' Claudia is thinking of the famous German model who looks like the young Brigitte Bardot). The problem also arises for utterances of the same that-clause. Thus, Lois Lane may say

(7) I believe that he flies, but I don't believe that *he* flies

where, as before, the first utterance of 'he' is accompanied by her pointing to a photo of a man in a superhero outfit and the second utterance of it is accompanied by her pointing to a photo of a bespectacled man wearing a suit and tie. Intuitively, her utterance of (7) may be true even when both utterances of 'he' refer to the same person. Or, to take an example made famous by Saul Kripke,[12] two simultaneous utterances of 'Herbert believes that Paderewski was musical' may have different truth-values even though both occurrences of 'Paderewski' refer to the same person. This could happen when Herbert mistakenly believes there were two famous Poles named Paderewski, one a statesman, the other a pianist, and when what matters in the conversational context of the first utterance is Herbert's willingness to say 'I've no idea whether Paderewski was the slightest bit musical', while what matters in the other conversational context is Herbert's willingness to say 'Paderewski was astoundingly musical'. The Russellian who accepts the face-value theory is evidently committed to denying the intuitive data, since for her both utterances of the belief sentence must have the same truth-value.

There is another problem for the Russellian worth mentioning, but since it is a problem for every theory of structured propositions, I will raise it later.

They were the problems for which the Fregean sought a circumventing theory; she thought she found it in Fregeanism. The Fregean holds that the referents expressions have in that-clauses are not the objects and properties our beliefs are about but are rather things she calls *concepts*, or *modes of presentation* (or *guises*, or *ways of thinking*), of the objects and properties our beliefs purport to be about. (Henceforth, I'll for the most part drop 'mode of presentation', which

12 Kripke (1979).

was Frege's own metaphor, and use just 'concept', even though this use of 'concept' differs from Frege's own technical use. When confusion doesn't threaten, I may also use 'concept' with its current non-technical sense, as when one says that so-and-so doesn't have the concept of an electron.) Fregean propositions, then, are structured entities whose basic building blocks are concepts of the objects and properties our beliefs purport to be about. Thus, whereas the Russellian will hold that in the that-clause in

Ralph believes that Fido is a dog

'Fido' refers to Fido, 'dog' refers to doghood, and the whole that-clause therefore refers to the Russellian proposition we represent as $\langle$Fido, doghood$\rangle$, the Fregean will hold instead that there is some concept of Fido c_f and some concept of doghood C_d such that in the that-clause 'Fido' refers to c_f, 'dog' refers to C_d, and the whole that-clause therefore refers to the Fregean proposition we may represent as the ordered pair $\langle c_f, C_d \rangle$. For any possible world w, $\langle c_f, C_d \rangle$ is true in w iff in w: some thing x uniquely falls under c_f, some property Φ uniquely falls under C_d, and x instantiates Φ. Falsity conditions are a little trickier for the Fregean. She will hold that, for any possible world w, $\langle c_f, C_d \rangle$ is false in w *if* in w: some thing x uniquely falls under c_f, some property Φ uniquely falls under C_d, and x doesn't instantiate Φ. But the Fregean is evidently free to regard $\langle c_f, C_d \rangle$ as either false or neither true nor false in w if either one of its constituent concepts has nothing uniquely falling under it in w.

Just as the Russellian may take $\langle \langle x_1, \ldots, x_n \rangle, R^n \rangle$ to represent the form of every proposition, so the Fregean may take it to be represented by $\langle \langle c_1, \ldots, c_n \rangle, C^n \rangle$. The possible-worlds truth and falsity conditions are a generalization of those just illustrated for the Fregean proposition that Fido is a dog.[13]

For the Fregean, then, propositional building blocks are not the objects and properties our beliefs are about, but rather 'concepts' of them. But what are they? Although the word 'concept' and its ilk— 'mode of presentation', 'way of thinking', 'guise', etc.—are chosen for

---

[13] That is, for any possible world w, $\langle \langle c_1, \ldots, c_n \rangle, C^n \rangle$ is *true in* w iff in w: $\exists x_1, \ldots, x_n$, $R^n(x_1, \ldots, x_n)$, R^n uniquely fall under $c_1, \ldots, c_n$, C^n respectively & $\langle x_1, \ldots, x_n \rangle$ instantiates R^n), *false in* w if in w: $\exists x_1, \ldots, x_n$, $R^n(x_1, \ldots, x_n)$, R^n uniquely fall under $c_1, \ldots, c_n$, C^n respectively & $\langle x_1, \ldots, x_n \rangle$ doesn't instantiate R^n). Again, Fregeans are free to dispute whether $\langle \langle c_1, \ldots, c_n \rangle, C^n \rangle$ is false in w or neither true nor false in w if one or more of its constituent concepts has nothing uniquely falling under it in w.

the suggestiveness of their pre-theoretic meanings, no one of those pre-theoretic meanings does all the technical work the Fregean requires. There isn't much to be gleaned about concepts from the generic Fregean theory, and Fregeans can, and do, disagree among themselves about what exactly concepts are. What we do get from generic Fregeanism is that concepts are whatever propositional building blocks must be in order to avoid the problems that arise for Russellianism. As regards the problem of empty names, the Fregean can hold that in the counterfactual situation in which George Eliot never existed, we can account for the truth of

(3) Ralph believes that George Eliot was a man, but in fact there was no such person; a committee wrote all the novels

by claiming that 'George Eliot' there refers not to George Eliot but to a concept of her. As regards the problems of rational belief and disbelief, the Fregean can account for how

(4) Ralph rationally believes that George Eliot adored groundhogs and Mary Ann Evans did not adore woodchucks

and

(5) Ralph rationally believes that George Eliot adored groundhogs and George Eliot did not adore groundhogs

can take different truth-values by claiming either that the occurrences of 'George Eliot' and 'Mary Ann Evans' refer to distinct concepts (albeit of the same person) or that 'groundhog' and 'woodchuck' refer to distinct concepts (albeit of the same property), which means that in either case Ralph isn't rationally believing both a proposition and its negation, but rather a proposition and the negation of some other proposition.

The Fregean handles the third problem for the Russellian in similar fashion. Nothing prevents

(6) Ralph believes that George Eliot adored groundhogs but doesn't believe that Mary Ann Evans adored woodchucks

from being true, since its two that-clauses refer to distinct propositions. Similarly for Lois's utterance

(7) I believe that he flies, but I don't believe that *he* flies.

The two that-clauses refer to distinct propositions owing to the two occurrences of 'he' referring to distinct concepts of Superman; and likewise for the two simultaneous utterances of 'Herbert believes that Paderewski was musical' that have different truth-values: the two that-clauses again refer to distinct propositions, this time owing to the two occurrences of 'Paderewski' referring to distinction concepts of Paderewski.

The Russellian will be quick to point out that Fregeanism is also not without some problems.

First, the Russellian theory is complete in a way that the Fregean theory isn't, and there may be some question about the Fregean's ability to complete it. For the Russellian's conception of a proposition is fully specified in a way the Fregean's is not. The Russellian conception is fully specified because we know what the components of Russellian propositions are, and thus know what those propositions are. Not so for the Fregean conception. There's the *illusion* that we know what the components of Fregean propositions are, because the Fregean has borrowed familiar terms—'concept', 'mode of presentation', 'way of thinking', and so on—to stand for those components; but it's an illusion because, as we have already noticed, in the context of her theory these terms are technical terms meaning not a whole lot more than *the basic components of propositions, assuming those components are not the objects and properties our beliefs are about.* The Fregean owes a more complete specification of what concepts, and therewith Fregean propositions, are, and on this further specification Fregeans can, and do, differ. The Russellian may feel justified in calling this a *problem*, as opposed merely to a task in need of completion, because, he may feel, in the one hundred plus years since the theory was proposed, no theory of concepts has won anything close to wide acceptance even among Fregeans.[14]

Secondly, it is widely believed that names and other singular terms rigidly designate their referents, and that this affects the truth conditions of propositions referred to by that-clauses containing those rigid designators, so that, for example, the proposition Ralph believes when he believes that George Eliot was a man is one that is true in any arbitrary possible world just in case George Eliot exists and is a man

---

[14] The most fully developed, and perhaps the most promising, Fregean theory of concepts is to be found in Peacocke (1992).

in that world.[15] How, one may wonder, can the Fregean assign the right possible-worlds truth conditions to the proposition that George Eliot was a man, given that for him, the Fregean, the referent of the that-clause occurrence of 'George Eliot' is not George Eliot but rather a concept of her?

Thirdly, there are numerous instances where singular terms occur in that-clauses apparently as referring not to concepts of things but to the things themselves. According to my stipulated Fregean, the referent of a term in a belief report's that-clause is a concept of an object or property the belief purports to be about, yet it is obvious that terms in that-clauses often refer to things that aren't concepts but are the very things the belief is about. When your husband's brother says to you, 'I believe that I'm falling in love with you', isn't it obvious that both utterances of 'I' refer to him and that his utterance of 'you' refers to you?

Fourthly, one may suspect there is something fishy about the Fregean's claim that occurrences of terms in that-clauses refer to concepts. The problem is most salient in cases where the Fregean is constrained to say that a term makes a contextually determined reference to a concept. Consider first a typical case of contextually determined reference. Walking down the street with a friend, you point to an unusually coiffed man and say, 'That's how my father combed his hair', where your utterance of 'that' refers to a certain hairstyle. Now, a large part of what makes it the case that your utterance of 'that' referred to that hairstyle is that your intention in uttering the demonstrative was to refer to that hairstyle. Intending is a propositional attitude like believing, and if the Fregean is right, then what she says about believing applies, *mutatis mutandis*, to intending. One thing this means is that the proposition that provides the content of an intention is a Fregean proposition, so that your referential intention in uttering 'that' must, if the Fregean is right, involve a proposition containing a concept, a mode of presentation, of the hairstyle to which you referred. This is not unintuitive for the case at hand. But now suppose you say to your friend,

(8) I met a high school English teacher who actually believes that George Eliot was a man!

[15] The notion of a rigid designator is from Kripke (1980). We may say that the occurrence of the singular term t in an occurrence of $S(t)$ rigidly designates a just in case that occurrence of t refers to a and the proposition expressed by the utterance is true in any possible world w iff a has in w the property actually expressed by $S(x)$.

According to the Fregean, in uttering 'George Eliot' you're referring to some concept, or mode of presentation, of Eliot, and in uttering 'man', you're referring to some concept, or mode of presentation, of the property of being a man. On any version of Fregeanism worth considering, these will be contextually determined references, since it is enormously implausible to suppose that 'George Eliot' and 'man' have associated with them particular concepts involved in every literal use of those expressions.

Very well, then you should be able to answer the following questions. According to the Fregean, whenever you refer to anything, you do so under some particular concept of that thing. What then is the concept under which you are referring to a concept of George Eliot in uttering the token of 'George Eliot' in your utterance of (8), and what then is the concept under which you are referring to a concept of the property of being a man in uttering the token of 'man' in your utterance of (8)? Your referential intentions in this case should be as accessible to you as your referential intentions in any clear case of contextually determined reference, and in every such clear case we have the same privileged access to our referential intentions as we do with any of our conscious intentions. Might the Fregean say that concepts, or modes of presentation, are the one sort of thing we can think about directly, in a way unmediated by a concept, or mode of presentation, of it? What would explain that strange anomaly? And what is the concept of George Eliot to which you're referring in uttering 'George Eliot' in (8), and what is the concept of the property of being a man you're there referring to in uttering 'man'? Since the referents in (8) of the tokens of 'George Eliot' and 'man' are determined by your referential intentions, one would think you should be able to say. After all, in every clear case of contextually determined reference one has no trouble in saying to what one is referring. And if one can't say, what, again, would explain this strange anomaly? I dare say it's clear that no one can say what concepts are the referents of 'George Eliot' and 'man' in (8) or what the concepts are under which one is referring to those concepts, and that no one can say why it is that no one can say.

Fifthly, it is apt to seem that, whatever concepts turn out to be, there are cases where it is implausible to think anything that could be called reference to a concept is going on. An example of such a case is the belief report

> Just about everyone who visits New York City believes that it's noisy,

which is both true and easily understood, even though, one would think, there is nothing to which the occurrence of 'it' might there refer that could, in any sense, constitute the way in which nearly every visitor to New York thinks of the city. Similarly, you may believe what I tell you when I say

> Hilda believes that that guy is on his way there from Paris,

but would you thereby know the concepts under which Hilda, who is not party to the utterance, is thinking about Jacques Derrida, the *x-is-on-the-way-to-y-from-z* relation, Yale, and Paris?

Sixthly, there is an argument against the Fregean theory—due to Adam Pautz[16]—which complements some of the preceding problems, especially the fourth problem mentioned. The argument may be put thus:

(1) If the Fregean theory is true, then (α) 'Fido' occurs in 'Ralph believes that Fido is a dog' as a singular term whose referent is a concept of Fido.

(2) If (α), then the following inference is valid:
Ralph believes that Fido is a dog
∴ $\exists x(x$ is a concept & Ralph believes that x is a dog).

(3) But the inference isn't valid; given the truth of the premiss, the conclusion is also true only in the unlikely event that Ralph mistakes a concept for a dog.

(4) ∴ The Fregean theory is not true.

This little argument is valid, so if it's unsound, it's because one of its premisses is false. Which one might that be?

By stipulation the Fregean theory requires names in that-clauses to refer to concepts of their bearers, but one might challenge premiss (1) by claiming that while the that-clause occurrence of 'Fido' refers to a concept, the name doesn't occur in the that-clause as a *singular term*, and if it doesn't occur as a singular term, then it's no objection to the Fregean that the inference displayed in premiss (2) isn't valid. After all, there is a sense in which 'dog' in 'Fido is a dog' refers to, or

---

[16] Pautz gives his own statement and defence of the argument in Pautz (forthcoming).

denotes, the set of dogs, but we don't on that account consider the inference

Fido is a dog

∴ $\exists x(x$ is a set & Fido is a $x)$

to be valid. But given that the that-clause is a singular term that refers to a Fregean proposition and that the referent of the that-clause is partly a function of the referent of 'Fido' in the that-clause, what could 'Fido' be in the that-clause if not a singular term? Let '$c_f \wedge C_d$' refer to the Fregean proposition that Fido is a dog in the way that '$\langle c_f, C_d \rangle$' refers to the ordered pair that we're using to represent the Fregean proposition. Then '$c_f \wedge C_d$' in

(9) Ralph believes $c_f \wedge C_d$

has the same referent as the that-clause in

Ralph believes that Fido is a dog.

Now, 'c_f' is plainly functioning as a singular term in (9), and the inference from (9) to

$\exists x(x$ is a concept & Ralph believes $x \wedge C_d)$

is plainly valid. Yet if the Fregean is right, shouldn't 'Fido' be functioning as a singular term in the that-clause if 'c_f' functions as a singular term in (9)?

The Fregean might try denying premiss (3). She might say that the inference displayed in premiss (2) is really valid; it merely sounds odd to assert the conclusion. But why would it sound 'odd' if 'Fido' really refers to a concept of Fido? One can't just mention the word 'implicature' and go home. If Gricean considerations shy us away from a literal reading, there must be an explanation of how the relevant implicatures are generated, and it is far from clear what such an argument would look like in the present case.[17] It might be thought that the technical word 'concept' in '$\exists x(x$ is a concept & Ralph believes that x is a dog)' is what is causing the trouble, but the displayed inference might just as well have had the conclusion '$\exists x$(Ralph believes that x is a dog)', the claim then being that only a dog could be a witness to that generalization. Besides, the generalization of Pautz's argument

---

[17] For the notion of implicature, see Grice (1989a).

I am about to consider would seem to rule this response out, for its counterpart in the generalization is wholly implausible, and one should think that whatever is wrong with the one argument is wrong with the other.

If the argument is unsound, it is most likely because premiss (2) is false. The problem is to explain why the inference displayed in the premiss isn't valid if the that-clause is a complex singular term whose referent is partly a function of the reference 'Fido' has in that singular term. After all, there is no problem with the validity of

> Ralph believes that Fido is a dog
>
> So, there is something—namely, Fido—such that Ralph believes that it is a dog

when we suppose 'Fido' occurs in the premiss as a name of 'Fido', or with the validity of

> I believe that I am a paragon
>
> So, there is someone—namely, myself—such that I believe that he is a paragon

when we suppose that the that-clause occurrence of 'I' refers to me. So why isn't

> Ralph believes that Fido is a dog
>
> So, there is something—namely, the such-and-such concept of Fido—such that Ralph believes that it is a dog

valid if the that-clause occurrence of 'Fido' refers to a certain concept of Fido? Notice that it is no objection to premiss (2) that the Fregean theory precludes substitution *salva veritate* of 'the concept of Fido' for 'Fido' in the that-clause, since when ensconced in the that-clause, 'the concept of Fido' would refer not to the concept of Fido but to the concept of the concept of Fido. The argument proceeds in full awareness of that aspect of Frege's theory and doesn't challenge it; the force of the argument turns only on the fact that, if the Fregean theory is right, a concept is *the referent* of 'Fido' in the that-clause. If anything about substitutivity is relevant to the falsity of (2), if (2) is false, one would need to show how it is relevant. It would help if one could even give a rationale for why exportation *should* fail for referring expressions in that-clauses if the Fregean account of that-clauses is correct. One can't be completely confident that Pautz's objection is correct, since one can't be certain that the failure of exportation can't be explained. At the same time, until the explanation is produced, the objection has some force.

A final problem is the generalization of Pautz's objection to which I alluded two paragraphs back. This problem, however, is a problem not just for the Fregean but for *every* theory of structured propositions. The problem may be stated as the following argument:

(1) If any theory of structured propositions is true, then (α) 'barks' in 'Ralph believes that Fido barks' functions as a *singular term* whose referent is a constituent of the structured proposition to which the that-clause refers (for all intents and purposes, that referent would be either the property of being a barker or else a concept of that property).

(2) If (α), then the following inference is valid:
Ralph believes that Fido barks
$\therefore \exists x$(Ralph believes that Fido x).

(3) But the inference isn't even coherent, let alone valid.

(4) $\therefore$ No theory of structured propositions is true.

Premiss (1) may strike one as surprising, but the theorist of structured propositions seems to be committed to it. For example, for the Russellian 'that Fido barks' in 'Ralph believes that Fido barks' is a semantically complex singular term whose referent is, or may be represented as, ⟨Fido, the property of being a barker⟩. This means that both '⟨Fido, the property of being a barker⟩' and 'that Fido barks' are co-referential semantically complex singular terms, in the first of which 'the property of being a barker' refers to the property of being a barker, and in the second of which 'barks' refers to that property. This isn't a role 'barks' could perform if it were functioning as a verb; to perform its referential role in the that-clause it must be functioning as a singular term on all fours with the co-referential expression 'the property of being a barker'. Likewise, *mutatis mutandis*, for the Fregean, only in her case the reference is not to the property of being a barker but to a concept of it. If the displayed argument is unsound, it is because premiss (2) is false. This argument and Pautz's stand or fall together, in each case the second premiss being the crux of the issue. The difficulty in suggesting that (2) is false in the argument just displayed lends support to its counterpart premiss in Pautz's argument.

Before asking how Russellians and Fregeans might respond to their respective problems, let's return to the partitioning of logical space which initiated this section's discussion. Having discounted the combination of the face-value theory and unstructured propositions on the assumption that the compositionality hypothesis (CH) holds, we asked what the options were as regards structured propositions. The distinction between Russellianism and Fregeanism is not an exhaustive classification of theories of structured propositions, but, for all that matters, it does yield an exhaustive and exclusive distinction concerning the referent of a given expression in a given that-clause: given what the generic Fregean means by 'concept', this referent will be either an object or property or else a concept of one. This in turn yields the following partitioning of theories of structured propositions, which is exhaustive as regards structured propositions:

- The referent of a that-clause is always/sometimes a Russellian proposition (strong/weak Russellianism).
- The referent of a that-clause is always/sometimes a Fregean proposition (strong/weak Fregeanism).
- The referent of a that-clause is sometimes a Fressellian proposition (if I may), such as the proposition represented by

$$\langle\langle \text{Bob}, c_c\rangle, C_L\rangle,$$

  which could result from the referent of 'Bob' in 'Alice believes that Bob loves Carol' being Bob, while the other terms have Fregean referents.[18]

The problems I have just finished mentioning are either for the position now called strong Russellianism or for the position now called strong Fregeanism, and the question must be, at this point, whether any advantage with respect to those problems is gained over either of the strong positions by any of the three new positions. It is doubtful any such advantage is conferred.

According to weak Russellianism, only some that-clauses have Russellian propositions as their referents. The theorist who might be drawn to this position would be one who accepts the face-value theory and wants to accommodate Fregean intuitions (it's *true* Lois believes that Superman flies but doesn't believe that Clark Kent flies); her idea is to keep Russellian propositions when she can get away with it. The question for this theorist, however, is where will she find

---

[18] Cf. Horwich (1998: 122).

a that-clause whose referent is a Russellian proposition? The problem to which I am alluding may be elaborated in the following way. When t appears to enjoy a Russellian reference in the true utterance

A believes that $S(t)$

it will nearly always be possible that there should be another utterance

A believes that $S(t')$,

where t' may or may not be the same as t, such that, first, the two utterances have different truth-values, and, secondly, t' also appears to enjoy the same Russellian reference as t (this was illustrated in Claudia Schiffer's true utterances of 'I don't believe that I'm German' and 'I believe that she is German'). I take this to be obvious, and obviously obvious to anyone who accepts the Fregean intuitions for the relevant examples already considered. Now, there is the example already used against the Fregean, the true utterance of 'Just about everyone who visits New York City believes that it's noisy', but this merely supports the idea that 'New York City' occurs only as referring to New York City; there is still, say, 'believes' and 'noisy' to contend with. It might be that the utterances of the preceding example and 'Just about everyone who visits New York City believes that it's clangorous' have different truth-values. Finally, even if one could find one or two examples that seemed to support weak Russellianism, the mere paucity of examples ought to suggest that a more satisfying account is in the offing.

If weak and strong Russellianism are rejected as completers of the face-value theory, then the only other structured-proposition position to consider is the Fressellian position. Perhaps this is supported by the pair of examples just considered. Perhaps; one should again worry about the paucity of examples that even *seem* to support the proposal. Besides, the Fressellian alternative, in addition to requiring that some terms in that-clauses occur merely as referring to some thing or property the belief is about, also requires that adequate Fregean references—concepts—can be found for other terms in the that-clause, and that idea has already been found problematic. In any event, even if the Fressellian account is true, its truth, one would expect, ought to be explicable in terms of some illuminating underlying generalization.

1.5 RUSSELLIANS AND FREGEANS
ON THEIR PROBLEMS

Can either the Russellian or the Fregean reply to the problems raised in the preceding section? Let's start with the Fregean.

There isn't much to say about the first 'problem', which merely laments the absence of an account of what concepts are, unless one is prepared to offer the Fregean the account she needs. I'll have something to say about this in the next chapter. In the meantime, we might notice that quite a bit in philosophy turns on its outcome. Think, for example, of the issue of whether phenomenal properties can be identical to physical or topic-neutral properties.[19] Various thought experiments have been proposed to show that they can't be. Reductionists respond in Fregean fashion: the intuitions pumped by the thought experiments rely on the fact that, for example, one can know that one is in pain without knowing that one is in a Φ state, where 'Φ' holds the place for any physicalistic or topic-neutral candidate (e.g. a c-fibre-stimulation state), but, they continue, this doesn't show that the property of being in pain is not identical to the property of being in a Φ state, since it is consistent with there being one property that is thought of under two distinct concepts. Unfortunately, those taking this line never really tell us what concepts, and in particular phenomenal concepts, are supposed to be. There is no way of assessing the Fregean–reductionist response until we are told what concepts are supposed to be. I have nothing more to say about this now.

The second problem wondered whether the Fregean could assign the right possible-worlds truth conditions to, say, the proposition that George Eliot was a woman, given that for the Fregean the referent of 'George Eliot' in the that-clause is not George Eliot but is instead a concept of her. Related to this, the third problem pointed out that there are numerous instances where it is simply obvious that terms in that-clauses refer to some object the belief is about, as when in uttering 'I believe that I'm falling in love with

---

[19] A 'topic-neutral property' is a property that per se leaves open the nature of the things having it. The property of occurring at noon is a topic-neutral property, since it may be had by physical, mental, or any other kind of events. The topic-neutral properties of most concern to philosophers are functional properties, which encapsulate causal and transitional relations of the things having them.

you' your brother-in-law is plainly referring to himself and to you, respectively, by his that-clause utterances of 'I' and 'you'. The Fregean may claim to have an answer, an answer that I believe was first clearly articulated by Gareth Evans.[20] The Fregean might say that the problematic referring expressions have as their referents *object-dependent* concepts, concepts that are individuated partly in terms of the objects of which they are concepts and that wouldn't exist if those objects didn't exist. The Fregean can then distinguish between (i) x's being *the referent* of t and (ii) t's merely *referring to x*. The idea would be that t refers to x if x is the referent of t, but not necessarily conversely. An object may be so transparently contained (so to say) in an object-dependent concept of it that one can't refer to the concept without thereby indirectly referring to the object. Moreover, object-dependent propositions will have the objects contained in object-dependent concepts entering rigidly into the possible-worlds truth conditions of those propositions. In this way, the Fregean may say, the that-clauses in, for example, Claudia Schiffer's two utterances when she suffered amnesia—'I don't believe that I'm German' and 'I believe that she's German'—may refer to distinct object-dependent propositions about her that have the same possible-worlds truth condition: each is true in a possible world w just in case Claudia herself exists and is German in w.

The answer the Fregean might give might not be a correct answer, at least as regards the second of the foregoing two problems (the third problem raised for the Fregean). The glitch I have in mind is related to Adam Pautz's objection (p. 27). As a preliminary to making my point, consider the following unproblematically valid inference:

Ralph believes ⟨the woman next to Henry, humility⟩
∴ $\exists x$(Ralph believes ⟨the woman next to x, humility⟩).

An inference that would of course be problematic would be:

Ralph believes ⟨the woman next to Henry, humility⟩
∴ $\exists x$(x = Henry & Ralph believes ⟨x, humility⟩).

Existential generalization on a singular term having a secondary occurrence can't result in an existential quantifier binding a variable having a primary occurrence. Even if Henry is the referent of 'Henry' in 'Ralph believes that the woman next to Henry is humble', there is no way we could existentially generalize on 'Henry' in

Ralph believes that the woman next to Henry is humble

and validly get

$\exists x$(Ralph believes that x is humble),

as opposed to

$\exists x$(Ralph believes that the woman next to x is humble).

To be sure, the inference

Ralph believes that the woman next to Henry is humble
∴ $\exists x$(Ralph believes that x is humble)

remains valid (provided 'the woman next to Henry' there refers to someone); but it would not have Henry as its witness—as the value of 'x' that makes the conclusion true—unless he were a woman standing next to himself. The problem for the Fregean is that an inference such as

I don't believe that I'm German
∴ $\exists x$(I don't believe that x is German)

is unproblematically valid, but it wouldn't be if the referent of the occurrence of 'I' in the that-clause was not the person self-ascribing the belief but an object-dependent concept of her. We don't know what object-dependent concepts are supposed to be like, other than that they are object-dependent and satisfy Frege's constraint, so one can't give formal representations of inferences involving them. Yet the formal point is the same as the one illustrated, and the inference just displayed is valid only if, *pace* the Fregean theory, the referent of the occurrence of 'I' in the that-clause is a person, not a concept, object-dependent or otherwise.

What is the Fregean's best response to the fourth problem? The fourth problem is actually a package of three problems: (i) Belief reporters are not aware of referring to anything that might be called a Fregean concept; they don't understand a literal utterance of a belief sentence to require them to be making contextually determined references to concepts. Although Claudia's two utterances ('I don't believe that I'm German' and 'I believe that she [unknowingly referring to herself] is German') would intuitively both be taken to be true, she would not be aware of her that-clause utterances of 'I' and 'she' requiring reference to anything other than to herself and the woman to whom she is referring in uttering 'she'. Contrast this with clear cases of contextually determined references: the reference to a certain woman in uttering 'she'; an implicit reference to a certain comparison class in uttering 'He's tall'; an implicit reference to a certain place in uttering 'It's raining'. Now, there are cases where speakers don't realize that their utterances require certain implicit references—e.g. someone's making a simultaneity judgement in ignorance of the fact that events can be simultaneous only relative to a frame of reference, or a child's utterance of 'It's six o'clock' in ignorance that it can be six o'clock only relative to a time zone. But in these cases it can't be said that the ignorant speakers are making the required implicit references (the child doesn't mean that it's six o'clock EST), whereas belief reporters in the cases at issue are not failing to do something required by the literal meanings of the sentences they are uttering. (ii) If they are implicitly referring to concepts, they are unaware of that to which they are referring. After all, no one seems to be in a position to say what concepts are! This is consistent with the way in which we can appreciate what is relevant to the assessment of a given belief report. Claudia's utterance of 'I believe that she's German', when her utterance of 'she' refers, unbeknown to her, to herself counts as true, even though her concurrent utterance of 'I don't believe that I'm German' also counts as true, because we recognize that it is essential to the evaluation of the statement that Claudia thinks of the referent of 'she' as being a famous supermodel named 'Claudia Schiffer'. But this isn't to say that her utterance of 'she' in her utterance of 'I believe that she's German' refers to the concept of being a famous supermodel named 'Claudia Schiffer'. Her utterance of 'she' refers only to Claudia Schiffer, i.e. to herself. (iii) Not only are belief reporters not aware either of what concepts are or that they are referring to them; even less are they aware of the concepts under which they're referring to those concepts. Perhaps in uttering 'she' Claudia may be said to be referring to an object-dependent concept of herself which identifies her as a famous supermodel named 'Claudia Schiffer', but who can say what the concepts are under which the belief reporter is, if the Fregean is right, referring to the concepts to which he is referring in uttering the words in the that-clause he utters? Might the Fregean say that propositional attitudes about concepts don't require concepts of those concepts? If so, she may be opening a floodgate. I see no good response for the Fregean to make to the fourth problem.

Nor do I see what half-way promising reply to put in the mouth of the Fregean for her remaining problems.

What might the Russellian respond to the problems raised for her?

The problem of empty names has always been a nemesis of Russellianism. Russell's way of staying a Russellian was to deny that most ordinary singular terms—proper names, demonstratives, and pronouns—functioned as genuine singular terms. They functioned rather as disguised definite descriptions, so that the propositions to which that-clauses containing them referred were general propositions of the kind famously associated with Russell's theory of definite descriptions. Most, if not all, current Russellians consider this description-theoretic solution to have been refuted by Kripke's assault on the description theory of names.[21] Currently, Russellians have no way that is generally accepted among them for dealing with the problem of empty names. The Russellian Nathan Salmon has recently sought to resolve the problem by proposing that even when a speaker intends her use of a name in a that-clause to refer to a bearer of that name, the occurrence of the name refers to a certain sort of *mythical entity* should it turn out that the intended bearer of the name doesn't exist.[22] This has the unfortunate consequence of making it impossible to be an atheist, since, if Salmon is right, it is impossible to express a true belief by saying 'I believe that God doesn't exist'. One is apt to feel that the cons attaching to Salmon's solution far outweigh whatever pros Russellianism might enjoy.

Russellians have tended to deal with the second and third problems in one of two ways, one of which stays wedded to the face-value theory, the other of which rejects a key component of it. A Russellian who is aware of these problems and continues to accept the face-value theory has no choice but to bite the bullet: *pace* common sense,

(4) Ralph rationally believes that George Eliot adored groundhogs and Mary Ann Evans didn't adore woodchucks

and

(5) Ralph rationally believes that George Eliot adored groundhogs and George Eliot didn't adore groundhogs

must have the same truth-value; and, again *pace* common sense,

[21] Kripke (1980).   [22] Salmon (2001).

(6) Ralph believes that George Eliot adored groundhogs but doesn't believe that Mary Ann Evans adored woodchucks

is necessarily false. The theorist recognizes the need to explain away common-sense intuitions, but his strategy for doing that considerably narrows the conceptual space between Russellians and Fregeans, since it adopts the Fregean's notion of a concept (mode of presentation, guise, way of thinking) under which one believes a thing to be such-and-such. For Salmon,[23] the strategy takes the form of analysing the two-place belief relation, which is said to hold between believers and the Russellian propositions they believe, in terms of a three-place relation BEL which holds among believers, Russellian propositions, and the concepts, or modes of presentation, under which the believers believe the propositions they believe. These concepts are typically made up of concepts of the objects and properties contained in the proposition believed; for all intents and purposes, one can think of a typical propositional concept for a Russellian proposition

$$\langle\langle x_1,\ldots,x_n\rangle, R^n\rangle$$

as the Fregean proposition

$$\langle\langle c_1,\ldots,c_n\rangle, C^n\rangle$$

where $c_1,\ldots,c_n$ are concepts of $x_1,\ldots,x_n$, respectively, and C^n is a concept of R^n. In other words, the two-place belief relation that relates believers to the Russellian propositions they believe is analysed in terms of the three-place BEL thus:

$B(y, \langle\langle x_1,\ldots,x_n\rangle, R^n\rangle)$ iff $\exists c_1,\ldots,c_n, C^n$ [$c_1,\ldots,c_n, C^n$ are concepts of $x_1,\ldots,x_n, R^n$, respectively & BEL($y, \langle\langle x_1,\ldots,x_n\rangle, R^n\rangle, \langle\langle c_1,\ldots,c_n\rangle, C^n\rangle$)].

The next part of the idea is that utterances of sentences like (4)–(6), notwithstanding their face-value semantics, typically carry conversational implicatures about the third term of the BEL relation, so that in uttering, say, 'Lois believes that Superman flies but not that Clark Kent does', the speaker would be literally saying something necessarily false but implicating something true—namely, that Lois stands in the BEL relation to the proposition that Superman–Clark Kent flies

---

[23] Salmon (1986).

under a concept that identifies Superman as a guy who flies around in a caped spandex outfit but doesn't stand in the BEL relation to that proposition under a concept that identifies him as a bespectacled mild-mannered reporter.[24] In my estimation,[25] this effort fails, but my present concern isn't to repeat the case against it so that a final verdict can be issued on the matter; it is merely to make salient a certain portion of the logical geography within which the face-value theory is located. It should be clear, however, that in taking on the Fregean apparatus of concepts, without an accompanying account of what they are, the current Russellian theory of belief reports loses any appearance of advantage over the Fregean account with respect to completeness, and it makes one realize that at the level of psychology, as opposed to the level concerned with the semantics of that-clauses, the two theories are only notionally distinct.

The way of dealing with the second and third problems that involves a departure from the face-value theory is to retreat to the *hidden-indexical theory of belief reports*.[26] This is the theory for you if you want a theory of the semantics of

(1) A believes that S

according to which substitution instances of 'that S' refer to Russellian propositions and Fregean intuitions about the truth-values of belief reports are respected, so that an utterance of, for example, 'Lois believes that Superman flies but not that Clark Kent flies' may be literally true. The hidden-indexical theory holds, first, that that-clauses in sentences of form (1) refer, or purport to refer, to Russellian propositions, and, secondly, that a literal utterance of (1) states that:

(10) For some c, A believes that S under c and c is of type Ψ^*

where Ψ^* is some contextually determined type of concept to which implicit reference is made in the utterance of (1). Concepts of propositions may be construed, as they were in connection with Salmon's BEL proposal above, as Fregean propositions composed of concepts of the constituents of the Russellian proposition occupying the

---

[24] Scott Soames pursues a variant of this line in his (2002).   [25] Schiffer (1987b).

[26] See Schiffer (1977), where I first proposed a version of the hidden-indexical theory, and Schiffer (1992), where I cast a more critical eye on it. A version of the theory was also put forward by Crimmins and Perry (1989) and Crimmins (1992).

second argument slot. It is because the reference to the contextually determined type of mode of presentation isn't carried by any term in (1) that I call this theory the *hidden-indexical* theory. It assimilates (1) to other sentences having a hidden-indexical semantics, such as 'It's raining', whose utterance requires a contextually determined reference to a place at which it is raining, that reference not carried by any term in the sentence uttered. In a limiting case, the hidden-indexical theorist may see the reference to a *type* of concept as being in effect a reference to some particular concept, but the hidden-indexical theorist does best to state her theory in a way that requires merely the reference to a type of concept, as opposed to a particular concept, because whatever she finally ends up taking concepts to be, she will find that in many cases of correct belief attributions, the belief reporter is in no position to refer to any *particular* concept, but only to the *sort* of concept under which the person to whom the belief is being attributed is thinking about some constituent of the Russellian proposition to which the belief reporter is referring. Indeed, if the belief reporter were always making reference to particular concepts, it is difficult to see why the Fregean version of the face-value theory would not be the theory of choice. The hidden-indexical theory owes the same account of the technical notion of a 'concept' it employs as does the Fregean, as it is the same technical notion in both cases, the only difference being that for the Fregean, but not the hidden-indexical Russellian, concepts are the referents expressions have in their that-clause occurrences. As with Fregeans, hidden-indexical theorists may disagree among themselves about the proper explication of that notion.

The hidden-indexical theory has apparent problems. One problem is that it does nothing to ameliorate the Russellian's problem of empty names. It will still be impossible for

(3) Ralph believes that George Eliot was a man, but in fact there was no such person; a committee wrote all the novels

to be true, unless, like Nathan Salmon,[27] one cooks up some other thing to be the name's referent, should the name fail to have a bearer.

A second problem is that it forces us to say that ordinary speakers are in error about what they are stating when they make belief reports. One uttering 'It's raining' knows that she is stating that it's raining at such-and-such place, where the place to which reference is

[27] Salmon (2001).

made is determined by her referential intentions in uttering the sentence.[28] No one who utters 'It's raining' would suppose he simply means that it's raining. Yet one uttering, say, 'I believe that $1^2 + 1^2 = 4$' is in no way aware of stating [that there is a c such that he believes that $1^2 + 1^2 = 4$ under c and c is of type Ψ^*], where Ψ^* is a type of concept to which he referred in ascribing to himself this belief. He will not be at all aware of making such an implicit reference, and by his lights all he was stating was that he believes that $1^2 + 1^2 = 4$. One would think that if in uttering a sentence a speaker were implicitly referring to a thing and saying something about it, she'd be aware of that. This is evidently true of all the non-contentious examples of such implicit reference, such as utterances of 'It's raining'.[29]

A third problem is that the hidden-indexical theory makes it more difficult to account for the validity of those inferences that motivated the face-value theory in the first place, inferences such as

> Harold believes everything that Fiona says.
> Fiona says that there is life on Venus.
> So, Harold believes that there is life on Venus.[30]

If the hidden-indexical theory is correct, then the first premiss apparently has a scope ambiguity that would have to be resolved in the context of utterance to determine whether it is saying that

> For any p, c, if Fiona says p under c, then Harold believes p under c

or that

> For any p, if Fiona says p under some c, then Harold believes p under some c'.

If the first reading is operative, then a token of the expressed argument will be invalid unless the utterance of the second premiss implicitly refers to a particular concept (as opposed merely to a type of concept) and the utterance of the conclusion implicitly refers to the same particular concept. Such reference to a particular propositional concept, as opposed to a type of concept, would be a very rare occurrence. If the second reading is operative, then any token of the

---

[28] Typically one uttering 'It's raining' is referring to one's own location at the time of the utterance, but this is not required by the sentence's meaning. A speaker in New York can say 'It's raining' in response to a question about the weather in Paris.

[29] See Schiffer (1992: 512–18).   [30] Cf. Salmon (1995).

argument will be invalid, for whatever implicit reference is made in the utterance of the conclusion, the resulting statement will not be entailed by the premises.

A fourth problem may be the most serious. In claiming that (10) is what is stated in an utterance of (1), does the hidden-indexical theory retain or reject the face-value theory's claim that 'believes' in (1) is a *two*-place relation? That is to ask, does 'believes' in (10) express a two-place relation, or does it rather express a three-place relation that holds among a believer, a proposition, and a mode of presentation under which the believer believes the proposition? It would seem that it must be the two-place relation alleged by the face-value theory. For if it were the three-place relation BEL (to borrow Salmon's term), then 'μ', construed as a name of a concept in

Ralph believes that Fido is a dog under μ,

would occur as the name of an argument of the relation. But it does not; it occurs as part of the adverbial phrase (what linguists call an *adjunct*) 'under μ', and thereby behaves semantically exactly like 'under the mistletoe' in

Carmelina kissed Ralph under the mistletoe,

and no one supposes that kissing is a three-place relation holding among kissers, kissees, and things under which kissers kiss kissees. The problem for the hidden-indexical theory is that if 'believes' in (1) expresses the two-place belief relation that relates believers to the propositions they believe, then it is extremely implausible that a literal utterance of (1) should require the speaker to mean (10). For it ought to be possible simply to report that so-and-so believes that such-and-such without further embellishment, and how else is that to be done, given that believing is the two-place relation, other than by uttering an appropriate sentence of form (1)? Moreover, if 'believes' expresses a two-place relation and that-clauses are singular terms that refer to propositions, then just the semantics for the form '$a R b$' alone will determine belief reports to have the semantics the face-value theory attributes to them—unless there is some special ad hoc convention that gives belief reports an idiomatic meaning wherein they must be used only to make statements of form (10). It is extremely unlikely that there is any such convention.[31]

---

[31] When in (1977) I first introduced the hidden-indexical theory, I *stipulatively defined* it as holding that 'believes' in (1) expressed a three-place relation holding among a believer,

Finally, we should look a bit more closely at the perceived weakness in the face-value theory which is thought to motivate the hidden-indexical theory. We have already encountered one pretty decent motive for taking the hidden-indexical theory seriously: the need to explain how Claudia's utterances of 'I don't believe that I'm German' and 'I believe that she's German' can be true simultaneously when the sole referent of both that-clause pronouns is Claudia. Whether this forces us to conclude that that-clauses refer to Russellian propositions is a question I won't resolve until the next chapter. What I want to comment on now is a certain two-part motivation that I believe moves many to hold the hidden-indexical theory, but which I think is not a very good motivation.

Part of what recommends the hidden-indexical theory is that it respects Fregean intuitions, and the motivation for wanting to respect those intuitions should be transparent. Anyone who wields the concepts employed in belief reports will be disposed to judge, even if defeasibly, that Lois may both believe that Superman flies and fail to believe that Clark Kent flies; that part of the hidden-indexical theory's motivation needs no argument. The same cannot be said for the theory's commitment to the claim that that-clauses in sentences of form (1) always refer to Russellian propositions. What is supposed to motivate that? Russell's own view of propositions was forged from views no one now shares—logical atomism and an epistemology based on the dubious distinction between knowledge by description

---

a proposition the believer believed, and a mode of presentation under which the believer believed the proposition. I did this because it was clear to me that, for the reasons just given in the text, the theory would be a virtual non-starter if 'believes' expressed the face-value theory's two-place relation. Then in Schiffer (1992) I pointed out that this stipulative requirement was inconsistent with what the theory said was meant by utterances of belief reports of form (1) (namely, a proposition of form (10)). Peter Ludlow (1995) replied that the inconsistency did not tell against a version of the hidden-indexical theory that recognized the adverbial status of 'under m', and therewith the two-placedness of 'believes' in both (1) and (10). I replied (1996) that if 'believes' were a two-place predicate, then the projective meaning rules for English would give sentences of form (1) a meaning that was inconsistent with a hidden-indexical account wherein 'under m' was an adverb. Ludlow (1996) rejoined that there might be a special convention requiring speakers to mean propositions of form (10) in uttering belief reports of form (1), notwithstanding that 'believes' expressed a two-place relation and 'under m' in (10) was an adverbial phrase. But of course there *could* be such a special convention. There could be a special convention that required one not to utter 'I bought a hat' unless one means that one bought a pink hat that was too small for one's head. Such a special convention would make belief reports idioms, and one might be hard-pressed to explain why there should be such a special idiomatic meaning.

and knowledge by 'acquaintance'.[32] Besides, the Russellian general proposition Russell would take to be the referent of the that-clause containing an actual proper name is, notoriously, not the Russellian 'singular' proposition the contemporary Russellian would take to be its referent. Philosophers who nowadays think they need to construe that-clauses as referring to Russellian propositions seem to be moved by two things. First, they feel that the 'direct reference' semantics that is identical to the commitment to Russellian propositions is required by insights growing out of Saul Kripke's *Naming and Necessity* and subsequent work by David Kaplan and others.[33] This is a bit ironic in that Kripke himself refused to endorse a Russellian account of that-clause reference. Kripke's views do motivate a certain theory of the possible-worlds truth conditions of the propositions referred to by that-clauses containing proper names, but one does not need Russellian propositions to capture those truth conditions. We've already noticed (p. 39) that Fregean object-dependent propositions capture the truth conditions engendered by 'rigidity', and in the next chapter we'll see that they may be captured in other ways as well. If there is a good argument for taking that-clauses to refer to Russellian propositions, I don't know what it is.

Well, some claim to find this good argument in the doctrine of 'semantic innocence', and this is the second source of commitment to Russellian propositions to which I earlier alluded. This motivation strikes me as both weak and confused. At the end of 'On Saying That', wherein Donald Davidson presented his so-called 'paratactic' account of belief reports, Davidson offered the following method-ological homily:

Since Frege, philosophers have become hardened to the idea that content-sentences in talk about propositional attitudes may strangely refer to such entities as intensions, propositions, sentences, utterances, and inscriptions. What is strange is not the entities, which are all right in their place (if they have one), but the notion that ordinary words for planets, people, tables, and hippopotami in indirect discourse may give up these pedestrian references for the exotica. If we could recover our pre-Fregean semantic innocence, I think it would seem to us plainly incredible that the words 'The earth moves', uttered after the words 'Galileo said that', mean anything different, or refer to anything else, than is their wont when they come in other environ-ments. No doubt their role in *oratio obliqua* is in some sense special; but

---

[32] Russell (1910*a*).   [33] Kaplan (1978).

that is another story. Language is the instrument it is because the same expression, with semantic features (meaning) unchanged, can serve countless purposes.[34]

There are two questions we need to ask. First, does the theory that that-clauses refer to Russellian propositions adhere to Davidson's 'semantic innocence'? Secondly, whether or not it does, is there anything to recommend semantic innocence?

It ought to be plain that no theory whereby that-clauses are singular terms can satisfy what Davidson meant by 'semantic innocence'. Semantic innocence, as Davidson makes very clear in the first sentence just quoted, is being invoked precisely to rule out any theory whereby content sentences—the sentences following the 'that' in that-clauses—form singular terms when prefixed by 'that'. Neo-Russellians who claim semantic innocence do so because names and certain other singular terms have for them the same reference they have out of that-clauses. That gives semantic innocence for *names*, but not for *that-clauses*, since the sentence occurs as the bulk of a singular term whose referent is a proposition, which is not the sort of thing to which sentences ordinarily refer, or have as their extension, out of that-clauses. Moreover, the use of general terms in that-clauses is far from innocent. The referential semantic value of 'dog' in

    Fido is a dog

is the set of dogs, but that can't be its referent in

    Ralph believes that Fido is a dog,

for if it were and the set of dogs were identical to the set of creatures belonging to the species most beloved of fleas, then we could infer that Ralph believed that Fido belonged to the species most beloved of fleas, and this, needless to say, isn't something that can be validly inferred. Russellians depart from semantic innocence in holding that the referent of 'dog' in a that-clause is not the set of dogs but rather the property of being a dog.

As for the second question, I see nothing to recommend semantic innocence except the very weak maxim that counsels one not to multiply anything (in this case semantic assignments) without good reason; but who ever thought of 'postulating' propositions without good reason? And if the last sentence of the quotation from Davidson

[34] Davidson (1984a: 108).

is intended to scare one into thinking that one who treats that-clauses as singular terms can't account for the uses of language in the sort of compositional ways favoured by Davidson, then it is simply mistaken. The idea that that-clauses refer to propositions is about as threatening as the idea that terms sometimes refer to themselves, as when, for example, someone says that his name is Donald.

1.6 WHAT NOW?

The face-value theory has a default status, and it is the only theory of belief reports that has an initial *intuitive* basis (all the other theories are designed to replace the face-value theory for this, that, or the other reason). When conjoined with the compositionality hypothesis (CH), the most plausible further assumption is that believing is a relation to structured propositions. But this, for all that matters, is tantamount to the claim that believing is a relation either to Russellian or to Fregean propositions, and neither of those two options has yet shaken its not inconsequential problems. Should we next question CH, or should we question one or another tenet of the face-value theory? Merely questioning CH would do no good, unless the questioning is accompanied by a plausible account of propositions that coheres with denying CH. As for questioning the face-value theory, there are those, in addition to hidden-indexical theorists, who support theories that are incompatible with it. Except for the hidden-indexical theory, these are, at least for the most part, theories motivated by their supporters' wanting nothing to do with propositions. Most of these theories take believing to be a two-place relation to sentential, or quasi-sentential, entities of one stripe or another, but not all of those theories take that-clauses to refer to things believed.[35] On one unusual variation of a theory that takes that-clauses to refer to quasi-sentential entities—Mark Richard's theory[36]—it is denied that 'believes' makes a constant contribution to utterances of sentences of form (1) ('*A* believes that *S*'); there are, the idea goes, numerous distinct but similar belief relations, and 'believes' is an

---

[35] e.g. Donald Davidson's 'paratactic' theory (1984*a*) doesn't.
[36] Richard (1990).

indexical that makes contextually determined references to these various belief relations.[37]

I have no interest in rehashing a debate with sententialist theories of propositional attitudes,[38] but I will make two quick remarks. Theories that take believing to be a relation to sentential, or quasi-sentential, entities are motivated entirely by objections their proponents have to propositions. If those objections are not any good, those theories give way to the best version of the face-value theory. Whether there are any good objections to propositions, rightly construed, remains to be seen. My other comment is that while each version of sententialism will have its own unique flaws, there is one they all share, and I doubt that it is surmountable. A theorist who eschews contents in favour of things that merely have content must say that a person will believe one of those things S just in case she is in a belief state that has the same content as S. For example, if believing that the earth moves is standing in the belief relation to the sentence 'the earth moves', then my utterance of 'Galileo believed that the earth moves' will be true just in case Galileo was in a belief state whose content matched that of 'the earth moves'. The problem every sententialist account of propositional attitudes confronts comes to this for the example at hand: no one can know that Galileo believed that the earth moves without knowing *what Galileo believed*, the content of his belief, but one (e.g. a monolingual speaker of Hungarian) can know that Galileo was in a belief state whose content was the same as the content of 'the earth moves' without having any idea of what Galileo believed, of the content of his belief.[39]

---

[37] I criticize Richard's theory in (1990).

[38] I'm content to rest with what I said against these theories in (1987a, ch. 5).

[39] Hartry Field (2001a) has recently made a proposal designed to get around this objection. Field's proposal boils down to two claims: (a) an utterance of (1) is true just in case A is in a belief state whose content matches the content 'S' has for the one uttering (1); and (b) a special convention attaches to sentences of form (1) conformity to which requires one uttering (1) to intend her audience to believe that A is in a belief state whose content matches that of σ—where σ is any sentence that means for the audience what 'S' means for the speaker of (1). But I don't see how this helps. For suppose Al said to Betty, a fellow speaker of English, 'Ralph believes that embryos have souls'. It still remains that a monolingual speaker of Hungarian could know the truth expressed by Al without knowing the first thing about what Ralph believes.

There is a further problem for any version of sententialism which holds that that-clauses refer to the sentences embedded in them, as, for example, it might be held that the

In any event, I think there is a successful completion of the face-value theory, and in the next chapter I try to say what it is.

that-clause in 'Ralph believes that there is life on Venus' refers to 'there is life on Venus'. For consider the identity statement

That there is life on Venus = Fiona's theory.

The theorist in question must also hold that the that-clause in this identity statement also refers to the English sentence 'there is life on Venus', lest he be unable to account for the validity of an inference such as

Ralph believes that there is life on Venus.
That there is life on Venus = Fiona's theory.
∴ Ralph believes Fiona's theory.

But if the that-clause in the second premiss refers to 'there is life on Venus', then it's true iff Fiona's theory is identical to that sentence, which is absurd, since the English sentence has no greater claim to being Fiona's theory than any other sentence, of any other language, with the same meaning. The only way out I can see for the sententialist is to claim that the two occurrences of the that-clause in the displayed inference both refer to the class of sentences equivalent in meaning to 'there is life on Venus'. The sententialist may, however, have his reasons for not wanting to make this move.

2

Pleonastic Propositions

2.1 INTRODUCTION

The close of the preceding chapter left us realizing that if there is a successful version of the face-value theory, it will have to employ a notion of propositions which satisfies certain demands. Should I now rehearse those demands and then try to cook up an account of propositions to meet them? Not if I can arrive first at an account of propositions shown to be plausible on independent grounds, and then display its relevance to the face-value theory. That is what I'll try to do.

I call the account of propositions I'll offer an account of *pleonastic propositions*, because calling it that serves as a useful reminder of a crucial feature of the account, presently to be explained. But the label should not obscure what I'm up to. I aim to be revealing the nature of the propositions we believe, the actual referents of that-clauses, not inventing a new species of abstract entity especially assembled to do a certain job.

Pleonastic propositions are but one kind of pleonastic entity. In introducing the notion of a pleonastic entity, it will be helpful to start with a kind of pleonastic entity a little removed from more familiar arenas of dispute concerning the existence and nature of abstract entities—not that I'm so naive as to think this will give me an entry into the fray which escapes the axes of those protecting long-hardened positions. (Fortunately, inter-theoretical rivalries have cooled somewhat in recent times. Dugald Stewart, a nineteenth-century Scottish philosopher, tells us that, after a dormant period, the dispute between realism and nominalism was revived in the fourteenth century by William of Occam:

From this time the dispute was carried on with great warmth in the universities of France, of Germany, and of England; more particularly on the two former countries, where the sovereigns were led, by some political views, to interest themselves deeply in the contest [between realism and nominalism], and even to employ the civil power in supporting their favourite opinions. The Emperor Lewis of Bavaria, in return for the assistance which, in his disputes with the Pope, Occam had given to him by his writings, sided with the Nominalists. Lewis the Eleventh of France, on the other hand, attached himself to the Realists, and made their antagonists the objects of a cruel persecution.[1]

We may be thankful that current political leaders show less interest in metaphysics.) The pleonastic entities with which I'll begin, in the next section, are fictional entities, such as the fictional character Hamlet. Section 2.3 discusses the way in which properties are pleonastic entities, since that will have relevance to later discussions in the book, and in 2.4 I arrive at the way in which the propositions we believe are pleonastic entities. Section 2.5 discusses the way in which pleonastic propositions complete the face-value theory and considers a couple of challenges to the claim that they do give a successful completion of it. Section 2.6 clarifies my theory in relation to the notion of a possible world and to the modal notions of necessity and possibility; and 2.7 gives the direction of a more complete understanding of content, and thereby the further direction of this book.

2.2 FICTIONAL ENTITIES

James Joyce's novel *Ulysses* begins with the sentence

Stately, plump Buck Mulligan came from the stairhead, bearing a bowl of lather on which a mirror and a razor lay crossed.

This occurrence in the novel of the name 'Buck Mulligan' neither refers nor purports to refer to anything. Joyce was not trying to refer to a man named 'Buck Mulligan' and failing miserably; he was, in the way characteristic of fiction, *making as if* to refer to a man with that name and to tell us something about him, and we, in reading the novel, collude in this make-believe when we read the novel as a novel. What is remarkable is that this *pretending use* of the name 'Buck Mulligan' should create the existence of something whose name *is* 'Buck Mulligan', thereby making it possible to use the name in a

---

[1] Stewart (1970: 136–7).

genuinely referential way in true statements about that referent. The thing brought into existence is a certain abstract entity, the *fictional character* Buck Mulligan. Thus, from the fact that

(1) Joyce wrote a novel in which he used 'Buck Mulligan' in the pretending way characteristic of fiction

we may infer

(2) Joyce created the fictional character Buck Mulligan.

Since this thing, the fictional character Buck Mulligan, now exists in its own right, it will, like any existing thing, have numerous properties, and these may be ascribed to it in true statements. For example:

Buck Mulligan isn't as well known as certain of Joyce's other characters, such as Molly Bloom.

Buck Mulligan isn't a fictional detective.

Buck Mulligan was based on someone Joyce knew.

In these statements, 'Buck Mulligan' occurs as a genuinely referential singular term whose referent is a certain fictional character, and each statement says something true or false about that character. We may call this use of fictional names the *hypostatizing use* of fictional names. I call valid inferences like that from (1) to (2) *something-from-nothing transformations* since they take one from a statement in which no reference is made to a thing of a certain kind (in this case, to a fictional entity) to a statement in which there is a reference to a thing of that kind. 'Pleonastic' entities are entities whose existence is secured by something-from-nothing transformations (I call these things 'pleonastic' entities because something-from-nothing transformations often take us to pleonastic equivalents of the statements from which they are inferred). Fictional entities, as revealed in the something-from-nothing transformation from (1) to (2), are pleonastic entities.

How is it possible to get something from nothing in this way, to infer from statements in which a fictional name is used in the pretending way to a true statement in which it is used in the hypostatizing way? When Joyce wrote the displayed first sentence of his novel he was not referring to anything by 'Buck Mulligan', neither to a real person nor to a fictional person. Yet, as a result of that use of the name, there now exists a certain thing whose existence supervenes on Joyce's using the name 'Buck Mulligan' in the pretending way. How is it possible for the existence of a fictional character to be entailed by, to supervene on, a fact that doesn't involve that fictional character and can thus be fully specified without reference to it?

Before trying to answer this and related questions, let's ask another one: How is it possible for us to have *knowledge of* fictional entities, abstract entities whose existence supervenes on the pretending use of words? We may put this question in proper perspective in the following way. Imagine a possible world β exactly like the actual world, α, except that no one in β has the concept of a fictional entity, and hence no one has knowledge of the existence of any fictional entities. They have the pretending use in β, and, by stipulation, all the fiction that exists in α exists in β, and therefore every fictional entity that exists in α also exists in β (for it belongs to our concept of a fictional entity that the existence of such an entity supervenes solely on the pretending use of its name). But while β is heavily populated with fictional entities, no one in β is aware of the existence of any fictional entity. What would it take to bring the people in β up to epistemological snuff with us? What would the people in β have to do in order to discover the existence of the fictional entities in their world?

The answer is easy: what they would have to do, and all that they would have to do, would be to play a certain language game—namely, to adopt our hypostatizing use of fictional names. But how can that be? How can adopting a certain linguistic, or conceptual, practice give one knowledge of things that exist independently of that practice? Because to have the practice is to have the *concept*, and *it is a conceptual truth—* a truth knowable a priori via command of the concept—*that the existence of fictional entities supervenes on the pretending use of their names.*

Maybe you feel like reading Kant to me. For Kant, in response to the ontological argument for the existence of God, famously held that 'existence isn't a predicate', where by this he meant that no mere concept, however defined, can secure that there exist things that fall under the concept. Hartry Field, endorsing Kant's point, has succinctly restated it thus: 'An investigation of conceptual linkages can reveal conditions that things must satisfy if they are to fall under our concepts; but it can't yield that there are things that satisfy those concepts (as Kant pointed out in his critique of the ontological argument for the existence of God).'[2] For consider the concept of a *wishdate*,

---

[2] Field (1989: 5).

which I hereby stipulatively introduce thus:

> x is a *wishdate* = $_{df}$ x is a person whose existence supervenes on someone's wishing for a date, every such wish bringing into existence a person to date.

The point that Kant and Field are making implies that while this is a perfectly kosher definition, it doesn't result in its being true that there are any wishdates, no matter who wishes for a date. All that follows from the stipulative definition of a wishdate is that *if* (*per impossibile*) wishdates exist, *then* their existence supervenes on the mere wish for a date.

At the same time, isn't it *obvious* that, if there are fictional entities, then it is a conceptual truth that their existence supervenes on the pretending use of their names? I put the qualification 'if there are fictional entities' not because the existence of fictional entities is in doubt but because there are philosophers who doubt it. By my lights, it is true that

> The fictional spy James Bond is a lot more famous than the fictional detective Adam Dalgleish

and that in this displayed statement the names 'James Bond' and 'Adam Dalgleish' occur as genuinely referential singular terms whose referents are fictional characters.[3] So, there must be an important difference between the concept of a fictional character and that of a wishdate such that by virtue of that difference it can be a conceptual truth that the existence of a fictional character supervenes on the pretending use of its name but it can't be any kind of truth that the existence of a wishdate supervenes on the wish for a date. It can hardly be any kind of truth, let alone a conceptual truth, that wishing for a date brings into existence a person to date. That sort of wishing does not have that power, and if it did, it would be a contingent causal power; the wishing would not *entail* that there springs into existence someone to date. Yet it seems clear that it is a conceptual truth that using the name 'n' in writing a fiction creates the fictional character n. How should we characterize the crucial difference by virtue of which it can be a conceptual truth that fictional entities supervene on the

---

[3] Saul Kripke gave convincing arguments for the existence of fictional entities in his unpublished John Locke Lectures, given at Oxford University in 1973. See also Searle (1979, ch. 3).

pretending use of fictional names, but the existence of a date does not supervene on the wish for a date? Perhaps in the following way.

There is a crucial difference between the concept of a wishdate and the concept of a fictional entity (or of any other kind of pleonastic entity, although for now my focus will be just on fictional entities). To a first approximation, the difference is that:

> There are numerous theories T such that when we add to T the concept of a wishdate together with the claim that wishing for a date entails the existence of a wishdate, the resulting theory is *not* a *conservative extension* of T. But if we add to *any* theory T the concept of a fictional entity together with its attendant claim that using a name in the pretending way entails the existence of a fictional entity, the resulting theory *is* a conservative extension of T.

A theory T' is a *conservative extension* of a theory T provided that T' includes T and nothing statable in the vocabulary of T is logically entailed by T' but not by T. (The notion of 'adding a concept' is vague; it should be taken to mean that the canonical expression for the new concept has its full meaning when introduced, and that as much of that meaning as can be made explicit via defining conditions is made explicit, especially whatever existence-entailing something-from-nothing conditionals are partly definitive of the concept.)

Suppose T is a fairly rich true physical theory that doesn't employ the concept of a wishdate or the concept of a fictional entity, but does assert that someone wished for a date and that James Joyce wrote *Ulysses*, where this is understood to include the text of the novel. Adding to T the claim that wishing for a date entails the existence of a wishdate will entail that there exists a person—the person brought into existence by the wish for a date—whose existence wasn't recognized in T but was statable in the vocabulary of T. The resulting theory is therefore clearly not a conservative extension of T. Indeed, should the new person exist, he or she would be a substantial physical object that would enormously disturb the pre-existing causal order. But when we add the concept of a fictional entity to T, and with it its something-from-nothing entailment claims, what can we get that we couldn't get from T alone? Well, we can get the statement that the fictional character Buck Mulligan was created by James Joyce but (subject to a small qualification) we can assert nothing new that can be said in the language of T. Adding fictional entities to one's ontology via legitimate something-from-nothing entailments does nothing to disturb the pre-existing causal order. That is why adding those entailment claims to *T* yields a conservative extension of *T*.

The first shot needs refinement; as it stands it is too strong to account for what makes the truths expressed by instances of (roughly) 'If someone uses the name "*n*" in the pretending way, then there is a fictional entity *n*' conceptual truths; and it is also arguably too weak, that it lets in things that shouldn't be let in.

The first shot is too strong because there are ways of adding the concept of a fictional entity together with its something-from-nothing entailment claims and getting a theory that isn't a conservative extension of the original theory. For example:

- The new theory, but not the original theory, may entail that more than such-and-such many things exist, which was statable in the original theory.
- In addition to asserting that Joyce wrote *Ulysses*, the original theory may also assert that if there are abstract entities, then it will snow in Miami in August. When we add the concept of a fictional entity to that theory, along with its something-from-nothing entailment claim, we get a theory which entails that fictional entities—and therefore abstract entities—exist, in which case the resulting theory will also entail that it will snow in Miami in August, which was assertable but unasserted in the original theory.
- In addition to asserting that Joyce wrote *Ulysses*, the original theory may assert that there are no abstract entities, so that when we add the concept of a fictional entity and its something-from-nothing entailment claim, we get an inconsistent theory from which everything follows.

That the first shot may also be too weak is implied by a type of example independently suggested to me by Kit Fine and by Josh Schechter. For consider the concept of an anti-fictional entity, where that is stipulated to be the concept of an abstract object whose existence both supervenes on anything one likes and rules out the existence of fictional entities. It is arguable that the concept of an anti-fictional entity is on a par with the concept of a fictional entity as regards conservative extension, so that adding the concept of an anti-fictional entity to a theory will conservatively extend it to whatever extent adding the concept of a fictional entity would, thereby frustrating hopes of accounting for pleonastic concepts in terms of conservative extension (since if the concepts of a fictional entity and of an anti-fictional entity were both pleonastic concepts, then that would imply that fictional entities did and did not exist).[4]

These problematic examples motivate a strategy employed by Hartry Field when he wanted to say that the result of adding a mathematical theory to a nominalistic theory conservatively extends the nominalistic theory but had to contend with a nominalistic theory that says things that rule out the existence of abstract entities.[5] Field's solution to this problem was, roughly speaking, to say that a mathematical theory can't be assured of conservatively extending every nominalistic theory, but can be assured of conservatively extending the result of restricting the quantifiers of any given nominalistic theory to things that aren't mathematical entities. (We restrict T's quantifiers to things that satisfy a predicate 'Px' thus: if T asserts '$\forall xGx$', then we replace that with '$\forall x(Px \rightarrow Gx)$', and if T asserts '$\exists xGx$', then we replace that with '$\exists x(Px \& Gx)$'.) I believe that a suitable deployment of Field's strategy will enable me to put together a definition that will capture what I want from the notion of a pleonastic entity.[6] The definition should be regarded as stipulative, substantive claims coming in the form of claims about what kinds of things are pleonastic entities. For now, the definition needs only to get right the distinction between wishdates and fictional entities. I start with some preliminary definitions.

Where '$\Rightarrow$' expresses metaphysical entailment,[7] '$S \Rightarrow \exists xFx$' is a *something-from-nothing F-entailment claim* iff (i) its antecedent

[4] The parasitic nature of the concept of an anti-fictional entity raises a problem familiar from other problems created by parasitic concepts. So you think that hypothesis H is true because it provides the best explanation of all observable evidence. But how can you justifiably reach that conclusion when you have done nothing to rule out another hypothesis which explains the same evidence—namely, the hypothesis Anti-H, which says that H is false but that all the observable evidence is as it would be if H were true?

[5] Field (1980: 11–12).

[6] The idea of accommodating certain difficulties for a conservative extension test by restricting a theory's quantifiers to things in its recognized ontology is also used by Bob Hale and Crispin Wright in their discussion of conservativeness in connection with Hume's Principle. Their way of putting the qualification is that the extending theory 'must not introduce fresh commitments which (i) are expressible in the language as it was prior to the introduction of its [additional material] and which (ii) concern the previously recognized ontology of concepts, objects, and functions, etc., whatever in detail they may be' (Hale and Wright 2000: 302).

[7] A *metaphysically entails B* just in case the material conditional $A \rightarrow B$ is metaphysically necessary. As I understand the notion, metaphysical necessity is that strong form of necessity

is metaphysically possible but doesn't *logically* entail either its consequent or any statement of the form '$\exists x(x = \alpha)$', where 'α' refers to an F, and (ii) the concept of an F is such that if there are Fs, then $S \Rightarrow \exists x F x$. (I'll say that the concept of an F 'implies' a something-from-nothing F-entailment claim if it satisfies (ii).)

A *pleonastic entity* is an entity that falls under a *pleonastic concept*; and a pleonastic concept is the concept of an F which implies *true* something-from-nothing F-entailment claims.

For any theory or sentence T, $T^{\sim F}$ is the theory or sentence that results from restricting each quantifier of T to things that aren't F.

I now offer the following conservative-extension criterion for being a pleonastic concept.

(CE) The concept of an F implies true something-from-nothing F-entailment claims—and is therefore a *pleonastic concept*—iff (i) it implies something-from-nothing F-entailment claims, and (ii) for any theory T and sentence S expressible in T,[8] if the theory obtained by adding to $T^{\sim F}$ the concept of an F, together with its something-from-nothing F-entailment claims, logically entails $S^{\sim F}$, then $T^{\sim F}$ logically entails $S^{\sim F}$.[9]

In other words, adding pleonastic entities to any theory conservatively extends that theory, relative to the restriction on quantification. We can see how CE handles the problems for the first shot in the following way (in considering each example, 'T' will designate the original theory).

The first problem was that the theory obtained when we add to T the concept of a fictional entity may entail that more than such-and-such many things exist, when this isn't entailed by T. But since the new

---

such that whatever is logically, arithmetically, or conceptually necessary is *ipso facto* metaphysically necessary, but something can be metaphysically necessary without being necessary in any of those ways (such as, perhaps, the proposition that water is composed of H_2O molecules). Something can be 'physically necessary'—e.g. the proposition that nothing travels faster than the speed of light—without being metaphysically necessary. I don't think metaphysical necessity can be defined. This is touched on again in 2.6.

[8] S's being expressible in T doesn't imply its being asserted in T; it merely means that S can be formulated in the vocabulary of T.

[9] CE supersedes the criterion proposed in Schiffer (2001a).

theory doesn't entail that more than such-and-such many *non-fictional* things exist, it is a conservative extension of $T^{\sim F}$ (where '*Fx*' abbreviates '*x* is a fictional entity'), whose claims about how many things exist are limited to claims about how many *non-fictional* things exist.

The second problem for the first shot was that T may assert that if there are abstract entities, then it will snow in Miami in August. But $T^{\sim F}$ merely says that if any non-fictional entities are abstract entities, then it will snow in Miami in August, and thus nothing statable but unstated in $T^{\sim F}$ is forthcoming when we add the concept of a fictional entity to $T^{\sim F}$.

The third problem was that T may assert that there are no abstract entities. But since $T^{\sim F}$ merely asserts that nothing exists that is both a non-fictional entity and an abstract entity, there is again no problem for CE.

Nor is CE threatened by Fine and Schechter's anti-fictional entities. If there is a threat here, it is either (*a*) that the concept of an anti-fictional entity would, unacceptably, be a pleonastic concept if CE were correct, or (*b*) that the result of adding fictional entities to the required restriction of a theory that asserts the existence of anti-fictional entities would not conservatively extend that theory. It is clear (*b*) is not a threat. Suppose $T = (S \& \exists x Ax)$, where '*Ax*' abbreviates '*x* is an anti-fictional entity'. Now, '$\exists x Ax$' for all intents and purposes is equivalent to

$$\exists x(x = x \& \forall y(\sim Fy))$$

where '$\sim Fy$' abbreviates '*y* is not a fictional entity'. Thus, when we restrict T with the formula '$\sim Fy_i$' (for appropriate variable 'y_i'), $T^{\sim F} =$

$$S^{\sim F} \& \exists x(\ (\sim Fx \& x = x) \& \forall y(\sim Fy \rightarrow \sim Fy)\ ),$$

which is conservatively extended by the theory that adds fictional entities. Nor is (*a*) a threat, since the result of adding anti-fictional entities to the required restriction of a theory that asserts the existence of fictional entities is an inconsistent theory from which everything follows. For let $T = (S \& \exists x Fx)$, where '*Fx*' abbreviates '*x* is a fictional entity'. When we restrict each quantifier in T with the formula '$\sim Ax_i$', $T^{\sim A} =$

$$S^{\sim A} \& \exists x(\sim Ax \& Fx)$$

so that when we add to this the claim that anti-fictional entities exist, we get the inconsistent

$$S^{\sim A} \,\&\, \exists x(\,(\sim Ax \,\&\, Fx)\, \&\, \exists y(y = y \,\&\, \forall z(\sim Fz)\,)\,).$$

It might be thought that CE still faces problems. An example of Hartry Field's (Cian Dorr raised a similar problem) might again suggest that CE is too weak, that it lets in things I don't want to let in. Field's example concerns the concept of an undetectable non-interfering god. Won't that conservatively extend any theory that the concept of a fictional entity will conservatively extend? I don't think so. What are we to make of the concept of a 'god'? If the concept of an undetectable and non-interfering god is simply the concept of an undetectable and non-interfering thing, then there is no problem, since that is what fictional entities are. If the concept of a god is to be non-vacuous, it must entail that gods have propositional attitudes. But now consider a theory that entails the existence of propositional attitudes. When we add to that theory the claim that an undetectable and non-interfering god exists, we get a theory that introduces new propositional attitudes and therefore isn't a conservative extension of the original theory.[10]

CE, as I said, should be read as a stipulative definition of 'pleonastic concept', with substantive claims coming in the form of claims that such-and-such concept is, or isn't, a pleonastic concept. The concept of a fictional entity is a pleonastic concept, fictional entities therefore pleonastic entities. Fictional entities are that thin and inconsequential. We overgeneralize Kant's insight when we lump concepts that pass the CE test with the concept of a wishdate and the concept of God. Fictional entities are mere shadows of the pretending use of their names;[11] they come softly into existence, without disturbing the pre-existing causal order in any way. That is why claims that they exist may be conservatively added to the truths we had before those claims were added. There is nothing more to the nature of fictional entities than is determined by the hypostatizing language game that recognizes

[10] Kit Fine has wondered about changing Field's non-interfering god to a prime mover, or first cause. But I don't think that adding a first cause can be assured of conservatively extending all relevant theories. A theory that doesn't say anything was caused but in which causal claims are expressible won't be conservatively extended by the addition of the assertion that there's a first cause, since the resulting theory will entail that some event was caused.

[11] The 'shadows' metaphor is borrowed from David Armstrong's (1989) metaphor of properties as shadows of predicates.

them in our ontology. This is in contrast with cats, islands, electrons, and whatever else enjoys the highest degree of ontological and conceptual independence from our linguistic or conceptual practices. Their essential natures must be discovered by scientific investigation, not by an armchair perusal of our talk about them. But there can be nothing more to the nature of fictional entities than is determined by our hypostatizing use of fictional names. The 'science' of them may be done in an armchair by reflective participants in the hypostatizing practice; fictional entities can have 'no hidden and substantial nature for a theory to uncover. All we know and all we need to know about [them] in general'[12] is determined by our hypostatizing use of fictional names. As we shall see, this sort of thinness is an important feature of the pleonastic entities that most interest us.

Let's briefly take stock. Sherlock Holmes is a much more famous fictional detective than Adam Dalgleish. The statement I just made is literally true, and its literal truth requires the existence of the fictional characters Sherlock Holmes and Adam Dalgleish. Given the existence of these fictional characters, it ought to be clear that even slightly reflective people have a priori knowledge of the conceptual truth that the existence of any fictional entity supervenes on the existence of a work of fiction in which the character's name is used in the pretending way characteristic of fiction. This explains how we are well enough *en rapport* with certain fictional entities to have knowledge about them. It is, however, one thing for us, as philosophers, to know that it is a conceptual truth that the existence of fictional entities supervenes on the pretending use of their names and another, more difficult thing to discern and state clearly what it is about the concept of a fictional entity that allows the relevant something-from-nothing entailment claims to be conceptual truths. I'm more confident that these are conceptual truths than I am that the stuff about conservative extension captures what's essential to that, and I'm more confident that the general idea about conservative extension is on the right track than I am about whether CE has everything exactly right. Anyway, I hope I've succeeded in getting at what is crucial with CE, but, philosophy and the effort to state necessary and sufficient conditions being what they are, I wouldn't be completely shocked to learn that what I've written needs further qualification. Even approximate truth may do pretty well for my further purposes, and at this point it

---

[12] Johnston (1988: 38).

should be plain what those purposes are. My strategy has been to begin with things—fictional entities—subject to something-from-nothing entailments that are fairly undeniably conceptual truths; next, to discern what it is about the concept of a fictional entity that permits its something-from-nothing entailment claims to be conceptual truths; next, to state the result of that discernment as a general principle; and eventually to show that the propositions we believe, along with other things of interest, satisfy that principle. I turn now, in the next two sections, to other things, closer to what matters in this book, which, I claim, also fall under concepts that satisfy CE.

2.3 PLEONASTIC PROPERTIES

Pleonastic entities are entities whose existence is typically secured by something-from-nothing transformations—'secured' not necessarily in the sense that they are brought into existence (like fictional entities) but in the sense that their existence supervenes on the premisses of something-from-nothing transformations. We have a something-from-nothing transformation when from a statement involving no reference to an F we can deduce a statement that does refer to an F. The property of being a dog is a pleonastic entity. From the statement

(3) Lassie is a dog,

whose only singular term is 'Lassie', we can validly infer the pleonastic equivalent

(4) Lassie has the property of being a dog,

which contains the new singular term 'the property of being dog', whose referent is the property of being a dog.

Just as we asked about the licence for the something-from-nothing transformations that yield fictional entities, so we may repeat the question for properties: What explains the validity of the something-from-nothing transformation that takes us from (3) to (4)? How *can* (3) entail (4), thereby entailing that the property of being a dog exists? The answer, of course, mirrors that given for fictional entities; it is the answer that applies to all pleonastic entities. It is a *conceptual truth* that if Lassie is a dog, then Lassie has the property of being dog. The intuitive rightness of this can be glossed in the same way we glossed the intuitive rightness of its being a conceptual truth that the existence of a fictional entity supervenes on the pretending use of a fictional name. For how, one might ask, are we able to have knowledge about properties, mind- and language-independent abstract entities that are wholly incapable of causally interacting with us? This question, as before, is made more vivid in the following way. Suppose there is a possible world exactly like ours except that our counterparts in that world don't have any property-hypostatizing linguistic or conceptual practices, and hence have no concept of a property. These people can think that Lassie is a dog, but they can't infer from this that Lassie has the property of being a dog, even though in that world, as in every world in which Lassie exists, it is necessarily true that if Lassie is a dog, then Lassie has the property of being a dog. Lacking the concept of a property, these people are entirely ignorant of properties, even though they live in a world as rich in properties as the actual world. What would it take to bring these people up to epistemological snuff with us?

What it would take, and all that it would take, would be for them to engage in a certain manner of speaking, a certain language game—namely, our property-hypostatizing practices, in particular our property-yielding something-from-nothing transformations. But how can this be? They certainly couldn't discover the existence of *volcanoes* by engaging in any language game. How can merely engaging in a linguistic, or conceptual, practice give one knowledge of things that exist independently of that practice? Because to engage in the practice is to have the concept of a property, and to have the concept of a property is to know a priori the conceptual truths that devolve from that concept, such as the conceptual truth that every dog has the property of being a dog.

We should expect these conceptual truths to be explained by the fact that the concept of a property is a pleonastic concept, properties therefore pleonastic entities. And it is clear that the concept of a property passes the CE test. For take any theory that doesn't employ the notion of a property. It says that Fido is a dog and that dogs bark, but it doesn't say that Fido has the property of being a dog or that things that have the property of being a dog also have the property of being barkers. When we add to this theory the concept of a property, which carries with it its something-from-nothing property-entailment claims, the theory that results is (modulo the point about restriction of quantifiers) a conservative extension of the original theory. Once again, properties are that thin and that inconsequential; properties, to borrow again Armstrong's metaphor, are mere shadows of predicates; adding them to a theory does nothing to disturb the output of that theory, does nothing to alter that theory's take on the pre-existing causal order.

Thus, as with all pleonastic entities, properties have 'no hidden and substantial nature for a theory to uncover.'[13] The essential truths about them are directly or indirectly determined by the hypostatizing practices constitutive of the concept of a property, together with those necessary a priori truths applicable to things of any kind, such as that if $x = y$, then whatever property x has, y has, and vice versa. As regards the principles by which properties are individuated, it means that if a question of individuation is left unsettled by the practices constitutive of the concept of a property, then that question has no determinate answer. The same applies to any other kind of pleonastic entity. This has important implications for the mind–body problem. Before illustrating this with respect to properties, let me first illustrate it with respect to pleonastic entities of another kind, events.

Events are pleonastic entities, for they, too, enter our ontology via something-from-nothing transformations. From

> Jane was born on a Tuesday,

whose only singular term is 'Jane', we may validly infer the pleonastic equivalent

> Jane's birth was on a Tuesday,

which contains the new singular term 'Jane's birth', whose referent is Jane's birth, an event. Leibniz's law gives us a means for establishing numerous non-identities. If Jane's birth occurred in 1850 and her death occurred in 1933, then Jane's birth ≠ Jane's death. But there is a paucity of principles determined by our conceptual practices that enable us to establish interesting identifications; evidently, such principles aren't required by the purposes for which we have the concept of an event.[14] For example, consider Donald Davidson's claim that while no mental event *type* is identical to any physical or functional

---

[13] Johnston (1988).

[14] Here (and elsewhere in this book) I flout the Quinean principle that in order for there to be Fs there must be a non-trivial criterion of identity for Fs. After all, there are pains, but where is the non-trivial criterion of identity for pains? As implied in the text, very often the lack of a non-trivial criterion for Fs will render the proposition that x is the same F as y indeterminate, but not always, as is obvious from the fact that I can know, say, that the Φ is the same F as the Ψ without a non-trivial criterion just by virtue of knowing of some given F that it's both uniquely Φ and uniquely Ψ.

event type, every mental event *token* is identical to a physical event token; that is to say, every token of a mental event type is also a token of a physical event type.[15] But there is nothing in the principles by which events are individuated that could make any identification of a mental event token with a physical event token determinately true, given that no mental event type is identical to any physical or functional event type. It is given, let's suppose, that at time t there occurs in you a certain twinge and an X-fibre firing. How might you determine whether there is one event token in you at t that is both the twinge and the X-fibre firing, as opposed to one event that is the twinge and a distinct co-temporal event that is the X-fibre firing? It should be clear that there is no procedure you could in principle carry out to resolve the question. This isn't because the answer can't be known, or can be known only on the basis of some abstruse methodological principle of simplicity or the unity of science, but because there is nothing in our concept of an event to determine the issue. It is, at best, indeterminate.

The same is true for properties and the claim that mental properties are identical to physical or functional properties, where the correct identity claim is one that is supposed to be knowable only a posteriori, if knowable at all. For what procedure might you follow to determine whether, say, the property of being a pain = the property of being a c-fibre stimulation? We can, to simplify more than a little, know a posteriori that water = H_2O because our concept of water is the concept of whatever it is that we drink, swim in, etc., and we then discover that that stuff is composed of H_2O molecules. But we don't think of the property of being a pain under a concept that identifies it in terms of one of its contingent properties, and there is nothing in the practices constitutive of our concept of a property, or of the property of being a pain, that leaves a conceptual space for it to be determinately true that the property of being a pain is identical to any physical property.

It might be helpful to think of a contrasting view. Consider the property of being a dog. On my view, there isn't a lot more to this property than can be culled from the something-from-nothing transformation that allows us to move back and forth between

(5) x is a dog

15 Davidson (1980*b*).

and its pleonastic equivalent

(6) x has the property of being a dog.

Now, suppose (what is probably not the case), that, necessarily, a thing is a dog just in case it belongs to such-and-such genotype. Can we then say that the property of being a dog = the property of belonging to such-and-such genotype? I don't see that we can, for there is nothing in the something-from-nothing practice or in any ancillary practice to establish either that

> The property of being a dog = the property of belonging to such-and-such genotype

or that

> The property of being a dog and the property of belonging to such-and-such genotype are distinct metaphysically equivalent properties.

On the contrasting view, 'doghood' is simply a proper name of a thing enjoying the same conceptual and ontological independence from our hypostatizing practices as a volcano. Perhaps the link between 'doghood' and doghood by virtue of which the former names the latter is a causal link. In any case, once we grasp the bearer of 'doghood', it is then a matter for some sort of further, a posteriori investigation to determine the nature of, and hence the individuating conditions for, the property that bears that name. For all we yet know, we may discover that this property is identical to this, that, or the other thing.

Consider the difference between volcanoes and fictional characters. We can first discover volcanoes and then explain the introduction of 'volcano' in terms of the discovered volcanoes, but we can't first discover fictional characters and then explain the introduction of 'fictional character' in terms of the discovered fictional characters. This is because of the way, already made a big deal of, fictional entities enter our ontology only *qua* fictional entities, via the something-from-nothing transformations that give us our knowledge of them. The problem with the contrasting view is that it makes properties out to be like volcanoes when they're really like fictional entities. There can be no intrinsically identifying the property of being a dog apart from identifying it as the property of being a dog. If something falls under the concept of doghood, we can't look at what it is apart from its falling under that concept, for there is nothing there apart from its falling under that concept. There can be nothing more to the identity and individuation of a particular property than is determined by the canonical concept for that property. This is why the property of being a dog has no hidden nature for empirical investigation to unearth; it is a shadow of the word 'dog'.

I turn now to certain critical questions whose answers will further clarify the notion of a pleonastic entity.

The way properties enter our conceptual scheme via something-from-nothing transformations and the way they take to the metaphor of being shadows of predicates may suggest that in some sense they are creations of our hypostatizing linguistic or conceptual practices. I believe there is something to this. Conceptualism about properties is the view that properties are creations of our conceptual or linguistic practices. I don't see how this can be literally true, since properties exist in every possible world, and thus in possible worlds in which there are neither thinkers nor speakers. Since it is a metaphysically necessary truth that properties exist, they can hardly be created by anything we do. Indeed, their being independent of us in this way is a consequence of the pleonastic conception of them. For example, from

Necessarily, there are dogs or there are not dogs

we may infer

Necessarily, there are things that have the property of being a dog or there are not things that have the property of being a dog,

which entails

Necessarily, the property of being a dog is or is not instantiated,

which entails

Necessarily, the property of being a dog exists.

The property of being a dog, in other words, exists in every metaphysically possible world (although, to be sure, it is only in some of these possible worlds that it is instantiated).

So, conceptualism about properties is false: nothing we do creates properties. At the same time, I believe that the theory of pleonastic properties is a conceptualist *manqué* theory: it is a theory that should relieve the need to be a conceptualist, a theory the conceptualist would have accepted had she thought of it. In this sense, the doctrine of pleonastic properties, and of pleonastic entities generally, is a deflationary theory, but that quasi-evaluative term has in recent years been used in so many diverse ways that it is now almost entirely devoid of descriptive content.

There are three questions about something-from-nothing transformations that must be addressed. The questions arise for any kind of pleonastic entity, but I'll address them, for the most part, with respect to properties, although what I say is intended to apply, *mutatis mutandis*, to other kinds of pleonastic entities.

The first question is about the validity of the inference schema

(7) x is F.
    So, x has the property of being F.

For virtually all substitution instances of 'F', e.g.

Fido is a dog
So, Fido has the property of being a dog,

the schema (7) yields a valid inference; but, notoriously, we can't safely conclude that (7) is valid for all substitution instances, as is shown by the at first sight seemingly innocuous inference

(8) Doghood is a property that doesn't instantiate itself.
    So, doghood has the property of being a property that doesn't instantiate itself.[16]

For what are we now to say about *the property of being a property that doesn't instantiate itself*? Does it instantiate itself? If it does, it doesn't; if it doesn't, it does. We are landed with a contradiction. Let me cautiously say that it can't be said that (8) is determinately valid. My reason for putting it in this coy way will be apparent in Chapter 5, when I present my own views on the 'determinately' operator. For now, however, it doesn't really matter whether we say either that there can be no such property as the property of being a property that doesn't instantiate itself or that it is indeterminate whether there can be such a property. The important thing for now is that any claims about the validity of the schema (7) must be qualified, and the question of

---

[16] Another exception to the unqualified validity of the schema (7) is provided by a sentence such as 'Cell phones are ubiquitous', from whose truth we shouldn't want to infer that every cell phone has the property of being ubiquitous.

moment, for me, is how to qualify (7) without undermining the pleonastic conception of properties.

Before directly addressing this question I want to say something about the nature of philosophical paradoxes and the bearing of that on the nature of our quotidian concepts. A philosophical paradox is a set of apparently mutually incompatible propositions each one of which enjoys some significant degree of plausibility when viewed on its own. The problem of free will is a paradigm of such a paradox. Here there are three evidently mutually incompatible propositions: (i) that we have free will, i.e. that we sometimes act freely; (ii) that everything we do is such that we were caused to do it by events that occurred even before we were born and, therefore, over which we had no control; and (iii) that the foregoing two propositions can't both be true. Now, a *happy-face solution* to a philosophical paradox would do two things. First, it would identify the odd guy out: it would tell us that the apparently incompatible propositions were not really incompatible, or that a certain one of the plausible propositions wasn't the truth it appeared to be; and secondly, it would, in unmasking the odd guy out, do so in a way that removed its patina of plausibility, so that we would never again be taken in by it. Most of the traditional solutions to the classical philosophical paradoxes aspire to be happy-face solutions. For example, the problem of free will admits in principle of three potential happy-face solutions, each with its school of proponents: 'compatibilism', which accepts (i) and (ii) but denies (iii); 'hard determinism', which accepts (ii) and (iii) but denies (i); and 'libertarianism', which accepts (i) and (iii) but denies (ii).

A nice example of a genuinely happy-face solution is the solution to the 'paradox' of the barber who shaves all and only those who don't shave themselves. Does he, or doesn't he, shave himself? Here the solution is that it is logically impossible for there to be such a barber, and once this is appreciated there is nothing whatever paradoxical or puzzling about the barber. But what classical philosophical problem enjoys a happy-face solution? The trouble in each case is that while any given 'solution' offers an identification of the odd guy out, none succeeds in removing from it its patina of plausibility. This is illustrated by each position in the space of potential happy-face solutions to the problem of free will. Consider compatibilism, no doubt the most widely held solution. If to say that an act is free is just to say that the actor would have acted otherwise if she had decided to (or, anyway, something in that direction), then how did the problem ever come to be a problem, and why has no one succeeded in eliminating the worry that we can't be free in any sense that matters if everything we do is caused by factors over which we had no control? When one thinks of the classical philosophical paradoxes—scepticism about the external world, the problem of induction, the sorites, the liar, etc.—it seems clear that none of them truly enjoys a happy-face solution. There are competing solutions to each paradox, and none succeeds in getting us to see through the alleged spurious plausibility of its chosen odd guy out.

It is my view that most, if not all, of these paradoxes don't have happy-face solutions; they have *un*happy-face solutions.[17] An unhappy-face solution to a paradox would do two things. First, it would tell us that there can be no determinately correct complete identification of the odd guy(s) out; and secondly, it would tell us what it is about the concepts involved that explains this. In each case, the explanation will find a glitch in the concept or concepts involved, a tension in the underived conceptual roles that individuate those concepts. For example, as regards the problem of free will, our concept of free will has one component that inclines us to ascribe free will in certain conditions ('paradigm cases' of free acts, if there are any), whereas another component disinclines us to ascribe free will when we know that the agent's decision was caused by factors over which he or she had no control, and there is nothing else in the concept or else-where to adjudicate the issue. The troublesomeness of the paradox-inducing conceptual glitch may vary from case to case. In some cases it may be disastrous, as it arguably is for our concepts of free will and moral responsibility, but in other cases it may be benign. One way in which it may not be disastrous is nicely illustrated by an example made up by Charles Chihara.[18] A group of secretaries of clubs they are not allowed to join themselves form a club whose condition of mem-bership is that one be a secretary of a club one isn't allowed to join. All works well until one day the club itself hires a secretary. Is this person eligible to join the club? If yes, then the condition of membership is violated, and so, no. But if no, then yes, for then the condition of membership is satisfied. Chihara suggests that something like this lies behind the semantic paradoxes, and I'm inclined to agree.

I would put the point this way as regards the version of Grelling's paradox represented by 'the property of being a property that doesn't

---

[17] Schiffer (1995–6).   [18] Chihara (1979).

instantiate itself.' Our concept of a property is governed by an under-ived conceptual role that disposes us to accept instances of (7); it is *as if* the notion of a property had been explicitly introduced without qualification by the schema. All goes well until we hit upon the para-doxical instance (8), at which point it is not clear what to say, and for which there may well be no determinately correct thing to say (here I look ahead to Chapter 5). What is crucial to the present discussion is that we must not suppose that the paradox generated by 'the property of being a property that doesn't instantiate itself' has a happy-face solution. Our concept of a property *is* largely determined by our disposition to accept instances of the property-hypostatizing something-from-nothing transformation (7) (that's why the paradox is a paradox); it is just that the concept of a property, like the concepts of truth, knowledge, free will, and more, has a glitch, one revealed in the present version of Grelling's paradox. The existence of the paradox neither shows that the uninfected instances of (7) are invalid, nor that our concept of a property isn't based on the underived conceptual role that leads us to take uninfected instances of something-from-nothing property-entailment claims as conceptual truths. Where we go from here is another matter, but I will defer further discussion of what can be done when confronted with an unhappy-face solution to Chapter 5.

A second point of clarification concerns the scope of something-from-nothing entailments. It is important to appreciate that it doesn't follow from the fact that '*x* has the property of being *F*' is a pleonastic equivalent of '*x* is *F*' that *every* statement containing a singular term whose referent is a property is pleonastically (or in *any* way) equiva-lent to a statement containing no such singular term. The statement that so-and-so is humble is pleonastically equivalent to the state-ment that so-and-so has humility, the property of being humble, but I doubt that the statement that humility is a virtue is pleonastically equivalent to any statement not containing a singular term referring to humility.[19] When we get to propositions in the next section, it will be especially important to appreciate that what is stated by a belief report of the form '*A* believes that *S*' can't be stated without reference to the proposition to which the belief report's that-clause refers.

[19] Cf. Armstrong (1989).

Finally, what about inexpressible properties? A property isn't inexpressible simply by virtue of not having a single *word* to express it: from the fact that x is a figure having fourteen sides and a fuzzy texture we may infer that x has the property of being a figure that has fourteen sides and a fuzzy texture. Still, there might be properties that are ineffable, or perhaps effable only in the languages of vastly more intelligent creatures, or of creatures with much different sensory abilities. My view here is that we can make sense of such properties just by virtue of our ability to make sense of there being a language—an enrichment of our own language or a completely different language—in which such properties are expressible.

2.4   PLEONASTIC PROPOSITIONS

Propositions, the things to which that-clauses refer, are also pleonastic entities. They have their something-from-nothing transformations, such as the one that takes us from

>   Lassie is a dog,

whose only singular term continues to be 'Lassie', to another of its pleonastic equivalents,

>   That Lassie is a dog is true

(more colloquially, 'It is true that Lassie is a dog'), which contains the singular term 'that Lassie is a dog', whose referent is the proposition that Lassie is a dog. Consequently, the concept of a proposition—that is to say, of a that-clause referent—satisfies CE, the conservative extension criterion. When we add the concept of a proposition, which carries with it its something-from-nothing proposition-entailment claims, to a theory that doesn't employ the notion of a proposition—that is to say, to a theory whose language is devoid of that-clauses—the resulting theory (modulo the stuff about restricted quantifiers) is a conservative extension of the original theory. Merely adding propositions does nothing to disturb the pre-existing causal order; as properties are shadows of predicates, so propositions are shadows of sentences.

Of course, the language game we play with that-clauses isn't limited to something-from-nothing transformations, or even to what is indirectly implied by them. Crucially, there is also the use of that-clauses in ascriptions of meaning, speech acts, and psychological states like belief. These practices presuppose the validity (subject to certain qualifications[20]) of the something-from-nothing transformation schema that yields the familiar truth schema for propositions—namely,

The proposition that S is true iff S

—but the role of that-clauses in propositional-attitude discourse is not deducible from the something-from-nothing practice and is essential to completing the account of pleonastic propositions. What we are about to see is of signal importance for the theory of content—namely, that, in certain crucial respects, *the relation between that-clauses and the propositions to which they refer is importantly different from the usual relation between singular terms and their referents.*

Assume that the face-value theory is correct and that, therefore, utterances of the form 'A believes that S' share the form $R(a, b)$ with other sentences containing a two-place relational predicate flanked by two singular argument terms, such as 'She loves him' and 'Austria is next to Germany'. Trivially, if in an utterance of

(9) $t_1 R s\, t_2$

the uttered token of t_1, τ_1, refers to a and the uttered token of t_2, τ_2, refers to b (and assuming that 'R' expresses the R relation), then the utterance will be true just in case a $R s$ b. Thus, the referent of τ_2 will help in this logical sense to 'determine' the truth condition for the utterance. This much holds for every utterance of form (9), including belief reports. It is after this commonality that important differences take over. I'll list a few things that normally hold of utterances of form (9) when the term in the t_2 slot is other than a that-clause which, as we'll presently see, don't hold when the term is a that-clause in a belief report.

(*a*) Normally, in order to evaluate an utterance of form (9), we must first identify the referent of τ_1 and the referent of τ_2, and then determine whether the former stands in the R relation to the latter. Consequently, the referent of τ_2, once itself determined, partially

---

[20] I allude to the semantic paradoxes, on which my line is the same as the one I took in the preceding section regarding the Grelling-type paradox that arises for 'the property of being a property that does not instantiate itself'. The topic recurs in Ch. 5.

determines the criteria for evaluating the statement made by the utterance of (9): we fix the referent of τ_2, and thereby partially fix the criteria for truth-evaluating the utterance of (9). What we absolutely do *not* do is *first* fix the criteria for evaluating the utterance of (9) and *then* use that to fix the referent of τ_2. This is an obvious and familiar point, but it is important that it be made vivid. To this end, consider the pair of statements

(10*a*) Henri admires Picasso
(10*b*) Henri admires Braque.

In order to evaluate the utterance of (10*a*), we must first identify the referents of 'Henri' and 'Picasso'; likewise, *mutatis mutandis*, for (10*b*). It would be laughable to suppose we *first* fix the criteria of evaluation and *then* use those criteria to determine the referents. We evaluate the statements made in (10*a*,*b*) by idenfying the referents of 'Henri', 'Picasso', and 'Braque' and then determining whether the first stands in the admiration relation to the other two. This is brought home by the absurdity of supposing that we know that Picasso ≠ Braque because we know that the statements made in (10*a*) and (10*b*) may differ in truth-value. Just the opposite, of course: we know that the two statements may differ in truth-value *because we know that Picasso ≠ Braque.*

(*b*) Normally, if the referent of τ_2 is contextually determined, the determination of reference proceeds via the speaker's conscious referential intentions. For example, the literal meaning of the pronoun 'she' constrains one to be referring to a female; what makes it the case that a particular utterance of 'she' refers to so-and-so is that so-and-so is the female to whom the speaker intended to be referring in his utterance of 'she'. Likewise for so-called 'incomplete' definite descriptions, such as 'the dog', and complex demonstratives, such as 'that dog'. In these cases, the speaker in producing τ_2 intends, and knows that he intends, to be referring to a certain thing, and τ_2 refers to its referent at least partly by virtue of that intention.

(*c*) Normally, if τ_2 in the utterance of (9) refers to *b*, then there will be a condition *Cxy* such that (i) τ_2 refers to *b* by virtue of $\langle \tau_2, b \rangle$ satisfying *Cxy* and (ii) the condition *Cxy* is independent of both (9) and the fact that its utterance has the truth condition it has: satisfaction of *Cxy* entails nothing per se about those things, and its specification involves no mention of them. For example, the occurrence of 'Picasso' in (10*a*) refers to Picasso by virtue of a certain conventional

practice of referring to Picasso by the name 'Picasso', and if in uttering 'She fed that pigeon' my utterance of 'that pigeon' refers to a certain pigeon, then that is by virtue of the fact that the pigeon was the
contextually salient pigeon to which I intended to refer in uttering
'that pigeon'.

(d) Normally, if τ_2 is a semantically complex singular term, then
the referent of τ_2 is determined by its structure and the referents—
broadly construed so as to include the extensions of predicates, func-
tors, and so on—of its component expressions.

(e) A consequence—indeed, a precondition—of (a) is that in the
normal case the identity and individuation of the referent of τ_2 owes
nothing to the criteria of evaluation it helps to determine. It is
because Picasso and Braque each has an identity and individuation
that is entirely independent of the criteria for evaluating the statements about them that we immediately see the absurdity of supposing that we know that Picasso ≠ Braque because we know that the
statements made in ($10a$) and ($10b$) may differ in truth-value.

That-clause reference differs with respect to each of (a)–(e).

(a') As we just observed in (a), when t_2 in an utterance of (9) is not
a that-clause, we first fix the referent of the token of t_2, τ_2, and then
use that to help fix the criteria for evaluating the utterance of (9), as
illustrated in the examples ($10a$) and ($10b$). Matters are just the
opposite when we turn to that-clauses and their referents. In a belief
report, we *first* have contextually determined criteria of evaluation,
and *then* those criteria determine the proposition to which the that-
clause refers. In every case of an utterance of form (9)—whether it is
an utterance of 'She loves him' or of 'Ralph believes that George Eliot
was a woman'—what is asserted is a proposition of the form $R(a, b)$,
which proposition is therefore true just in case a is related in way R
to b. The asymmetry I'm flagging is pretty radical. In the case of the
first utterance we must first identify the referent of 'him' in order to
determine the criteria for truth-evaluating the utterance. That is to
say, roughly speaking, that we can't determine the truth-value of the
utterance of the sentence until we know the proposition asserted in
that utterance. In the case of the second utterance, the belief report,
we first have a contextual determination of the criteria for truth-
evaluating the utterance, and it is these criteria which determine the
referent of the that-clause, and thereby (at least in part) the proposition asserted by the entire belief report. What this means is that in the

case of the belief report, you don't evaluate the utterance by first
determining the proposition expressed by it; rather, you first have
contextually determined criteria of evaluation that are statable without reference to the proposition asserted by the belief report, and it is
these contextually determined criteria which determine, as though by
an afterthought, what proposition is asserted by the belief report. The
key to this is that the referent of the belief report's that-clause isn't a
factor in determining the contextually determined criteria of evaluation for the belief report but is itself determined by those criteria.
These criteria of evaluation are in part determined by contextual
factors pertaining to the communicative interests of speakers and
their audiences, even after disambiguation and obvious reference-
fixing has taken place.[21]

It should be fairly uncontentious that the referent of a that-clause
is nearly always contextually determined. Two literal utterances of

(11) Ralph believes that George Eliot was a woman

may have different truth-values, owing to the fact that in one conversational context but not the other the truth of the utterance requires
thinking of George Eliot as a famous author. If, as I'm defeasibly
assuming, the face-value theory is correct, then the two utterances of
'that George Eliot was a woman' refer to different propositions—
albeit, no doubt, to propositions with the same possible-worlds truth
condition: each is true in a possible world w just in case George Eliot
is a woman in w. But I'm saying considerably more than that the
referent of a that-clause is contextually determined; I'm also saying
something about the way that referent is determined. If we were
evaluating an utterance of 'Ralph admires her' we would first
determine the referent of 'her' and that would in turn complete the
determination of the criteria for evaluating the statement. In evaluating the statement made in the utterance of (11), however, we first
implicitly fix the criteria for evaluating the statement, and that is
what fixes the referent of the that-clause. The same applies to two
utterances of

(12) Ralph believes that she wrote *Ivanhoe*

when the occurrences of 'she' in both utterances refer to George Eliot.
None of this is to say that the semantic properties of expressions in a

---

[21] The point of the 'obvious' qualification will soon be apparent.

that-clause are not crucial to the determination of the that-clause's referent; in order to fix the criteria of evaluation for the utterances of (11) and (12) we must first know to whom the utterances of 'George Eliot' and 'she' refer. My point is that these semantic properties on their own don't determine the referents of that-clauses; rather, those semantic properties help to determine the criteria of evaluation for belief reports, which criteria in turn fix the referents of that-clauses. (At the same time, the contextually determined criteria of evaluation may themselves determine the operative semantic properties of expressions in that-clauses. We noticed in Section 1.4 that a problem for the Russellian was that an utterance of 'Mary believes that George Eliot wrote *Middlemarch*' may possibly be true even if it turns out that George Eliot never existed, the novels credited to a bearer of that name having been written by a committee. The contextual factors determining criteria of evaluation, and thus determining the proposition to which the utterance of the that-clause refers, may depend on how much the belief reporter and her audience know. If, for example, they believe that George Eliot existed, then the proposition to which the that-clause refers will most likely be an *object-dependent* proposition, a proposition that would not have existed if George Eliot had not existed and is partly individuated in terms of her. But if they knew, or even believed, that George Eliot didn't exist, then the contextually determined criteria of evaluation would determine an object-independent proposition as the referent of the that-clause.[22])

In glossing (*a*), I illustrated the left-to-right direction of

$$\text{fixing the referent of } \tau_2 \to \text{determining the criteria of evaluation}$$

for the normal case when τ_2 is not a that-clause by the absurdity, as regards (10*a,b*), of supposing that we know that Picasso $\neq$ Braque because we know that (10*a*) and (10*b*) can differ in truth-value. When we compare (10*a,b*) with the pairs (13*a,b*) and (14*a,b*), we see how the latter two pairs nicely illustrate the right-to-left direction of

$$\text{fixing the referent of } \tau_2 \leftarrow \text{determining the criteria of evaluation}$$

---

[22] I was pleased to see essentially this point made by Richard Holton (2000) when he conceded that the thought that, for example, Ronald Reagan is retired is essentially about Reagan, but then pointed out that 'that does not preclude...that, were he to turn out not to exist...we would still have a mistaken but contentful thought....It is just that this thought would not have the same content as it has given that he does exist' (p. 13).

when τ_2 is a that-clause in a belief report:

(13a) Nobody doubts that whoever believes that all ophthalmologists are ophthalmologists believes that all ophthalmologists
are ophthalmologists.

(13b) Nobody doubts that whoever believes that all ophthalmologists are ophthalmologists believes that all ophthalmologists
are eye doctors.[23]

(14a) Lois believes that Superman flies.

(14b) Lois believes that Clark Kent flies.

We know that the two members of all three pairs—(10a,b), (13a,b)
and (14a,b)—may well differ in truth-value, but there is a very important difference between (10a,b), on the one hand, and, on the other
hand, (13a,b) and (14a,b). As already noted, it is absurd to suppose
we know that Picasso ≠ Braque because we know that (10a) and (10b)
may differ in truth-value; rather, we know that (10a) and (10b) may differ in truth-value *because* we know that Picasso ≠ Braque. But just the
opposite obtains as regards the other two pairs. We don't know that
(13a) and (13b) may differ in truth-value because we know that the
proposition that whoever believes that all ophthalmologists are ophthalmologists believes that all ophthalmologists are ophthalmologists ≠
the proposition that whoever believes that all ophthalmologists are
ophthalmologists believes that all ophthalmologists are eye doctors;
rather, we know that the proposition that whoever believes that all
ophthalmologists are ophthalmologists believes that all ophthalmologists are ophthalmologists ≠ the proposition that whoever believes
that all ophthalmologists are ophthalmologists believes that all ophthalmologists are eye doctors *because we know (13a) and (13b) may differ in truth-value*. Likewise for (14a) and (14b): we first know that they
may differ in truth-value, and on this basis we know that the proposition that Superman flies ≠ the proposition that Clark Kent flies.

The asymmetry I have been rehearsing explains and partially justifies Crispin Wright's understanding of Frege's 'doctrine of syntactic
priority', that 'for Frege it is the syntactic category which is primary,
the ontological one derivative'.[24] As I understand it, Frege, according
to Wright, held that syntactic criteria establish numerals as genuine

---

[23] The examples, but not the use to which they're put, are borrowed from Mates (1952).
[24] Wright (1983: 13).

singular terms, and that we can infer that these singular terms do refer, and therefore that numbers do exist, because the truth of certain numerical sentences is established by ordinary arithmetical criteria. Wright explains:

it must not be coherent to suggest the possibility of some sort of independent, language-unblinkered inspection of the contents of the world, of which the outcome might be to reveal that there was indeed nothing there capable of serving as the referents of what Frege takes to be numerical singular terms.... Rather, it has to be the case that when it has been established, by the sort of syntactic criteria sketched, that a given class of terms are functioning as singular terms, and when it has been verified that certain appropriate sentences containing them are, by ordinary criteria, true, then it follows that those terms do genuinely refer.[25]

One coming to this afresh is apt to be puzzled. Doesn't the view Wright is attributing to Frege simply beg the question about the existence of numbers? 'OK,' one is apt to protest, 'let's assume that numerals are singular terms, and that therefore "1" refers to the number 1 if it succeeds in referring to anything. But then "$1 + 1 = 2$" is true provided that a certain number, identified as the sum of 1 and 1, is identical to the number 2. Surely, the "ordinary criteria" to which Wright is alluding must require us to identify the numbers in question and see whether the alleged identity obtains. But then, of course, application of these "ordinary criteria" presupposes that the numbers in question exist, and that we know that. So what coherent doctrine is being attributed to Frege?' The answer to this puzzle is the asymmetry, now applied to numbers, that I have been labouring with respect to propositions. True, ordinarily the criteria for establishing the truth of a sentence containing a singular term requires one first to identify the referent of that singular term and then to determine whether it, so identified, satisfies a condition provided by the criteria; but the arithmetical criteria—Wright's 'ordinary criteria'—are an exception to what is ordinarily the case. These criteria make no mention of numbers, and thus can be applied to determine the truth-value of an arithmetical sentence without first identifying anything as the referents of the numerical singular terms. This asymmetry vis-à-vis the typical case, such as an utterance of 'She loves him', is what cashes Frege's doctrine of syntactic priority. Appreciation of this enables us to appreciate Michael Dummett's mistake when he objected that the meaning of abstract singular terms can't 'be construed after a realistic model, as determined by a relation of reference between them and external objects; for at no point in the explanation of the truth-conditions of sentences in which they occur is there any need to invoke such objects'.[26] Dummett is right that the criteria of evaluation for arithmetical sentences don't invoke numerical objects; his mistake is to think this entails that numerals aren't genuine singular terms whose referents are numbers.[27] Likewise, *mutatis mutandis*, for propositions.[28]

(*b'*) The referent of every, or virtually every, that-clause token is contextually determined, which means that although the token's reference may be constrained by the semantic properties of the type of which it is a token, the referent of the token is not a function of those properties. The evidence for this is that for any, or virtually any, substitution instance of the form '*A* believes that *S*', it is easy to conceive of circumstances where different utterances of it at the same time would have different truth-values. The point is illustrated by examples already in play, but here is a new one to pump intuitions. Let's imagine two distinct utterances of

(15) Harold believes that Claudia Schiffer teaches philosophy at NYU.

One utterance is false. The conversation is about whether Harold may have confused Claudia Schiffer with a certain other Schiffer who does teach philosophy at NYU. Harold knows all about Claudia Schiffer,

---

[26] Dummett (1981: 508); quoted by Wright (1983: 69–70).

[27] In replying to a talk based in part on the material of this chapter, which I gave at the Oxford Philosophical Society in November 2001, Ian Rumfitt said: 'I am sympathetic to the claim that a speaker's grasp of a simple ascription's truth conditions is prior to his identification of the proposition that may (in the relevant context of utterance) be associated with its complement clause. But I confess to being baffled how this claim is supposed to cohere with the face-value theory. According to the face-value theory, a simple ascription of belief just *is* a relational statement, relating a person to a proposition. But if that theory is correct, then how *can* somebody understand such an ascription in advance of identifying its second relatum?' I hope that the bafflement expressed by Rumfitt is relieved by what I've just said in the text.

[28] I was slow to appreciate that what I was saying about propositions was probably what Crispin Wright was, in the name of Frege, attributing to numbers. Somehow, the connection occurred to me when I was giving seminars based on a draft of this book at the University of Heidelberg in February 2002.

whom he thinks of by face and by name as a famous German super-model, but, even though he's an undergraduate philosophy major at NYU, he has never even heard of this other Schiffer who teaches philosophy. A second utterance of (15), made at the same time as the first, is, however, true. Harold has lately seen a professorial-looking woman in the philosophy department on a few occasions, and on one occasion he passed a classroom where she was writing on the blackboard and speaking to the class; Harold inferred that the woman was a member of NYU's philosophy faculty. It happens (I spare you the details) that that woman was Claudia Schiffer, and the facts just recounted are what make true the second utterance of (15). Now, we saw that when t_2 in an utterance of a sentence of form (9) ('t_1 Rs t_2') has no context-independent referent and is not a that-clause, the speaker, in producing the token τ_2 typically has something in mind to which he intends to refer in producing τ_2, and that this conscious referential intention is a key ingredient in determining τ_2's referent.[29] In the utterance of a that-clause in a belief report, however, the speaker does not have a conscious, or even unconscious, referential intention, and consequently no such intention helps to determine the proposition to which a given utterance of a that-clause refers.

Suppose that-clauses were on a par with other contextually dependent singular terms. Then we might expect parallels such as the following one.

> *Case 1.* There is some particular person Ralph has in mind—namely, Jane—such that Ralph wants to tell Alice that Jane is admired by Harold. In a context in which Jane is salient, Ralph says 'Harold admires her', intending his utterance of 'her' to refer to Jane.

> *Case 2.* There is some particular proposition Ralph has in mind—namely, ... [?]—such that Ralph wants to tell Alice that Harold believes that proposition. In a context in which the proposition is salient, Ralph says 'Harold believes that Claudia Schiffer teaches philosophy at NYU', intending his utterance of 'that Claudia Schiffer teaches philosophy at NYU' to refer to that proposition.

---

[29] Referring expressions like 'I' and 'you' aren't exceptions; they are merely cases where the constraint on the speaker's referential intention limits her to one thing.

The point is that while it is easy to imagine cases that would fit the description of case 1, it is not easy to think of cases that would fit the description of case 2. For one thing, there is nothing for me to put in place of the '...' in case 2, because no that-clause available to me has a context-independent reference (what would that that-clause be if not 'that Claudia Schiffer teaches philosophy at NYU'?), and our context can't generate the same context that generates the reference in Ralph's imagined utterance. Yet that isn't the main problem. The crucial disanalogy with case 1 is that, imagining oneself in Ralph's position, it is difficult to find in oneself referential intentions that would determine a particular one of the that-Claudia-Schiffer-teaches-philosophy-at-NYU propositions. This is because the particular referent is not determined by the speaker's referential intentions. It is determined by what the speaker and audience mutually take to be essential to the truth-value of the belief report. For example, would the belief report be deemed false if Harold were unacquainted with the name 'Claudia Schiffer'? If so, then that is an individuating feature of the proposition to which the utterance of the that-clause refers. The point at issue segues into the next disanalogy with the typical case in which the context-dependent t_2 is not a that-clause.

(c') When t_2 is not a that-clause, there is associated with it a condition Cxy that is independent of the truth condition and criteria of evaluation for the utterance of (9) and which determines the referent of the utterance of t_2. There is no such condition when t_2 is a that-clause. This is because the truth conditions for the utterance determine the referent, not the other way around, as is usually the case. There is the utterance, and the contextually determined criteria for evaluating the utterance, which fixes the truth conditions of the utterance, and therewith the proposition to which the that-clause refers.

(d') When τ_2 is a semantically complex term other than a that-clause, its referent is determined by its structure and (nearly enough) the referents of its component expressions. Consequently, in the normal case one fixes the referent of τ_2 by first fixing the referents of its component expressions. It follows from (a') that we don't fix the referent of a that-clause by first fixing the referents of its component expressions; what fixes the referent of the that-clause are the criteria for truth-evaluating the belief report. The fact that we don't fix the referent of a that-clause by way of fixing the referents of its component expressions doesn't preclude the referent of a that-clause from being a function of the referents of its component expressions. It may be that the criteria of evaluation that determine the proposition to which the that-clause refers also determine, *pari passu*, entities suitable to play the role of Fregean concepts *qua* components of those propositions, and thereby suitable to be the referents of expressions in that-clauses, so that, once those referents are in place, we can say that the referent of the that-clause is a function of the referents of its component expressions. It is important, however, to see that the criteria of evaluation don't *have* to determine referents for a that-clause's component expressions in order to determine a referent for the that-clause, for the criteria of evaluation already provide the way of determining the referent of τ_2 that would normally be provided by the referents of τ_2's component expressions.

Still, a stronger point can be made: the contextually determined criteria of evaluation seem not to determine anything adequate to be propositional building blocks, the referents of expressions in that-clauses. I don't have a proof that they don't, merely a plausibility argument which simply amounts to the fact that I can't think of any plausible candidates together with there being no good reason why the referent of a that-clause must be a function of the referents of its component expressions. If pleonastic propositions are structured propositions, then they are Fregean propositions—structured propositions whose basic components, the propositional building blocks, are concepts. This follows from the functional meaning of 'concept' for the Fregean together with the way in which pleonastic propositions are fine-grained (the proposition that George Eliot admired groundhogs $\neq$ the proposition that Mary Ann Evans admired woodchucks). Now, Fregean concepts must do two things: they must make it possible rationally to believe and disbelieve what would otherwise be the same Russellian proposition, and they must have the wherewithal to determine the things of which they are concepts. In other words, if c is a concept of x, then there must be an account of what makes c a concept of x—a theory of reference for concepts, what Christopher Peacocke calls a 'determination theory' for concepts.[30] What I can't find are entities that are well suited to do this. Uniqueness properties (properties of the form *the property of being uniquely F*) would do the trick, but only if we could, implausibly, be assured of properties of which we had 'knowledge by acquaintance'—that is, properties that could be thought about directly, without having to think of them

[30] Peacocke (1992).

under a concept. For if we supposed that concepts must be unique-ness properties, then we would need concepts for the properties occurring in any uniqueness property functioning as a concept, and since those concepts of concepts would be uniqueness properties, we would need concepts—concepts of concepts of concepts—for them, and so on, either ad infinitum, which would be self-refuting, or else until we got to properties of which we had knowledge by acquain-tance.[31] If pleonastic propositions have components, it seems to me, then the pleonastic concepts composing pleonastic propositions would have to be abstractions from the propositions containing them, with no identity of their own apart from those propositions. They would perforce be individuated in terms of the propositions containing them and would be tantamount to equivalence classes of propositions: the concept to which an expression in a that-clause refers would, for all intents and purposes, be *the class of propositions equivalent in such-and-such respect to the proposition to which the that-clause refers*. For example, the that-clause in a particular utterance of 'Ralph believes that George Eliot was a man' may refer to a propo-sition that, intuitively speaking, requires thinking of George Eliot as a famous author, along with various other George Eliot related things not so easily articulated, and we may trivially think of the token of 'George Eliot' as associated with a certain equivalence class of propo-sitions: the class of propositions equivalent to the one in question with respect to how they require thinking of George Eliot.

There are three problems with supposing that such equivalence classes might be the referents of expressions in that-clauses and therewith the building blocks of Fregean propositions. First, it is hard to see how there could be a suitable general account of what would make such an equivalence class a concept *of* a given object or property. If the equivalence class is defined with respect to the object or prop-erty (so that the resulting concept would be an object-dependent con-cept of that object or property), there wouldn't be a problem, but we probably don't want to require all concepts to be object-dependent, and I doubt there could be a general account of the concept-of relation for non-object-dependent concepts, if concepts are con-strued as equivalence classes of propositions. Secondly, things that can be individuated only as equivalence classes of propositions don't have an identity and individuation apart from the propositions that

---

[31] See Schiffer (1987*a*, sect. 3.5).

determine the equivalence relation, but it is arguable that (i) in order for propositions to be structured, there must be a constructive account of how each proposition is determined by the building blocks that are its ultimate constituents—for how else could the referent of a that-clause be a function of the referents of its component expressions?—and that (ii) such a constructive account won't be possible if the things we want to take as propositional building blocks can't be identified and individuated apart from the propositions they build. This point raises some difficult technical questions, and I won't try to puzzle it through; I raise it now just as a point worth considering should one be tempted to think of the propositions we believe as structured entities whose basic components are equivalence classes of those very propositions. Thirdly, taking Fregean concepts to be equivalence classes of pleonastic propositions helps with none of the problems raised against the generic Fregean in Section 1.4, and those problems—especially the two Pautzian problems (pp. 27–30)—continue to suggest that the referent of a that-clause is *not* determined by its structure and the referents of its component expressions.

The foregoing considerations thus favour the conclusion that when τ_2 is a that-clause, we can't construe its referent as determined by its structure and the referents of its component expressions, and that believing isn't a relation to structured propositions. *It is a relation to unstructured but very fine-grained propositions.*

My claim that that-clauses refer to fine-grained but unstructured propositions requires me to be very clear about referential occurrences of singular terms in that-clauses. Pretend, yet again, that the Superman story is fact, and suppose that Harold points to Superman, who is wearing his Superman outfit, and says

(16) Lois believes that he flies.

Along with common sense, I count this utterance true. I also want to say that the occurrence of 'he' in (16) refers to Superman—*in this sense*: first, *Harold* clearly counts as referring to Superman by his utterance of 'he' in our pre-theoretic sense of speaker reference; secondly, 'he' occurs there as a rigid designator of Superman, in that the proposition to which (16)'s that-clause refers is true in an arbitrary possible world just in case Superman flies in that world; and thirdly, that proposition is also an object-dependent proposition centred on Superman, in that the proposition wouldn't have existed had Superman not existed and is therefore partly individuated with respect to Superman. I do *not*, however, claim that the occurrence of 'he' in (16) refers to Superman in any sense that allows us to say that it follows from the truth of (16) that Superman has the property expressed by the 'open sentence'

(17) Lois believes that x flies.

I had better not, for if I did I would also have to say that, owing to the falsity of 'Lois believes that Clark Kent flies', Superman both has and doesn't have that property. In the technical sense of 'open sentence', a one-place open sentence expresses a property which a given thing either does or doesn't have; if it has the property, we say that the thing satisfies the open sentence, and if it doesn't have the property, we say that it fails to satisfy the open sentence. In that sense, my view is that (17) is not an open sentence, since it expresses no property, and this because the occurrence of 'he' in (16) does more than refer to Superman in the sense in which I allow; it also plays its contextual role in determining the proposition to which (16)'s that-clause refers, even though the referent of the that-clause isn't compositionally determined by its structure and the referents of its parts (i.e. 'he' in (16) refers to nothing other than Superman). We can have different substitution instances of (17)—e.g.

Lois believes that Superman flies

and

Lois believes that Clark Kent flies

—such that the two substitution instances have different truth-values, even though the singular terms replacing 'x' refer to the same thing, in the sense of reference I have explained.

Now, I also recognize that from the truth of (16) we may infer

(18) There is someone such that Lois believes that he flies.

On my view, we don't explain the truth of (18) by saying that someone satisfies (17); rather we explain its truth in terms of Lois's believing an object-dependent proposition to the effect that so-and-so flies:

$\exists x$(Lois believes that x flies) iff $\exists x$(Lois believes an object-dependent proposition that's true iff x flies).

A slight awkwardness remains. If I'm to allow that (16) entails (18), then I had better also allow that the true statement

Lois doesn't believe that Clark Kent flies

entails that

> There is someone such that Lois doesn't believe that he flies,

which, put together with (18), permits

> (19) There is someone—namely, Superman–Clark Kent–such that Lois does and does not believe that he flies.

The awkwardness is superficial, since on my theory (19) is true (since when is predicate logic the correct account of all ordinary-language quantifications?); it is true because Lois believes that Superman flies but doesn't believe that Clark Kent flies. But wouldn't common sense regard (19) as a contradiction? I don't think so. Uttered out of the blue, it would no doubt provoke a 'Come again?' response. But, first, when we get to this level of complexity, it is not clear what philosophy should make of the reactions of ordinary speakers, and, secondly, I don't see why the non-philosopher in whom the response was provoked shouldn't be assuaged by the explanation that (19) is true because, after all, Lois believes that Superman flies but doesn't believe that Clark Kent flies.

(e') When τ_2 is other than a that-clause, its referent enjoys criteria of individuation that are independent of the criteria of evaluation which that referent helps to determine. Think of Picasso and Braque. When, however, τ_2 is a that-clause in a belief report, the criteria of individuation for the proposition to which the that-clause refers depend on the criteria of evaluation. More specifically, the propositions we believe enjoy no more intrinsic conditions of individuation than those provided by their truth conditions and the requirements for believing those propositions that are determined by the criteria for truth-evaluating belief reports in which reference is made to them. This doesn't mean that there must be believers in order for there to be propositions; it means the conditions that individuate propositions in the range of the belief relation can be individuated only with respect to what it would take to believe them. This is suggested by the points made in (d'), since it is evidently the only option for the identity and individuation of propositions if they are not structured entities whose basic components themselves have an identity and individuation that is independent of the propositions they build. This conception of the propositions we believe as owing their identity and individuation to criteria for evaluating belief reports is confirmed by an otherwise very puzzling feature of propositions. This is that we have no way of identifying a proposition other than as the proposition *that such-and-such*. This inseparable bond with that-clauses would be hard to explain if propositions were made up of propositional building blocks with an identity and individuation of their own apart from the propositions they build; it is explained by the conceptual status of something-from-nothing proposition entailments and the role of that-clauses in the evaluation of belief reports.

So much for how the relation between a that-clause and the proposition to which it refers differs from the way things typically are between a singular term and its referent. Before moving on to the next section, I should comment on a feature of my account of pleonastic propositions which may seem problematic. Consider the inference

(20) Julius Caesar died before 1933.
     So, that Julius Caesar died before 1933 is true.

I am committed to this being a valid something-from-nothing transformation. But now consider the proposition to which (20)'s that-clause refers, the proposition that Julius Caesar died before 1933. How, given the conceptual nature of such a something-from-nothing transformation, can the proposition to which its that-clause refers be in any way individuated by criteria for evaluating belief reports, or reports of any other kind of propositional attitude? Must I say that the propositions deployed in something-from-nothing transformations are of a radically different nature from those we believe? That would leave me hard-pressed to explain the validity of, say,

Hilda believes that Julius Caesar died before 1933.
That Julius Caesar died before 1933 is true.
So, Hilda believes something true—to wit, that Julius Caesar died before 1933.

There is no problem here. The validity of (20), like of that of, say,

Mary is a widow
So, Mary has a dead husband,

is non-formal and depends on what in the olden days would have been said to be the 'meaning' of the sentences involved. In this enlightened age, we know that the meaning of a sentence type, which probably expresses no context-independent proposition, is the wrong thing to invoke, and that the correct thing to invoke is the propositional content of the particular occurrence of the premiss and conclusion. But the 'propositional content' of the utterance of a sentence is just the proposition stated in the utterance, and stating is a propositional attitude on all fours with believing. The validity of (20) is owed to the fact that the proposition to which the that-clause in its conclusion refers is the proposition stated in the utterance of the premiss. What applies to the propositions we believe also applies, *mutatis mutandis*, to the propositions we state.

2.5 PLEONASTIC PROPOSITIONS AND THE FACE-VALUE THEORY

The face-value theory of sentences of the form '*A* believes that *S*' holds that these sentences say, as it were, that *A* believes the proposition that *S*. If the face-value theory is to be plausible, it must allow us to recognize the truth of a sentence such as 'Ralph believes that George Eliot adored groundhogs but not that Mary Ann Evans adored woodchucks'. This rules out both Stalnakerian, unstructured propositions, which are individuated by their possible-worlds truth conditions, and Russellian propositions, which are individuated by the objects and properties they are about. Fregean propositions are, literally, tailor-made for the face-value theory, but, alas, they may not be well enough made to help anyone. Both Russellian and Fregean propositions are structured entities whose ultimate components are propositional building blocks, the Russellian and the Fregean disagreeing about the nature of those blocks. The need for such structured entities was thought to be motivated, in part, by the compositionality hypothesis, CH, which holds that the referent of a that-clause token is determined by its structure and the primary references made in its utterance. If CH is rejected, then the face-value theory can look to unstructured but fine-grained propositions, which is what pleonastic propositions seem to be. It behoves us, therefore, to ask what was supposed to motivate CH in the first place. The most immediate answer is that it was thought to be needed to account for how a semantically complex singular term can have its referent, but we have seen (2.4) that it isn't needed for that if that-clauses refer to pleonastic propositions. CH may also seem to be needed in order for a natural language to have either a compositional truth theory or a compositional meaning theory, where the former is a finitely axiomatized theory whose theorems ascribe to each truth-evaluable sentence type the conditions under which a token of it would be true, and where the latter is a finitely axiomatized theory whose theorems ascribe to each expression of the language its meaning in the language. These will be topics for later discussion (in 4.3 and 4.5), where we will find that in whatever sense natural languages have truth or meaning theories, it is compatible with the falsity of CH.

Now I want to discuss a couple of questions whose answers might seem to threaten the face-value theory when it is conjoined with the claim that the propositions we believe are pleonastic propositions.

One question is whether we really need to recognize the existence of pleonastic propositions. Is it so clear that we can't account for the intuitive evidence for the existence of pleonastic propositions without going so far as to recognize their existence? I don't here have in mind so-called 'fictionalist' accounts of abstract entities wherein statements that ostensibly make reference to them are not literally true, but merely 'true in the fiction of those entities'. For one thing, such fictionalist accounts don't succeed in accounting for the intuitive data. I can assure you, it seems extraordinarily intuitively correct to me that I believe that I exist and believe many other things as well. Yet according to the fictionalist about propositions, the statement

I believe that I exist

can't be literally true, since its truth requires its that-clause to refer to a proposition, and there are no propositions for it to refer to. It is not much consolation to be told that such statements are 'true in the fiction of propositions'. For another thing, talk of 'the fiction of Xs' may seem credible when there is a sustained story, such as in arithmetic, but when it comes to other things, like properties or fictional entities, the claim that a statement is 'true in the fiction of Xs' is devoid of any explanatory force, since it is merely tantamount to saying that the statement would be true if its vacuous singular terms had the referents they purport to have.

A more promising way of doing without pleonastic entities without sacrificing clearly intuitive claims is the way I offered in *Remnants of Meaning*. That way has two parts. First, it says that while there are sound substitution instances of

A believes that S
∴ There is something A believes—to wit, that S,

'that S' is not a referential singular term and the existential quantification in the conclusion is a kind of *non-objectual* quantification. To say
that the quantification in

(21) $\exists x F x$

is objectual is to say that there exists some entity in the domain of
quantification which satisfies the open sentence

(22) Fx.[32]

This is not an analysis or definition of objectual quantification, however, since it uses objectual quantification ('there exists some entity in
the domain...') to explain objectual quantification. Now, to say that
the quantification in (21) is non-objectual is simply to say that it can
be true even though there doesn't exist anything that satisfies (22).
There is, it is important to notice, no reason why non-objectual
quantification must be construed as 'substitutional' quantification,
which, when (21) is read substitutionally, requires the open sentence (22)
to have a true substitution instance of the form

(23) Fa

where 'a' is syntactically a singular term, but where it need not be
required that 'a' refer in order for (23) to be true. Non-objectual
quantification may be taken to be a primitive, indefinable species of
quantification in just the way that objectual quantification is. As far
as I know, there are no *technical* problems with this way of treating
non-objectual quantification. Secondly, the approach is tied to a
denial of the claim that natural languages have finitely axiomatizable
truth theories. This allows one to deny that that-clauses are singular
terms without giving them a different truth-theoretical role.

The reason I switched from the no-reference, non-objectual-
quantification line to my present view, which sees that-clauses as
referring to pleonastic propositions and sees no obstacle to reading
true quantifications with respect to that-clauses as objectual quantification over pleonastic propositions, was that I came to think that
if that was the solution, then what the hell was the problem? Let me
explain, although the point to be made will emerge more clearly if
made with respect to properties rather than propositions.

---

[32] Here I ignore quantification into that-clauses.

As regards properties, the line advanced in *Remnants of Meaning* allows one to say everything common sense wants to say. Thus, 'Humility is a virtue' and 'Fido has the property of being a dog' are true, and the following inference is sound: 'Fido and Lassie are dogs; so, there is a property that they both have—to wit, the property of being a dog'. We simply deny that 'humility' and 'the property of being a dog' are referential singular terms, and we deny that the quantification ostensibly over properties is objectual. We can even allow the truth of

'Humility' refers to humility.

Now comes the rub. Imagine a dispute between my old self and a realist about properties. She and I agree that humility is a virtue, that Fido has the property of being a dog, that there are many properties that she and I both have, and even—why not?—that 'humility' refers to humility. We disagree on just one thing: she affirms while I deny that properties exist. What came to unsettle me were two related things. The first was that I couldn't see either how that dispute could have a determinate resolution or what the cash-value of the dispute really amounted to. Relative to all the agreement, what could the further question about existence amount to such that it could be answered? I didn't see that this could have a happy answer, and it even seemed to me that the only concept of existence I had any grip on made it pretty difficult to deny the existence of properties and propositions given all I wanted to say about them. The second thing to move me was the realization that whatever established the truth of statements ostensibly about properties and propositions, and whatever allowed us to know the truths those statements expressed, would establish the existence and nature of properties and propositions, and would explain our ability to have knowledge of those things, if those statements really were about the abstract entities they're ostensibly about. Putting all this together yields the pleonastic conception of properties and propositions. For example, there is no problem in saying what justifies one in believing that Fido has the property of being a dog or that (the proposition) that Fido is a dog is true: both these things believed are conceptually entailed by my belief that Fido is a dog. And so on. The doctrine of pleonastic propositions and properties is merely, so to speak, a hypostatization of what I used to say when I denied that there were such things as properties and propositions— except 'pleonastically speaking', as I said even then.

The second question whose answer might seem to threaten the conjunction of the face-value theory and pleonastic propositions is about the ability to generalize the face-value theory of belief reports to other kinds of propositional-attitude reports (as well as certain other problematic constructions). One should be suspicious of the claim that in their belief-report occurrences that-clauses refer to propositions if they don't refer to them elsewhere, especially in other propositional-attitude reports, and the question to be considered asks whether other relevant occurrences of that-clauses do refer to propositions. The problem to which I allude reveals itself in a sentence such as

(24) Jane hopes that Slovenia will win the World Cup.

According to what would be the face-value theory of (24), (24)'s that-clause refers to the proposition that Slovenia will win the World Cup. Now, one thing that adds plausibility to the face-value theory of belief reports is that the that-clause in

(25) Jane believes that Slovenia will win the World Cup

behaves exactly as the face-value theory says this referentially transparent singular term should behave, thus making (26) unproblematically valid:

(26) Jane believes that Slovenia will win the World Cup.
     That Slovenia will win the World Cup = the proposition that
     Slovenia will win the World Cup.
     ∴ Jane believes the proposition that Slovenia will win the
     World Cup.

By parity of reasoning, (27) should also be valid:

(27) Jane hopes that Slovenia will win the World Cup.
     That Slovenia will win the World Cup = the proposition that
     Slovenia will win the World Cup.
     ∴ Jane hopes the proposition that Slovenia will win the
     World Cup.

But it isn't valid; the conclusion isn't even well formed.[33] Of course, there are other contexts in which the prefix produces garbage,

---

[33] Cf. Bach (1997) and Moltmann (2002).

such as:

> Jane predicts/guesses [the proposition] that Slovenia will win the World Cup.

> It's true [the proposition] that Slovenia will win the World Cup.

Other contexts don't produce garbage, but they change the meaning drastically:

> Jane fears/expects [the proposition] that Slovenia will win the World Cup.

> [The proposition] that you do it quickly is more important than [the proposition] that you do it thoroughly.

How serious a problem is this? If it is a serious problem, it shows that the that-clause in (24) doesn't refer to *anything*. For suppose it refers to an *F*, be that a sentence, a mental representation, or anything else. Then 'Jane hopes the *F* that Slovenia will win the World Cup' will be as ill formed as 'Jane hopes the proposition that Slovenia will win the World Cup'.

I don't think the problem is serious; I think it is based on a confusion about substitutivity *salva veritate*. There are clearly non-trick contexts where co-referential singular terms can't be substituted *salva veritate*. For example, if Pavarotti is the greatest tenor, we still can't substitute 'the greatest tenor' *salva veritate* for 'Pavarotti' in

> The Italian singer Pavarotti never sings Wagner

since

> The Italian singer the greatest tenor never sings Wagner

isn't even well formed.[34] There are even clear cases where one can't substitute *synonymous* expressions *salva veritate*. The sentence

> Betty gave her tiara to Oxfam

permits the dative movement that yields

> Betty gave Oxfam her tiara.

---

[34] I'm grateful to Paul Horwich for pointing out to me the way in which apposition provides counter-examples to the principle of substitutivity *salva veritate*.

But while in this context 'give' and 'donate' are (nearly enough) synonyms,

> Betty donated her tiara to Oxfam

doesn't (at least in American English) permit the dative movement that yields

> Betty donated Oxfam her tiara.

As Jerry Fodor points out in a discussion of examples like these, 'there's a *morphological* constraint on dative movement, in that poly-syllabic verbs resist double-object movement'.[35] There are even synonymous, or nearly synonymous, constructions where one of a pair of synonymous sentences allows 'the proposition' to prefix its that-clause while the other doesn't. For example,

> It's true that Fido is a dog

and

> That Fido is a dog is true

are synonymous, but whereas

> The proposition that Fido is a dog is true

is fine,

> It's true the proposition that Fido is a dog

is ill formed. Likewise,

> She said that it will rain

is fairly synonymous with

> She stated that it will rain

but to my ear

> She said the proposition that it will rain

sounds odd in a way that

> She stated the proposition that it will rain

doesn't.

---

[35] Fodor (1998: 67).

I conclude that there is no good reason to suppose these failures of substitutivity constitute counter-examples to the claim that the that-clauses involved in them refer to propositions. At the same time, there are reasons to suppose they do refer to propositions. First, there is the way propositional attitudes interact in reasoning. If I predict that Alice will go to the party if Bob doesn't and believe that Bob won't go to the party, then I'll predict that Alice will go to the party. It is hard to see how this could make sense if the that-clause in the belief statement but not the prediction statement referred to a proposition, and the case for taking that-clauses in belief statements to refer to propositions remains pretty compelling. Secondly, some of the problematic examples have pleonastic equivalents in which that-clauses do refer to propositions, for example:

> It's true that Fido is a dog/The proposition that Fido is a dog is true.
>
> She said that it will rain/She stated the proposition that it will rain.

And in other cases there are strong conceptual connections involving propositions, as, for example, that a person with the concepts of truth and of a proposition can't hope that it will rain without hoping that the proposition that it will rain is true.

Still, I would feel more confident about my conclusions if I knew the principled distinction that explains the asymmetry between 'believes' and 'hopes' *et al.*—if, that is, there is a *principled* distinction, as opposed to, say, a quirk of certain Indo-European languages. Unfortunately, if there is a statable difference that accounts for the asymmetries, I don't know what it is, nor do I know anyone who does.[36]

---

[36] After writing the foregoing, I read Jeffrey King's (forthcoming) illuminating discussion of the substitution failures. King claims to have explained the substitution failures in a way that is compatible with the face-value theory, but while I agree with his conclusion that the substitution failures are compatible with the claim that that-clauses refer to propositions, I don't see that he provides the kind of explanation of the failures I was in search of. For example, as regards 'Jane hopes that Slovenia will win the World Cup', King says that verbs like 'hopes' 'simply do not take (most) NP complements' and that therefore 'substitution failure [of the sort displayed in the inability to substitute "the proposition that Slovenia will win the World Cup" for the that-clause in the hope report] is very easily explained ... when we substitute an NP complement for a [that-clause] complement where the verb whose complement it is takes only [that-clause] complements, we go from a grammatical sentence to an ungrammatical sentence'. But I don't see how this explains what

2.6 PLEONASTIC PROPOSITIONS, NECESSITY, AND POSSIBLE WORLDS

The purpose of this section, which contains more proclaiming than arguing, is to get certain things out in the open. That confessed, let me more or less baldly state some plausible claims which together have interesting implications for the modal notions of necessity and possibility and the metaphysical notion of a possible world, and which may shed further light on the doctrine of pleonastic propositions, the propositions to which, I claim, that-clauses refer.

1. Pleonastic propositions are *sui generis* abstract entities. In no sense are they constructions out of possible worlds. I take it this is already a consequence of what I have argued up to this point.

2. Strictly speaking, there are no such things as possible worlds. The notion of a possible world is a metaphor, albeit a metaphor that has proved extremely useful in logic and philosophy (I myself will continue throughout this book to gloss modal truth conditions in terms of the metaphor of possible worlds). The only literal sense to be made of the metaphor of possible worlds is as a construction out of propositions of some kind or other, most happily, I suspect out of Russellian propositions, something along the lines of possible worlds being maximally consistent sets of Russellian propositions.

3. Necessity and possibility are *properties* of propositions—of pleonastic propositions, but also of things of any other kind that might legitimately be called propositions, such as Russellian propositions. No one who believes in propositions seems to doubt that truth is a property of propositions (although there is considerable debate about the nature of that property). This is primarily because the best account of the logical form of

The proposition that S is true

needs to be explained. If, as the report claims, Jane stands in the hope relation to the proposition to which the that-clause refers, then one would expect 'Jane hopes x' to express a property which that proposition has and that, accordingly, a truth will be expressed by any sentence that results from replacing the free variable 'x' with a singular term that refers to that proposition. But, even though 'the proposition that Slovenia wins the World Cup' refers to the same proposition as 'that Slovenia wins the World Cup', we don't get a true sentence when we put the first singular term in place of 'x', and what requires explanation is precisely why that should be. Merely pointing out that 'hopes' takes only that-clause complements exacerbates rather than explains this mystery.

treats 'is true' as a predicate: sentences of the displayed form say that the propositions they are about have the property of being true. Accordingly, forms like

It's true that S

and even

Truly, S

are taken to be pleonastic equivalents of the explicitly predicational form. The syntactical behaviour of 'necessary' mimics that of 'true', giving us

The proposition that S is necessary

and encouraging us to take

It's necessary that S

and even

Necessarily, S

as pleonastic equivalents of the explicitly predicational form. It is therefore a mistake to speak of necessity *et al.* as modal *operators*. Trivially, 'It's necessary that' is *syntactically* an operator in that it takes a sentence and makes a sentence, but there is no interesting *semantic* sense in which 'necessary' is anything that might be called an operator. The way '□' is handled in modal logic is perfectly legitimate, but it can provide no model for the treatment of ordinary-language modal notions. None of this should be at all surprising, if truth is held to be a property of propositions, for the property of being necessary/possible = the property of being necessarily/possibly true.

4. Necessity and possibility are *underived* properties of propositions; i.e. propositions are the ultimate bearers of these properties. Linguistic entities, such as sentences or utterances, have modal properties only by virtue of expressing propositions with those modal properties, but the propositions don't inherit their modal properties from anything else. Thus, the sentence '7 + 5 = 12' is necessary by virtue of expressing the proposition that $7 + 5 = 12$ and that proposition's being necessary. (The truth-values of sentences or utterances are also inherited from the propositions they express.)

5. Necessity and possibility are interdefinable (p is possible iff not-p isn't necessary; p is necessary iff not-p isn't possible), but no modal

notion is explicable in wholly non-modal terms. In particular, meta-physical necessity, of which logical, arithmetical, and conceptual necessity are species, is an irreducible property of propositions. It enjoys no reductive explication or non-trivial definition.

A corollary of the foregoing points is that the notion of a possible world, despite its undeniable heuristic value, plays no serious or ineliminable role in the metaphysics, epistemology, semantics, or logic of modality. If a truth is expressed using the metaphor of possible worlds, it will be expressible without that metaphor. So much for my *ex cathedra* pronouncements; they are not arguments but are intended to clarify this book's agenda.

2.7 REQUISITES FOR A COMPLETE THEORY OF CONTENT

So far I've argued that that-clauses refer to pleonastic propositions. Taken together with some fairly uncontestable stuff, this implies that propositional attitudes and propositional speech acts are relations to pleonastic propositions, and that truth and necessity (and the other modalities) are properties of pleonastic propositions. A more complete account of these fundamental units of content can be gained by seeing what work they do for us, and by ascertaining whether other things might not do that work just as well. We also want to know, if indeed it's something additional, what other notions are to be explicated in terms of pleonastic propositions.

In one way or another, the rest of this book is concerned with the uses to which we put our notion of content and with how that notion is able to do what it does. I begin with the role of content in the philosophy of language.

3

Meanings and Knowledge of Meaning

3.1 INTRODUCTION

The semantic properties of linguistic expressions must be understood in terms of the propositional contents of speech acts, and they are pleonastic propositions. I will approach the study of semantic properties obliquely, via an attempt to say what it is to know what an expression means. There are two reasons for this. First, it proves to be a useful structuring device, since the attempt to explicate knowledge of meaning provides an insightful slant on what it is we have knowledge of when we have knowledge of meaning. Secondly, knowledge of meaning is an important topic in its own right in the study of meaning, especially as it seems to play an essential role in language understanding—our ability to know what speakers are saying when they utter sentences, even sentences we haven't heard before.

The next section raises the question about knowledge of meaning and explores what to many theorists *ought* to seem the inescapable answer to it. Sections 3.3 and 3.4 negatively assess other answers to the question before settling, in 3.5, on what I take to be the right answer. Section 3.6 suggests there are no such *things* as expression meanings— a suggestion that has less to it than meets the eye—and identifies things I call 'characters*' as being meaning surrogates, or the things that are meanings if there are meanings. Section 3.7 compares and contrasts characters* with David Kaplan's characters,[1] and the final section continues the discussion of two-dimensional semantics into the realm of propositional-attitude content, even ending with a modest reflection on the problem of phenomenal properties.

---

[1] Kaplan (1989).

3.2   AN EASY ANSWER TO THE KNOWLEDGE OF MEANING QUESTION?

Every speaker knows what numerous expressions mean. In what does such knowledge consist? In other words, what is it to know what an expression means? In asking this question, I'm using 'know' and 'means' in ordinary, non-technical ways. There may be legitimate technical senses of 'know' or 'means' that would yield a different question and have a different answer, and later I'll touch on this, but for now my question is the non-technical one. The question needs refinement, but some progress can be made with it even before it is recast.

For a lot of theorists, the question ought (at least initially) to be perceived as having an easy answer—namely (where 'e' ranges over meaningful expressions and ambiguity is ignored) that:

> (I) To know what e means is to know that e means m, for suitable way m of identifying e's meaning.

The reference to a suitable way of identifying a meaning should be understood on analogy with, for example, knowing to whom Jane is married. You don't have that knowledge just by virtue of knowing that Jane is married to her husband, but you do if you know that she is married to Bill Bloggs in the history department. To know to whom x is married is to know that x is married to m, for suitable way m of identifying x's spouse.

To be married is to stand in the marriage relation to someone, and if x stands in that relation to y, then y, by that very fact, is x's spouse. Likewise, it is natural to suppose, to have meaning is to stand in the meaning relation to something, and if x stands in the meaning relation to y, then y, by that very fact, is x's meaning. This conception of meaning is implied both by a face-value reading of our use of 'means' as a transitive verb, as displayed in

> 'Existence precedes essence' *means something,*

and by a face-value reading of our use of 'meaning' as a sortal noun, as displayed in

> 'Bank' has *two meanings.*
> What's *the meaning of* 'hermeneutics'?
> 'Il pleut' means *the same thing* as 'It's raining'.

Evidently, anyone who accepts the relational conception of meaning ought to accept (I), since accepting (I) for this theorist is, on the face of it, simply acceding to a platitude about all relations expressed by transitive verbs—namely, that if *a* Rs *b*, then to know what *a* Rs is just to know that *a* Rs *m*, for suitable way *m* of identifying *b* (that is, a way of thinking of *b* which enables one to satisfy contextually appropriate standards for knowing what *a* Rs). For example, if Henry believes *that there was a hailstorm yesterday*, then even if the proposition that there was a hailstorm yesterday = the first proposition Jane asserted today, you don't *ipso facto* know what Henry believes by knowing that he believes the first proposition Jane asserted today. But you would know what he believes by knowing that he believes that there was a hailstorm yesterday.

Nevertheless, I doubt that the easy answer is correct. To begin, it's doubtful (I) holds for *every* meaningful expression. There are numerous expressions *e* such that one's knowing what *e* means seems not to consist in one's knowing that *e* means *m*, where *m* identifies that which *e* means. Sally, a normal speaker of English, knows what 'Stop singing!', 'It's raining', 'Is she there yet?', 'of', 'spells badly', 'run', and 'a lonely cyclist' mean, but when any of these expressions is taken to be the value of '*e*' in

> Sally knows that *e* means *m*,

it is doubtful that anyone can go on to replace '*m*' with a singular term that both refers to the expression's meaning and yields a knowledge ascription that would secure Sally's knowing what the expression in question means. Where, for example, is the singular term that would turn

(1) Sally knows that 'Is she there yet?' means *m*

into such a true statement?

Theorists who hold that meaning is a relation between an expression and its meaning have adopted various conventions for forming names of an expression's meaning. A currently popular convention has one form a name of the meaning of an expression by writing the expression in capital letters.[2] Clearly, however, we no more answer our question about (1) by writing

> Sally knows that 'Is she there yet?' means IS SHE THERE YET?

---

[2] See e.g. Fodor (1998) and Horwich (1998).

than we do by writing

> Sally knows that 'Is she there yet?' means the meaning of 'Is she there yet?'

Notice that it does no good to suggest that Sally's propositional knowledge of the meaning of 'Is she there yet?' is merely 'implicit' or 'tacit', for what seems impossible is to say what it is that she knows implicitly or tacitly. If a theorist is to insist that (I) isn't refuted by Sally's knowledge of what 'Is she there yet?' means, then he must hold either (i) that there is a relevant substituend for 'm' in (1) even though we can't now say what it is, or (ii) that although there is no relevant substituend for 'm' in (1), this is because the value of 'm'—that way of thinking of the meaning of 'Is she there yet?'—that makes (1) true is ineffable. I see nothing further to discuss on this score until the proponent of (i) gives some reasonable account of why we can't say what 'Is she there yet?' means, or the proponent of (ii) gives some reasonable account of why the canonical way of identifying the meaning of the sentence resists effability.

Given that (I) doesn't hold for *every* meaningful expression, one should expect it not to hold for *any* expression. It is implausible that our ordinary notion of expression meaning should encompass two disparate notions, one on which knowing what an expression means consists in a suitable identification of the thing that is the expression's meaning, the other requiring no such identification. We should therefore expect there not to be any relevant substitution instance of 'e means m' which expresses a truth knowledge of which suffices for knowing what the expression it concerns means. This is borne out, I hazard, by a search for counter-examples. Is there a single substitution instance that would do the trick? If we knew that there was something that was the meaning of, say, 'dog', then we could utilize the capital-letter convention and write

> 'Dog' means DOG.

But, in the first place, we can't be assured that there is anything that 'DOG' names; if there were, wouldn't there be a more revealing way of referring to it than by a made-up technical convention, and wouldn't we then have no need for the made-up convention? I'll return to this thought later. And, in the second place, even if the displayed meaning ascription expressed a truth and one knew that truth, it still wouldn't follow that one knew what 'dog' meant. Given the nature of the capital-letter naming convention, there is nothing to guarantee that one's knowledge of the meaning of 'dog' is under a suitably revealing mode of presentation; the cash-value of what one knew, we have already noticed, might be nothing more than that 'dog' means the meaning of 'dog'.

Nor would (I) find support in examples like

'Vixen' means 'female fox',

for the truth it conveys is merely that 'vixen' means the same as 'female fox' and implies nothing about any *thing* being the meaning of either expression. The best support for (I) comes from an example like

(2) 'Snow is white' means that snow is white.

For 'means' here expresses a dyadic relation, 'that snow is white' refers to a proposition in the range of that relation, and knowledge of the truth expressed by (2) would provide knowledge of what

(3) Snow is white

means. Nevertheless, I don't think (2) shows that (I) is true of any expression. I don't think (2) provides a *relevant* substitution instance of the schema '*e* means *m*'. It doesn't provide a relevant substitution instance of the schema because the sense of 'means' in (2) isn't the sense of 'means' applicable to any sentence. The reading of (2) on which it is true involves not the sense of 'means' strictly applicable to sentences in their own right, that is, the sense of 'means' on display in, say,

'It's raining' and 'Is it raining?' both mean something,

but is rather the sense of 'means' applicable to *speaker-meaning*, which *is* a relation between a person and a proposition. What is actually conveyed by (2) is that in uttering (3) the *speaker*, if speaking literally, would mean that snow is white. That is to say, 'that snow is white' in (2) refers to the proposition that the speaker would mean and not to anything the sentence (3) means in its own right, in the sense of 'means' at issue when we ask what it is to know what any sentence means. For consider the sentence

(4) Is snow white?

A literal utterance of either (3) or (4) requires a speech act whose propositional content is, or involves, the proposition that snow is white.[3] With what right, then, would that proposition be the meaning of (3) but not (4)?

If there are such things as sentence meanings, then those things should have something in them that marks the difference in meaning between (3) and (4). Better candidates for those meanings would be something along the lines of

  (5) ⟨asserting, the proposition that snow is white⟩
  (6) ⟨asking-whether, the proposition that snow is white⟩

respectively. At the same time, there doesn't seem to be any ordinary, non-technical sense of 'means' according to which it is true to say that

  (7) 'Snow is white' means ⟨asserting, the proposition that snow is white⟩
  (8) 'Is snow white?' means ⟨asking-whether, the proposition that snow is white⟩.

If we could say that, one would think, then we could also say that Sally knows the truths expressed by (7) and (8), since she certainly knows what (3) and (4) mean; but I don't think there is anything that warrants ascribing to Sally the knowledge that, for instance, 'Is snow white?' means ⟨asking-whether, the proposition that snow is white⟩.

Does this mean, as it certainly seems to imply, that there are no such *things* as the meanings of linguistic expressions, since (I) would be true if there were such things as expression meanings, and (I) isn't true? I think that on balance it probably does mean that, but the situation is complicated by there being abstract entities that do much of what meanings would do if there were meanings. This question will be addressed in Section 3.6, after I've tried to resolve the question about knowledge of meaning. (But, one might ask even at this point, how can I even entertain the possibility that the syntax of 'means' and 'meaning' is misleading, suggesting, as it were, that there are such things as meanings when there aren't? Isn't my refusal to take the misleading syntax at face value inconsistent with my doctrine of 'pleonastic entities', which claims to pull ontological rabbits from syntactical hats? Just the opposite, actually. A pleonastic entity is an entity that owes its entry into our conceptual scheme to a something-from-nothing transformation like

---

[3] I'm here ignoring my view that no that-clause has a wholly context-independent reference.

the one that takes us from

Fido is a dog,

whose only singular term is 'Fido', to its pleonastic equivalent

Fido has the property of being a dog,

which contains the new singular term 'the property of being a dog', whose referent is the property of being a dog. We couldn't get the pleonastic entity doghood in this way if 'Fido is a dog' didn't have a pleonastic equivalent that contained a singular term that referred to doghood. What's distinctive about expression meanings is that there is no something-from-nothing transformation that takes us from a statement which doesn't involve a singular term that refers to a meaning to a statement that does involve such a singular term.)

3.3 KNOWLEDGE OF MEANING AS KNOWLEDGE HOW

Our question—What is it to know what an expression means?—needs to be refined before considering further attempts to answer it. I've been asking what it is to know what an expression means, as though that question could be answered in those terms. It can't, of course, since an expression has its meaning only relative to a language, a person, or a group of persons. Our question shouldn't be 'What is it to know what e means?' but rather 'What is it to know what e means in language L, or for person x, or for group of persons G?' Nor is that enough. Meaning something is one thing when it is a matter of the kind of meaning an expression has when it is used in interpersonal communication, but it is something else when it is a matter of the kind of meaning an expression has when it is used in a *lingua mentis*, an inner system of mental representation. Meaning in a public language is a matter of how the expression is used, or apt to be used, in communication, while meaning in a system of mental representation is a matter of how the expression is used, or apt to be used, in thought. Moreover, use in communication is a matter of *intentional action*, of intentionally performed speech acts, whereas there is nothing intentional about the kind of processing role that defines use in thought.

The question I mean to ask is 'What is it to know what an expression means in the public language of a given group?' By 'the public language of a given group' I have in mind natural languages and dialects of them, used in the familiar interpersonal way. A lot could be said in explication and refinement of these notions, but I don't think doing so is necessary for my purposes. If my question demands further refinement, those demands should be met as they arise in my attempt to answer the question. Henceforth I'll take the restriction to shared public languages to go without saying.

The first attempt to answer our question construed knowledge of meaning as a kind of *propositional* knowledge, a matter of knowing that such-and-such is the case. The next attempt construes it as a kind of knowing how, a kind of ability or skill.[4] The idea is familiar and even has long-standing slogans. In the later Wittgenstein,[5] we are advised not to ask for an expression's meaning, but for its use. His thought, no doubt, was that knowing what an expression means is knowing how to use it. But use it to do what? As money is used to buy things, so words are used to...? Perform *speech acts* of certain kinds was J. L. Austin's famous way of making Wittgenstein's idea more precise.[6] A simplification of Austin's idea is that to know what an expression means is to know how to use it to say things.

At best, Austin's slogan merely provides a sufficient condition for knowing what an expression means, since one can know what an expression means in a language one doesn't speak. A revision of Austin's slogan—that to know what an expression means is to know how to use it to perform speech acts—points to a way of putting the knowledge-of-meaning-as-knowledge-how idea which helpfully loosens the connection between knowing what an expression means and being able to say something with it. One knows what an expression means if one is able to use it to say things that are consonant

---

[4] Knowing how to *X* may not entail having the ability to do *X*. A former ballerina, thirty years older and thirty pounds heavier, may still know how to do jumps she is now unable to do. What is crucial to the proposal about knowledge of meaning presently under consideration is having the ability to use language and to know what others are saying when they use language. Recently, Jason Stanley and Timothy Williamson (2001) have argued that knowing how is a kind of knowing that, and this would affect the proposal in question, since if one is able to understand utterances, then, presumably, one knows how to understand them. But, as I try to show in Schiffer (2002), the claim for which Stanley and Williamson argue is implausible, notwithstanding their ingenious arguments for it.

[5] See esp. Wittgenstein (1953).   [6] Austin (1962).

with the expression's meaning.[7] One also knows what the expression means if one is able to *understand* what others are saying when they use it. In fact, understanding trumps saying in that one can understand utterances containing an expression without being able oneself to say things with it, but if one is able to say things with an expression, then one is able to understand utterances containing it. The knowledge-how idea, then, may be put in terms of a certain understanding ability. But first we need a narrowing of our question.

We can't simply ask what it is to know what an expression *e* means in a language *L*, since we can't assume that knowledge of meaning will be the same for every kind of expression. For example, we should expect that knowing the meaning of a word is significantly different from knowing the meaning of a sentence. I propose to begin with the question

(9) What is it to know what sentence *s* means in language *L*?

where a sentence is taken to be something that occurs on its own, not contained in a larger expression. I allude to the contrast between, for example, 'Snow is white.' and 'snow is white'. The former can't occur as part of another sentence, but the latter can, as in 'Either snow is white or grass is green'.

To a first approximation, the idea is that:

(II) To know what *s* means in *L* is to have the ability to know what speakers of *L* are saying when they utter *s*.

This is very much a first approximation, since, among other things, we need to know what 'saying' is meant to involve, and since it is clearly not a requirement on one's knowing what *s* means in *L* that one be able to understand *any* utterance of *s* by *any* speaker of *L*. At the same time, the problems confronted by (II) make it doubtful that there is enough here to be worth trying to fix.

Knowledge of meaning plays an important explanatory role in language understanding, and thereby in language production, and it is hard to see why we should care much about it if it didn't. A big

---

[7] This may need qualification. I have enough mastery of the word 'titanium' to enable me to say that my new eyeglasses have titanium frames, but I don't know much more about titanium than that it's a strong, light metal called 'titanium'. Do I know what 'titanium' means? The question may not have a determinate answer, although there is some temptation to say that I don't fully know what 'titanium' means. There are interesting and important things to be said on this issue, but for now I'll ignore them.

problem with the knowing-how account, (II), is that even if having the ability to know what speakers are saying when they utter a sentence were a necessary and sufficient condition for knowing what the sentence means, that ability still couldn't be *identified* with knowing the sentence's meaning, for such an identification would preclude knowledge of meaning from playing its explanatory role in language understanding. The point is simple: we are able to understand utterances of sentences—that is, to know what is being said in those utterances—in part because we know what the uttered sentences mean; but that couldn't be the case if knowing what a sentence means was being able to understand utterances of it. Sally, facing Al, utters 'He refuses to take it', and Al straight away knows that Sally is telling him that their son Ludwig refuses to take his medicine. Al's information-processing transition manifests his understanding of Sally's utterance, his knowledge of what she said in it. How was Al able to move from his perception of Sally's utterance to his knowledge of what she said? We may not yet know the complete answer, but it is reasonable to suppose that part of it is that Al knew what the sentence type 'He refuses to take it' meant. This could hardly be part of the explanation of Al's ability to know what Sally said in uttering the sentence if Al's knowledge of what the sentence meant simply was his ability to know what someone was saying in uttering the sentence.

A second problem with (II) is that it fails to state a sufficient condition for knowing what *s* means in *L*. Leona doesn't know what any Hungarian sentence means but she's able to understand what Hungarians are saying. This is because her Siamese twin, Fiona, knows Hungarian and tells her what's said whenever anyone speaks Hungarian to them, which is often, as they live in Budapest. Thus, although Leona has the ability to know what a speaker of Hungarian is saying when he utters a Hungarian sentence, she still doesn't know what the sentence means.

A third problem with (II) is that it fails to state a necessary condition for knowing what *s* means in *L*. I might know what a certain spoken Japanese sentence means because I was told its English synonym but yet not be able to recognize the sentence in normal Japanese speech (I can't make any kind of meaningful division in any stream of Japanese speech). In this case I know what the sentence means in Japanese but I don't have the ability to know what Japanese speakers are saying when they utter it.

Is there some other version of the knowledge-of-meaning-as-knowledge-how idea that would not be subject to such quick collapse? Paul Horwich has proposed that a word's having a certain meaning is constituted by its having a certain non-intentional 'use' property and that one qualifies as knowing what the word means if one's deployment of the word results from that use property.[8] If this proposal worked for words, it wouldn't be hard to make it the basis of an account of one's knowing what an expression of any kind means. The proposal would help with the first problem raised against (II)—namely, that it precludes knowledge of meaning from playing a role in understanding utterances—if we could take the categorical use property to be a property that plays the knowledge-of-meaning role in the processing that results in one's knowing what was said in the utterance of a sentence containing the word. That would have to be spelled out in some detail. If we understand Horwich's use properties to apply to expressions that one doesn't deploy, perhaps because they belong to a language one doesn't speak, but which one understands, then a Horwichian revision of (II) yields:

(II′) x knows what s means in L iff $\exists\Phi(\Phi$ is that non-intentional 'use' property such that $\Phi(x, s)$ both constitutes s's having the meaning it has for x & 'grounds' x's ability to know what speakers of L are saying when they utter s).

Although this improves on (II) in at least one respect, it has problems of its own. One problem is that one may reasonably doubt that public-language meaning is constituted by Horwichian use properties.[9] A more serious problem is that Horwichian use properties are not well suited to play a role in the processing that takes one from the perception of an utterance of a sentence to the knowledge of what was said in that utterance. As I'll later emphasize, in order for a property of a sentence to enable one to know what was said in the utterance of the sentence, the property must somehow serve to connect the sentence both with the kind of speech act performed in the utterance and with the kind

---

[8] Horwich (1998: 16–18). Horwich combines this knowledge-how idea with the just-rejected (I), to which he is evidently committed by virtue of his holding that having meaning is a matter of being related to a meaning. He says that 'although understanding is indeed a practical ability, it may none the less be characterized as an instance of "knowing that"—providing we recognize that the knowledge is *implicit*' (p. 18). This combination stands vulnerable to the objections raised against proposal (I).   [9] See Schiffer (2000).

of propositional content that speech act enjoys. Horwich's use properties, however, can make no such connection; they are non-relational and have nothing about them to connect sentences bearing them with any particular kind of speech act or with any particular kind of propositional content. In any case, the deep moral as regards knowledge of meaning as knowing how to do things with words is that nothing can come of it unless it is somehow made to incorporate something categorical that can play the knowledge-of-meaning role in language processing. More on this presently.

3.4 'CHARACTERS*' AND KNOWLEDGE OF MEANING AS A DIFFERENT KIND OF PROPOSITIONAL KNOWLEDGE

To know what an expression means isn't to know that it has the property of meaning such-and-such; but maybe it is to know that it has a different property. We can help to motivate this idea by considering these three sentences:

(10) You sing it.
(11) Do you sing it?
(12) You, sing it!

These sentences differ in meaning, but they also share a common meaning feature. They differ in meaning in that each sentence is associated with a different kind of speech act—a speech act that a person must be performing if she utters the sentence in conformity with its meaning. Thus, a literal utterance of (10) requires the speaker to be performing a speech act of *stating*, or *saying that*; a literal utterance of (11) requires the speaker to be performing a speech act of *asking whether*; and a literal utterance of (12) requires the speaker to be performing a speech act of *ordering*, or *telling someone what to do* (or something along those lines). The meaning feature the three sentences share is that they impose the same constraint on the propositional contents of the speech acts they require—the content of each speech act must be a proposition of the form *m sings m'*, where *m* identifies the speaker's audience and *m'* the thing to which the speaker's utterance of 'it' refers. Two sentences will differ in meaning just in case they differ in the kind of speech act they require or in the kind of propositional content they require the speech act to have. These two constraints characterize what a sentence means. This suggests that to know what a sentence means in a language is to know what kind of speech act, with what kind of propositional content, a speaker of that language must perform in a literal utterance of the sentence.

In other words, we reach the following account of what it is to know what a sentence s means:

> (IIIs) x knows what s means in L iff $\exists A, P(x$ knows that in a literal utterance of s the speaker of L performs a speech act of kind A with a propositional content of kind P).

For example, to know what 'Is it raining?' means is to know that in a literal utterance of the sentence the speaker is asking her audience whether it's raining at some contextually determined place. A literal utterance of a sentence is one in which what the speaker means in uttering the sentence is in conformity with what the sentence means, as when 'It's raining' is uttered to say that it's raining, as opposed to when it's uttered to test one's voice, make a joke, or speak metaphorically.[10] Even if an ordinary person lacks the vocabulary to mark the distinction between literal and non-literal utterances, he has at least implicit knowledge of the distinction. It will be convenient to speak of the propositional content of a literal utterance of a sentence, where that is the content of the speech act performed in conformity with the sentence's meaning.

To a first approximation, a word's having meaning may be characterized in terms of its contribution to the propositional constraints imposed by the sentences containing the word. This contribution will itself be a kind of proposition: corresponding to a word w is a kind of proposition P such that the propositional content of a literal utterance of *any* sentence containing w must be a proposition of kind P. The same goes for all sub-sentential expressions, and we reach the following first approximation of an account of what it is to know the meaning of any sub-sentential expression e:

> (IIIe) x knows what e means in L iff $\exists P(x$ knows that the propositional content of a literal utterance in L of a sentence containing e is a proposition of kind P).

---

[10] But see n. 12 for a more illuminating gloss of 'literal utterance', which I'm not yet in a position to give because I haven't yet introduced the notion of 'character*'.

(IIIe) is a first approximation because it can't be assumed that an unambiguous expression imposes the same constraint in every sentential context. Whether the account is worth correcting in this regard will be determined after a brief digression.

Different utterances of the word 'she' make different contributions to the propositional contents of the utterances containing them, but there is a meaning factor shared by all tokens of 'she', *qua* English pronoun. In recent years it has become customary to follow David Kaplan in calling this common factor *character*.[11] But Kaplan's 'character' also stands for a particular conception of what these common meaning factors are, and while it is eminently reasonable to suppose there are common meaning factors, it is considerably less reasonable to suppose that Kaplan was right about their nature. I will consider Kaplan's characters, and two-dimensional semantics generally, in the next section, but for now let me dub the shared meaning factors *characters**.

I propose that we represent the character* of a sentence by an ordered pair $\langle A, P \rangle$, where A is the kind of speech act that must be performed in a literal utterance of the sentence, and P is the kind of propositional content that speech act must have. The character* of a sub-sentential expression will be a kind of propositional content, and we should expect the character* of a complex expression to be determined by its syntax and the characters* of its component expressions.[12] A *kind* of speech act or proposition is simply a *property* of speech acts or propositions, and these kinds can be very general or very specific. The kind of proposition determined by '$2 + 3 = 5$' is very specific, very constraining, but the kind of proposition determined by 'It doesn't look like that' is fairly unspecific, fairly unconstrained. And the kind of speech act determined by 'Come in!' is any kind of imperatival speech act—a request, an order, an entreaty, and so on.

---

[11] Kaplan (1989).

[12] We can now define what it is for an utterance of a sentence S to be *literal* in the following way. There is some relation R such that $\langle A, P \rangle$ is S's character* iff $R(S, \langle A, P \rangle)$. Clearly, R will be some use-dependent relation, and in the next chapter I try to give an account of it. But let's suppose that a particular relation R^* is the character* relation. Then we can say that an utterance of a sentence S is literal just in case $\exists A, P(R^*(S, \langle A, P \rangle)$ & in uttering S the speaker performs an act of kind A whose propositional content is of kind P).

In 3.6 I will ask whether, or to what extent, we can say that an expression's character* is its meaning. In the meantime we can at least take note of the fact that there seems not to be anything in our common-sense concept of meaning that would enable us to *discover* that, say,

(13) 'Is it raining?' means ⟨asking-whether, a proposition of the form *it's raining at place m at time m'*, where *m* identifies a place implicitly referred to by the speaker and *m'* identifies the time of the utterance⟩.

At the same time, it is not *unreasonable* to suppose that your understanding an utterance of 'Is it raining?' is in part enabled by your knowing that one uttering that sentence literally is asking you whether it's raining at the time of the utterance at a place implicitly referred to by the speaker. Given this, we are still motivated to ask whether (III)—i.e. the conjunction of (III*s*) and (III*e*)—is the correct account of knowledge of meaning.

Well, it does seem to supply a sufficient condition for knowing what a sentence means, and it satisfies the important requirement of supplying something that is capable of playing the 'knowledge-of-meaning' role in language processing. The reasonable worry is whether (III) yields a necessary condition for knowledge of meaning. One worry is whether ordinary people—say, your Uncle Clyde in Cleveland—really can be said to have the propositional knowledge (III) implies they have. It is not clear they do; it is also not *entirely* clear they don't. We have lots of knowledge we can't easily articulate, and perhaps we can be relaxed as to how exactly Uncle Clyde conceptualizes the notion of a 'literal utterance' and related matters. Still, things look worse for Uncle Clyde's knowing when we consider that getting a sentence's propositional constraint right can require some real analytical skill (think of debates about the logical form of belief reports). In any case, a more serious worry is whether anything like the propositional knowledge (III*s*) ascribes *actually* plays, or is needed to play, the knowledge-of-meaning role in language processing. If something else plays that role in the processing that takes you from your perception of an utterance of 'Is it raining?' to your knowledge that the speaker was asking you whether it was raining in your locale, then shouldn't *it* be what constitutes knowledge of meaning? This leads me to a final proposal about knowledge of meaning.

3.5 KNOWLEDGE OF MEANING AS
A ROLE IN LANGUAGE PROCESSING

Sally utters

(14) Eating clams is morally permissible

and says thereby that eating clams is morally permissible. Now consider three people who understood her utterance, that is, three people who knew that in uttering (14) Sally said that eating clams was morally permissible. The first is Mao, a monolingual speaker of Mandarin Chinese who knew, as a result of having been told, that the English sentence (14) was such that in a literal utterance of it a speaker of English would be saying that eating clams was morally permissible. This propositional knowledge of Mao's, propositional knowledge of the kind implied by (IIIs), is part of what enabled Mao to move from his perception of Sally's utterance of (14) to his knowledge of what she said in uttering it. In this bit of information processing, Mao's type-(III) propositional knowledge about (14) played the knowledge-of-meaning role. The second person who understood Sally's utterance is Al, who is one of us, and it is an empirical question as to what played the knowledge-of-meaning role in him, though it seems clear that something did. There is something he brought to the utterance without which he wouldn't have been in a position to know what Sally said in uttering (14), something of a type he brings to every English utterance he understands and which, by virtue of the role it plays in his language understanding, constitutes his knowledge, on each occasion, of the meaning of the sentence uttered. The third person to understand Sally's utterance of (14) is clever Pierre. Nothing plays the knowledge-of-meaning role in the information processing that took him from his perception of Sally's utterance to his knowledge of what she said in uttering (14). Pierre correctly inferred what Sally said just on the basis of contextual clues. Having correctly inferred what Sally said, he may still not know what (14) means, since several English sentences, all differing in meaning—e.g. 'That's morally permissible', 'Eating clams is OK', etc.—may have literal utterances in which the speaker says that eating clams is morally permissible. In any event, Pierre didn't know what (14) meant when he correctly inferred what Sally said in uttering it.

Intuitively, we want to say that Al and Mao, but not Pierre, knew what (14) meant when they encountered Sally's utterance of it. The basis of this intuition is that in the case of Al and Mao, there was something, though not necessarily the same thing, playing the knowledge-of-meaning role in the information processing that resulted in the knowledge of what Sally said in uttering (14). Nothing played that role in Pierre, and that's why we're unwilling to say he knew what (14) meant. What this suggests is that *knowledge of meaning needn't be any one kind of state but is rather any state that plays the 'knowledge-of-meaning' processing role.* I'll try to be a little more specific.

Many different kinds of information processing can take one from the perception of the utterance of a sentence to the knowledge of what was said in that utterance. For example, typically when in conversation we hear an English sentence, we instantaneously know, without any conscious thought, what the speaker said; that is, we instantaneously know what primary speech act she was performing and what propositional content that speech act had (of course, we don't have any conscious thoughts about what the speaker said; we don't, for example, say to ourselves *sotto voce*, 'She just asked me whether it's raining'; but we know what the speaker said all the same). On other occasions, we may have to do some conscious reasoning to figure out what, if anything, the speaker was saying; even more is this so when we struggle to know what someone said in a foreign language in which we are something less than fluent. It might also be that utterances of different kinds of sentences are processed in interestingly different ways, or that not everyone processes utterances in quite the same way. Moreover, there is no one kind of process that must subserve the normal case where we hear the utterance straight away as the performance of a certain speech act with a certain content. Perhaps the unconscious part of the process involves a state that pairs the uttered sentence with its character*, or perhaps it pairs it with a Mentalese synonym. Thus, whatever is meant by 'the knowledge-of-meaning processing role', it must be a role that can be played in very different kinds of information processing. What I mean by the knowledge-of-meaning processing role may be put in the following way.

Consider any instance of an information-processing sequence that begins with an agent x's perception of the utterance of a sentence s of a language L and ends with x's knowing what was said in that utterance, and where it is clear to us that this information processing was owed in part to x's knowing what s means in L. In saying that x knows what was said in the utterance of s, what I mean, more specifically, is that (i) there is a kind of speech act A and a kind of proposition P

such that $\langle A, P \rangle$ is the character* of s; (ii) in uttering s, the speaker Ψed q, where Ψing is a speech act of kind A and q is a proposition of kind P; and (iii) x knows that in uttering s the speaker Ψed q. Now, whatever the specific details of how this information processing is effected—and they may be extremely various—the explanation of how x came to know that the speaker Ψed q will entail that the information processing that resulted in x's knowledge included a token of a state type that represents s as directly or indirectly linked with its character*, $\langle A, P \rangle$. *Whatever state represents that linkage is the one that plays the knowledge-of-meaning role.*

The linkage needn't be of any one sort. Perhaps the state that represents it represents $\langle A, P \rangle$ as the value of a certain function which utilizes semantic information about the parts and structure of s; perhaps the state is a token of the belief that a literal utterance of s in L requires the speaker to be performing a speech act of kind A with a content of kind P; perhaps the state is simply a representation of the ordered pair $\langle s, \langle A, P \rangle \rangle$; perhaps it links s with its character* only indirectly, either by representing it as paired with a synonymous sentence of x's idiolect or of x's neural system of mental representation, perhaps à la Harvey of my *Remnants of Meaning* (chapter 7), whose language-understanding ability is, by construction, explicable without recourse to any kind of compositional semantics for the language he understands. But even where the linkage is indirect, the complete explanation of how x came to know that the speaker Ψed q will advert to the state's effecting a linkage with the kind of speech act and kind of content that comprise s's character*. In the typical case, where s is a sentence of the public language dialect x shares with the speaker, the state that represents s as linked with its character* will itself be determined by other states in the information-processing sequence, which states effect linkages of the words in s with their characters*; but, as previous examples illustrated, someone can know what a sentence (for example, of a foreign language) means without even knowing how to parse it into its component words. Presently I'll make a speculation about the kind of state that might in fact play the knowledge-of-meaning role in us.

My final proposal, then, for knowing what a sentence means is that:

(IVs) x knows what s means in L iff x is in (or disposed readily to be in) a token of a state-type capable of occupying the knowledge-of-meaning role in x's understanding of a literal L utterance of s.

This can be mimicked to produce a corresponding account of what it is to know what a sub-sentential expression means:

> (IVe) x knows what e means in L iff x is in (or disposed readily to be in) a token of a state-type capable of occupying the knowledge-of-meaning role in x's understanding of a literal L utterance of e.

But what constitutes the knowledge-of-meaning role for words and other sub-sentential expressions?

Let '$\Sigma(sLx)$' designate the state type that plays the knowledge-of-meaning role with respect to x's knowing what sentence s means in L. In the normal case, where x knows what s means by virtue of knowing the language to which s belongs, the information-processing sequence in which $\Sigma(sLx)$ is tokened will see that token produced via an algorithm that starts with state tokens that represent the words composing s as directly or indirectly linked with their characters*, yields states tokens that represent larger sub-sentential expressions contained in s as linked with their characters*, and so on, until one gets to $\Sigma(sLx)$. The algorithm, or algorithms, utilized in the processing will be based, *inter alia*, on functions that map sequences of word-size characters* onto sentence-size characters*. Roughly speaking, we may expect the same state to play the knowledge-of-meaning role for a word whenever one understands the utterance of a sentence containing that word, and this will be a state that directly or indirectly links the word with its character*.

It may be helpful to illustrate this account of knowledge of meaning with a speculation about the kind of states that in fact play the knowledge-of-meaning role in our normal understanding of public-language utterances. A *compositional character* theory for a language L* is a finitely axiomatized theory of L that assigns characters* to the words of L and associates recursive functions with basic syntactical structures in such a way that the theory entails, for each meaningful expression of L, a theorem that pairs the expression with its character* in L. If such a theory is internally represented, understanding the utterance of a novel sentence might work in the following way. Al hears Sally's utterance of s, a sentence he's never before encountered but which is composed of familiar words in familiar ways. Al's perception of the utterance of s combines with other stuff to form a representation of the uttered sentence, which representation serves as input to Al's internally represented compositional character* theory for his English dialect, which theory in turn yields as output a representation of *s* as paired with its character*, ⟨*A, P*⟩. This representation is fed into certain higher, more consciously accessible information processing to enable Al defeasibly to believe that Sally is performing a speech act of kind *A* whose propositional content is of kind *P*. Still further consciously accessible, but not necessarily conscious, information processing results in the knowledge that Sally, in uttering *s*, was *A*-ing that such-and-such. It is the state that pairs *s* with its character* ⟨*A, P*⟩ which plays the knowledge-of-meaning processing role.

The foregoing raises several questions, such as: What relation must obtain between two things in order for the first to be the character* of the second? How does the answer to that question bear on issues about the supervenience of the intentional on the non-intentional? How does my speculation about compositional character* theories bear on questions about compositional semantics generally? (This last is of special concern to me, given previous writings in which I argued that languages neither had nor needed either compositional meaning theories or compositional truth theories, where these notions were understood as requiring finitely axiomatized theories of a certain sort.[13]) Can characters* be construed as meanings, contrary to what the discussion in Section 3.2 may seem to imply? How are my characters* related to David Kaplan's characters, and to other uses of so-called two-dimensional semantics? The rest of this chapter deals with these two last questions, while the next chapter takes on the other questions.

3.6   ARE CHARACTERS* MEANINGS?

On the one hand, characters* seem primed to be meanings. On the other hand, we seemed at the end of 3.2 to have a good argument to show that there are no such *things* as the meanings of expressions.

Characters* are primed to be meanings because an expression has meaning just in case it has a character*, and two expressions have the same meaning just in case they have the same character*.

---

[13] See e.g. Schiffer (1987*a*, 1994).

The good argument implied by 3.2 is that it is a platitude that if *a* Rs *b*, then knowing what *a* Rs requires knowing that *a* Rs *m*, for a contextually suitable way *m* of identifying *b*, and we seem not to have such knowledge for any expression, which shows that for no expression is there some thing which that expression means. Certainly the suggestion that characters* are meanings gives no support to the rejected thesis

(I) To know what *e* means is to know that *e* means *m*, for suitable way *m* of identifying *e*'s meaning.

For it seems, as already remarked, that knowing what, say, 'Is it raining?' means doesn't require knowing that it means ⟨asking-whether, a proposition of the form *it's raining at place m at time m'*, where *m* identifies a place implicitly referred to by the speaker and *m'* identifies the time of the utterance⟩.

So we have a choice. We could say that we have in the case of meaning an exception to the just-mentioned platitude about knowing what *a* Rs. Characters* are meanings and (I) is false. It is both *true* that

'Is it raining?' means ⟨asking-whether, a proposition of the form *it's raining at place m at time m'*, where *m* identifies a place implicitly referred to by the speaker and *m'* identifies the time of the utterance⟩

and *false* that

Knowing what 'Is it raining?' means = knowing that it means ⟨asking-whether, a proposition of the form *it's raining at place m at time m'*, where *m* identifies a place implicitly referred to by the speaker and *m'* identifies the time of the utterance⟩.

It is precisely the *meaning relation* that *x* must bear to *y* in order for *y* to be a character* of *x*; the character* relation = the meaning relation.

Alternatively, we could say that the failure of characters* to satisfy (I) shows they aren't meanings, that the relation that *x* must bear to *y* in order for *y* to be a character* of *x* is not the meaning relation; there is no meaning *relation* for the character* relation to be identical with. This is supported by the fact that, while knowing what, say, 'Is it raining?' means isn't the same as knowing that it means ⟨asking-whether, a proposition of the form *it's raining at place m at time m'*, where m identifies a place implicitly referred to by the speaker and m' identifies the time of the utterance), knowing what the character* of 'Is it raining?' is *is* the same as knowing that its character* is ⟨asking-whether, a proposition of the form *it's raining at place m at time m'*, where m identifies a place implicitly referred to by the speaker and m' identifies the time of the utterance⟩.

It is probably indeterminate which of these two alternatives is correct, but if I *had* to choose, I would choose the second thing to say: notwithstanding their role in meaning, characters* aren't meanings. But why should we *care* about saying whether or not characters* are meanings once all the facts are in? As far as I can see, all that matters is that we know that having meaning consists in having a character* and that knowledge of meaning consists not in any sort of propositional knowledge but rather in occupation of the processing role described in 3.5.

3.7   CHARACTERS AND CHARACTERS*

In a recent paper Robert Stalnaker writes: 'We can all agree that natural languages contain context-dependent expressions, and that an adequate descriptive semantics for such languages will make the kind of distinction between character and content that Kaplan makes in his theory of demonstratives.'[14] Actually, we can't all agree—unless Stalnaker simply means, what has always been obvious, that some sentence types have meaning factors that don't determine the propositions expressed by literal utterances of their tokens.

The intuitive idea of Kaplan's notion of character may be put in the following way. To grasp the meaning of a word or other semantically simple expression type is to know a rule that allows one to determine the content of a token of that type given relevant facts about the context in which the token is produced, and to grasp the meaning of a sentence or other semantically complex expression type is to know a rule that allows one to determine the content of a token of that type given its structure and the contents of the expression tokens that compose it (and together with whatever implicit references are

---

[14] Stalnaker (2001).

involved in the utterance of the token). For Kaplan, the propositional contents of sentence tokens are Russellian propositions,[15] the contents of semantically simple sub-sentential expression tokens are the objects and properties that are the building blocks of Russellian propositions, and the contents of semantically complex sub-sentential expression tokens can be objects ('that pigeon') or complex properties ('a silly boy'). Thus, for Kaplan, we can say that, roughly speaking: the character of 'I' determines the content of each of its tokens to be the speaker producing it; the character of 'now' determines the content of each of its tokens to be the time at which it is produced; the character of 'you' determines the content of each of its tokens to be the audience in the context in which the token is produced; the character of 'David Kaplan' determines the content of each of its tokens to be David Kaplan, and the character of 'square' determines the content of each of its tokens to be the property of being square. Kaplan's notion of character is easily transposed to any other conception of the propositions utterances express, provided that conception is compatible with the compositionality hypothesis (see Section 1.3), but, for simplicity of exposition, I'll continue my discussion in terms of Kaplan's Russellian account (later in this section I'll ask what account of character best suits the Fregean).

More formally, characters are functions from 'contexts of utterance' to contents. We've seen what contents are for Kaplan; contexts of utterance are supposed to be n-tuples, or *indices*, containing all that's needed to fix the content of an expression token relative to those indices. Indices are thus to include a possible world, a person, a place, a time, and whatever else is needed to get a package that contains all the factors on which the content of an expression token depends. The *actual* content of an expression token will be the value of its character given the token's actual context as argument. The actual context of an expression token is the index whose world, speaker, time, etc. are those of the token.

---

[15] It's characteristic of discussions of content to ignore non-indicative sentences and act as though the whole content of a sentence token was a proposition. Clearly, this needs revision when non-indicative moods are taken into account. I'll assume that we can speak of the propositional contents of even non-indicative sentence tokens (although in some cases it may be better to speak of the contents as being propositional forms), recognizing that there will be more to the whole content of the token than its propositional content. However, when confusion doesn't threaten, I'll go along with standard expositions in speaking as though propositions are the whole contents of sentence tokens.

Kaplan's construal of contexts of utterance as indices containing all the factors needed to determine content is problematic. The problem doesn't emerge for 'I', for here there does appear to be a contextual factor sufficient to determine the content of a token of 'I', but it is not plausible that there are suitable 'indices' to provide a character for, say, 'she'. The problem with 'she' is that there are no contextual factors that suffice to fix the content of any of its tokens. The reference of a token of 'she' is determined by the speaker's referential intentions, and in a literal utterance of 'she' the speaker is merely constrained (roughly speaking) to refer to a female. (The literal speaker is further constrained to refer to a female who is contextually salient with respect to the topic of conversation, but that is only because the speaker can't hope to have his referential intentions recognized unless his audience can single out a particular female as the most likely candidate for being the referent of the speaker's utterance of 'she'.[16]) Kaplan himself came to appreciate that the reference of a term like 'she' or 'that' is determined by the speaker's referential intentions and not by any reference-independent contextual factor, but it is not clear that he realized that this in effect ruined his conception of characters as functions from *indices* to contents.[17] For the only way of keeping indices along with the fact that reference is determined by the speaker's referential intentions is to take the speaker's referential intentions as a component of the index for 'she' *et al.* The trouble is that then the notion of an 'index' is rendered superfluous. If Kaplan is intent on construing the meaning-factors associated with expression types as functions to the contents of the tokens of those types, then he should take the 'character' of an indexical or demonstrative (or any other expression type whose tokens can have different contents) simply to be a function that maps tokens of the expression type onto their contents, where such a function is definable in terms of the way a literal speaker's referential intentions are constrained. Thus, Kaplan should take the character of 'she' to be that function that maps a token of 'she' onto x just in case x is the female to whom the speaker intended to refer in producing the token, and so on. The character of 'I' can likewise be taken to be that function that maps any given token of 'I' onto x just in case

---

[16] There are other problems with thinking that the notion of salience should enter into the meaning rule for a term like 'she'; see Schiffer (1995a: 115).   [17] Kaplan (1989).

x = the speaker and the speaker intended, in producing the token, to be referring to herself.[18]

Suppose that the corrected Kaplanian notion of character is a correct representation of the meaning, or meaning-factor, of an expression type. A further issue, made topical by David Chalmers and Frank Jackson,[19] concerns the characters of proper names, of mass terms like 'water', and of natural kind terms like 'dog'. First, let's assume—as Kaplan, Chalmers, and Jackson would assume[20]—that the content of every actual token of a proper name is the thing it actually names, the content of every actual token of 'water' is H_2O, and the content of every actual token of 'dog' is the property of belonging to *Canis familiaris*, the biological species to which all actual dogs belong (for present purposes we may pretend that such species are individuated by genotypes).[21] The issue to which I'm alluding concerns the kind of *character* these terms have. Do they have, using Kaplan's technical terms, *context-sensitive* or *fixed* characters? To say that a character is context-sensitive is to say that it doesn't necessarily map all of its arguments onto the same content; if it does necessarily map all of its

---

[18] There is another problem with Kaplan's notion of character. Kaplan claims that, necessarily, the meaning of every meaningful expression type is a character; but that seems too strong. For even if propositions are structured Russellian propositions, nothing precludes there being meaningful expressions that can't have contents, in which case the meaning of such an expression can't be a function from contexts to contents. Definite descriptions are such expressions on Russell's theory of them, and it's what Russell meant when he said that definite descriptions have no meaning of their own, although every sentence in which one occurs has a meaning of its own. The point is that on Russell's theory the proposition expressed by 'The F is G' = the proposition expressed by '$\exists x \, (\forall y(y = x \leftrightarrow Fy) \, \& \, Gx)$', and that proposition contains nothing that could be the content of 'the F'.

[19] Chalmers (1996) and Jackson (1998).

[20] Chalmers and Jackson speak not of Russellian propositions but of functions from possible worlds onto truth-values, but they would allow that this difference is irrelevant for the present exposition.

[21] It may be useful at this point to have certain ancillary technical notions before us. A singular-term token t in a sentence token $S(t)$ (the sentence S which contains t) *rigidly designates* x just in case (nearly enough) t refers to x and for any possible world w, the proposition expressed by $S(t)$ is true in w only if x has in w the property actually expressed by '$S(\ )$'; and a token t in a sentence token $S(t)$ is *directly referential* just in case $S(t)$ expresses a Russellian proposition containing the referent of t. Given the truth conditions of Russellian propositions, it follows that every directly referential singular-term token also rigidly designates its referent. But a term can be a rigid designator of its referent without being directly referential. For example, 'the sum of 1 and 2' is a rigid designator of the number 3 since, for example, 'The sum of 1 and 2 is odd' is true in an arbitrary world just in case 3 is odd in that world; but since 'the sum of 1 and 2' contributes the property of being the

arguments onto the same content—if, that is, it is a constant function—then it is a fixed character. According to Kaplan, 'I' has a context-sensitive character and 'square' has a fixed character. It will be useful to use Gareth Evans's famous example of the name 'Julius', explicitly introduced as the name of whoever invented the zipper, as our example of a proper name.[22] Kaplan would hold that 'Julius', 'water', and 'dog' all have fixed characters, but Chalmers and Jackson seem to suggest that these terms have context-sensitive characters.[23] In so far as they did hold this, it was a view they were pleased to hold because of what they took to be its consequences for a priori knowledge and its relevance to the mind–body problem, but for now I'll be concerned merely with its plausibility as an account of character given Kaplan's Russellian framework (the next section touches on the relevance of two-dimensional semantics to issues about a priori knowledge, necessity, and content).

If these terms have context-sensitive characters, what are those characters? The issue is a little tricky in the case of 'Julius', because the theorist who claims 'Julius' has a fixed character and the theorist who claims that it has a context-sensitive character would agree that the character is such that every *actual* token of the name refers to Whitcomb L. Judson, the man who in fact invented the zipper.[24] The difference emerges when we ask who would have been the content of

sum of 1 and 2, and not the number 3 itself, to the proposition expressed, it's not directly referential. The notion of rigid designation is also commonly glossed in terms of the notion of a *circumstance of evaluation*: a token *t* rigidly designates *x* just in case *t* refers to *x* in every counterfactual circumstance of evaluating what is expressed by the sentence token containing *t*—that is, just in case the truth-value of the proposition expressed by the sentence token in an arbitrary counterfactual world is determined by how things are with respect to *x*. Neither the notion of rigid designation nor that of direct reference is well defined for non-singular terms. If one wants to use these notions in connection with, say, 'square', then we should say, assuming Kaplan's Russellian framework, that if we take the referent of 'square' to be its extension, the set of square things, then it doesn't rigidly designate that set (and hence doesn't 'directly refer' to it), since different things will be square in different possible worlds. But if one takes the referent of 'square' to be the property of being square, then, for Kaplan, it both rigidly designates and directly refers to that property. The real issue with non-singular terms like 'water' and 'dog', as we're about to see, is with the kind of *character* they have.

[22] Evans (1982).

[23] Chalmers (forthcoming *a*) concedes that this was an implication of his (1996) but now disowns any such rendering of character. The reading is explicitly endorsed in Jackson (1998: 72 n. 26), but he, too, might not want to be held to the endorsement.

[24] This nugget is reported by Stalnaker (2001), who got it from an MIT web site about inventors.

'Julius' if, holding its actual meaning constant, someone other than Judson had invented the zipper. Sometimes this question is put, not altogether felicitously, as who would be the referent of 'Julius' in a counterfactual world considered as actual in which Judson exists but someone else invented the zipper. The proponent of fixed character would claim that no matter which world is taken to be actual, the content of 'Julius' is Whitcomb L. Judson, the person who in actual fact invented the zipper, whereas the proponent of context-sensitive character would claim that the character of 'Julius' maps a token of it onto whoever uniquely invented the zipper, so that the content of Julius would be Lionel Frumbush in a possible world in which 'Julius' has its actual character but Frumbush, not Judson, invented the zipper. The motivating idea of the context-sensitive theorist is seen to good advantage when we consider the use of 'Julius' after it has been introduced as the name of whoever invented the zipper and before it is known that that person is Whitcomb L. Judson. At that time, the bearer of the name—which is to say, the inventor of the zipper— could turn out to be any one of myriad people, and it is apt to seem counter-intuitive to suppose that what the name means in the language depends on who that person turns out to be.

In the case of a general term like 'square', theorists in both camps would agree that its character was fixed, mapping tokens of the word onto squareness, no matter what possible world is considered as actual. In the case of 'water', Kaplan would hold that its fixed character yields H_2O as the content of any token of that word, given that the type of which the token is a token has the character 'water' actually has among us. I put the point in this convoluted way because of what Kaplan would say about Twin Earth, where the watery stuff is XYZ, not H_2O. Earth and Twin Earth are, by construction, two locations in the same possible world. When you say 'I drank water' on Earth, you speak truly, as does twin-you, when she says 'I drank water'. Thus, the *content* of 'water' on Earth differs from its content on Twin Earth: H_2O on Earth, XYZ on Twin Earth. Kaplan, the fixed-content guy, would explain this by saying that the sequence of marks 'water' has a *different meaning* on Earth and Twin Earth by virtue of having different fixed characters. English, Kaplan would say, is spoken on Earth, but a different language, Twin-English, is spoken on Twin Earth. In English 'water' has a fixed character, and thus a fixed content (i.e. the character of 'water' is a constant function that maps all possible tokens onto the same content), which happens to be H_2O, and in

Twin-English 'water' has a fixed character, and thus a fixed content, which happens to be XYZ. For terms that have a fixed character, there is only a notional difference between character and content; in these cases, character and content are, for all that matters, the same thing (thus, for Kaplan, it must be a matter of indifference whether one says that the meaning of 'Saul Kripke' is Saul Kripke or that it is that constant function which maps all possible tokens of the name onto Saul Kripke). Likewise, as regards 'dog', Kaplan would say that, given its fixed character, no matter what possible world one considers as actual, its content is the species *Canis familiaris*. On Twin Earth, where the doggy-looking-and-behaving creatures belong to a different biological species (maybe they're mutant turtles), 'dog' has a different meaning, i.e. a different fixed character, which yields as its fixed content the species of the doggy things on Twin Earth.

There is another position on 'water' and 'dog' that differs from the one Kaplan would take but which also gives those terms fixed characters and, thereby, fixed contents. According to this position, 'water' and 'dog' have the same fixed character *and the same content* on Earth and Twin Earth; English is spoken in both places, and in both 'water' has as its content the property of being the such-and-such looking and behaving liquid, and 'dog' has as its content the property of being a such-and-such looking and behaving animal. Since both H_2O and XYZ have the property of being such-and-such looking and behaving liquids, both are water. Likewise, *mutatis mutandis*, for 'dog'. Some philosophers feel that this is the correct account of terms like 'water' and 'dog' and that the Putnamian thought experiments merely succeeded in altering the intuitions of philosophers. At the least it must be said that it is by no means clear what ordinary speakers would say if they were actually to come across a twin earth.

The proponents of the Chalmers-and-Jackson-inspired context-sensitive characters for 'water' and 'dog' would claim that English is spoken on Earth and on Twin Earth. The content of 'water' on Earth is H_2O and on Twin Earth is XYZ, but that's because 'water' has the same context-sensitive character which maps a token of 'water' onto the watery stuff with which the utterer has been in direct or indirect contact, thus yielding tokens on Earth that have a different content from the tokens on Twin Earth. Likewise, *mutatis mutandis*, for 'dog'. This line enjoys the same sort of motivation that supports the context-sensitive-character line for 'Julius'. When we imagine the use of 'water' before it was known what the chemical constitution of water was, or even if it was of any one chemical kind, it is apt to seem counter-intuitive that what 'water' means in English should depend on what the chemical constitution of watery stuff is; surely, the thought goes, 'water' would have its actual meaning no matter which chemical-constitution world turns out to be actual.

Which side is right, the side for fixed character or the side for context-sensitive character? And if the fixed-character side, which version of it as regards 'water' and 'dog'? In the case of proper names, the answer should be clear. The character of an expression type is, by definition, that which gives the expression type whatever meaning it has, and, as we've seen, it is even reasonable to suppose that if expression types have characters, then those characters are the meanings of those expression types. As such, an expression's character is what gets attached to the expression by whatever conventional or other regularities in linguistic behaviour fix an expression's meaning. Thus, it is reasonable to suppose that 'square' has come to express the property of being square because that is what English speakers have used it to express. Now, by virtue of what does 'David Chalmers' name David Chalmers? Is it because there is a practice among those who use the name to use it to refer to David Chalmers, or is it because there is a conventional practice to use the name to refer to whoever satisfies a certain condition? Clearly the former; the linguistic practice, or convention, which makes 'David Chalmers' a name of David Chalmers is one that can be specified only by referring to David Chalmers; that practice, or convention, doesn't pick out Chalmers by first attaching to a condition he satisfies; Chalmers himself is that to which the practice, or convention, directly links the name. Even if I think of Chalmers under one description, say as the author of *The Conscious Mind*, and you think of him in another way, say, in terms of features derived from personal acquaintance, I can still refer to him by using his name when speaking to you because we both know of him, albeit under different ways of identifying him, that there is a practice of referring to him by the name 'David Chalmers'. The meaning-establishing link for a proper name is with its bearer, and we can speak of its meaning as being a fixed character (relative, of course, to ongoing assumptions about the probity of that way of speaking in the first place) because, as noticed, when an expression has a fixed character, there is no significant difference between its character and its fixed content. The same holds for 'Julius': a name doesn't change its meaning when it continues to name its bearer even after the description in terms of which the name was introduced has lost its exclusive connection with the name. When I say 'Just one person invented the zipper, and I hereby name that person "Julius" ', I'm *quantifying into* my name-establishing stipulation to link the name not to the property of being the inventor of the zipper but to the person who invented the zipper; the link to the property is merely the means to that end. Proper names are unique among singular terms in that the conventional correlation whereby a name can be used to refer to a thing can be specified only by reference to that thing: there is a practice of using the name to refer to *it*. In the case of every other kind of singular term, the term is able to refer to a thing because the term is conventionally correlated with something—a character, a constraint, a rule, whatever—that is specifiable without reference to anything to which the term might be used to refer. For example, when I refer to David Chalmers using the name 'David Chalmers', I rely on its being common knowledge between me and my audience that there is a practice of referring to Chalmers by that name; but when I refer to Chalmers using 'he', I rely on its being common knowledge that the meaning of 'he' requires the speaker to be referring to a contextually salient male and that Chalmers is a contextually salient male. Yet what of the motivating intuition that underlies the context-sensitive-character line on 'Julius', the intuition that tells us that the meaning of 'Julius' doesn't depend on who turns out to have invented the zipper. We serve the context-sensitive theorist better by having this sort of intuitive motivation dealt with in the case of a term like 'water' or 'dog'.

So what about 'water' and 'dog'? What's the correct account of their character and content relative to Kaplan's Russellian framework? Kaplan's version of the fixed-character view, I think. There is reason to think the other two views confuse how we ordinarily identify water and dogs with what, respectively, 'water' and 'dog' mean. I dare say I know what both 'alligator' and 'crocodile' mean, even though I keep forgetting the characteristics that distinguish them. Likewise, a person who was unreliable at identifying dogs—perhaps because he never personally encountered one—might nevertheless know what 'dog' means; similarly for 'water'. Although a group of people may think of the same material object in different ways, they may tend to think of a substance or natural kind in uniform ways. Even so, it would be a mistake to conflate the way of thinking of a substance or natural kind with its meaning if it is possible for someone who thinks of those things in a different way to use the general terms for those things with the meanings they have for us. There may, for example, be some question whether 'red' means the same for a blind person as it does for a sighted person, but there doesn't seem to be any question whether 'dog' means the same for a blind person as it does for a sighted person. But what about the intuition that for someone who doesn't know the chemical composition of water, what 'water' means in her idiolect shouldn't turn on which chemical-composition world—the XYZ, the H_2O, or whatever world—turns out to be actual? The intuition is being made too much of, in part because of its being characterized in a tendentious way. Consider, Horace, who is an English speaker on earth but doesn't know whether he's in an H_2O world or in an XYZ world. Even though 'water' in Horace's idiolect refers to H_2O, it is *epistemically possible* for him that water is XYZ. What 'water' means in Horace's idiolect doesn't turn on any chemical discovery. 'Water', having a constant character (supposing Kaplan to be right), for all intents and purposes means water, i.e. H_2O, and Horace knows what 'water' means; he just doesn't know what it means under a description that identifies water as H_2O. In a counterfactual world exactly like our world except that 'water' refers to XYZ, 'water' in Horace's idiolect will mean water, i.e. XYZ, although it will be epistemically possible for Horace that water is H_2O. Since 'water' has a fixed character (relative to ongoing assumptions), it has a different meaning in the two worlds, notwithstanding the striking similarities between them. Described thus, I submit, there is nothing counter-intuitive about the Kaplanian view—not, at least, anything that should make us say that 'water' has a context-sensitive character relative to Kaplan's Russellian framework.

I conclude that if we assume that Russellian propositions are the things we mean, then, subject to the qualification about the domain of character functions (Kaplan's 'contexts'), Kaplan was right that proper names, mass terms like 'water', and natural kind terms like 'dog' have fixed characters. But I reject the Russellian assumption, and my characters* are not characters. Before turning to an explicit discussion of characters versus characters*, however, I would like to raise a different question, of some interest on its own and whose answer will help to set up some points I want to make in connection with my own notion of character*. The question is, What should the Fregean say about character?

The Fregean will want characters as the meanings, or meaning factors, of expression types as much as the Russellian wants them for that. For both theorists the character of a semantically complex expression type is a function that maps tokens of the type onto contents that are themselves a function (nearly enough) of the contents of the expression tokens that compose the semantically complex token, and for both theorists the characters of words and other semantically simple expression types are functions that map tokens of those types onto their contents. Moreover, propositional contents for both theorists are structured propositions, and the contents of sub-sentential expression tokens are the components of those structured propositions. The only difference is that the Russellian's structured propositions are Russellian propositions, structured entities whose basic components are the objects and properties our thoughts can be about, while for the Fregean they are Fregean propositions, structured propositions whose basic components are 'concepts' of the objects and properties our thoughts can be about. We've seen what the Russellian should say about the characters of proper names, mass terms like 'water', and natural kind terms like 'dog', and the interesting question now is what the Fregean should say about those terms.

For the Fregean, the content of the token of 'Bertrand Russell' in a token of 'Bertrand Russell was a pacifist' is whatever concept that token contributes to the Fregean proposition that is the content of the sentence token, and any version of Fregeanism that stands any chance of surviving must claim that different tokens of 'Bertrand Russell', or any other proper name, can have different contents. The character of a proper name, therefore, must be a *context-sensitive* character for the Fregean. What, then, should the Fregean say is the nature of the content-determining rule embodied in the characters of proper names? I think he should say that, subject to a certain qualification, the only constraint on the concept is that it be a concept of the bearer of the name. So, the 'meaning rule' for 'Bertrand Russell', *qua* name of the philosopher, is, roughly speaking: utter a sentence '... Bertrand Russell...' only if you mean $\langle\langle...c...\rangle,...\rangle$, where c is a concept of Bertrand Russell. While the concept one must intend to express is unconstrained apart from its having to apply to Russell, one should nevertheless expect an invisible hand to be at work to assure that there is a significant overlap in the concepts expressed by tokens of 'Bertrand Russell' over and above their being concepts of Russell. This is so because when we speak we typically intend to be understood, so when a speaker utters 'Bertrand Russell', she must expect her audience to have a concept of Russell and to know that the speaker has one, too. This kind of mutual expectation would be hard to realize if there weren't a certain degree of commonality in the contents of the concepts expressed by tokens of the name. The qualification to which I alluded a few lines back is that the Fregean will want to make the nature of the concept expressed by a name token dependent on its sentential context, and perhaps on other things as well. I have in mind primarily negative existentials—'Moses didn't exist'—but there are also occurrences of names in that-clauses ('She believes that God is all-good', uttered by an atheist) and there may be other contexts. Perhaps here the Fregean can do no better than to say that the character of a name maps tokens of it in these special sentential contexts onto any concept intended by the speaker, provided it is a concept under which at least some users of the name thought they had knowledge of the bearer of the name.

On the account of name characters recommended to the Fregean, 'Superman' and 'Clark Kent' would, supposing the fiction to be fact, have the same character. But do we really want to stick the *Fregean* with having to say that 'Superman' and 'Clark Kent' are synonymous names? There is no problem here for the Fregean. The fact that both names have the same character doesn't imply that one who employs those names will know that they have the same character. Lois Lane, for example, knows that the meaning rule for 'Superman' is, as it were, to use that name to express some concept of Superman, and she knows that the meaning rule for 'Clark Kent' is to use that name to express some concept of Clark Kent. Since she doesn't know that Superman is Clark Kent, she doesn't yet know that the two names have the same character. This also secures that were she to utter 'Superman flies', she would be expressing a different proposition from the one she would be expressing were she to utter 'Clark Kent flies'.

Another thing we should note is that although 'Bertrand Russell', as used by us on Earth, has a context-sensitive character, according to what the Fregean should say, it would still be the case that when my doppelgänger on Twin Earth uses 'Bertrand Russell' to refer to Twin-Russell, he is referring to Twin-Russell, since the character of 'Bertrand Russell' among those in my doppelgänger's circle requires a concept that applies to Twin-Russell. For the Fregean, 'Bertrand Russell' has different context-sensitive characters on Earth and Twin Earth.

What should the Fregean say is the character of 'water' and 'dog'? I think the Fregean would do best to treat 'water' as a name of the stuff *we* call 'water' and to treat 'dog' as a name of doghood, the property of belonging to the species of those things *we* call 'dogs'. This is to accommodate the fact that 'water' and 'dog' can mean the same thing for someone—Helen Keller, for example—who thinks of water and doghood quite differently from the way we think of them. There would, as in the case of names, be an invisible-hand mechanism securing that we tend to use those terms to communicate with people who think of water and doghood in ways similar to the ways we think of those things. This doesn't imply that 'water' has the same character as 'collection of H_2O molecules' or that 'dog' means the same as 'has such-and-such ancestry and genotype', since, if for no other reason, 'water' and 'dog' have characters suitable to semantically simple expressions, whereas the semantically complex expressions just mentioned have characters, for the Fregean, that are a function of the characters of their component expressions.

So much for character. My notion of character* is importantly different. Characters are (best construed as) functions that map tokens of expression types onto their contents, but one can coherently speak of the 'content' of an expression token only if one thinks that the propositional content of a sentence token is a function of the contents of its semantically relevant parts, and I have argued that there is reason to doubt that that is so. My characters* serve not to *determine* propositional contents but rather to *constrain* them. But constrain them how? I hope I can answer this adequately by giving my view of the characters* of the following expressions, where we'll see that what I say about these characters* isn't unlike what the Fregean should say about her characters:

- 'I'. The character* of 'I' constrains the literal speaker who utters a token of 'I' to be performing a speech act whose content is a self-ascriptive proposition, a proposition of the sort one could refer to by using a that-clause that contains 'I'. Such a proposition would be an object-dependent proposition where the thing on which the proposition's identity and existence was dependent was the person who could use 'I' to refer to the proposition. Now, to at least a first approximation, one refers to x in uttering a token t in a token of a sentence $S(t)$ just in case the proposition expressed by $S(t)$ is, owing to t, an x-dependent proposition. In this way, the character* of 'I' secures that the literal speaker refers to herself in uttering a token of 'I'.

- Proper names. Subject to a certain qualification, the character*
  of a name n constrains the literal speaker who utters a token of a
  name to be performing a speech act whose propositional content
  is an x-dependent proposition, where x is the bearer of the
  uttered name. The qualification concerns negative existentials
  and that-clause occurrences, and perhaps other special contexts.
  In these cases the literal speaker will, to a first approximation, be
  constrained to mean a proposition that involves a contextually
  pertinent property associated with the practice of using the
  name in the linguistic community relevant to the utterance, as,
  for example, in an utterance of 'George Eliot never existed;
  Middlemarch and those other novels were written by a committee' the pertinent property would be the property of being the
  author of such-and-such novels.
- 'Red'. To a first approximation, and roughly speaking, the character* of 'red' constrains the literal speaker who utters a token of
  'red' to be performing a speech act whose propositional content
  is a redness-dependent proposition. The way in which a proposition is redness-dependent will affect its truth conditions. Thus,
  an utterance of 'That car is red' predicates redness of the car
  referred to, and is therefore true in an arbitrary possible world
  just in case the car is red in that world. All this is consistent with
  the contextually determined criteria of evaluation—which individuates the proposition expressed by an utterance of the sentence—doing its individuating work in such a way that to believe
  the expressed proposition requires that one have this, that, or the
  other perspective on, or way of thinking about, redness. The
  reason the foregoing characterization is a first approximation is,
  as we'll see when we get to the chapter on vagueness and indeterminacy (Chapter 5), that there really is no such thing as *the*
  property ascribed by 'red', and hence no such thing as *the* property of redness. For vague properties—which includes any property expressed by an utterance of 'red'—are partly individuated
  by their penumbras, their range of borderline cases, and the
  penumbra of the property expressed by an utterance of 'red' can
  dilate or constrict from one utterance to the next.
- 'Water'. To a first approximation, the character* of 'water'
  constrains the literal speaker who utters a token of 'water' to be
  performing a speech act whose propositional content is a water-
  dependent proposition. If water $= H_2O$, then water-dependent

propositions are H_2O-dependent propositions. This may need qualification to accommodate 'Water doesn't exist and never has existed; we've been suffering from a colossal illusion'. 'Water' has a different character* on Twin Earth.

- 'Dog'. To a first approximation, the character* of 'dog' constrains the literal speaker who utters a token of 'dog' to be performing a speech act whose propositional content is a doghood-dependent proposition. If doghood = has genotype G, then dog-dependent propositions are having-G-dependent propositions. This may need qualification to accommodate 'Dogs don't exist, and never have existed; we've all been suffering from a colossal illusion'. 'Dog' has a different character* on Twin Earth.

3.8 TWO-DIMENSIONAL SEMANTICS AND PROPOSITIONAL-ATTITUDE CONTENT

If we were doing semantics for a non-indexical language, we might assign to each non-logical expression type an *intension*, where that is taken to be a function that maps each possible world for which the function is defined onto the expression's *extension* in that world, where the extension of a name or other singular term is its referent, the extension of an n-ary predicate is the set of n-tuples to which it applies, and the extension of an indicative sentence is its truth-value.[25] Such a semantics, whose only extension-determining

---

[25] Strictly speaking, talk of 'the extension of e in w' is at least two ways ambiguous. It could mean the extension e has in w as determined by how e is used *in w*, or it could mean the extension e has in w as determined by how e is *actually used*. It's the latter that is intended in formal semantics when theorists of one-dimensional semantics speak without qualification of the extension of an expression in a possible world. But what does it mean to speak in this way of the extension of an expression in a possible world? Suppose a sentence $S(e)$ (a sentence S containing the expression e) says p, which happens, let's say, to be false; we might nevertheless want to know what p's truth-value would have been had things been thus and so. This is to wonder about p's truth-value—and a fortiori about $S(e)$'s—in a certain counterfactual world, a certain possible world other than the actual world. To a rough approximation, the extension of e in a possible world w is that semantic value associated with e that is essential to determining the truth-value of p—and a fortiori of $S(e)$—in w. As we'll presently see, in addition to asking about an expression's extension in w considered as a counterfactual circumstance of evaluation, one might also want to ask about an expression's extension in w on the supposition that w is, or turns out to be, the actual world.

apparatus is a function from possible worlds onto extensions, is a *one-dimensional semantics*.

A one-dimensional semantics can't accommodate indexical language, where numerous singular terms, predicates, and sentences may have no context-independent extension. A constraint on how a one-dimensional semantics should be modified to accommodate indexical language is that a sentence like 'I am here now' is to be true whenever it is uttered, while what is said in each such utterance is only contingently true. To get this right, we shall want to move to a *two*-dimensional semantics. One dimension will be a function that (at least in effect) maps each possible token e_t of an expression type e onto another function—the second dimension—which maps each possible world for which it is defined onto the extension of e_t in that world. Kaplan's character–content distinction determines a two-dimensional semantics: an expression type's character is a function from tokens of the type onto the contents of those tokens, and the content of a token determines a unique function that maps each possible world for which it is defined onto the extension of the token in that world. For example, the character of 'I' can be viewed as a function that maps each token of 'I' onto a function that maps each possible world for which the function is defined onto the extension of the token in that world. Given Kaplan's Russellian framework, the character of 'I' maps each of its tokens in my idiolect onto a function that maps each possible world onto me, provided I exist in that world.

The intensions that comprise a two-dimensional semantics are set-theoretic entities that can be deployed in ways that are less tightly connected to the literal meanings of expressions. For example, even if one agrees with Kaplan that, say, 'water' has a fixed character, one may nevertheless think that 'water' refers to whatever is the clear liquid we drink and bath in, so that what 'water' refers to turns on what in fact has that extension-determining property. If it turns out that XYZ is the liquid we drink and bath in, then 'water' has XYZ as its extension, and if it turns out, as it has in fact turned out, that H_2O has the extension-determining property, then it will be the extension of 'water'. In this way, one will want to recognize a third intension distinct from either the character or content of 'water', which, in effect, maps tokens of 'water' onto extensions in possible worlds considered as actual, that is, an intension that tells us how the extension of 'water' depends on what world turns out to be one's actual world (to consider a possible world as actual is to regard it as epistemically possible—i.e. possible

for all one knows—that that world is one's actual world). Such intensions, nearly enough, are David Chalmers's *primary intensions* and
Frank Jackson's *A-intensions* (Chalmers's *secondary* intensions and
Jackson's *C*-intensions are the same as the extension-determining
functions determined by Kaplan's contents; i.e. they map possible
worlds considered as counterfactual circumstances of evaluation onto
the extensions of expressions in those worlds).[26]

One might also try to use a two-dimensional semantic apparatus
to illuminate propositional-attitude content, and this, too, is one of
the pay-offs Chalmers and Jackson hope to gain, Chalmers with his
distinction between primary and secondary intensions, Jackson with
his virtually identical distinction between *A-* and *C*-intensions. I
want now to consider a two-dimensional theory of propositional-
attitude content that is very closely based on the work of Chalmers
and Jackson, and especially that of Chalmers.[27] In fact, so far as I can
see, the theory to be sketched is entailed by what Chalmers has written (subject to the qualification mentioned in footnote 27), but I'm
going to present the theory, which I'll call *Theory C*, without regard
to who may or may not subscribe to it, so that we may consider its
merits directly, without getting embroiled in exegesis. I want to discuss this theory in part because it has become influential and occu-
pies a certain position on the current philosophical landscape, but
more importantly for two other reasons. First, I have so far discussed
the issue of belief content only in connection with the semantics of
that-clause-containing belief reports, but it is possible to approach
the issue of belief content independently of the semantic concern, as
Chalmers does, and that will give us a different perspective on some
of the issues I have already discussed and the conclusions I have
drawn about them. Secondly, the two-dimensional theory of content
to be sketched as Theory C is quite different from the account of
content presented in this book, and indirect light will be shed on my
theory by a critical discussion of this other theory. And while I will
(big surprise) end up arguing against Theory C, one reason I'm interested in discussing it is that it is very close, as we'll see, to a certain
Russellian theory, one whose pull I have experienced myself.[28]

Let's assume that we think in an inner system of mental representation, a *lingua mentis* I'll call *Mentalese*. As a useful heuristic, we can

---

[26] Chalmers (1996); Jackson (1998); and Chalmers and Jackson (2001).
[27] See esp. Chalmers (2002a, forthcoming a).   [28] See Schiffer (1977, 1978).

pretend that Mentalese is neural English, the neural expressions standing to spoken English expressions in roughly the way the spoken expressions stand to their orthographic counterparts. I'll refer to Mentalese expressions by way of referring to their orthographic counterparts, and I'll assume that for any kind of semantic value—an extension, an intension, or whatever—the semantic value of a complex expression is determined, roughly speaking, by its structure and the semantic values of its component expressions. Before stating Theory C, we should first gloss some of the technical notions it deploys.

Centred worlds. Formally, a centred world may be taken to be an ordered pair whose first member is a metaphysically possible world and whose second member is an n-tuple of things (of any ontological category) in that world. This n-tuple constitutes the 'centre' of the centred world. Informally, a centred world is a metaphysically possible world in which certain things have been flagged for special consideration. What that 'special consideration' comes to is determined by the use to which those items are put in the theory which employs those centred worlds. As we'll see, Theory C needs centred worlds in order to determine what things would fall under a person's concepts were the actual world of that person to have a certain character, and the way this plays out requires the centre of a centred world to contain at least a given agent and time. For example, suppose my concept of water is the concept of the clear, tasteless liquid that I currently drink, that comes out of my taps, and that fills the lakes, rivers, and oceans in my environment. This means that water will turn out to be whatever satisfies the *uniqueness condition* that defines my concept: if H_2O satisfies that condition, then it's water, but if XYZ satisfies it, then it's water. The uniqueness condition that determines what falls under my concept of water has, roughly speaking, the form *the stuff that is R to me now*, and there is no replacing these references to me and the current time by some general condition. Now, suppose we want to represent this uniqueness condition as a function that maps a possible world w onto some stuff x (XYZ, H_2O, or whatever) just in case x falls under my concept of water, should w be my actual world now. This function will be defined only for possible worlds that contain me and the present time. This motivates the introduction of centred worlds where the centre consists of me and the present time. Instead of representing the uniqueness condition as a partial function undefined for most possible worlds (so to speak), we can more perspicuously represent it as a function from those centred worlds whose centres consist of myself and the present time onto the substances in those worlds that satisfy the uniqueness condition in question.[29] Bertrand Russell and every other theorist who has taken a description theory of reference determination seriously has recognized the need for uniqueness properties that ineliminably contain oneself and the present time.

Considering a world as <u>actual</u> versus considering a world as <u>counterfactual</u>. This has already been touched on, but it is important that it be made explicit. Talk of 'the reference of "water" in a possible world *w*' is three ways ambiguous. First, it could mean the reference 'water' has in *w* as the word is used in *w*. In this sense, the reference of 'water' would be the Eiffel Tower in a world in which 'water' was a proper name of that tower. This sense can be put aside, as it will never be at issue in the discussion of Theory C. The second thing it could mean is the stuff in *w* relevant to the determination of the truth-value of the statement that water is such-and-such when that statement is evaluated with respect to *w*. Since (we may suppose) 'water' rigidly designates the stuff that is water, which happens to be H_2O, the reference of 'water' in *w* would be H_2O, *even if the watery stuff in w is XYZ.* To consider a possible world as counterfactual is to consider it in this sense. The reference of the word 'water' or the concept of water in any world considered as counterfactual is always H_2O, the stuff that satisfies the relevant uniqueness condition in the actual world. The third thing talk of 'the reference of "water" in a possible world *w*' could mean is the stuff that satisfies the uniqueness condition in *w*. For example, if my actual world turns out to be an XYZ, rather than an H_2O, world, then 'water' would refer to XYZ. To consider a possible world as actual is to consider it in this sense. The reference of 'water' in a possible world considered as actual is whatever 'water' would rigidly designate if that world were our actual world.

1-intensions and 1-extensions. By stipulative definition, a function *f* from centred worlds onto things of a certain category (individuals, sets of *n*-tuples, truth-values, etc.) is an expression *e*'s *1-intension* just in case *x* is *e*'s extension in *w*-considered-as-actual iff $f(w) = x$. If *f* is *e*'s 1-intension and $f(w) = x$, then, by stipulative definition, *x* is *e*'s *1-extension in w*.

<hr />

[29] This is by way of illustration only; the condition determining what falls under my concept of water would need to be finessed in one way or another in order to allow for the possibility that water turns out to be no *one* kind of thing.

2-intensions and 2-extensions. By stipulative definition, a function g from metaphysically possible worlds onto things of a certain category (individuals, sets of n-tuples, truth-values, etc.) is an expression e's *2-intension* just in case x is e's extension in w-considered-as-counterfactual iff $g(w) = x$. If g is e's 2-intension and $g(w) = x$, then, by stipulative definition, x is e's *2-extension in w*.

Theory C may now be stipulated to make the following claims (attention will be restricted to Mentalese expressions capable of having extensions, such as singular terms, predicates, and sentences).

1. Every Mentalese expression token has a 1-intension. That is, for every Mentalese token e there is a function f, whose domain is a set of centred worlds, such that $f(w) = x$ iff x is the 1-extension of e in w, i.e. the extension e has in w-considered-as-actual.[30] Some examples by way of rough illustration. The 1-intension of 'Julius' is that function which maps a centred world onto the inventor of the zipper in that world, if there is a unique such person, and is undefined otherwise. Thus, the 1-extension of 'Julius' in the actual world is Whitcomb L. Judson, but David Chalmers is the 1-extension of 'Julius' in a centred world in which he alone invented the zipper. The 1-intension of 'water' is that function which maps a centred world onto whatever in that world is the watery stuff, if anything is, and is undefined otherwise. Thus, the actual 1-extension of 'water' is H_2O, but XYZ is the 1-extension of 'water' in any centred world in which it is the watery stuff. The 1-intension of 'circular' is that function which maps a centred world onto the set of things that are circular in that world. And the 1-intension of 'dog' is that function which maps a centred world onto the set of things in that world which belong to the zoological species of the such-and-such looking and behaving creatures in that world. Thus, the actual 1-extension of 'dog' is the class of dogs, i.e. the class of things belonging to the species *Canis familiaris*, but there are centred worlds in which dogs don't comprise the 1-extension of 'dog', as the such-and-such looking and behaving creatures in that world belong to a zoological species other than *Canis familiaris*.

---

[30] As Chalmers develops his theory in (forthcoming), he uses a generic notion of an epistemically possible world and then asks how these epistemic worlds are best construed. He allows that epistemic worlds can be taken to be centred metaphysically possible worlds, and, owing to their familiarity, usually presents his theory using those centred worlds, but he also allows for at least one other possible construal of epistemically possible worlds. Although I can't go into the matter, it's my view that centred worlds are best suited to Chalmers's overall semantic and metaphysical project.

2. For every Mentalese expression token e, there is a relation R such that, for any f, f is e's 1-intension iff $R(e, f)$. Two important things are true of R. First, it holds *contingently* between the things it relates. That a Mentalese expression token has a particular 1-intension has at the least something to do with the conceptual role of the expression type of which the token is a token. Secondly, bearing R to a 1-intension is an *individualistic* property, in that whether a thinker's expression bears R to a particular f is determined entirely by the internal state of the thinker, thereby securing that 1-intensions are so-called *narrow contents*.

3. Every Mentalese expression token has a 2-intension. That is, for every Mentalese token e there is a function g, whose domain is the set of metaphysically possible worlds, such that $g(w) = x$ iff x is the 2-extension of e in w, i.e. the extension e has in w-considered-as-counterfactual. There are two kinds of 2-intensions and two correspondingly different ways in which an expression's 2-intension may be determined.

Some expressions, such as 'circular', have the same 2-intension in every centred world. For such expressions, their 2-intensions are directly determined by their 1-intensions, and there's a sense in which these 2-intensions are mere copies of the 1-intensions that determine them. This is because both the 1-extension and the 2-extension is determined by the same condition. For example, the 1-intension of 'circular' maps each centred world onto the set of circular things in that world, and the 2-intension of that word maps every world onto the set of circular things in that world.

Other expressions—including many that are rigid designators—have different 2-intensions in different centred worlds. For such an expression, its 2-intension in a given centred world is determined by its 1-extension in that world, and the expression can have different 1-extensions in different centred worlds. If in these cases the expression's 1-extension in a centred world is x, then its 2-intension in that centred world is that function which maps every world onto x (or perhaps onto x in every world in which x exists, a qualification I'll henceforth ignore). In these cases, the expression's 1-intension determines a certain *uniqueness property* for each centred world—a property of the form *the property of being the only thing that's such-and-such*—and the 1-extension in a given centred world is whatever in that world has the uniqueness property. Such a uniqueness property may be a composite property containing an ineliminable occurrence of whatever agent or time (or whatever else) belongs to the 'centre' of a particular centred world. The expression's 2-intension in that centred world will map each possible world onto the thing in the centred world that has the uniqueness property determined by the expression's 1-intension. Some examples by way of rough illustration. The 1-intension of 'Julius' determines the 1-extension of the name in a centred world to be whatever in that world has the property of being the unique inventor of the zipper. Since Whitcomb L. Judson actually has that property, he's the actual 1-extension of 'Julius', and therefore the actual 2-intension is that function which maps every possible world onto Judson. Thus, 'Julius' has Judson as its 2-extension in every possible world. In a centred world in which Chalmers is the 1-extension of 'Julius', then the name's 2-intension in that centred world maps every world onto him. Let's call the 1- and 2-intensions of sentences *propositions*. Then we see that the 1-proposition expressed by 'If Julius exists, then Julius invented the zipper' is the *necessary* proposition that (so to say) if the inventor of the zipper exists, then he or she invented the zipper, whereas the 2-proposition expressed is the *contingent* proposition that (so to say) if Judson exists, then Judson invented the zipper. The 1-intension of 'water' determines the 1-extension of the word in a centred world to be whatever in that world has the property of being the unique watery stuff in that world. Since H_2O actually has that property, it is the actual 1-extension of 'water', and, accordingly, its actual 2-intension is that function which maps every possible world onto H_2O. But in a centred world in which XYZ is the 1-extension of 'water', its 2-intension in that world maps every world onto XYZ. In this way we see that the 1-proposition expressed by 'Water is H_2O' is the *contingent* proposition that (so to say) the watery stuff in our environment is H_2O, whereas that sentence's 2-proposition is the *necessary* proposition that (so to say) H_2O is H_2O.

4. There are very important epistemological and psychological asymmetries between 1- and 2-propositions, and some of the more striking ones are inventoried here and in the points to follow. The first point has virtually been made already, but it is worth repeating. It is that whereas 1-propositions are always *narrow* contents, 2-propositions, when they are not mere copies of 1-intensions, are typically *wide* contents. That all 1-propositions are narrow contents follows from the claim, made in glossing what it is for a function to be an expression's 1-intension, that having a certain 1-intension always supervenes on

what's in the head of the person for whom the expression has that 1-intension. That many 2-propositions are wide contents is an obvious consequence of the way in which 2-intensions are determined.

5. If p is a 1-proposition, then it is in principle possible to know a priori whether p is metaphysically necessary, impossible, or possible. It follows that all metaphysically necessary 1-propositions are a priori, in the sense that anyone who can think such a proposition is capable in principle of knowing it a priori. This is not true of metaphysically necessary 2-propositions that aren't mere copies of the 1-propositions which determine them. The points at play here give a neat way of explicating the necessary a posteriori–contingent a priori distinction as applied to Mentalese sentences. Necessary a posteriori sentences have necessary 2-propositions but contingent 1-propositions, while contingent a priori sentences have necessary 1-propositions but contingent 2-propositions. Thus, 'Water is H_2O' is necessary a posteriori; it has a contingent 1-proposition that determines a necessary 2-proposition. One counts as knowing both propositions by virtue of knowing the contingent proposition that H_2O is both self-identical and the watery stuff in one's environment. And 'If Julius exists, then Julius invented the zipper' is contingent a priori by virtue of having a necessary 1-proposition and a contingent 2-proposition.

The foregoing also yields an obvious way of deploying the two-dimensional apparatus to defend Kripke's claim that phenomenal properties such as pain are irreducibly phenomenal, not identifiable with either physical or topic-neutral properties.[31] If pain is a physical or topic-neutral property, then the proposition that pain = physical or topic-neutral property X is a necessary a posteriori 2-proposition, and this 2-proposition is determined by a contingent proposition to the effect that X happens to be the property that satisfies that uniqueness condition determined by the 1-intension of 'pain'. But the 1-intension of 'pain' determines no such condition: the reference of 'pain' isn't fixed by a uniqueness property that pain contingently instantiates, for, like 'circular', the 2-intension of pain is a mere copy of its 1-intension.

6. Rationality relations are determined by 1-propositions, in the following sense. You can't rationally have in your belief box at the same time two sentences where p is the 1-proposition of one of the

---

[31] Kripke (1980).

sentences and not-p is the 1-proposition of the other. But you *can* rationally have in your belief box at the same time two sentences where p is the *2-proposition* of one of the sentences and not-p is the 2-proposition of the other. For example, suppose the 1-proposition of one sentence is the proposition that the F is H and the 1-proposition of another sentence is that the G isn't H. Suppose further that, unbeknown to you, the F = the G, thereby securing that the two sentences have the same 2-proposition. In this case, nothing has yet been ascribed to you that impugns your rationality.

7. The rationality claim just made implies an account of *modes of presentation*, since it offers an explanation of rational belief and disbelief, as when someone rationally believes both that George Eliot adored groundhogs and that Mary Ann Evans didn't adore woodchucks, notwithstanding that George Eliot was Mary Ann Evans and the property of being a groundhog is the property of being a woodchuck. Given the way this works, we may take 1-intensions to be modes of presentation of the 1-extensions they determine, where the notion of a mode of presentation is playing the Fregean role of being that in terms of which one explicates, e.g., how it is that one can rationally believe that George Eliot adored groundhogs and that Mary Ann Evans didn't adore woodchucks, notwithstanding the identities involved.

How adequate is Theory C?

(*a*) My first point is more of a comment than a criticism. The comment is that Theory C is for all intents and purposes a notational variant of a familiar Russellian theory. This familiar theory starts with the distinction between 'knowledge by acquaintance' and 'knowledge by description'.[32] One has knowledge by description of x provided x is uniquely such-and-such and one knows that something is uniquely such-and-such. One has knowledge by acquaintance of x provided one knows that x is such-and-such, and this knowledge isn't possessed by virtue of one's having knowledge by description of x, or by virtue of having knowledge of x under some non-descriptive mode of presentation. One's epistemic acquaintance with x isn't mediated by anything. This doesn't preclude one from characterizing a thought's content by reference to a singular proposition containing an object known only by description. But that can only be done when

---

[32] Russell (1910*a*).

the primary content of the thought is a proposition that contains a uniqueness property instantiated by the object in the singular proposition. In this way, our Russellian can say that the primary content of a thought is a proposition constructed from objects and properties with which the thinker is directly acquainted—i.e. things that can be thought of without the aid of a distinct mode of presentation—and that a thought will also derivatively have as part of its content a singular proposition containing an object or property known only by description, provided that the thought's primary content contains a uniqueness property that's instantiated by the thing known only by description. Our Russellian can go on from here to mimic Theory C's claims about rationality, modes of presentation, narrow content, the contingent a priori and the necessary a posteriori, and epistemic and metaphysical modalities.

I said that Theory C is 'for all intents and purposes' a notational variant of the Russellian theory, but actually a much stronger point can be made: the best literal reading of Theory C *is* the Russellian theory. In 2.6 I proposed that anything true expressed using the metaphor of possible worlds should be expressible without that metaphor, and it should be immediately clear that the essential ideas of the Chalmers–Jackson line on mental content can be borrowed by theorists who employ Russellian or Fregean propositions and want no truck with the metaphor of possible worlds. So let's see how Theory C appears when cashed out in terms of Russellian propositions. The idea here, not altogether unfamiliar, might be put in the following way.

For every belief state there is a Russellian proposition that is its *un*derived content, and there may or may not be another Russellian proposition that is its *derived* content.

If the proposition that...the such-and-such...is the underived content of a belief state and α = the such-and-such, then the proposition that...α...is a derived content of that belief state. For example, the underived content of the belief state expressed by 'Julius is probably dead' is the proposition that the person who invented the zipper is probably dead, and since Whitcomb L. Judson = the person who invented the zipper, that belief state has the proposition that Judson is probably dead as a derived content. The underived content of the belief state expressed by 'Water = H_2O' is the proposition that the watery stuff in my environment = H_2O, and since H_2O = the watery stuff in my environment, that belief state has the proposition that $H_2O = H_2O$ as a derived content. The underived content of the belief state expressed by 'Dogs bark' is the proposition that the things that belong to the zoological species of the such-and-such looking and behaving things in my environment bark, and since *Canis familiaris* is that species, that belief state has as its derived content the proposition that the things that belong to *Canis familiaris* bark. Russell held that among particulars, as opposed to universals, the only things that could enter into an underived content were oneself, the current time, and one's current sense data.

Underived contents are narrow contents: the fact that your belief states have the underived contents they have supervenes entirely on what's in your head, on individualistic facts about you. Derived contents are typically wide contents: they don't supervene on individualistic facts about the believer but depend on the believer's relation to the environment. For example, one believes the derived content that H_2O is the stuff that comes out of one's taps by virtue of the fact that H_2O happens to be the watery stuff in one's environment.

The distinction between underived and derived contents yields a neat way of explaining the contingent a priori–necessary a posteriori distinction. A statement is contingent a priori when the underived content of the belief state it expresses is metaphysically necessary but the derived content it determines is contingent. Thus, the statement that if Julius exists, Julius invented the zipper is contingent a priori by virtue of its having as its underived content the necessary proposition that if the inventor of the zipper exists, then he or she invented the zipper, and as its derived content the contingent proposition that if Judson exists, then Judson invented the zipper. The statement that water is H_2O is necessary a posteriori by virtue of its having as its underived content the contingent proposition that H_2O happens to be the watery stuff in my environment, and as its derived content the necessary proposition that $H_2O = H_2O$. The application of this to Kripke's famous argument about the non-identity of pain with any physical or topic-neutral property is again straightforward; it follows from the foregoing together with the fact that we don't think about pain under one of its contingent uniqueness properties.

One can't rationally both believe and disbelieve an underived content, but one can rationally both believe and disbelieve a derived content. Thus, Lois Lane can't rationally believe both that the superhero known as 'Superman' flies and that he doesn't fly, but, because she rationally believes both that the superhero known as 'Superman' flies and that the nerdy reporter named 'Clark Kent' doesn't fly, and because Superman–Clark Kent satisfies both descriptions, she can rationally both believe and disbelieve the derived content that Superman–Clark Kent flies.

One important corollary is that 'modes of presentation' are the uniqueness properties (the properties expressed by proper definite descriptions) that enter into those Russellian propositions that are underived contents, and that the objects and properties that enter into underived contents do so directly, not via modes of presentation. This means that in Russell's sense of 'knowledge by acquaintance', one has knowledge by acquaintance of every object and property contained in a proposition capable of being an underived content of one of one's propositional attitudes (for although I have, for simplicity, been putting things in terms of belief, what applies to it of course applies, *mutatis mutandis*, to every other kind of propositional attitude).

I mention the equivalence with the familiar Russellian theory not to accuse Chalmers and Jackson of putting old wine in new bottles (still less to suggest that they were in any way motivated by the Russellian theory), but for two other reasons. First, the familiar problems that plague the Russellian theory also plague Theory C, and seeing the parallel will help us to appreciate this. And secondly, I think the Russellian version is the best literal construal of the Chalmers–Jackson theory; it is the most promising way of restating their theory without the metaphor of possible worlds.[33]

(*b*) One familiar problem with the Russellian theory is that it requires modes of presentation to be *uniqueness properties* (albeit uniqueness properties that may ineliminably contain particulars known by acquaintance, such as oneself, one's current sense data, and the present moment), and the same is in effect true of Theory C. For according to Theory C, a 1-intension that determines different 2-intensions in different centred worlds always picks out its 1-extension in a given centred world as whatever in that world has a certain uniqueness property determined by the 1-intension. For example, the 1-intension of 'Hesperus' tells us that the name's 1-extension in any given centred world is whatever in that world is the such-and-such heavenly body that appears in the evening. Now, it might seem that Kripke refuted the Russell–Chalmers–Jackson theory, since it relies

---

[33] Byrne (forthcoming) also emphasizes the similarity between Chalmers's theory and the Russellian theory.

on modes of presentation being uniqueness properties, and Kripke showed, with his Gödel and Feynman examples,[34] that the thoughts expressed by sentences containing proper names need involve no such uniqueness properties. But Kripke's 'refutation' paid insufficient attention to the metalinguistic modes of presentation available to his subjects in the Gödel and Feynman examples. Would the person who appears to know merely that Feynman was a famous physicist have her beliefs about Feynman if she didn't know that there was someone who was uniquely such that he was a famous physicist named 'Richard Feynman' and to whom those from whom she acquired the name were referring when they used the name?

Nevertheless, there remain apparent counter-examples to the description-theoretic account of modes of presentation even when metalinguistic modes of presentation are taken into account. Consider, for instance, the following example suggested to me a long time ago by Gareth Evans as a counter-example to the description theory of *de re* thought and mistreated by me in 'The Basis of Reference'.[35] A person is looking at a large array of qualitatively identical balls and his attention alights on one of them, and he believes that that ball is just like all the others. In this case, the believer isn't able to single the ball out by its position in the array, since the array is too large and the ball too far towards the centre of the array. If the description theorist is to accommodate this example, she must find a way in which the believer can single out the ball in terms of its relation to herself. Two suggestions come to mind. First, the believer has knowledge by acquaintance of a certain patch of her visual field and believes that some ball is uniquely causally responsible for that patch in such-and-such way. Secondly, the believer thinks of the ball as 'the ball to which I'm now attending'. The problem with the first suggestion is that very few adults can replace the 'such-and-such' in the designation of the required uniqueness property, and even if they could, it is very unlikely that we can account for the belief of a 5-year-old child in this way. The problem with the second suggestion is that attending is itself a propositional attitude that requires a mode of presentation for the ball, and there is no uniqueness property available to be the mode of presentation under which the believer is attending to the ball. Certain memory-based beliefs also present a

[34] Kripke (1980).   [35] Schiffer (1978).

problem. Five-year-old Johnny has a fuzzy memory image of a certain woman who visited his family and believes that she was funny. Johnny has no uniqueness property available in terms of the woman's appearance or behaviour or visit. If his belief about her is under a uniqueness property, it must evidently be the woman's being the person uniquely causally responsible for Johnny's current image. But it is doubtful that he believes that just one person is causally responsible in such-and-such way for his current memory image. Many ordinary perceptual beliefs provide the same sort of problem. Come to think of it, our beliefs expressed by sentences containing ordinary proper names also provide this problem, for what 5-year-old child, or even adult, knows a relevant completion of 'the thing causally responsible in... way for my current use of the name'? Kripke was right after all, and although he should have paid better attention to metalinguistic properties, he had the wherewithal to dismiss them once considered. Notice that the problem here isn't that the reference isn't determined by some uniqueness condition. We should expect there to be a uniqueness condition that determines reference. The problem is that the uniqueness condition might not be available as part of a thought's *content*. An analogy may be helpful. There is evidently a uniqueness condition, however complex and however unknown, whose satisfaction by 'circular' in my mouth determines it to mean circularity, but that condition isn't available to me to do any psychological work as part of the content of any of my thoughts. In like manner, whatever condition determines the *reference* of a name, demonstrative, or any other kind of term may also be unavailable as a thought content.

It may seem that the Russellian and, a fortiori, the proponent of Theory C have a quick and easy fix whenever a needed uniqueness property fails to materialize. The Russellian allows that certain particulars can be objects of acquaintance, such as oneself, the present moment, and one's current sense data, and the centres of Theory C's centred worlds can be defined with respect to anything at all. So, when a suitable uniqueness property fails to materialize for a certain kind of referent, why can't the Russellian simply say that we have knowledge by acquaintance of referents of that kind, and, what comes to the same thing, why can't the proponent of Theory C simply add those referents to the centres of his centred worlds? But such a move can work only if the kind of object in question is one that we can plausibly think about without the aid of a distinct mode of presentation, and that would have to be motivated. Perhaps objects of the problematic kind need modes of presentation all right, but modes of presentation other than uniqueness properties. Perhaps they need *object-dependent* modes of presentation, modes of presentation that can't exist unless the things of which they are modes of presentation exist and which are individuated partly in terms of those things. In recent years many theorists have appreciated the need for object-dependent concepts and for object-dependent propositions other than stark singular propositions, but it is not easy to see how such concepts and propositions can be accommodated either by Theory C or by its Russellian translation.[36]

(*c*) Another problem with the Russellian theory should be familiar to those acquainted with the travails of logical atomism: there don't seem to be enough things at the end of the line with which we're directly acquainted; that is to say, there don't seem to be enough Russellian propositions capable of serving as underived contents to determine all the propositions we believe. Modes of presentation are supposed to be not merely uniqueness properties, but uniqueness properties that don't themselves require modes of presentation; when they constitute a belief content, they do so directly—that is what it means to belong to an underived content. Yet it is arguably doubtful

---

[36] I presented some of this material at a symposium on two-dimensional semantics, with David Chalmers as the principal speaker, at the Pacific Division meeting of the American Philosophical Association, in Seattle, March 2002. In reply to my counter-example about the boy who remembers that a certain woman was funny, Chalmers said that 'the boy is presumably in a position to make judgements about extension, given relevant information about the world and rational reflection. The resulting intension may well have something to do with causal responsibility, but Stephen's objection that the boy may have no beliefs about causal responsibility is irrelevant here, since no such belief is required.' Chalmers's point is this. Suppose the child had a complete description of his world in non-intentional terms. Then the child could pick out the woman his thought was about, even if he didn't have command of a sophisticated causal uniqueness property. There are at least two problems with this reply. First, it's by no means guaranteed that the child could pick the woman out. It may be that he met several similar-looking women on the same occasion and has no way to select which of them is the one his memory thought is about. Secondly, it's hard to see what the relevance of this reply could be. The primary intension of the child's concept of the woman his memory belief is about is a function from centred worlds onto individuals. Can Chalmers be suggesting that what makes that function the primary intension of the child's concept (of, as it were, his Mentalese memory demonstrative) is a complex counterfactual about what selections the child would make in various possible worlds considered as actual? Among numerous other problems, that would be entirely circular, since 'selecting' is a contentful propositional attitude. The description-theoretic component of Chalmers's theory is also criticized in Byrne and Pryor (forthcoming).

that there are enough such properties to serve as modes of presentation of all the objects and properties we're capable of thinking about. Even more is this so when we take Burgean Twin Earth cases into account along with the Putnamian cases.[37] I'd like to be told the uniqueness property constructed wholly from things with which I'm directly acquainted under which I think about Saddam Hussein.

Theory C faces the same sort of problem. 1-propositions are narrow contents, we can know their modal status a priori, and they constitute modes of presentation but don't themselves need modes of presentation. In short, they count as objects of 'acquaintance'. It is not at all clear that there are enough 1-propositions to determine all the 2-propositions we're capable of believing. This objection becomes more forceful when one realizes the extent to which I cheated in presenting Theory C. The whole point of the distinction between 1- and 2-intensions is as an account of our concepts of the objects and properties our beliefs are about—things like Richard Nixon and water. If, however, the concepts of those things involve objects and properties that can themselves be thought about only under concepts, then if we are to avoid an infinite regress, we must get to concepts that don't themselves need concepts in order to enter into the contents of our thoughts. But now consider the alleged 1-intension of 'water'. The reference-fixing uniqueness property that intension determines made reference to liquidity. But what is the difference between doghood and water, on the one hand, and liquidity, on the other, such that by virtue of that difference the former can't, but the latter can, be definitive of a 1-intension?

(d) According to Theory C, 1-intensions are 'narrow contents', determined entirely by the internal state of the thinker. There are two problems with this. First, whether or not this is so depends entirely on the nature of that relation that must hold between a Mentalese term and a function in order for the latter to be the former's 1-intension, but Theory C gives no account of that relation which earns the narrow-content claim. How, then, can the theory confidently assert it? Who is to say but that a lot of externalistic stuff won't find its way into the explication of this content-determining relation? Consider such a basic word as 'red'. Is it really plausible that the word in my head could express the property of being red even if I wasn't directly or

---

[37] Burge (1979, 1982a,b) and Putnam (1975a).

indirectly in causal contact with red things? Secondly, since virtually any concept can be subject to a Burgean Twin Earth scenario, it is hard to see how there could possibly be enough 'narrow contents' to sustain the claim that *every* 1-intension is a narrow content. Appealing to deference here is to no avail, since the same problem arises for 1-intensions expressed by the terms of the deferrer.

(*e*) Finally, Theory C has at least one problem that is gratuitous with respect to its equivalence to the Russellian theory. This is that it requires that it be possible to know whether any 1-proposition is metaphysically necessary, impossible, or possible. But examples like Goldbach's conjecture or the continuum hypothesis make that assumption doubtful.

I also believe we can pinpoint where the Russell–Chalmers–Jackson approach goes wrong. It is a point already touched on above and starts with a plausible idea, namely that it is a contingent fact that a word or thought-state component has the referent or content it has, and this fact evidently means that there is some uniqueness condition satisfaction of which makes a thing or property the referent or content of the word or thought-state component. So why not take that uniqueness condition to play the role Russell, Chalmers, and Jackson assign to their reference-fixing conditions? Because, if for no other reason,[38] there is a big difference between (1) a condition specifiable in terms of language use or conceptual role on which meaning supervenes and (2) a further reference- or content-determining uniqueness condition which is itself determined by the type of uniqueness condition at issue in (1). The Russell–Chalmers–Jackson approach requires *both* types of uniqueness conditions, but in many cases there is no is reason to suppose that a condition of type (2) is needed. A (2)-type condition is needed by the Russell–Chalmers–Jackson approach, because that is the only way their uniqueness conditions can be cognitively accessible in a way that would enable them to play the mode-of-presentation and related roles claimed for them. What I mean can be illustrated with respect to two competing accounts of proper names. Suppose that in x's public language or Mentalese idiolect n is a name of y. On a broadly Kripkean picture, in the typical case (since few names are like Evans's 'Julius') there is but

---

[38] I allude to my own non-compositional account of propositional content, not presently in play.

one condition satisfaction of which makes n a name of y for x, and in the normal case it isn't epistemically available to x. It is a condition having to do with the use of n by x and, perhaps, others with whom x interacts who also use n as a name of y, and this use may involve causal relations between y and these uses of n. Since even highly skilled philosophers are unable to say what this condition is in any detail (although they're convinced there is such a condition, since, after all, being a name of a thing is a use-dependent property of the name), it is most unreasonable to suppose that it is a condition that enters into the content of the propositional attitudes of ordinary speakers and thinkers. An exception to this one-condition account would be a name like 'Julius', introduced by stipulation as the name of whoever uniquely invented the zipper. In this case, a (1)-type use-dependent condition, which need in no way be cognitively or epistemically accessible to the language user, determines a (2)-type reference-fixing uniqueness condition, which is cognitively and epistemically accessible to the language user. On the competing Russell–Chalmers–Jackson account, *every* term has a (2)-type condition (except for terms like 'circle', where the two-condition account is abrogated), as though the theorist advancing the account conflated conditions of types (1) and (2). The fact is, (2)-type uniqueness conditions don't exist, and don't need to exist, for many terms; many terms, that is, fail to have 1-intensions that are not 'mere copies' of their 2-intensions.

I can't resist adding a comment or two about the mind–body problem, comments that further elaborate comments I made about this problem in 2.3. The way in which the Russell–Chalmers–Jackson account fails defeats its defence of the Kripkean line on the irreducibility of phenomenal properties and the possibility of their being instantiated without the co-instantiation of any particular physical or topic-neutral property. At the same time, there may be other things to say that support a sort of watered-down Kripkean line.

For one thing, I doubt that any claim that a particular phenomenal property is identical to a particular physical or topic-neutral property can be determinately true. Ned Block and Robert Stalnaker propose that we might be justified in inferring, for example, that pain = such-and-such physical property by the principle of inference to the best explanation. For suppose we find that in every one of a lot of examined cases a person is in pain when, and only when, that person has physical property Φ at precisely the times she is in pain, and vice versa. What would explain this strange coincidence? We might infer that the best explanation of it is that pain = Φ. Block and Stalnaker give an analogy:

Suppose one group of historians of the distant future studies Mark Twain and another studies Samuel Clemens. They happen to sit at the same table at a meeting of the American Historical Association. A briefcase falls open, a list of the events in the life of Mark Twain tumbles out and is picked up by a student of the life of Samuel Clemens. 'My Lord,' he says, 'the events in the life of Mark Twain are exactly the same as the events in the life of Samuel Clemens. What could explain this amazing coincidence?' The answer, some-one observes, is that Mark Twain = Samuel Clemens.[39]

The trouble with the analogy is that it overlooks a crucial disanalogy between persons and pains—namely, that whereas we have a clear sense of what it would be like for person x to be identical to person y, we have no clear sense of what it would be like for a pain to be ident-ical to a physical or topic-neutral property. As a result of this asym-metry, it can easily be a determinate fact that person x = person y, but it is doubtful in the case of pain whether, for any physical or topic-neutral property, the way is clear for it to be a determinate fact that pain is identical to that property. It is because it may be a determinate fact that person x = person y that it may in a given case be legitimate to conclude that person x = person y via an inference to the best explanation. An inference to the best explanation that pain = such-and-such physical or functional property is to no avail, however, if there can be no determinate truth that the identity holds. The pos-sible indeterminacy to which I allude is indirectly owed to the pleonastic nature of properties, but the point can be made without direct appeal to that: it is that it's a determinate fact whether an F is identical to a G only when the concept of an F or of a G contains a criterion whose satisfaction in a given case determinately establishes whether a particular F is identical to a particular G, and while such a criterion is available in the case of persons, it is doubtful it is available in the case of properties in a way that allows us ever to conclude that pain is determinately identical to such-and-such physical or topic-neutral property.

   To illustrate what I mean, suppose that we didn't have the concept of a property and that the concept was then introduced simply by

---

[39] Block and Stalnaker (1999: 24).

the stipulation that instances of the following introduction and elimination rules were deemed valid (and let's ignore Grelling-type paradoxes):

a is F
∴ a has the property of being F.
a has the property of being F
∴ a is F.

And now suppose it is given that it's metaphysically necessary that a thing is F iff it is G, where 'F' and 'G' represent distinct non-synonymous predicates. Given the way the concept of a property has been introduced by the displayed introduction and elimination rules, it can't be determinately true that the property of being F is, or is not, identical to the property of being G. To think that there might be a determinate truth about the identity notwithstanding the way the concept of a property has been introduced would be like supposing that 19-year-old Lester is determinately a shminor or determinately not a shminor, when the notion of a shminor has been introduced just by these two stipulations: a person is a shminor if he or she has not reached his or her seventeenth birthday, and a person is not a shminor if he or she has reached his or her twentieth birthday. My claim about properties isn't that the notion of a property was introduced by the two rules just displayed; that was just for purposes of illustration. My point is that nothing can determinately establish the identification of pain with a physical or topic-neutral property because there is nothing in the notion of a property to give us any sense of what such an identification would be like. A good test of whether we have such a clear sense is whether we know what would in principle determinately establish that a claimed identity held. Mark Twain and Samuel Clemens obviously pass that test: we need only trace Twain's and Clemens's spatio-temporal worms to establish that they coincide. But what in principle would determinately establish the mooted identity in the case of pain? The point is made vivid by the following consideration. Suppose we had a physical property P we thought was a good candidate for being identical to pain. Most likely, P will be the unique realizer of a certain functional property F, thereby making F a good candidate, too, for being identical to pain. What in principle would determinately show that pain was one of those two properties as opposed to the other?

The issue about the *identification* of phenomenal properties with physical or topic-neutral properties isn't the most interesting or the most pressing issue. The more important question is whether the phenomenal supervenes on the physical, on whether, if you will, zombies are possible.[40] But I don't see that this has a determinate answer either. We have criteria for establishing that something is metaphysically possible, and we have criteria for establishing that something is metaphysically impossible. Unfortunately, the criteria we have don't exhaust all cases; they leave a large penumbra. That zombies fall in the penumbra is indicated by the fact that philosophers have been debating this issue for a few hundred years without any resolution. Those who think zombies are possible are impressed with the ease with which we seem to be able to imagine, or conceive, 'possible worlds' with zombies, and with the evident impossibility of explaining away those thought experiments in anything like the way we can, as Kripke taught us, explain away our seeming to conceive possible worlds in which water isn't H_2O.[41] But, *pace* Chalmers and Jackson, we lack any plausible general account of metaphysical possibility, let alone one that would resolve the problem of phenomenal properties, and those who deny the possibility of zombies are impressed with the difficulty of accounting for the relation between phenomenal states and their underlying physical states if that relation doesn't see the physical states as metaphysically necessitating the phenomenal states. I think the question we should really be asking is one I don't think I've ever seen asked—namely, What are we to make of the mind–body problem if it is indeterminate whether zombies are possible? Is that a coherent, or stable, view? Must we then say that it is indeterminate whether underlying physical states *cause* or *metaphysically necessitate* phenomenal states? If so, how does that help, since the problem, as many see it, is that we can make no coherent sense of the relation being a causal one? These questions partly depend on how the notion of determinate truth is to be explicated (see Chapter 5), but, I predict, even with such an explication we shall still be left with a mind-body problem as puzzling as ever.

---

[40] A zombie is a creature that is physically and behaviourally just like us but who has no phenomenal states.   [41] Kripke (1980).

4

Having Meaning

4.1 INTRODUCTION

So far we know (ahem!) that things I call *pleonastic propositions*, and about whose unusual nature I have held forth, are the basic units of content. They are the representational contents of our thoughts and utterances, and it is in terms of them that all other semantic notions must be explained. Linguistic expressions have meaning just in case they have things I've called *characters**, abstract entities that represent constraints on what speech acts, and with what propositional contents, literal speakers must be performing when they utter those expressions. I've questioned whether there are such *things* as the meanings of expressions, but if there are, they are characters*. We should therefore want to know in what having a character* consists. What, that is, is the nature of the character* relation, that relation that one thing must bear to another in order for the second to be the character* of the first? Tackling this question will lead to others, some left over from the preceding chapter: The actual-language-relation problem: What relation must a person, or group, bear to a language in order for that language to be a language of the person or group? In what sense does the intentional 'supervene' on the non-intentional, and what explains that supervenience? I have speculated that natural languages have compositional character* theories. Are there any other kinds of compositional semantics that natural languages have? If so, what are those compositional semantics needed to explain? These questions are the concerns of this chapter.

4.2 THE CHARACTER* RELATION

Characters* do much of what meanings would do if there were meanings, for having meaning consists in having a character*, and sameness or difference of meaning always consists in sameness or difference of character*. For a theorist who takes having meaning to consist in standing in the meaning relation to a meaning, the two big questions are: What are meanings? and What is the nature of the meaning relation, that relation that must obtain between two things in order for the first to mean the second? For me, therefore, the two big corresponding questions are: What are characters*? and What is the nature of the character* relation, that relation that must obtain between two things in order for the first to have the second as its character*? Chapter 3 gave my answer to the first question. How should I answer the second? The character* of an expression is clearly determined by use, either by how the expression itself is used, if the expression is semantically simple, or by how the expressions and structures composing the expression are used, if the expression is semantically complex. But how exactly does use determine character* (and therewith meaning)?

This question isn't easy to answer. Paul Horwich's book *Meaning* develops what he calls a use theory of meaning,[1] but the use properties he claims determine meaning, while potentially relevant to the theory of content generally, seem not to have direct application to public-language meaning, since they have nothing to do with use in interpersonal communication.[2] David Lewis, however, has suggested what I think is the most promising approach to our problem,[3] although I will give my own reconstruction of Lewis's leading idea.

Let's say that a *potential public language* is any function L that satisfies the following conditions:

(1) There is a finitely specifiable recursive function G (the 'grammar' of L) whose arguments are sequences of marks or sounds or whatever drawn from some finite list (the 'lexicon' of L) and whose values are infinitely many finite sequences of those marks or sounds or whatever (the 'sentences' of L).

(2) L's domain of arguments consists of G's range of values—the 'sentences' of L.

(3) L's range of values consists of ordered pairs $\langle A, P \rangle$, where A is a kind of speech act and P is a kind of proposition. If $L(s) = \langle A, P \rangle$, we may say that $\langle A, P \rangle$ is s's character* in L. The fact

---

[1] Horwich (1998).   [2] There may be other problems as well; see Schiffer (2000*a*).
[3] Lewis (1983*c*).

that s's character* in L is $\langle A, P \rangle$ is a necessary truth that
has nothing to do with how anyone uses s or the words
composing it.

(4) There is a compositional character* theory for L, whose base
axioms assign word-size characters* to the 'words' of L (i.e. the
items in L's 'lexicon'), which issues in a theorem of the form
$L(s) = \langle A, P \rangle$ for each sentence of L. If the compositional character* theory assigns a kind of proposition P' to an expression
e—either in an axiom, if e is a word, or in a theorem, if e is
complex—then we may say that P' is the character* of e in L.

The question now—the *public-language-relation problem*—is: What
relation must obtain between a person x and a potential public language L in order for L to be x's *actual* public language (or one of x's
actual public languages)? To ask this question relative to the Lewisian
set-up is precisely to ask the question raised two paragraphs back
about the character* relation. For the character* relation that interests us is the one that holds contingently: it is that relation that holds
among a person x, an expression e, and a character* c when c is the
character* e has for x, or, in other words, the character* of e in x's
public language idiolect. How is the public-language-relation problem to be solved?

Not by saying that L is a public language of x's if x belongs to
a group of communicators G such that:

- members of G frequently communicate with one another;
- whenever a member of G communicates with another member
of G, she does so by uttering a sentence of L; and
- if $L(s) = \langle A, P \rangle$ and a member y of G utters s, then $\exists\Psi\exists q(A(\Psi)$ &
$P(q)$ & $y\,\Psi\text{s}\,q)$.

The reason this doesn't give a sufficient condition for x's using L is
that if L satisfies the foregoing condition, then so will infinitely many
other languages which x clearly doesn't use. For suppose that English
is Jones's public language and let English$^+$ be the same as English as
regards every sentence that anyone is ever likely to utter but departs
radically from English thereafter. For example, 'giraffe' means
the same as 'grapefruit' in every sentence of English$^+$ in which
'giraffe' occurs more than 100 times. If English satisfies the foregoing
condition, then so will English$^+$, but English$^+$ is not a language that

anyone uses.[4] Nor will it help to go counterfactual by saying that if a member of G *were* to utter s and $L(s) = \langle A, P \rangle$, then she would Ψq, where Ψ is a speech act of kind A and q is a proposition of kind P; for it may be that if Jones were to utter a sentence in which 'giraffe' occurred more than 100 times, that would trigger a neurological event that would result in her suddenly becoming a speaker of English[+] rather than of English.

What's needed is something that will nail down all of L at once. Perhaps this nailing down may be done by utilizing the empirical speculation, which I made in 3.5, about what in fact plays the knowledge-of-meaning role in the processing that subserves our understanding of public-language utterances. I suggest that a sufficient condition for L's being used by x as a public language is that x belongs to a group of communicators who regularly communicate by uttering sentences of L, and, when they do, the knowledge-of-meaning role is played by states that pair expressions with characters* via an internal representation of the compositional character* theory for L in terms of which L is defined. Yet this condition's being a sufficient condition isn't of much interest unless compositional character* theories in fact play the proposed role in the processing that subserves our understanding of public-language utterances, and that it does remains an empirical speculation. If our language processing doesn't use a compositional character* theory, then the sufficient condition is plainly neither a necessary condition for using a language as a public language nor a sufficient condition that does any work for us. At the same time, I doubt that the public-language-relation problem has a more a priori solution—unless, not implausibly, we can say that *whatever* plays the knowledge-of-meaning role will provide the relation that resolves the public-language-relation problem. For example, I suggested in 3.5 that the states that play the knowledge-of-meaning role might indirectly link expressions with their characters* by first linking them with Mentalese synonyms; so perhaps the mechanism that generates these states uses not a compositional character* theory for the understood language but rather a compositional translation manual that maps public-language expressions onto their Mentalese synonyms.[5] Then the explanatory sufficient condition for L's being

---

[4] I first raised (in conversation) this sort of objection to Lewis's account of the public-language relation in 1967. Lewis discusses the objection in (1983c: 187–8).

[5] This idea is elaborated in Schiffer (1987a, ch. 7; 1993).

used by x as a public language is that x belongs to a group of communicators who regularly communicate by uttering sentences of L, and, when they do, the knowledge-of-meaning role is played by states that indirectly pair expressions with characters* via an internally represented translation manual that maps each expression of L onto a Mentalese expression that in one way or another correlates the L expression with the character* assigned to it by the axioms or theorems of the compositional character* theory that is definitive of L. This, of course, raises still another difficult question—namely, What is it for a potential language of thought to be someone's actual language of thought?

4.3 COMPOSITIONAL MEANING THEORIES

In other writings I have argued that natural languages neither have nor need compositional semantics, neither compositional meaning theories nor compositional truth theories.[6] Is my current speculation about compositional *character** theories an apostasy of my scepticism? Yes and no.

Yes in that characters* are tantamount to expression meanings—or at least the closest things to expression meanings we can have—and I've conceded that natural languages have compositional character* theories and that, as a matter of empirical fact, these are essential to the explanation of our ability to hear the utterance of a novel sentence and know what the speaker was saying in uttering it.

No for the following reasons.

First of all, if what I suggested in 3.6 is correct, it may be that no language can have a correct compositional meaning theory for the simple reason that there may not be any correct ascriptions of meaning, and this because there are no such things as expression meanings. But even waiving that point, there are difficulties with the idea of a compositional meaning theory even relative to an often made simplifying assumption most favourable to the idea that natural languages have correct such theories. The simplifying assumption that is typically made in discussions of compositional meaning theories is that

---

[6] e.g. Schiffer (1987a, 1994).

the languages in question are non-indexical and indicative, so that all canonical meaning specifications are of the form

(1) *s* means that such-and-such,

as, for example,

'Snow is white' means that snow is white,

or

'La neige est blanche' means that snow is white.

It is then concluded that such a language must have a correct compositional meaning theory that issues in theorems of form (1). There are several problems with this.

1. There can be no generalization from a language all of whose sentences are the subjects of truths of form (1) to a language that is either indexical or contains non-indicative sentences. In other words, the 'simplifying assumption' provides no basis for the construction of a compositional meaning theory for a natural language. This is because, as suggested in 3.2, meaning specifications of form (1) aren't, strictly speaking, proper meaning specifications for sentences. This is unimportant when the pretence is that every sentence is indicative and non-indexical, but it is disastrous when that simplifying assumption is dropped, because no theory can issue in a true theorem that completes, say,

'She isn't there yet' means . . .

as that form has no true completion.

2. While there are truths of form (1), it is not obvious that any finitely axiomatized theory could issue in infinitely many theorems of that form. If sentences meant Russellian propositions, then perhaps there could be a finitely axiomatized meaning theory that issued in theorems such as

(2) 'Fido is a dog' means $\langle$Fido, doghood$\rangle$,

and if sentences meant Fregean propositions, then perhaps we could have theorems such as

(3) 'Fido is a dog' means $\langle c_f, c_d \rangle$.

What *I* can't see how to do is devise a compositional meaning theory that will take us from either (2) or (3) to

(4) 'Fido is a dog' means that Fido is a dog.

Getting from (3) to (4) seems especially problematic, although I haven't an impossibility proof for either case. Whether or not this matters depends on the purposes for which one thinks one needs a compositional meaning theory. If it is to account for language understanding, where the idea is that one knows what's said in an utterance via knowing what the uttered sentence means, then it matters a lot, since someone who knows that 'snow is white' means that snow is white might not know that 'snow is white' means either ⟨snow, whiteness⟩ or ⟨c_s, c_w⟩.

3. This problem is one we noticed in Section 2.4—namely, that there is reason to think that mere equivalence classes of propositions are the best we can do by way of identifying propositional building blocks, and that they won't enable us to construct a compositional meaning theory. In order to have a compositional meaning theory, it is not enough that we have a finitely axiomatized theory that issues in theorems of the form

(5) *s* means *t*

where the substituend for '*t*' denotes the proposition *s* means. A finitely axiomatized theory that issued in a theorem of the form

s means the meaning of *s*

wouldn't count as providing relevant specifications of meaning, and this because such a theory wouldn't provide the wherewithal to explain anything a compositional meaning theory is thought to be needed to explain. Likewise, I dare say, for the kind of theory that we would have if substituends for '*t*' in (5) were complex descriptions describing sequences of equivalence classes of particular propositions.

4. Even on the simplifying assumption that we speak a language for which each sentence enjoys a true meaning specification of form (1), there is a reason in addition to that given in problem 2 just above why no finitely axiomatized theory could issue in truths of form (1). This reason, already noted in 2.4, is that just as no belief sentence of the form '*A* believes that *S*' has a context-independent content, so no meaning ascription of the form '*s* means that *T*' has one either. We

noted that two utterances of

(6) Ralph believes that George Eliot was a man

might have different truth-values owing to the fact that in the one case, but not the other, the contextually determined criteria of evaluation might require Ralph to know that 'George Eliot' was the name of a famous author. Now, to utter

s means that George Eliot was a man

—even when s = 'George Eliot was a man'—is to say that in a literal utterance of s the speaker would mean that George Eliot was a man. But two utterances of

Ralph meant that George Eliot was a man

can have different truth-values in exactly the way two utterances of (6) can.

5. It is not clear we would *need* a compositional meaning theory even on the present highly artificial assumption that we speak a language for whose every sentence there is a truth of form (1). Theorists who think that natural languages have compositional meaning theories do so because they think that the assumption that they have them is needed to explain this, that, or the other thing. Theorists have thought that natural languages needed compositional meaning theories either:

(a) to explain language understanding: our ability to hear a novel sentence and to know either what it means or what was said in its utterance; or

(b) to explain the way the meaning of a complex expression depends on the meanings of its semantically relevant parts; or

(c) to explain the productivity of language: the fact that each of infinitely many expressions has its own unique meaning; or

(d) to explain the systematicity of language: the fact, roughly speaking, that expressions make the same meaning contribution in each of the expressions in which they occur, so that, for example, if one sentence can mean that John loves Mary, then another can mean that Mary loves John.

As regards (a), if any kind of compositional semantics is needed to explain language understanding, then that necessity is an empirical necessity. I believe my Harvey example in *Remnants of Meaning*[7] shows there is no conceptual or metaphysical necessity, since we can easily imagine someone who has our language understanding ability but whose ability can be explained without recourse to any kind of compositional semantics. In the case of Harvey, his language understanding was explained, roughly speaking, by his being programmed in such a way that his language processing realized algorithms that mapped spoken public-language sentences onto Mentalese sentences in a way that enabled him to form correct beliefs about what was said, where these algorithms made no appeal to any semantic properties of either public language or Mentalese expressions. A need for a compositional meaning theory would be at best a contingent need, whether or not the propositions our sentences were assumed to mean were structured or unstructured. But on the assumption that our sentences do mean *structured* propositions, then (b)–(d) would probably hold non-contingently. The interesting question is whether we must assume our sentences mean structured propositions *in order to explain the explananda mentioned in (b)–(d)*. If so, my claim that the propositions we mean and believe aren't structured is in jeopardy. Jerry Fodor, who agrees with me about language understanding, is happy to say that the productivity and systematicity of one's public language is inherited from that of one's language of thought, but he claims that without recourse to a compositional meaning theory of the sort presently at issue there can be no accounting for the productivity and systematicity of one's language of thought, and thereby of one's thought.[8] This is worth going into.

I believe the following is a good way of reconstructing Fodor's reasoning:

> Each person thinks in a *lingua mentis*, a system of mental representation, and to account for the productivity and systematicity of our thought is to account for the productivity and systematicity of one's system of mental representation. For simplicity, let's pretend we all think in the same neural language, Mentalese. Taking our cue from David Lewis, we may represent Mentalese ('M', for short) as a function from sequences of neural state types (the 'sentences' of M) onto propositions. If $M(s) = p$, then we may

---

[7] (1987a, ch. 7).   [8] Fodor (1990a).

say that s means p in M. Meaning facts of that sort are necessary truths that are independent of how anyone uses M. But if x *thinks in M*—if M is x's language of thought—then, letting 'means$_m$' stand for 'means *qua* mental representation', we may say that s means$_m$ p for x, and this is a contingent meaning fact that depends, no doubt, on the role of s in x's conceptual economy and on the way the semantically relevant parts of s are causally related to objects and properties in the extra-cranial world. What needs to be explained is how infinitely many mental representations can each mean$_m$ something for a person. We have infinitely many meaning facts of the form s *means$_m$ p for Jones*. What explains this infinity of meaning$_m$ facts? Broadly speaking, there are two answers one might offer. One says there is some finite basis from which the infinity of meaning$_m$ facts emanates; some complex but finitely statable state of affairs whose obtaining somehow determines that each sentence of M has the meaning$_m$ it has for Jones. The other answer says there is no finite state of affairs that generates the infinity of meaning$_m$ facts; *nothing* generates the infinitely many distinct meaning$_m$ facts, unless it's some separate infinity of generating facts, one for each meaning$_m$ fact. Now, the second answer is just crazy; the only sensible answer is the first. But if, as this answer entails, there is some finitely statable proposition whose truth determines each of the infinitely many meaning$_m$ facts, then how can one's language of thought fail to have a compositional meaning theory? The finite basis must certainly determine properties for the words of Mentalese as they occur in the head of one who thinks in Mentalese, and it must determine recursive conditions which use those properties to generate meaning-determining properties for the sentences of Mentalese, and, surely, in having all that one would have a finitely axiomatizable theory of Mentalese whose theorems told us what each sentence of Mentalese means, and was, thereby, a compositional meaning theory for Mentalese.

Let's go along, at least for a while, with Fodor's assumption that we think in a language of thought and that languages of thought can be represented as functions from sentences onto propositions. Then Fodor is right that the fact that there are infinitely many facts of the form s *means$_m$ p for Jones* must be shown to emanate from some finite state of affairs; but he's wrong in claiming that this requires Mentalese to have a compositional meaning theory.

Just as we have the public-language-relation problem, so we also have the *language-of-thought-relation problem*: What relation must obtain between a person and a potential language of thought in order for the latter to be a language in which the former thinks? This bears on Fodor's argument for compositional semantics, because s means$_m$ p for x just in case there is a language L in which x thinks and $L(s) = p$.

A first thought might be that we can solve the language-of-thought-relation problem (relative to the ongoing assumption about the nature of Mentalese) thus:

> x thinks in L iff $\forall p(x$ believes $p \rightarrow \exists s \exists \Phi(\Phi$ is a non-intentional property & Φs & $L(s) = p$ & it is metaphysically sufficient for x's believing p that $[\Phi s$ & s is tokened in x's belief box]$))$

—where being tokened in the belief box is a stand-in for a token of a mental representation's having whatever computational property is sufficient for its realizing a belief. In other words, you think in L just in case, for whatever proposition p you believe, your believing p is realized by a tokening in your belief box of a sentence that means p in L, where to say that your believing p is realized by a tokening of s in your belief box is to say that s has some non-intentional property Φ such that s's both having Φ and being tokened in your belief box is metaphysically sufficient for your believing p. But this runs afoul of a problem that is the counterpart of the problem that arose in trying to resolve the public-language-relation problem: it lets in infinitely many languages in which it is clear no one thinks. For suppose Jones thinks in neural English and let English$^+$ be exactly like English with respect to those sentences that have any chance of being tokened in Jones's belief box but departs radically from English thereafter. Then ⟨Jones, English$^+$⟩ will satisfy the displayed first shot if ⟨Jones, English⟩ does. As before, what's needed is something that will nail down all of English at once while leaving English$^+$ in the garbage dump where it was found. This can be done in the following way.[9]

---

[9] What follows was done at greater length in Schiffer (1994, 1995b).

Let's assume that the languages in which we're interested each have a fixed lexicon and syntax. Then let's say that

> x's having Ψ is a *minimal supervenience base* for x's believing p iff (1) x's having Ψ metaphysically necessitates x's believing p, (2) it's metaphysically possible that x has Ψ, and (3) there is no non-disjunctive property Ψ' such that (*a*) Ψ entails Ψ', but not vice versa, and (*b*) x's having Ψ' metaphysically necessitates x's believing p.[10]

Further, let's have this stipulative definition:

> T is a *compositional supervenience theory for a language L with respect to x* iff T is a finitely axiomatized theory whose axioms ascribe a non-intentional property to each word and primitive structure of L, and T has for each sentence s of L a theorem that ascribes to s a non-intentional property Φ such that (1) s's having Φ is logically equivalent to the parts and structure of s having the non-intentional properties T's axioms ascribe to them and (2) s's both having Φ and being tokened in x's belief box is a minimal supervenience base for x's believing $L(s)$.

Now we may say that

(7) x thinks in L iff there is a compositional supervenience theory for L with respect to x.

The relevance of this account to the issue of compositional semantics is that there being a compositional supervenience theory for L with respect to x doesn't entail that L enjoys a compositional meaning theory. Suppose we think in English. Then although the compositional supervenience theory for English with respect to us entails

(8) 'Snow is white' has Φ,

and although the truth of

(9) 'Snow is white' means that snow is white

[10] The 'non-disjunctive' qualification (which remains to be made exact) is needed for the following reason. Suppose that Ψ_1 and Ψ_2 are distinct minimal supervenience bases for Al's believing that Pavarotti sings. Then Al's having the disjunctive property of having Ψ_1 or Ψ_2 would also metaphysically necessitate his believing that Pavarotti sings, but that wouldn't preclude Ψ_1 from being a genuinely minimal supervenience base, even though it entails, but isn't entailed by, the disjunctive property.

supervenes on the truth of (8), the theory doesn't entail (9), and it is consistent with everything we have so far that no compositional meaning theory can be constructed that would entail (9), or even

'Snow is white' means ⟨snow, whiteness⟩

or

'Snow is white' means ⟨c_s, c_w⟩.

Even so, two questions confront us.

The first question is whether we *can* say that (7) is true. No one who thinks that intentional facts are metaphysically entailed by non-intentional facts can coherently deny that (7) is true, whether or not she also thinks languages of thought enjoy compositional meaning theories; but someone might deny that intentional facts are metaphysically entailed by non-intentional facts. As far as I'm concerned, the only reasonable basis for scepticism about the metaphysical necessitation claim derives from worries about phenomenal states. Specifically, the worry is that (i) some intentional states are individuated partly in terms of phenomenal states but that (ii) phenomenal states aren't metaphysically entailed by non-intentional (read: physical) facts. As I've already indicated, I accept (i) (see 2.4) and think (ii) is probably indeterminate (see 3.8). But I don't think this issue really matters as regards the question at hand, for no one, I take it, would deny that the intentional is at least *nomically* necessitated by the non-intentional, whether or not phenomenal states reduce to intentional states, and the foregoing account of a compositional supervenience theory can simply be restated, if need be, with supervenience understood as at least nomic necessitation. Nevertheless, merely for simplicity of exposition I shall for the most part write as though intentional facts were metaphysically entailed by non-intentional facts, since it ought throughout to be clear how to restate what I say to allow a weaker kind of supervenience.

The second question is apt to seem more serious, and deserves its own section before we return to the questions about compositional semantics I still haven't answered.

4.4 THE SUPERVENIENCE OF THE INTENTIONAL ON THE NON-INTENTIONAL

A compositional supervenience theory accounts for how the infinity of meaning facts emanates from a finite basis, but it leaves unexplained something else which may well be thought to demand explanation—namely, why it is that the meanings of Mentalese sentences supervene on precisely those properties on which they do supervene. Jane thinks in Mentalese, so each of infinitely many Mentalese sentences has some physical property that secures that in her head the sentence means the proposition it means in Mentalese. How is this infinite correlation of physical properties and propositions to be explained? What explains how just *those* meanings come to supervene on just *those* properties? As Paul Boghossian has aptly remarked,

in the absence of further comment, a relation of supervenience between sets of distinct and highly disparate properties is puzzling. How could there be a set of necessary connections between such properties as being a certain configuration of molecules and believing that *Lully was a better composer than Purcell*, given the admittedly highly divergent characters of the properties involved? We are entitled to be mystified.[11]

This mystery isn't dispelled by the compositional supervenience theory for Mentalese with respect to Jane. That theory gives a finite way of correlating each sentence of Mentalese with the physical property on which its meaning supervenes, but it does nothing to explain why any given meaning should supervene on the physical property that is its supervenience base. If the sentence s means the proposition that snow is white in Jane's head, then the supervenience theory will assign to s a physical property Φ such that s's meaning that proposition supervenes on s's having Φ; but nothing will have been done to account for why that particular meaning property should supervene on that particular property.

It might be thought that, while this explanatory demand must be met, having a compositional meaning theory in addition to a compositional supervenience theory would put one in no better position to meet it. The combination would give one a finitely specifiable way of matching up each propositional content with the physical property on which it supervenes, but it would do this by way of associating each word and primitive structure of one's Mentalese with a physical property on which that word or structure's meaning supervenes, and nothing would thereby be done to explain those match-ups of semantic values with the physical properties on which having those values supervene. For example, if the compositional meaning theory tells us that 'Fido is a dog' means ⟨Fido, doghood⟩ and the

---

[11] Boghossian (1991: 66).

compositional supervenience theory correlates 'dog' with physical property Φ, then, putting the two theories together, we know that the fact that 'dog' means doghood supervenes on the fact that 'dog' has Φ, but it would still remain to be explained why meaning doghood should supervene on having Φ. To this, however, the champion of compositional semantics might, while conceding the point just made, reply that she nevertheless enjoys an explanatory advantage. It is true, she might say, that a theorist equipped with a compositional super-venience theory and a compositional meaning theory would still need to explain her basic supervenience correlations, but the theorist possessed of the combination of compositional theories has *finitely* many *basic* supervenience correlations to explain, and therein lies her apparent explanatory advantage. If she can explain those finitely many correlations, she can explain all the (so to say) Φ/p correlations, but if one merely has a compositional supervenience theory, one still has infinitely many Φ/p correlations to explain, only now without the leverage of any finite stock of correlations from which to generate those infinitely many Φ/p correlations. So the question is, how, if at all, might the theorist of non-compositionally determined propositions solve (what we might call) *the Φ/p correlation problem*—the problem of explaining why it is that each Mentalese sentence means for a person the proposition it does mean for her? Actually, as we'll presently see, it is not entirely obvious that the theorist who has both a compositional meaning theory and a compositional supervenience theory really does enjoy a head start on the Φ/p correlation problem.

We can answer at least part of Boghossian's worry without much trouble. A given belief fact (I'll take belief facts as my exemplars of intentional facts) will supervene on numerous non-intentional facts, because many of the non-intentional facts on which it supervenes will themselves supervene on other non-intentional facts. But there will be one non-intentional fact N that is privileged in that the belief fact's supervening on N doesn't depend on N's supervening on any other fact, and if the belief fact supervenes on any other fact, that is just because N supervenes on that fact. The privileged subvening facts for belief facts will be facts pertaining to the functional roles of men-tal states and the external environment with which those states causally interact. (So, knowing how *molecular* facts can enter the supervenience picture, we have an answer to a small part of Boghossian's question.)

We can even say something—or at least begin to say something—about what determines privileged subvenience, that is, about what makes a particular (no doubt very complex) functional–environmental fact the one on which believing that Lully was a better composer than Purcell supervenes. Suppose, just to begin, that we think in a language of thought, a neural system of mental representation. Then the *proto-conceptual role* of a Mentalese sentence is that conceptual role determined for the sentence by the proto-conceptual roles of its primitive structures and constituent words. The conceptual role of a Mentalese expression is that complex counterfactual property that details how the expression interacts with other expressions, having their own conceptual roles, with sensory input, and with behavioural output. The proto-conceptual role of a primitive expression (roughly, a word) or structure is that original conceptual role the expression or structure has regardless of whatever functional states one might be in. The fact that a Mentalese sentence has its proto-conceptual role will belong essentially to an account of the conditions under which that sentence will, or will not, enter one's belief box. If A's Mentalese sentence s has the same proto-conceptual role as B's sentence s' and A and B share the same environment, then s and s' are synonymous. Consequently, the proposition A believes when s is in her belief box will be the same as the proposition B believes when s' is in his belief box.

But the content of a belief doesn't always supervene on just its proto-conceptual role. That is shown by Twin Earth examples. The proto-conceptual role of 'water' will be the same on Earth and on Twin Earth, but on Earth it will refer to water, i.e. H_2O, while on Twin Earth it will refer to water, i.e. XYZ. It is, however, plausible to suppose that a Mentalese expression's proto-conceptual role at least determines what sort of environmental thing will be needed to complete the determination of the term's content, although, of course, nothing has yet been said about how it effects that determination. In any event, the pressing question as regards the Φ/p-correlation problem is what accounts for why a given content should supervene on just the proto-conceptual-role, environmental state of affairs on which it happens to supervene.

Let's begin by asking how the compositional meaning theorist would answer this for Mentalese 'dog'. She knows, we may pretend, that 'dog' means doghood and that that fact supervenes on the fact that 'dog' in one's Mentalese has proto-conceptual-role, environmental property Φ.

What explains the fact that the one fact supervenes on the other?
Well, what do we mean by 'explains' in this context? One thing that
would no doubt count as an explanation would be a deduction of
the form

> Necessarily, x means y iff $x R y$
> 'Dog' R doghood
> ∴ 'Dog' means doghood

where R was a relation intrinsically specifiable in proto-conceptual-
role and causal terms. Stampe, Dretske, Stalnaker, and Fodor have
suggested explanations of roughly this kind, where the reducing relation R is held to be some sort of covariation relation, the starting idea
being that under certain sorts of ideal circumstances tokenings of
'dog' in one's belief box (presumably in sentences of the form 'a is a
dog') will covary with nearby instantiations of doghood.[12] For
reasons that I and others have laid out in various places,[13] I regard
this sort of reductive enterprise as hopeless, and I shall henceforth
proceed on that assumption. Even if having meaning consists in
standing in the meaning relation to a meaning, the non-intentional
properties on which meaning properties supervene won't themselves
be composite properties consisting of a non-intentionally specifiable
relation and a meaning.[14] Although meaning (or character*) properties
supervene on non-intentional properties, they can't be *identified*
with them. For if having a meaning/character* consists in standing in
the meaning/character* relation to something that is a meaning/
character*, then any *identification* of those properties with properties
that were intrinsically specifiable non-intentionally would have to
entail an identification of the meaning/character* relation with a
relation to meanings/characters* that was intrinsically specifiable in
non-intentional terms, and it is precisely this that is highly implausible (what on earth, for example, could be the non-intentionally
specifiable reducing relation in which 'immaterial' stands to the
property of being immaterial and by virtue of which the word means
that property?).

---

[12] Stampe (1977); Dretske (1981); Stalnaker (1984); and Fodor (1990c).
[13] See e.g. Schiffer (1987a, ch. 4), and the essays in Loewer and Rey (1991).
[14] Here I'm in complete agreement with what Paul Horwich (1998) says against supposing
that intentional relations must reduce to non-intentional *relations*.

Suppose we know that meaning doghood supervenes on the proto-conceptual-role, environmental property Φ. Whatever Φ is, it won't be of the form *bearing R to doghood*, where *R* in any way reduces the meaning relation.[15] Whatever property Φ is, our question for the compositionalist must be: What is to count as an explanation of the supervenience of meaning doghood on Φ, given that there is no reductive account of the meaning relation? The explanation can't be something that enables us to conclude that a word means doghood from premises that don't include that fact, for that would be possible only if we had something that was tantamount to a reduction of the meaning relation, in that it would at least have to include a sufficient condition for a word's meaning a property. So, on behalf of the compositionalist, we're in the following predicament. We seek something that might be called an 'explanation' of a necessary truth—namely, that having proto-conceptual-role, environmental property Φ metaphysically entails meaning doghood—that isn't a deduction of that truth from premises that make no assumption about what the word means. The most one can hope for, I submit, is something that, in some vague way, 'demystifies' the modal truth, makes it seem unremarkable or unsurprising, that somehow or other allows us to see why *that* particular property, as opposed to some other, is the one on which meaning doghood supervenes. And in this regard I suspect that the best we can do is simply to make the unexciting point that that property is the one that accounts for our intuitions about when a word does, or does not, mean doghood for someone (well, since we're dealing with Mentalese words, our concern is really with our intuitions about when someone does, or does not, have the, or at least a, concept of a dog). We can elaborate a little in the following way. For any propositional attitude Ψ, we have pretty nearly indefeasible intuitions about when a person determinately Ψs that...dog..., determinately doesn't Ψ that...dog..., and when it is indeterminate whether she Ψs that...dog... What would serve to explain, in the sense of demystify, why meaning doghood in a person's Mentalese supervened on a neural word's having the non-intentional property Φ would be our learning the word's having Φ accounted for our intuitions about whether the person Ψs that...dog... In the absence of

---

[15] In the case of meaning doghood, it's not implausible that an intrinsic specification of Φ will require reference to doghood, but there are many properties for which the corresponding claim isn't plausible—e.g. meaning the property of being a unicorn.

a full-blooded reduction of the Mentalese meaning relation, that sort of 'explanation' is the most one can hope for.

Let's now return to the question of whether the theorist who has both a compositional meaning theory and a compositional superven-ience theory enjoys an advantage over the theorist who merely has a compositional supervenience theory as regards the Φ/p-correlation problem, the problem of explaining why the meaning of each of infin-itely many Mentalese sentences should supervene on the particular proto-conceptual-role, environmental fact on which it happens to supervene. The answer, it should now be clear, is no. For precisely the same 'explanation' available to the theorist with both compositional theories is available to the theorist with just the one: each can explain that having Φ accounts for the 'intuitions' that entitle us to say any particular sentence means the proposition it means, and that is the best 'explanation' available to either theorist. This does presuppose that both theorists can help themselves to the assumption that the proto-conceptual role of a sentence is determined by the proto-conceptual roles of its component words and structures, but that seems a safe assumption, and it in no way presupposes that one's Mentalese has a compositional meaning theory.

So much for explaining the supervenience of the intentional on the non-intentional. A further question concerns how much can be said about the nature of the proto-conceptual-role, environmental prop-erties on which mental content supervenes. Paul Horwich, who accepts what I have so far said in this section, suggests, in effect, that these properties are all 'acceptance' properties having the form

> σ will be tokened in x's belief box in non-intentionally specifi-able circumstances of kind C.[16]

An example might be:

> 'That [perceptually demonstrated thing] is red' will be tokened in your belief box when and only when the demonstrated thing is clearly red.

However, while Horwich's proposal holds promise for some cases, I doubt that he's right that all the subvening properties are of the displayed form. I don't, for example, see how it can work for 'There is an invisible unicorn in my garden', or even for 'Fido is here'. As far as

---

[16] Horwich (1998).

I can tell, there is no one kind of non-intentional proto-conceptual-role, environmental property on which all propositional content supervenes.

4.5 COMPOSITIONAL TRUTH THEORIES

Natural languages are thought by many to have two kinds of compositional semantics—compositional meaning theories, which I have finished discussing, and compositional truth theories. A compositional truth theory for a language L would be a finitely axiomatized theory of L whose theorems would ascribe to each truth-evaluable sentence of L the conditions under which a token of the sentence would be true. What about warranted scepticism regarding compositional truth theories for particular languages?

The situation here is a little complex. On the one hand, compositional truth theories aren't possible in the sense in which they are usually thought to be possible, and they aren't needed for the reasons they are usually thought to be needed. On the other hand, there is a straightforward sense in which natural languages have compositional truth theories, and there is something they do serve to explain.

Philosophers who think that natural languages enjoy correct compositional truth theories do so because they think that such theories are needed to explain how the extension of a complex expression depends on the extensions of its semantically relevant parts. Some years ago there were also philosophers who, influenced by Donald Davidson,[17] thought that truth theories were needed to serve as meaning theories, but I think it is safe to say that that idea turned out to be a dead end.[18] Still, of course, natural languages might have and need compositional truth theories even if those theories can't in any way 'serve as' (and what's *that* supposed to mean?) meaning theories.

Just as discussions of compositional meaning theories typically commence with the simplifying assumption that our initial concern is with a homophonic meaning theory for non-indexical, indicative English which is to issue in theorems of the form

'S' means that S,

---

[17] Davidson (1984*b*).   [18] See e.g. Schiffer (1987*a*, ch. 5).

such as

'Snow is white' means that snow is white,

so discussions of compositional truth theories typically commence with the simplifying assumption that our initial concern is with a homophonic truth theory for non-indexical English which is to issue in theorems of the form

(10) 'S' is true iff S,

such as

(11) 'Snow is white' is true iff snow is white.

Such a theory, it is assumed, will do its work by way of assigning extensions to words in its base axioms, as well as associating suitable recursive rules with basic syntactic structures and other devices, which rules will enable the determination of a sentence's truth-value as a function of the extensions of its semantically relevant parts.

Perhaps a theory like that could crank out (11) as a theorem, but, if I'm right about that-clauses, we couldn't have a correct finitely axiomatized truth theory for a fragment of English that included belief sentences which had as a theorem, say,

(12) 'Ralph believes that George Eliot was a man' is true iff Ralph believes that George Eliot was a man.

One reason this is so is that the simplifying assumption is supposed to be that we're concerned only with non-indexical sentences and on my view that-clauses don't have context-independent referents. But what is presently of more interest is that no correct truth theory could yield (12) *even if its that-clause had a context-independent refer-ent*. The reason is that on my account of that-clauses, they are singular terms whose referents are not determined by the referents of their constituent expressions. To be sure, we noticed in 2.4 that there is a sense in which 'George Eliot' in (12) would probably refer to George Eliot and 'man' to the property of being a man, but the proposition to which the that-clause refers, not being the singular proposition ⟨G.E., the property of being a man⟩, isn't a function of those referents. That-clauses, on my view, are unique among semantically complex singular terms. Their referents aren't a function of the referents of their semantically relevant parts but, as I argued in Chapter 2, are instead determined by contextually determined criteria of evaluation which are not themselves a function of the referents of that-clauses' semantically relevant parts.

And yet, I claim, nothing prevents full-blown indexical natural languages from having correct compositional truth theories—from having, that is to say, finite theories that assign to each sentence capable of having truth-evaluable tokens a condition that is necessary and sufficient for the token's being true. Here, by way of illustration, is how things might work for

(13) Ralph believes that George Eliot was a man.

A truth theory might assign Ralph to 'Ralph', the belief relation to 'believes', George Eliot to 'George Eliot', and the property of being a man to 'man'. Then the theorem generated by the truth theory for (13) might be that

> An utterance of (13) is true iff $\exists p(\text{Nec}(p$ is true iff George Eliot was a man) & p is determined by such-and-such contextual factors & Ralph believes p).

This is merely for illustration, since the actual truth condition for (13) would have to assign an utterance of (13) a truth condition in the event that George Eliot is believed by the belief reporter and his audience not to exist (see Section 2.4); but I don't see why this sort of thing couldn't be done—if all that is meant by 'a compositional truth theory' is a finitely axiomatized theory that generates for each sentence that can be used to make a truth-evaluable statement a condition, however lightly informative, that is necessary and sufficient for the truth of an utterance of the sentence. But what would we need such a theory *to explain*? Evidently—and trivially—what it explains, and what it is needed to explain, is how truth conditions are determined by a language to the extent to which they are so determined.

5

Vagueness and Indeterminacy

5.1 INTRODUCTION

Up to this point I have been theorizing about linguistic and mental semantics pretty much as though vagueness didn't exist. In fact, however, almost every expression is to some extent vague, and we can't know the correct semantics and logic for any language until we know the correct semantics and logic for vague language. A theory of vagueness must lie at the heart of any complete theory of meaning. This chapter offers a theory of vagueness, and of indeterminacy generally, since the indeterminacy of vague borderline propositions is, as the two chapters after this will show, only one source of indeterminacy, albeit the most prevalent.

There is a philosophical problem of vagueness because of various conceptual puzzles to which vagueness gives rise. The most famous of these puzzles is the *sorites paradox*,[1] and it very quickly leads to all the other semantical and logical puzzles associated with vagueness. Accordingly, I begin, in 5.2, with the sorites paradox, and canvass some attempted solutions to it. Section 5.3, which recalls my distinction between happy- and unhappy-face solutions to paradoxes (see 2.3), sets the stage for my own response to the sorites. That response relies on a distinction between two kinds of partial belief, *standard partial belief* (SPB) and *vagueness-related partial belief* (VPB), and this distinction is introduced and partially explained in 5.4, while 5.5 explains vagueness, and indeterminacy generally, in terms of VPB. My account of vagueness and indeterminacy as a psychological notion explicable in terms of VPB raises a metaphysical puzzle which

---

[1] 'Sorites' derives from the Greek word for heap, *soros*, and the original paradox turned on the vagueness of that word, but paradoxes of the same form can be generated for virtually any vague concept, and *sorites paradox* is now used as a label for any paradox of that form.

is resolved, in 5.6, by appeal to the pleonastic notion of properties. After further explicating the notion of a VPB in 5.7, in 5.8 I re-examine the sorites in light of the new account of vagueness. The final section, 5.9, deals with two remaining questions: whether VPBs are really *beliefs* and whether vagueness and indeterminacy are products of the world or of thought and language, and here a famous argument of Gareth Evans is addressed.

5.2   THE SORITES PARADOX

The following inference, which I'll call *SI*, constitutes a sorites paradox:

(1) A person with $50 million is rich.
(2) $\forall n$(a person with $\$n$ is rich $\rightarrow$ a person with $\$n - 1$¢ is also rich)[2]—i.e. you can't remove someone from the ranks of the rich by taking 1¢ from her fortune.
(3) $\therefore$ A person with only 37¢ is rich.

This constitutes a paradox because it appears to be valid, each of its two premisses appears to be true (at least when considered on its own), and its conclusion certainly appears to be false.

It is reasonable to assume (at least initially) that a solution to the sorites, as manifested in SI, would do two things. First, it would tell us which of the four appearances just cited was deceptive; and secondly, it would explain away that deceptive appearance by explaining why that untrue proposition appeared to be true; it would strip from the masquerader its appearance of plausibility so that we were no longer duped by it. Most, if not virtually all, writers on vagueness assume that the sorites has such a solution, and the various theories of vagueness strain to provide it. Very well; what is that solution?

One may reasonably find it hard to question the validity of SI, as it turns just on modus ponens and universal instantiation, and we can remove the reliance on universal instantiation by replacing its *sorites premiss*, (2), with its millions of instances (if a person with $50 million is rich, then so is a person with $49,999,999.99; if a person with $49,999,999.99 is rich, then so is a person with $49,999,999.98,...).

---

2 '$\rightarrow$' is the material conditional.

Assuming the validity of SI, one's apt to suppose that, *faute de mieux*, the sorites premiss must be false. After all, it is plainly true that a person with $50 million is rich and that a person with only 37¢ isn't rich, and if SI is valid, then, one is apt reasonably to suppose, so is

> A person with $50 million is rich.
> A person with only 37¢ isn't rich.
> ∴ ~∀n(a person with $n is rich → a person with $n − 1¢ is also rich).

But if this little argument is valid and its premisses are true, then its conclusion, the negation of SI's sorites premiss, is true, and thus the sorites premiss is false.

Now, we don't solve the sorites merely by supposing that the sorites premiss is false. We would still need to explain why, though it is false, we're so tempted to think it is true. Well, we're tempted to think the sorites premiss is true to the extent that we're tempted to think the following argument for it, which I'll call *SPA*, is sound:

> (i) There is no 1¢ cut-off between those who are rich and those who aren't—i.e. there isn't some particular number *n* such that the proposition *that a person with $n is rich but a person with $n − 1¢ isn't* is true.[3] (In symbols: ~∃n(the proposition that [a person with $n is rich & a person with $n − 1¢ isn't rich] is true).)
>
> (ii) ~∃n(the proposition that [a person with $n is rich & a person with $n − 1¢ isn't rich] is true) → ∀n(a person with $n is rich → a person with $n − 1¢ is also rich).
>
> (iii) ∴ ∀n(a person with $n is rich → a person with $n − 1¢ is also rich).[4]

SPA must be unsound if the sorites premiss is false. But SPA generates its own paradox, since it appears to be valid, its conclusion seems unacceptable, and yet each of its premisses appears plausible when viewed on its own.

---

[3] Equivalently, there is no numeral α such that the sentence ⌜A person with $α is rich & a person with $α − 1¢ isn't⌝ is true.

[4] I'm grateful to Hartry Field for getting me to see that an earlier version of this argument was longer than it needed to be. His penetrating remarks on an earlier draft have led to various other changes in this chapter.

SPA appears to be valid, since its validity depends only on modus ponens, and we've already noticed why its conclusion, SI's sorites premiss, seems unacceptable (one pretty much has to say at least that if one deems the argument unsound).

Premiss (i) *looks* right. Isn't it patently absurd to suppose that there is a precise 1¢ cut-off between what suffices for being rich and what suffices for not being rich? Is it that $495,946.47 is the cut-off point such that if you have that much, then you're rich, but if you have only $495,946.46, then you're not rich? This is hard to take seriously.

Premiss (ii) also looks right. If there is no particular amount of money such that it is true that having *that amount* makes you rich but having 1¢ less than it doesn't, then, one might reasonably suppose, if any amount of money makes you rich, then so will 1¢ less than it.

One hasn't achieved a happy-face solution to the sorites of the kind typically sought by theorists of vagueness until one has both revealed what is wrong with SPA and explained why it is wrong in a way that allows us to see why we were wrongly tempted to think it was right.[5] Familiar would-be solutions of the kind typically sought don't question the validity of SPA, which, as we've seen, relies only on modus ponens, and may be grouped according to which of the two premisses they take not to be true. Here the contest has up to now mostly been played out in the literature between those who deny the truth of (i) and those who deny the truth of (ii).

Theorists who deny that (i) is true do so because they hold that there *is* a precise 1¢ cut-off between the rich and non-rich. These theorists hold that there is such a precise cut-off because they accept the principle of bivalence—the principle that every proposition, and thus every borderline proposition, is true or false. A theorist who is committed to bivalence is constrained to hold that there is a precise cut-off, that is, a particular number n such that the proposition *that a person with $n is rich but a person with $n − 1¢ isn't* is true, and no one who didn't think that borderline propositions were true or false would be tempted to suppose that there was such a precise 1¢ cut-off between the rich and the non-rich. A theorist who is committed to bivalence is constrained to hold that there is such a precise cut-off, because if she holds that every proposition of the form

A person with $n is rich but a person with $n − 1¢ isn't

---

[5] The notion of a happy-face solution to a paradox was explained in 2.3, and I return to it in 5.3.

is false, then that would be tantamount to accepting the sorites pre-miss, and that would force her either to accept that a person with only 37¢ is rich or else to deny that a person with $50 million is rich, and thus, accepting bivalence as she does, the theorist is committed to holding that some proposition of the displayed form is true.

The theorist who holds that borderline vague propositions are true or false has some serious debts. The first debt is epistemic. For con-sider borderline Harry, who isn't definitely bald and isn't definitely not bald. If, nevertheless, the proposition that Harry is bald is either true or false, then it is either a fact that Harry is bald or else a fact that he isn't bald. At the same time, no one can know which fact obtains; if borderline propositions have truth-values, no one can know what they are.[6] Presumably, there must be some explanation of this ineluctable ignorance. Thus, the first debt of the theorist who would deny (i) is to explain why we're necessarily ignorant of the truth-values of borderline propositions.

The second debt is semantic. If there is a precise 1¢ cut-off between what suffices to make a person rich and what suffices to make a person not rich, then the property of being rich is a precisely bounded property, which, being precisely bounded, determines a precise extension for the term. Suppose that the cut-off is $495,946.47 in that if you have that much, then you're rich, but you're not rich if you have 1¢ less than that. In the event, the property of being rich would be identical to the property of having at least $495,946.47, and, by an obvious generalization, something analogous would hold for every vague term. For example, if we pretend that baldness supervenes just on the number of hairs on a person's scalp, then there would be some

---

[6] Several writers—e.g. Raffman (1994) and Graff (2000)—have emphasized the context-sensitivity of vague terms, but I think these writers have been wrong to think that attention to this sensitivity enables us either to resolve the sorites or to suggest a new account of vagueness. For consider an utterance of 'She won't date him—he's bald'. The context of utterance will certainly affect what is to count as a borderline case, and raising the question whether So-and-so is bald after that utterance will have a new effect on what is to count as a borderline case of baldness, but that doesn't disturb the fact that we can focus on the first proposition asserted and ask if there is a precise hair condition such that that proposition is true if the man referred to satisfies that condition but is false if he satisfies the minutely and indiscernibly different hair condition that is the contiguous condition in the sorites series that marks the precise boundary between what makes the proposition true and what makes it false. It's just as absurd to suppose there is such a precise cut-off point here as there ever was, and, given this, it's hard to see how attention to the context-sensitivity of vague utterances can help solve any problem of vagueness.

number—say, 3,343—such that you're bald if, but only if, the number of hairs on your scalp isn't greater than that number, and in this case baldness would be identical to the property of having no more than 3,343 hairs on one's scalp. Now, the meaning of a predicate supervenes on its use, and the semantic question confronting the theorist in question would be to explain what it is about the use of our terms that makes the meaning of each general term such an absolutely precise property. What is it about the way we use 'rich' such that it expresses the property of having at least $495,946.47 and not the property of, say, having at least $495,946.48? What is it about our use of 'bald' such that it expresses the property of having no more than 3,343 hairs on one's scalp, rather than, say, 3,342 or 3,344? The situation is actually worse. The foregoing gloss of the semantic problem indulges in the fiction that words like 'rich' and 'bald' express context-independent properties, when, in fact, what property is expressed by a token of either word is very heavily dependent on contextual factors. What the epistemic theorist must say is that those factors determine an absolutely precise property for each token. For example, the epistemic theorist must hold that when I say that I worked for a little while this morning, there is some absolutely precise span of time such that my statement is true if, but only if, it falls within that span of time, and is false if the amount of time I worked was one nanosecond longer than the span of time to which my utterance of 'a little while' referred. What kind of 'factors' could with any degree of plausibility have that result? And, to add a third debt, the theorist who accepts bivalence must cash the two preceding debts in a way that makes clear why (i), which the theorist denies, strikes us as so very plausible.

There are theorists who embrace bivalence for borderline propositions and therefore deny (i). Such a theorist is said to hold an *epistemic theory of vagueness* if she defines the notion of a borderline proposition as a proposition of whose truth-value we must be ignorant for such-and-such reason. For these theorists, vagueness is a form of ignorance. Recent interest in such theories was partly generated by Roy Sorensen's *Blindspots*, but the view is most fully elaborated and defended in Timothy Williamson's *Vagueness*. According to Williamson, the reason we can't know a true borderline proposition even if we believe it is that had things been ever so slightly and indiscernibly different, the proposition we believed would have been a slightly different and false proposition, even though it would have been produced in us by the same belief-forming mechanism. But we are precluded from knowing a proposition if the mechanism that produces belief in it might just as well have caused us to believe a false proposition. Thus, if we pretend that 'bald' in fact expresses the property of having fewer than 3,344 hairs on one's scalp, then we shall have a true belief if we believe that Harry is bald, given that he has exactly 3,343 hairs on his scalp. But we would have believed the proposition expressed by 'Harry is bald' even if our use of 'bald' had been indiscernibly different but different enough so that 'bald' expressed the property of having fewer than 3,343 hairs on one's scalp, and in that case our belief about Harry would have been false. Since the factors that produced in us the true belief about Harry might just as easily have produced in us a false belief about him, our true belief that he's bald can't constitute knowledge. But Williamson's account presupposes what to my mind is incredible—namely, that every token of a vague predicate in every natural language always succeeds in picking out, as that token's meaning or reference, a single precisely bounded property, and that the factors which determine the contents of our thoughts determine those thoughts to have contents that are as exquisitely precise as can be. Moreover, Williamson offers no account of meaning or language use or content determination to make this bizarre claim credible; he accepts it because his theory of vagueness requires him to accept it, much as Leibniz accepted that this is the best of all possible worlds.[7] Hartry Field offers an especially telling objection against theorists, such as Williamson, who take there to be a determinate fact of the matter in borderline cases. It is a *conceptual truth* that a person who knows the complete hair situation on borderline Harry's scalp and has full command of the concept of baldness can't know that Harry is bald or that he's not bald, but the epistemic theorist can't hold this. He must hold that the fact that we have no means to detect the fact of the matter about Harry's baldness is 'a medical limitation on our part, not a conceptual necessity'.[8]

Other theorists who accept bivalence for borderline propositions, and thus accept that we are ineluctably ignorant of the truth-values of borderline propositions, resist calling themselves epistemic theorists, presumably because their programme isn't to *define* vagueness in terms of ignorance. For example, Hartry Field has suggested

---

[7] My problems with the epistemic theory are elaborated in Schiffer (1999). Timothy Williamson replies in Williamson (1999).   [8] Field (2001e: 286).

(nearly enough) that meaning is *not* a use-dependent property and that sentences such as

'Harry is bald' is true iff Harry is bald
'Bald' is true of a thing iff it's bald
'Bald' means baldness

are all conceptual truths—necessary, a priori truths that, being necessary, hold regardless of how anyone uses language. Thus Field adhered to the truth and falsity schemas

'S' is true iff S
'S' is false iff not S.

Since in the publication in question Field also accepted excluded middle (every proposition of the form *p or not-p* is true), he was thereby committed to bivalence.[9] But this is no more promising than Williamson's solution. There are three problems. First, meaning simply is *not* a use-independent property. What an expression means for someone is determined by how that expression is used, if the expression is semantically simple, or, if it's semantically complex, by how the expressions and structures composing it are used. If anything is a datum in these muddy waters, that is.[10] Secondly, Field still owes an account of why we can't know either the truth-values of borderline propositions or the precise criteria for belonging to the extensions of vague terms (the two points of ignorance are connected, since one could in principle know the truth-values of borderline propositions if one could know the precise extensions of vague terms, and vice versa). Thirdly, in order to achieve a fully satisfying solution, Field would still have to explain away our temptation to think that (i) was true. To be sure, if Field is right, then the temptation to think (i) true is due in part to a tendency to confuse truth with determinate truth, but we would still be owed an explanation of why we should be so tempted, given that truth and determinate truth are for him distinct notions.

---

[9] Field (2001*b*). Field no longer accepts excluded middle and now favours a non-classical logic in which excluded middle is neither asserted nor denied. See Field (forthcoming) and my own discussion relating to this in 5.8.

[10] Field may have intended his claims about the use-independent status of semantic statements to be a proposal for conceptual reform. My concern, however, is to understand the vagueness of actual expressions and to comprehend the sorites as it arises for those expressions. Also, Field, as I note again in n. 38, now favours a different account of vagueness, one which doesn't entail a commitment to bivalence (see Field forthcoming).

Paul Horwich is another theorist whose commitment to bivalence and the truth and falsity schemas for propositions forces him to deny (i) and to accept the existence of sharp cut-offs.[11] Thus, Horwich accepts that there is some precisely bounded property—say, the property of having at least $495,946.47—such that 'rich' expresses that property.[12] He also holds that the meaning of a term is determined by its use. How, then, does he avoid the complaint lodged against Williamson, that it is highly implausible that our use of predicates determines them to mean precisely bounded properties? And how does he explain the fact that no one can know the boundaries of the properties her words mean or the truth-values of borderline propositions? In response to the first question, Horwich claims that we won't find it incredible that our use of 'rich' determines it to mean a precisely bounded property such as the property of having at least $495,946.47 once a certain false assumption is removed. The false assumption is that if use determines meaning and meaning determines extension, then it must be possible to explain the term's having the extension by deducing that it has that extension from the proposition that it has whatever use happens to constitute its meaning. Use, Horwich holds, does determine meaning, but no reductive definitions of semantic relations are possible, and, therefore, there can be no explanations of the kind involved in the false assumption.[13] In response to the second question, Horwich says that the conceptual role of a vague term leads to unimprovable partial belief because the explanatorily basic fact which governs the term's use and thereby constitutes its meaning is 'gappy' in that, roughly, the predicate 'is confidently applied to things whose value of underlying parameter # is greater than y; its negation is confidently applied to things whose value of # is less than x; and neither is confidently applied to things whose value of # is in between x and y'.[14]

I don't think Horwich makes denying (i) any more palatable than Williamson or Field did. In the first place, Horwich is wrong in suggesting that only someone with a commitment to a reductionist brand of explanation could be puzzled about how language use could determine precisely bounded meanings. The puzzle isn't about

[11] Horwich (1998, 2000a,b).

[12] Horwich, of course, is harmlessly going along with the fiction that 'rich' expresses a context-independent property.   [13] Horwich (2000a: 277–9).

[14] Horwich (2000a: 277).

reductive accounts of meaning and reference; it's about there being any kind of coherent story to tell about how the facts about how we use a term could give it a meaning of the kind required. What is it about the way we use 'rich' such that it expresses the precise property of having more than $495,946.46 and not, say, the property of having more than $495,946.45? Secondly, this puzzle is exacerbated in Horwich's case by his explanation of the ineluctable ignorance to which he's committed: How could one's use of a term determine a precisely bounded property as its meaning or reference if the 'explanatorily basic fact which governs the term's use' is 'gappy' in the way he suggests?

I think the proper conclusion to draw isn't that we've yet to hit on the best way to defend sharp cut-offs; it is rather that no plausible case can be made for accepting sharp cut-offs. If there is a solution to the sorites, it doesn't entail the negation of (i). And if that is right, then it can't be right that the principle of bivalence is determinately true. More on this later.

Just as there are theorists who deny (i) and accept (ii), so there are theorists who accept (i) and deny (ii). There is more than one way to challenge the truth of (ii),[15] but by far the most prevalent way is that of those theorists who hold that the correct semantics for vague language is a *supervaluationist* semantics.[16] The supervaluationist on vagueness holds that (ii) is false: it has a true antecedent but a false consequent. The idea, roughly, is that a vague sentence is true just in case it is true under every admissible precisification of the language to which it belongs, false just in case it is false under every admissible precisification, and neither true nor false just in case it is true under some admissible precisification while false under another. A precisification is a model-theoretic interpretation of the language wherein the set assigned as extension to a vague term includes everything to which the term definitely applies, nothing to which it definitely doesn't apply, and may include none, some, or all of the term's borderline applications. A precisification is admissible just in case it respects all

[15] For example, Hilary Putnam (1983) brings intuitionistic logic to bear on the sorites in a way that could be used to challenge (ii), but Stephen Read and Crispin Wright (1985) offer a good critique of his effort.

[16] Supervaluationist semantics was first proposed by Bas van Fraassen (1966) as a way of accommodating truth-value gaps due to the sort of presupposition failure one finds in 'The present King of France is bald'. The classical supervaluationist treatment of vagueness is Kit Fine (1975).

analytic connections among vague terms (e.g. if x is assigned to the extension of 'tall' and y is taller than x, then y must also be assigned to the extension of 'tall'). Truth under a precisification is defined in the standard model-theoretic way. Thus, truth under a precisification is bivalent: for any given precisification of the language, a sentence of the language is either true or false under that precisification. But truth *tout court* isn't truth-under-a-precisification. Since a sentence can be true under some admissible precisification while false under another, truth *tout court* isn't bivalent. So suppose Harry is borderline bald. Then 'Harry is bald' is neither true nor false, but 'Harry is bald or not bald' is true, since on every admissible precisification one of the disjuncts will be true, and 'Harry is bald and not bald' is false, since on every admissible precisification one of the conjuncts is false— although, since both the atoms of these molecular sentences are borderline, which one is true and which false will vary from one admissible precisification to another. In this way the supervaluationist hopes to retain classical logic while rejecting the semantic principle of bivalence.

Now, let's abbreviate the negation of (ii)'s consequent as

$$\sim\forall n(R(\$n) \rightarrow R(\$n - 1\text{¢}\,)),$$

which for the supervaluationist is equivalent to

$$\exists n(R(\$n) \,\&\sim R(\$n - 1\text{¢}\,)).$$

This sentence is true for the supervaluationist, since in every admissible precisification there is some number or other that satisfies

$$R(\$x) \,\&\sim R(\$x - 1\text{¢}).$$

But since there is no one number which satisfies that open sentence in every admissible precisification, there is no number n such that the proposition *that a person with $\$n$ is rich but a person with $\$n - 1$¢ isn't rich* is true. It is in this way that the supervaluationist holds that (ii) has a true antecedent but a false consequent, and is therefore false.

But it is very hard to see how this can provide a solution to the sorites. There are several problems.

(*a*) Our concept of disjunction does seem to require that a disjunction can be true only if one of its disjuncts is true; our concept of conjunction does seem to require that a conjunction can be false only if one of its conjuncts is false; and our concept of the existential quantifier does seem to require that no existential generalization can be true without there being some particular thing of which the quantified open sentence is true. So, the supervaluationist is evidently just wrong if she is proposing an account of the meaning our connectives and quantifiers actually have, and if she is merely proposing a useful *revision*, then it is hard to see how that can be part of a *solution* to the sorites.

(*b*) Even if the supervaluationist's semantical claims were correct, she would still have done nothing yet to explain away (ii)'s appearance of being true, and so would again have failed to provide a solution to the sorites of the kind she seeks.

(*c*) The supervaluationist offers a semantics for vague language, but it is a semantics that makes it hard to see how to explicate vagueness. This is because the semantics uses the notion of a precisification, which is itself defined in terms of vagueness. One would hope that a solution to the sorites would throw light on what vagueness is and on what it is to be a borderline proposition.[17]

(*d*) There are apparent counter-examples to the supervaluationist semantics.[18] Suppose that Alice says to Bob, 'Harry's biggest problem is baldness', and Bob later says to Carla, 'Baldness, Alice said, is Harry's biggest problem', which we may pedantically but usefully restate as

(1) Baldness is such that Alice said that it was Harry's biggest problem.

We may suppose that, notwithstanding the vagueness of 'baldness', Bob's utterance (1) is determinately true. The problem for the supervaluationist is that he must say that (1) is determinately false.

There are two accounts of the semantics of (1) the supervaluationist might offer, but they come to the same thing. First, the supervaluationist might say that 'baldness' in (1) indeterminately refers to numerous precise properties, those that comprise the admissible precisifications of 'baldness' (I here ignore higher-order vagueness: borderline cases of borderline cases, borderline cases of borderline cases of borderline cases, and so on). Then (1) will be true iff it is true

[17] Why can't the supervaluationist simply say that a borderline proposition is a proposition that is neither true nor false? Because this theorist will almost certainly want to say that there are propositions other than borderline propositions that are neither true nor false, such as, for example, the proposition that the present King of France is bald.

[18] See also Schiffer (2000*b*,*c*).

on each of those precisifications, false iff it is false on each of them, and neither true nor false iff it is true on some of the admissible precisifications, false on others. Since, even allowing for the vagueness of the rest of (1), Alice quite clearly didn't say of *any* precise property (e.g. the property of having fewer than 3,137 hairs on one's scalp) that *it* was Harry's biggest problem, the supervaluationist must hold that on this first way of doing the semantics for (1), (1) is determinately false. On the second way of doing the semantics of (1), the supervaluationist holds that 'baldness' determinately refers to a single vague property, baldness, and (1) will be true just in case Alice said of that vague property that it was Harry's biggest problem. At first glance this is apt to look promising as a way of getting (1) to come out true. But not really. For the supervaluationist has to provide truth conditions for propositions involving the vague property baldness, and the only way he has of doing that is to hold that a proposition involving the property is true only if it is true on every admissible precisification of baldness, and this will, again, have (1) come out, unacceptably, as determinately false. (More generally put, when we take propositions into account, the supervaluationist must say, nearly enough, either that a vague sentence token indeterminately expresses a bunch of precise propositions, in which case the sentence is true just in case each of those propositions is true, or else it expresses a single vague proposition, in which case the proposition, and hence the sentence, is true just in case every admissible precisification of the proposition is true. Precisifications of propositions are easily understood on analogy with the precisifications of sentences.)

David Lewis, replying to remarks of Saul Kripke's which evidently raised something like the problem (1) raises, gives the impression that he would concede that such examples can't be accommodated by the supervaluationist but would also claim that this wouldn't show supervaluationism to be mistaken:

What's mistaken is a fanatical supervaluationism, which automatically applies the supervaluationist rule to any statement whatever, never mind that the statement makes no sense that way. The rule should instead be taken as a defeasible presumption. What defeats it, sometimes, is the cardinal principle of pragmatics: The right way to take what is said, if at all possible, is the way that makes sense of the message. Since the supervaluationist rule would have made hash of our statement of the problem, straightway the rule was suspended.[19]

---

[19] Lewis (1999a: 173–4).

This may be a good reply to Kripke's objection, but it makes no sense as applied to (1). For if the correct semantical treatment of (1) is non-supervaluationist, then what is that alternative semantics, and who's to say that it isn't the correct semantics for vagueness generally?

(e) While supervaluationism is incapable of giving a positive account of what vagueness is, it nevertheless succeeds in implying a false account of it. The point has been very nicely made by Crispin Wright. The main problem with supervaluationism, he would say, is that according to it 'indeterminacy consists ... in some kind of status other than truth or falsity—a *lack* of a truth-value, perhaps, or the possession of some other truth-value', and to such '*third-possibility views of indeterminacy*' he objected that

it is quite unsatisfactory in general to represent *in*determinacy as any kind of determinate truth-status—any kind of middle situation, contrasting with both the poles (truth and falsity)—since one cannot thereby do justice to the absolutely basic datum that in general borderline cases come across as hard cases: as cases where we are baffled to choose between conflicting verdicts about which polar verdict applies, rather than as cases which we recognize as enjoying a status inconsistent with both.[20]

In other words, when confronted with borderline Harry we have some temptation to say that he's bald and some temptation to say that he's not bald, but supervaluationism can't account for this. If supervaluationism were correct, we should recognize that the proposition that he's bald is neither true nor false and therefore have no temptation to say either that he's bald or that he's not bald.

So much for a supervaluationist solution to the sorites. Some theorists hope to resolve the sorites by appeal to a *degree-theoretic* notion of truth. On this way of reckoning truth, a borderline proposition and its negation will both be true to a degree greater than 0 and less than 1, given the convention typically adopted by degree-of-truth theorists that degrees of truth can be measured by real numbers in the interval [0, 1]. There is, however, more than one way of developing a degree-theoretic notion of truth, some of which comport with classical logic, some of which don't.

The degree-theoretic notion of truth that departs from classical logic is the one most commonly invoked in application to vagueness; it is a degree-functional account of the connectives due to

Łukasiewicz,[21] which, following Dorothy Edgington,[22] we may restate as follows for negation, conjunction, disjunction, and implication:

[~] $T(\sim p) = 1 - T(p)$
[&] $T(p \& q) = \text{Min}[T(p), T(q)]$
[v] $T(p \vee q) = \text{Max}[T(p), T(q)]$
[⊃] $T(p \supset q) = 1$ if $T(p) \leq T(q)$, $1 - [T(p) - T(q)]$ otherwise.

This requires a departure from classical logic in that, for example, excluded middle and non-contradiction fail: if $T(p)$ and $T(\sim p)$ are both .5, then both $T(p \vee \sim p)$ and $T(p \& \sim p)$ are also .5.

There are two apparent problems. The first is that the theory is a 'third-possibility view of indeterminacy', and thus subject to Wright's trenchant objection to all such theories.[23] The theory is evidently constrained to hold that p is true just in case p is T to degree 1 (or—allowing for the vagueness of ordinary language 'true'—to a contextually relevant high degree); false just in case p is T to degree 0 (or to a contextually relevant low degree); and neither true nor false just in case p is T to some (contextually relevant) degree greater than 0 and less than 1. But suppose Harry is borderline bald. Then, since it would be definitely wrong to say that 'Harry is bald' is T to degree 1 (or to some other contextually relevant high degree), the theory entails that it would also be definitely wrong to say it is true that Harry is bald. But if Harry is borderline bald, it would *not* be definitely wrong to say that he's bald, and thus not definitely wrong to say it's true that he's bald.[24] (But what if the Łukasiewiczian were to protest that we have no business identifying his degrees of T with degrees of *truth*. Why can't he say, for example, that '$T(p)$' in effect signifies the degree of belief one should have in p and is consistent with p's being true or false even when, say, $T(p) = .5$?[25] The problem with this response is that it renounces the Łukasiewiczian's claim to be presenting a non-classical *logic* in any non-Pickwickian sense of 'logic'. The fact that we can't derive instances of excluded middle ($p \vee \sim p$) from the empty set of premises would signify merely that we're not entitled fully to believe an instance of excluded middle just by virtue of its being an instance of excluded middle and would imply nothing about whether it is possible for there to be instances of excluded middle that aren't

---

[21] See Łukasiewicz and Tarski (1956). [22] Edgington (1996).
[23] See above, p. 191. [24] See the quote from Edgington (1996: 299) in the text below.
[25] Cf. Field (forthcoming).

true. Of course it would be absurd to refrain from fully believing some instances of excluded middle while also holding that every instance of excluded middle was true, but the fact that it would be correct to have something less than full belief in the proposition that borderline Harry is bald or not bald need only signify that it is indeterminate whether classical logic is correct. I return to these issues in 5.8, where I attempt to make better use of Łukasiewiczian continuum-valued fuzzy logic.)

The second apparent problem is that the theory requires us to hold that some determinately true propositions classically entail propositions that are determinately false to a degree close to 1, and this is apt to seem flat-out unacceptable. For consider the inference

A person with $50 million is rich.

A person with only 37¢ isn't rich.

Therefore, it's not the case that, for any n, if a person with n is rich, then so is a person with $n - 1$¢.

This inference is classically valid, and the Łukasiewiczian degree-of-truth theorist will of course recognize that the two premisses are completely true, T to degree 1. But this theorist must also hold that the conclusion is nearly completely false, for it is equivalent to a long disjunction of negations of conditionals of the form

~(a person with α is rich ⊃ so is a person with $\alpha - 1$¢)

and, given [⊃], each such negation will be either completely false or else very nearly completely false. But how, one might well wonder, can it be anything but determinately false that if having a given amount of money makes you rich, then so will having 1¢ less than it, given that it is determinately true both that a person with $50 million is rich and that a person with only 37¢ isn't rich? There are issues here that will recur in 5.8.

A degree-theoretic account of truth which comports with classical logic can be defined in terms of a supervaluational account of truth, for, on such an account, a proposition's degree of truth can be defined in terms of the proportion of admissible precisifications on which it is true.[26] And Dorothy Edgington shows how we can achieve the same effect by introducing a degree-theoretic construal of truth

---

[26] See Lewis (1970); Kamp (1975); McGee and McLaughlin (1994: 236–9).

wherein T mimics the behaviour of prob in classical probability theory.[27] For example, in probability theory, $\text{prob}(p \vee q) = \text{prob}(p) + \text{prob}(q) - \text{prob}(p \& q)$; accordingly, the Edgington-inspired proposal holds that $T(p \vee q) = T(p) + T(q) - T(p \& q)$. Whereas the Łukasiewicz-ian account is degree-functional (the degree of truth of a compound is a function of the degrees of truth of its components), the Edgingtonian T, like prob, isn't. Thus, even when both $T(p)$ and $T(\sim p) = .5$, it will still be the case that $T(p \vee \sim p) = 1$ and $T(p \& \sim p) = 0$, and, in the same way, $\exists x F x$ can be true to degree 1 even though no substitution instance of its quantified open sentence is true to degree 1. But there is no point going further with this theory, since, being a form of supervaluationism, it has the problems already levelled against that theory.

But Dorothy Edgington seems not to hold the supervaluationist account of degrees of truth just sketched, for she denies that truth is truth-under-all-admissible-precisifications.[28] Her reason for this refusal is based on her sensitivity to the crucial point with which Wright pokes 'third-possibility views of vagueness', that vagueness manifests itself in one's having some inclination to say that a border-line proposition is true and some inclination to say that it is false. She explains (where 'true$_A$' stands for our common-sense all-or-nothing notion of truth): 'Suppose "a is red" is definitely borderline: neither clearly true nor clearly false. It would not be definitely wrong to call it true$_A$; but it would be definitely wrong to give it a "degree of truth" of 1.'[29] Accordingly, she writes not '$T(p)$' but rather '$v(p)$', a new degree-theoretic technical term for 'degree of closeness to clear truth', which she calls 'verity'. Degrees of verity, then, aren't to be identified with degrees of truth. At the same time, Edgington emphasizes that degree-of-verity isn't degree-of-belief, as it would naturally be taken to be if the epistemic theory of vagueness were correct, and it seems clear from her exposition that Edgington would deny that borderline propositions are true or false. Evidently, then if, say, $v(p) = .5$, then p is neither true nor false, and this is enough to show that Edgington can't avoid the problem she hopes to avoid by refusing to identify degrees of verity with degrees of truth. For if $v(\text{'Harry is bald'}) = .5$, then it wouldn't be definitely wrong to say that it is true that Harry is bald, but Edgington must say that it would be definitely wrong.

---

[27] Edgington (1996).   [28] Edgington (1996).   [29] Edgington (1996: 299).

One might complain that I've exaggerated the difference between theories of vagueness that deny bivalence and those that accept it, since in some cases there will be a virtual equivalence between the two kinds of theories. Suppose that A is a conventional supervaluationist (except, we'll suppose, her theory is developed for propositions rather than sentences—which I take to be merely an expository convenience in the present context). According to A, a proposition is true just in case it is true under every admissible precisification, false just in case it is false under every admissible precisification, and neither true nor false just in case it is true under some admissible precisification and false under another. A holds that the proposition that borderline Harry is bald is neither true nor false. A counts, on my characterization, as a theorist who rejects bivalence for borderline propositions. Opposed to A is B. B accepts bivalence for borderline propositions but gives a supervaluationist account of *definitely true* and *definitely false*. That is, a proposition is definitely true just in case it is true under every admissible precisification, definitely false just in case it is false under every admissible precisification, and neither definitely true nor definitely false if it is true under some admissible precisification and false under another. But now suppose that, with no alteration of her theory, A introduces the predicates 'true*' and 'false*' via the stipulation that every instance of the schemas *The proposition that S is true* iff S* and *The proposition that S is false* iff not-S* is to be true. Since A's theory already entails excluded middle, propositions are for her bivalent with respect to their truth*-values. Yet now A and B hold equivalent theories, for B's truth = A's truth* and A's truth = B's definite truth.

Two points. First, this shows nothing of interest about vagueness. Any theorist who accepts classical logic can cast her theory in a supervaluationist guise, since the notion of an admissible precisification must itself be explicated in terms of vagueness: a precisification of Φ is admissible only if everything that *definitely* has Φ is assigned to the extension of Φ and everything that *definitely* doesn't have Φ is assigned to the anti-extension of Φ. No account of vagueness is given until a non-question-begging account of the definitely (or determinately) operator has been given. Secondly, it is trivial to introduce an operator of 'dispropositionalization' '#' whereby 'The proposition that S is #' expresses the same proposition as 'S'. But this can tell us nothing about *truth*. For the propositionalist, the semantic features of a sentence are entirely determined by the proposition it expresses,

and truth and falsity are in the first instance properties of propositions, the properties in terms of which we understand what it is for it
to be a fact that such-and-such. Given the introduction of the dispropositionalization operator '#', all we're told by, say, 'The proposition that the present King of France is bald is #' is that it expresses the
proposition that the present King of France is bald and, consequently,
has whatever truth-value that proposition has.

5.3   HAPPY- AND UNHAPPY-FACE SOLUTIONS

A paradox is a set of apparently mutually incompatible propositions
each one of which enjoys some non-negligible degree of plausibility
when considered on its own. Classical philosophical problems typically take the form of paradoxes. The problem of free will, for example, consists of the set of mutually incompatible propositions whose
members are the propositions that we have free will, i.e. that we
sometimes act freely; that everything we do was caused by factors
over which we had no control; and that if everything we do was
caused by factors over which we had no control, then we don't have
free will. The sorites inference with which I began this chapter, SI,
also presents a paradox, for it yields the classically inconsistent set
containing the proposition that a person with $50 million is rich, the
proposition that, for any n, if a person with $\$n$ is rich, then so is a per-
son with $\$n - 1¢$, and the proposition that a person with only 37¢
isn't rich.

Earlier in this chapter I implied that it is reasonable to expect a solution to any paradox to do two things: first, to reveal the odd guy(s)
out, that is, either to tell us that, despite first appearances, the members of the paradox set aren't really mutually incompatible, or that one
or more of them isn't true; and secondly, to tell us why the now undis-
guised masquerader, or masqueraders, seemed so plausible to us in the
first place, and to do this in a way that explains away the misleading
impression or impressions. Recalling the discussion of happy- and
unhappy-face solutions to paradoxes in 2.3, we know that a solution to
a paradox that does these two things is a *happy-face solution* to the
paradox. Philosophers who take on a philosophical problem typically
hope to provide a happy-face solution to it, and writers on vagueness
typically hope to give a happy-face solution to the sorites.

It may be reasonable to seek a happy-face solution to the sorites or to any other philosophical problem, but, to repeat what I said in 2.3, I doubt that the sorites or any of the classical philosophical problems has a happy-face solution. The 'paradox' of the barber who shaves all and only those who don't shave themselves has a happy-face solution: it is impossible for there to be such a barber, and when we realize this any air of paradox disappears. That no classical philosophical problem, including the sorites, yet has a happy-face solution is attested to by the fact that we are still debating each one of them. The sticking point in each case is in explaining away the plausibility of the selected odd guy(s) out. Why, if, say, compatibilism is the correct solution to the problem of free will, do we continue to feel a tendency to deny that an act can be free (and one morally responsible for it) if it was caused by events that occurred even before the agent was born?

It is my view that few, if any, classical philosophical problems have happy-face solutions. It is also my view that the reason a philosophical paradox lacks a happy-face solution, when it does lack one, is that there is a glitch in the concept, or concepts, generating the paradox. The glitch is an underived, or basic, feature of the paradox-generating concept, or concepts, that, without making the concept logically inconsistent, nevertheless pulls one in opposing directions without there being anything else in the concept or elsewhere to resolve that tug-o-war. Thus, the problem of free will doesn't admit of a happy-face solution because it is indeterminate which proposition in the paradox set is false, and this is because of a glitch in our concept of free will. The underived conceptual role of that concept has two parts that don't cohere. On the one hand, we're disposed to judge that an act was done freely when it satisfies certain paradigm conditions, while on the other hand we're disposed to deny that an act was done freely when we learn that the propositional attitudes which led to it were caused by factors over which the agent had no control. Further, there is nothing in the concept to resolve the conflict. The conflicting aspects of conceptual role don't mean that the concept of free will is inconsistent (it isn't like the concept of a round square), for we don't take the aspects of conceptual role to provide necessary conditions for the concept's application when we learn of their conflict. The extent to which one experiences these conceptual pulls can vary from person to person, and even within a person over time, but for anyone who has our concept of free will, both pulls are inherent in the concept, and they remain there even if one decides to ignore them in applying the concept. This is why the paradox of free will can have no happy-face solution.

If a paradox doesn't have a happy-face solution, it may still have an *un*happy-face solution. An unhappy-face solution to a paradox will do two things. First, it will explain what it is about the paradox-generating concept, or concepts, which precludes a happy-face solution; and secondly, it will tell us whether the paradox admits of a *weak* or a *strong* unhappy-face solution, in the following sense. A *weak* unhappy-face solution to any paradox will tell us that while there can be no happy-face solution involving the concept, or concepts, generating the paradox, a suitable conceptual revision is possible that would be paradox-free, where a conceptual revision is 'suitable' if it can do the primary work we wanted the 'defective' concept to do. Alfred Tarski in effect offered a weak unhappy-face solution to the semantic paradoxes.[30] He suggested that given the 'inconsistent' nature of our common-sense concept of truth, there could be no happy-face solution to those paradoxes. But Tarski, and those who have followed him, expected, and sought, a notion of truth on which the paradoxes wouldn't arise. A *strong* unhappy-face solution denies that any suitable conceptual revision is possible. I'm inclined to think the problem of free will has a strong unhappy-face solution.

The sorites, I believe, has no happy-face solution. To see why this is so, we must first inquire further into the nature of vagueness and indeterminacy. Once this is done, we can raise the question whether the sorites has a weak or a strong unhappy-face solution.

5.4 TWO KINDS OF PARTIAL BELIEF

Vagueness, I hold, is neither a semantic nor an epistemological notion but rather a *psychological* notion, for its correct explication is in terms of a certain kind of partial belief.

My account of vagueness turns on a distinction between two kinds of partial belief. Although we philosophers often suppress the point, we know that believing is a matter of degree having to do with how firmly—the degree to which—one accepts a proposition. One can believe a proposition more or less firmly, and to say that someone

---

[30] Tarski (1956*b*).

believes p *tout court* really means that she believes p to some contextually relevant high degree. What is less well known is that there are two distinct kinds of partial belief.

One kind is what philosophers usually have in mind when they think about partial belief; I call this kind of partial belief *standard partial belief* (SPB). SPB is the kind of partial belief which—subject to a qualification that I'll ignore until I get to it in 5.7—can under suitable idealization be identified with *subjective probability*. SPB, in other words, is the kind of partial belief philosophers have in mind in standard discussions of personal probability and decision theory. I take this to mean two things:

1. SPBs are those partial beliefs that under suitable idealization satisfy the standard axioms of probability theory. Given that there are SPBs, then we instantiate a partial-belief function, SPB, such that the following holds under suitable idealization:

$0 \leqslant \text{SPB}(p) \leqslant 1$.

If p and q are logically incompatible, then $\text{SPB}(p \vee q) = \text{SPB}(p) + \text{SPB}(q)$.

If p is a theorem of classical logic, then $\text{SPB}(p) = 1$.

Since my focus is to be on another kind of partial belief, I intend to be suitably vague about what I mean by 'suitable idealization'. I mean at least whatever writers on subjective probability mean when they take the probability calculus to model rational belief. Evidently, the idealization would involve perfect rationality and logical omniscience. I won't concern myself with how SPBs should be modelled for actual humans, as that won't be necessary for my purposes.

2. If there are SPBs, then

$\text{SPB}(q/p) = \text{SPB}(p \,\&\, q)/\text{SPB}(p)$

holds (under idealization) when, for the intended notion of partial belief, $\text{SPB}(q/p)$ represents the degree to which one believes q given p.[31] Now, the notion of *conditional belief*—believing q given p—is itself somewhat of a technical notion. The pre-theoretic notion it is intended to capture is the extent to which one would believe q to be true given that one took p to be true. In this sense, one takes p and q

---

[31] Since division by 0 is undefined, both sides of the equation are undefined when $\text{SPB}(p) = 0$.

to be independent when one's being certain that p would make no difference to the degree to which one believed q; that is, when $SPB(q/p) = SPB(q)$. Thus, suppose I regard p as extremely good evidence that q, so that if I were to become certain that p, then I would believe q to degree .9. Then to say that the displayed formula holds for the pre-theoretic notion of conditional belief implies that the values of $SPB(p \& q)$ and $SPB(p)$ are such that $SPB(p \& q)/SPB(p) = .9$.

SPB, as I said, is the familiar kind of partial belief that has long been an object of study. Examples of SPBs are your believing to some degree or other—i.e. more or less firmly—that you left your glasses in your office, that it will rain tonight, or that the Atlantic City Flounders will win the Super Bowl. Thus, if you, rational believer that you are, believe to degree .5 that you left your glasses in your office, then you believe to degree 1 that you either did or didn't leave your glasses in your office. And if you believe to degree .6 that you left your glasses in your office, believe to degree .2 that your nephew will pass his logic course, and take these two partially believed propositions to be independent, then you believe to degree .12 that (you left your glasses in your office and your nephew will pass his logic course).[32] Here are some further substantial things true of SPBs.

(*a*) SPB is the kind of partial belief we would have even if, *per impossibile*, our language were perfectly precise.

(*b*) SPB is a measure of *uncertainty*, and thus of *ignorance*. If one s-believes p to a degree less than 1 and greater than 0, then one takes the truth-value of p to be uncertain; there is some fact of the matter of which one is at least somewhat ignorant. As we'll presently see, uncertainty is quite distinct from indeterminacy. In fact, as will later be clear, one can't take the truth-value of a proposition to be uncertain unless it is epistemically possible for one that the proposition is determinately true or determinately false.

(*c*) SPBs generate corresponding likelihood beliefs. Thus, if Sally s-believes to degree .5 that she left her glasses in her office, then she thinks it is just as likely that she left them there as that she didn't; she thinks, as she would put it, that there's a fifty-fifty chance that her glasses are in her office. If she s-believes to degree .98 that it will rain

---

[32] It's a theorem of the probability calculus that if p and q are independent, then prob $(p \& q) = \text{prob}(p) \times \text{prob}(q)$ (otherwise, $\text{prob}(p \& q) = \text{prob}(p) \times \text{prob}(q/p)$, unless $\text{prob}(p) = 0$, in which case $\text{prob}(p \& q) = 0$).

tonight, then she believes that it will almost certainly rain tonight. If she s-believes to degree .32 that she'll pass her course in number theory, then she thinks it is somewhat unlikely that she'll pass. (Note that these beliefs aren't about any kind of 'objective probability'. They are really just *redescriptions* of a particular kind of partial belief. In the relevant sense, to say that Sally thinks there's a fifty-fifty chance that she left her glasses in her office is just another way of saying she s-believes to degree .5 that she left her glasses in her office.)

(*d*) Typically, if one s-believes *p* to some degree between 0 and 1, then one doesn't regard oneself as being in the best possible position to pronounce on the truth of *p*, even if one has no doubts about the integrity of the evidence one has for or against *p*. Often one thinks there is a better position it is at least possible for one to get into. So, I believe to degree .5 that I left my glasses in my office. Well, I can go there and resolve the matter. Sometimes one supposes there is no better position one can get oneself into, but that there is a better epistemic position someone else might have enjoyed. For example, there is probably nothing I can do to improve my opinion about the colour of Thales' eyes, but a contemporary of his could have satisfied herself on that score. Sometimes when one s-believes *p*, one supposes that no one can presently get into a better epistemic position with respect to *p*, but one thinks that theoretical advances may change that. This may be our position with respect to our ability to know what happens in a black hole. Still, there may be cases where no improvement is possible, and this is why I cautiously prefixed this discussion with the 'typically' qualifier.

So much for SPBs until I return to them in 5.7. I turn now to the other kind of partial belief, which I call *vagueness-related partial belief* (VPB).[33] A fuller characterization of VPB will come in 5.7; for now I just want to get enough of the intuitive notion before us so that we can see its bearing on vagueness and indeterminacy. The crucial claim for now is that VPBs are those partial beliefs that can't under any idealization be identified with subjective probability and are, moreover, such that the substantial things true of SPBs aren't true of

[33] This is what I called VPBs when I first introduced them in Schiffer (1998), where the only kind of indeterminacy of concern was that manifested in vague borderline propositions. As will later be apparent, vagueness-related partial belief might better be called *indeterminacy-related partial belief*, but since I have used the label 'VPB' in several publications by now, I shall stay with it.

them. I will, however, assume that, like SPBs, VPBs can under suitable idealization be measured by real numbers in the interval $[0, 1]$.[34] Thus:

(*a*) As we'll presently see, we couldn't have VPBs if our language were perfectly precise; VPBs go hand-in-hand with vagueness. One couldn't have a vague language without VPBs, and having VPBs secures one's having a vague language.

(*b*) VPB is *not* a measure of uncertainty or ignorance. When one is confronted with what one takes to be a paradigm borderline case of a bald man, one doesn't take oneself to be *uncertain* as to whether or not the man is bald; that is resolved by one's taking him to be a borderline case of a bald man. As we'll see, to take someone to be a borderline case of a bald man is, roughly speaking, just to v-believe to a degree between 0 and 1 that the person is a bald man.

(*c*) VPBs don't give rise to corresponding likelihood beliefs. If one v-believes that such-and-such to degree .5, one *won't* thereby think there's a fifty-fifty chance that such-and-such, and if one v-believes that such-and-such to degree .7, one *won't* believe that it is somewhat likely that such-and-such.

(*d*) If one v-believes p to any degree between 0 and 1, and one's epistemic circumstances are known by one to be ideal (in a way to be explained), then one won't feel that one, or anyone else, can get into a better epistemic position with respect to p.

It will help to illustrate VPBs with a somewhat artificial example. Sally is a rational speaker of English, and we're going to monitor her belief states throughout the following experiment. Tom Cruise, a paradigmatically non-bald person, has consented, for the sake of philosophy, to have his hairs plucked from his scalp one by one until none are left. Sally is to witness this, and will judge Tom's baldness after each plucking. The conditions for making baldness judgements— lighting conditions, exposure to the hair situation on Tom's scalp, Sally's sobriety and perceptual faculties, etc.—are ideal and known by Sally to be such. For simplicity of exposition, I'll assume that at any given time Sally believes to some determinate degree that Tom is bald. This assumption is highly artificial, but I intend my provisional use of it to be innocent. Let the plucking begin.

---

[34] In 5.7 we'll see that there can't really be a VPB held to degrees 1 or 0; formally we could say that in the degenerate case in which $VPB(p) = 1$ or 0, VPB is indistinguishable from SPB.

Sally starts out judging with absolute certainly that Tom is not bald; that is, she believes to degree 1 that Tom is not bald and to degree 0 that he is bald. This state of affairs persists through quite a few pluckings. At some point, however, Sally's judgement that Tom isn't bald will have an ever so slightly diminished confidence, reflecting that she believes Tom not to be bald to some degree barely less than 1. The plucking continues and as it does the degree to which she believes Tom not to be bald diminishes while the degree to which she believes him to be bald increases. At some point, we may pretend, the degree to which Sally believes both that Tom is bald and that he isn't bald is .5, and Tom thereby represents for Sally a solid borderline case of baldness. Having reached .5, Sally's degrees of belief that Tom is bald will gradually increase as the plucking continues, until she believes to degree 1 that he is bald.

I take it that the qualified judgements about Tom's baldness that Sally makes throughout the plucking express partial beliefs. After all, the hallmark of partial belief is qualified assertion, and, once she was removed from her ability to make unqualified assertions, Sally would make qualified assertions in response to queries about Tom's baldness. The assumption that Sally is expressing partial beliefs throughout the plucking is not immune to questioning, and later (in 5.9) I shall say more about why I make the assumption, but for now I'll simply assume that Sally's qualified assertions express partial beliefs. My claim is that Sally's partial beliefs that Tom is bald are VPBs; they are, that is, beliefs that can't under any idealization be identified with subjective probability. Given my earlier stipulation about what it is for partial beliefs to be identified with subjective probability, my claim that Sally's partial beliefs are VPBs means that either (1) her partial beliefs (under idealization) don't satisfy the standard axioms of probability theory or (2) the formula 'VPB(q/p) = VPB $(p \& q)$/VPB(p)' doesn't hold when, for the intended notion of partial belief, 'VPB(q/p)' represents the degree to which one believes q given p.

I take disjunct (2) to be straightforwardly true. As regards SPBs, SPB$(p \& q)$/SPB(p) *does* (under idealization) give the degree to which one would s-believe q given p. For suppose one s-believes to degree .5 both that Beetlebomb will win the Kentucky Derby and that Lithuania will win the World Cup, and suppose one takes these two partially believed propositions to be independent in that the degree to which one s-believes either proposition doesn't affect the degree to which one s-believes the other. Then one ought to s-believe the conjunction *that Beetlebomb will win the Kentucky Derby and Lithuania will win the World Cup* to degree .25. Intuitively, this is what we would expect of a rational believer. If asked to justify her .25 degree belief in the conjunction, the rational s-believer would say her evidence justifies her in thinking that either proposition could go either way, but it is a much stronger thing to suppose they'll both go the same way. This response relies on there being a gap between the partially believed proposition and her evidence for it, so that she can meaningfully wonder how things will turn out.

As regards VPBs, however, VPB$(p \& q)$/VPB(p) does *not* in any way give the degree to which one would v-believe q given p. Suppose that at the point in the plucking when Sally believes to degree .5 that Tom is bald, thereby making him a paradigm borderline case of baldness for her, she also believes to degree .5 that he is thin, making him also for her a paradigm borderline case of thinness (poor Tom has been entirely nude throughout the plucking). Suppose further that these two partially believed propositions are taken by Sally to be independent, in that for her the truth of neither proposition has any bearing on the truth of the other. Can we expect eminently rational Sally to believe to degree .25 that Tom is bald and thin? I submit not. I submit that she'll believe the conjunction to degree .5. I regard this as intuitively correct, but that doesn't preclude a rationale. The rational believer who takes the propositions that Beetlebomb will win the Kentucky Derby and that Lithuania will win the World Cup to be independent and s-believes each to degree .5 will believe the conjunction of those two propositions to degree .25, for that is the degree supported by the evidence. But for Sally, there is no gap between her partially believed proposition and her evidence for it; she's *ambivalent* but she's not *uncertain* about anything. For her, all the relevant factors are completely available to her; nothing more of relevance could possibly come to light. Sally can't wonder how, given her situation, the issue of Tom's baldness (or thinness) might turn out, nor will she wonder what the secret fact of the mater to which she can't have access might be. Thus, she v-believes to degree .5 that Tom is bald, that Tom is thin, and that Tom is bald and thin; yet the two propositions are for her independent. If, however, VPB$(p \& q)$/VPB(p) adequately represented conditional belief for VPBs, then the two propositions wouldn't be independent for her. Rather, Tom's being thin would be conclusive evidence for Sally of his being bald, since VPB(that Tom is bald and thin)/VPB(that Tom is thin) [i.e. .5/.5] $= 1$.

I also take disjunct (1) to be straightforwardly true. In the scenario just described, VPB(Tom is bald) = .5, VPB(Tom is bald and not thin) = .5, and VPB(Tom is bald and thin) = .5, and this is inconsistent with the probability calculus (if VPB satisfied the axioms of the probability calculus, VPB(Tom is bald) would be 1 when VPB (Tom is bald and not thin) and VPB(Tom is bald and thin) were both .5). Also, if Sally's .5 belief that Tom is bald were an SPB, then she would believe to degree 1 that Tom was bald or not bald. But Sally, who v-believes both that Tom is bald and that he's not bald to degree .5, is also apt to find it indeterminate whether excluded middle applies to borderline propositions. That is to say, she's also apt rationally to v-believe to degree .5 that Tom is bald or not bald, thereby, in effect, taking this instance of excluded middle to be indeterminate. Given this, she's also of course apt rationally to v-believe to degree .5 that the proposition that Tom is bald is either true or false, thereby, in effect, taking this instance of the principle of bivalence to be indeterminate. But more on this later.

Since Sally's partial beliefs about Tom's baldness can't be identified with subjective probability, they are VPBs and not SPBs. It is also easy to see that Sally's VPBs don't satisfy the substantial things true of her SPBs (see above, p. 200): (*a*) I said that SPBs were the sort of partial beliefs we could have even if, *per impossibile*, our language were perfectly precise; but, as we're about to see, VPBs go hand-in-hand with vagueness. (*b*) Sally's VPBs about Tom's baldness are no measure of any *uncertainty* she has about Tom's being bald. When her VPBs represent Tom as a borderline case of baldness, Sally is ambivalent as to how to judge Tom, but she doesn't take herself to be *ignorant* of the real state of affairs regarding Tom's baldness. It is because Sally appreciates that her situation isn't one of ignorance that she v-believes to degree .5 that Tom is bald and thin, even though she v-believes each conjunct to the same degree and takes the conjuncts to be independent.[35] (*c*) Sally's VPBs about Tom's baldness aren't accompanied by corresponding likelihood beliefs. If Sally v-believes to degree .5 that

---

[35] After writing Schiffer (1998), where I first put forward the SPB–VPB distinction, I became aware of Sainsbury (1986). There Sainsbury distinguishes between what he calls *epistemic* and *non-epistemic* degrees of belief. He holds that 'borderline cases for a vague predicate will give rise, in fully informed and rational beings, to degrees of belief. These resemble epistemic degrees of belief in that they are related to strength of tendency to act. But they are unlike epistemic degrees in that they represent no ignorance. Rather, they

Tom is bald, she doesn't thereby think there's a fifty-fifty chance that he's bald. Believing that there's a fifty-fifty chance that Tom is bald is not an appropriate epistemic stance when one feels, as does Sally, that one's evidence reveals the full story about Tom's baldness. Likewise, if Sally v-believes to degree .7 that Tom isn't bald, she won't thereby believe that it is somewhat unlikely that he's bald. (*d*) When, as we've already noticed, one s-believes a proposition to a degree midway between 0 and 1, one won't take oneself to be in the best possible epistemic position with respect to that proposition. But in a case such as Sally's, where epistemic conditions for judging Tom's baldness are known to be ideal, whatever the degree to which she v-believes that Tom is bald, she won't suppose that she, or anyone else, can get into a better epistemic position with respect to that proposition.

I think that, subject to a certain refinement, enough has been said about VPB to apply it to the problems of vagueness. I know there remain plenty of questions about VPB answers to which are needed for a full understanding of the notion, but these questions are best taken up after the main application to vagueness, and to indeterminacy generally, has been laid bare. The refinement to which I just alluded is needed for this application, and it is as follows.

Sally's VPBs are formed under ideal epistemic conditions, but VPBs may be formed under conditions that are less than ideal. For example, it may be that she would v-believe to degree .6 that Tom was bald if she were certain that the hair situation on his scalp was such-and-such, but since she only s-believes to degree .7 that that is the hair situation on his scalp, the degree to which she v-believes that

---

reflect the fact that there is no definite right or wrong: it would be as wrong to believe with total confidence that a borderline case is a positive case as to believe, with total confidence, the negation of this' (p. 99). He adds that 'epistemic degrees of belief reflect some lack in *us* (lack of information). They need give rise to no temptation to suppose that they answer to some feature of the world independent of ourselves. By contrast, the necessity for vagueness-induced non-epistemic degrees of belief, if we are to have as accurate and complete a picture of the world as possible, shows that these degrees *do* answer to some feature of the world. Omniscience, if it allows vague concepts at all, as we mortals do, could do no better than have an intermediate degree of belief about a borderline case' (p. 104). But Sainsbury's distinction isn't mine. Not only does he think that non-epistemic degrees of belief satisfy the same laws as epistemic degrees (they're both species of SPBs), but, even more significantly, he uses his non-epistemic degrees of belief to motivate a notion of degrees of truth, and it's in terms of this degree-theoretic notion of truth that he hopes to deal with vagueness. But degrees of truth can neither be identified with degrees of belief nor used to solve the problems of vagueness.

Tom is bald will be less than .6. How that degree is to be determined is a point to be taken up later. For now, let's say that a *VPB** is the kind of VPB Sally has when, during her presence at the plucking, she v-believes that Tom is bald. It is a VPB formed under ideal epistemic conditions as regards the supervenience base for the vague property that enters into the belief, for the sense in which Sally's VPBs about Tom's baldness are formed under epistemically ideal conditions is, roughly speaking, that she has, and knows herself to have, certain knowledge of the relevant hair situation on Tom's scalp, i.e. of that hair situation which determines the extent to which a person is bald. Later I'll offer a generalization that will allow a slightly better characterization of a VPB*, but what we have so far should do well enough for the applications to which I now turn.

5.5   VPB*, VAGUENESS, INDETERMINACY, AND BORDERLINE CASES

Tom is a borderline case of baldness. What makes him such? It is no help to say that Tom is neither determinately (definitely) bald nor determinately (definitely) not bald, since the problem of explaining the determinately (definitely) operator just is the problem of explaining the notion of a borderline case.

Semantic theorists of vagueness hold that a proposition's being borderline is at least in part constituted by its being neither completely true nor completely false, either because it is neither true nor false *tout court* or because it has some intermediate truth-value. In any case, we have already considered these 'third-possibility' views of vagueness—to use Crispin Wright's label (p. 191)—and found them inadequate as solutions to the sorites in ways that make them also inadequate as characterizations of vagueness and of being a borderline proposition. *Epistemic* theorists of vagueness hold that a proposition's being borderline is constituted by its being impossible for anyone to know the proposition's truth-value, notwithstanding that the proposition is either true or false, but this, too, was found wanting. If we think of the epistemic theorist as one who holds that borderline propositions have unknowable truth-values, then semantic and epistemic theories of baldness exhaust current attempts to explicate vagueness based on proffered happy-face solutions to the sorites.

Perhaps indeterminacy is an irreducible property of propositions. After all, what properties are reducible? Perhaps; but we should still want some sort of explication of why we can't know indeterminate propositions, of what it is about certain things and certain concepts that makes it impossible for the latter determinately to apply to the former, and what the relation is between being indeterminate and having a truth-value, and so on, and one might hope that such an explication would carry with it something like a reductive account of the problematic notions. I think this isn't an idle hope; I think that while vagueness is neither a semantic nor an epistemic notion, it is a psychological notion explicable in terms of vagueness-related partial belief.

Not every vague borderline proposition concerns a thing's being a borderline case of a vague property, but it will be useful to begin with that paradigm in seeing how the notion of a VPB* can be used in explicating vagueness, borderlineness, and indeterminacy generally. To this end I begin with the following proposed necessary condition for being a borderline case of a property:

(A) x is a borderline case of being F *only if* someone could v*-believe that x is F.

Obviously, a thing may be a borderline case of a property even though no one is, or ever will be, making a judgement about it. To say that someone could v*-believe that x is F is to say that there is *some* possible world similar in relevant respects to the actual world in which someone v*-believes that x is F. In many cases, the relevant respects are defined by the supervenience base for being F—e.g. the hair situation on Tom's scalp. The ability to v*-believe that x is F would fail to be a necessary condition for x's being a borderline case of being F only if there is a possible world in which x is a borderline case of being F and there is *no* possible world similar to that world in all F-relevant respects in which someone v*-believes that x is F. It is hard to see how this weak condition could fail to be satisfied, hard, therefore, to see how (A) can be false.

Is this necessary condition also a sufficient condition? That is to ask, is (B) also true?

(B) x is a borderline case of being F *if* someone could v*-believe that x is F.

Well, it would seem that (B) is false only if someone could v*-believe that x is F when x is definitely F or definitely not F. Yet it is difficult to see how such a state of affairs could obtain. If, for example, Tom is definitely bald and one's epistemic situation vis-à-vis the proposition that Tom is bald is ideal (which entails that one is ideally rational in relevant respects), then one won't v^*-believe that Tom is bald; one will *know*, and hence s-believe, that Tom is bald. I think this is right, subject to a small qualification, and it needs amplification.[36]

The qualification is that while there is no possible world in which x is definitely F and someone can v^*-believe that x is F, it is not the case that being able to v^*-believe that x is F entails that x is a *borderline* case of being F, and this because there are *indeterminate* propositions which aren't *borderline* propositions, propositions whose indeterminacy is owed to *vagueness*. The possibility of someone's v^*-believing *that x is F* is sufficient for its being *indeterminate* that x is F but not for x's being a *borderline case* of being F. For example, the proposition that Kennedy would have been elected to a second term if he hadn't been killed is indeterminate, but it is not a *borderline* proposition, and in the next chapter I'll argue that propositions that ascribe moral properties are indeterminate, even though the indeterminacy isn't owed to the vagueness of the ascribed property. Thus, while we can say that

(C) p is indeterminate iff someone could v^*-believe p,[37]

we can't quite say (B).

Given that being a vague borderline proposition isn't the same as being an indeterminate proposition, how can we explicate borderlineness? To answer this, we need to look more closely at what it is for a property to be vague, and this is where pleonasticity re-enters the picture.[38]

---

[36] The qualification wasn't made in earlier presentations of my account of vagueness.

[37] Recall that on my use of 'indeterminate' it's analytic that borderline propositions are indeterminate but it's not analytic that being indeterminate entails being neither true nor false.

[38] My account explicates indeterminacy in terms of an idealized epistemic agent whose degrees of belief in indeterminate propositions are normatively governed by quite different laws than those that govern her degrees of belief in propositions that are uncertain but regarded by the agent as determinately true or determinately false. Hartry Field (2001d, forthcoming) likes this idea but objects to my claim that VPB and SPB are distinct kinds of partial beliefs, as opposed to one being a special case of the other. Accordingly, Field introduces a special probability function that will keep what he likes while avoiding what he doesn't like. He starts with a classical probability function P and from it constructs a function Q that doesn't in all cases obey the laws of classical probability theory but can be regarded as an appropriate degree-of-belief function. Field's strategy, essentially, is to stipulate that $Q(p) = P(Dp)$, where 'D' is the determinately operator. Thus, if both Dp and

5.6 VAGUENESS AND PLEONASTIC PROPERTIES

Suppose it were true that

(D) x is a borderline case of being F iff someone could v^*-believe that x is F.

One is still apt to feel that (D) fails to capture the *essence* of vagueness, fails to capture what *constitutes* it, even if it provides a necessary and sufficient condition for being a borderline case. The worry is that

$D{\sim}p$ are completely false, as will be the case when both p and $\sim p$ are fully indeterminate, then $P(Dp) = 0$ and $P(D{\sim}p) = 0$. From this it further follows that $Q(p)$ and $Q(\sim p)$ both $= 0$ and that, accordingly, the rational agent who regards both p and $\sim p$ as fully indeterminate will believe both p and $\sim p$ to degree 0. For it is Field's leading idea that for an agent to treat a proposition as potentially indeterminate is for her to have degrees of belief in it and its negation that add to less than 1. But Field's account suffers from the same defect as 'third-possibility' views of indeterminacy. By having the rational agent believe both that Harry is bald and that he's not bald to degree 0, when Harry is a paradigm borderline case of a bald man, Field's account fails to reflect the *ambivalence* involved in treating a proposition and its negation as borderline; that is to say, it doesn't accommodate 'the absolutely basic datum that in general borderline cases come across as hard cases: as cases where we are baffled to choose between conflicting verdicts about which polar verdict applies' (Wright, 2001). This 'absolutely basic datum' is reflected in the fact that, when asked whether borderline Harry is definitely bald, the rational agent will unhesitatingly and fully assert no, thereby expressing her full belief that he isn't definitely bald, but will make an appropriately qualified judgement when asked if Harry is bald, thereby expressing a partial belief some way between complete belief and complete disbelief. Field can't reflect this because for him the agent will believe the proposition that Harry is bald to the same degree she believes the proposition that Harry is determinately bald. (The same objection to Field is made independently by David Barnett forthcoming.) Another, though related, problem for Field is that according to him the agent will believe to degree 0 that borderline Harry is bald no matter where Harry is in the penumbra of baldness. Intuitively, however, two people can both be borderline bald, even though one person is less or more bald than the other, and this difference should be reflected in the degree to which one believes each person to be bald. This was reflected in Sally's changing degrees of belief in the proposition that Tom was bald during the plucking even while Tom was squarely and determinately within the penumbra of baldness. The crux of the difference between Field and me is that for me, but not for Field, one can partially believe a proposition in one of two quite different ways. Thus, suppose you know that Al believes to degree .8 that Harry is bald. One thing this might mean is that Al thinks it's quite likely that Harry is determinately bald, but isn't in a position to believe that with total confidence. Another thing it might mean is that Al is in ideal circumstances for making baldness judgements and takes Harry to be borderline bald, but in a way that places Harry in that region of the penumbra that is close to determinate baldness (i.e. Al takes Harry to be balder than most other borderline bald men). And there are other possibilities when we consider the ways SPBs and VPBs can interact. For Field, however, Al's partial belief can mean only that he thinks it's quite likely that Harry is determinately bald.

a thing's being a borderline case of a property is a metaphysical status whose explication owes nothing to anyone's actual or potential propositional attitudes. The propositional attitude we have towards a borderline case can't be *constitutive* of a thing's being a borderline case of a property; it must merely be a *reflection of*, or *response to*, the thing's status as a borderline case. While it is perhaps true that VPBs track borderline cases, this is simply because a VPB is the appropriate attitude to have when confronted with a borderline case.

The problem with the feeling one is apt to have is that a VPB *couldn't* be the appropriate response to a borderline case if VPBs were trackers but not constituters. If being a borderline case were an ontological status explicable independently of VPBs or any other kind of propositional attitude, then a 'third-possibility' view of indeterminacy would be correct, and I agree with Crispin Wright that no such view is correct. Subject to a small qualification, I also agree with Wright when he further concludes: 'To reject the third possibility view is thus to reject the idea that in viewing the question, whether *P*, as indeterminate, one takes a view with any direct bearing on the question of the truth-value of *P*. I know of no way of making that idea intelligible except by construing indeterminacy as some kind of *epistemic* status.'[39] The small qualification is that I would conclude 'epistemic *or psychological* status', but I have it on the best authority that Wright didn't mean to exclude the kind of position I am advancing. In any case, if the epistemic theory *as defined above* were correct, then one would have an SPB, not a VPB, when confronted with a borderline case. This evidently means that the essence of being a borderline case would be captured by (D), were it true.

The philosopher who doubts that VPBs can constitute vagueness even though they might track it is perhaps coming at these issues from an entirely natural ontological view that owes something to Plato and that sees properties as entities that are in every sense ontologically and conceptually independent of whatever conceptual or linguistic practices govern our use of the predicates that express those properties. These properties, being vague, would admit of borderline cases, but their being borderline must be explained by characteristics of the vague properties, where these characteristics are in no sense explicable in terms of our linguistic or conceptual practices. On this view, we have seen, it makes no sense to suppose that VPBs track

---

[39] Wright (2001: 71).

vagueness; the appropriate response to a borderline case would be to s-believe that the borderline case had whatever characteristic of the vague property engenders borderline cases.

Standing opposed to this natural, albeit heavy-duty Platonic, conception of properties is my own pleonastic conception of them. On this, pleonastic, conception of properties, there is nothing more to the essence of a property than is determined for it by our property-hypostatizing linguistic and conceptual practices, and a property's being vague is explicable in terms of those practices. It is a *primitive and underived* feature of the conceptual role of each concept of a vague property that under certain conditions we form VPBs involving that concept, and *it is in this that vagueness consists*. To use a metaphor, what makes a property vague is simply the fact that its predicate name has an underived conceptual role that determines the name to go into a person's VPB box under certain conditions. When the sentence 'Tom is bald' goes into Sally's VPB box, it is not as a response to her perception of the independently explicable fact that he's a borderline case of baldness. His being a borderline case consists in the conceptual fact, and it is *this* that accounts for the familiar 'no-fact-of-the-matter' intuition many have about borderline cases. But since our conceptual practices exhaust what may be true of all properties and propositions, there can be no further question of what is 'really going on' at any non-conceptual level. In this regard, notice how unlike the case of vagueness is from a case where we really may want to say there is no fact of the matter. For suppose we are told that the concept of a shmadult is exhausted by these two conditions: anyone who has reached his or her twenty-second birthday is a shmadult, and anyone who has not yet reached his or her seventeenth birthday is not a shmadult. Confronted with someone we know to be 19 years old, we might well not v-believe that she is a shmadult but rather s-believe that it is not true that she is a shmadult and not true that she isn't a shmadult (which isn't to say that this inclination wouldn't land us with paradoxes of its own).

Let's say that one's VPB* that x is F is *F-concept-driven* when one is in ideal circumstances for judging x to be F and one's concept of being F precludes one from s-believing to any positive degree either that x is F or that x is not F and determines one to v-believe to some positive degree that x is F. Then we can say that:

(E) x is a borderline case of being F iff someone could have an *F*-concept-driven VPB* that x is F.

Needless to say, the notion of someone's having an F-concept-driven VPB* that x is F is, like everything else, vague, and one can v*-believe to some solidly intermediate degree whether the condition is satisfied in a given case, thereby starting the escalation known as 'higher-order vagueness'—borderline cases of borderline cases, borderline cases of borderline cases of borderline cases, and so on.

The way in which one's VPB* that x is F may be F-concept-driven permits a little more light to be thrown on what constitutes the 'ideal epistemic circumstances' required for a VPB to be a VPB*. There are two kinds of vague properties. If a vague property Φ belongs to the first kind, then there is some other property Ψ, however complex, such that Φ instantiations supervene on Ψ instantiations, and Φ judgements are based on Ψ judgements. Baldness is a property of this type, since baldness supervenes on the hair situation on a person's scalp and baldness judgements are based on hair-on-scalp-situation judgements. If a vague property Φ is of this kind, then to v*-believe that a thing has Φ is, possibly subject to a small qualification, to have one's VPB that the thing is Φ based on certain knowledge of the thing's Ψ situation (the possible qualification, discussed a couple of paragraphs below, pertains to the area where unqualified belief gets ever so slightly qualified). In our Tom Cruise thought experiment, Sally's VPBs are VPB*s because all of her judgements about Tom's baldness are based on certain knowledge of the hair situation on his scalp. For vague properties of this type, being in ideal epistemic circumstances for making a Φ judgement about a thing consists (possibly subject to the aforementioned qualification) in having certain knowledge of the thing's Ψ situation.

If a vague property Φ belongs to the second kind, then whether or not instantiations of that property supervene on instantiations of some other property Ψ, Φ judgements are not necessarily based on Ψ judgements. The canonical concepts of these properties have non-inferential applications that constitute knowledge when the believer knows that her non-inferentially based belief is undefeated. If one's VPB that x is F is non-inferential in this way and one knows that one's belief is undefeated, then one's VPB is a VPB*. Pain, for example, is a vague property of this type. A sensation which one knows oneself to have with certainty may be a borderline case of a pain. In the event, one's VPB that one is in pain is a VPB* if, as would normally be the case, one knows that nothing can be forthcoming to make one rationally revise one's partial belief. Colours are also vague properties of this type. One's belief that a thing before one is red will in the normal case not be based on inference; one's belief will be directly caused by one's sense experience. When the thing before one is borderline red, one's VPB that the thing is red will be non-inferential. If, as would normally be the case, one knows that nothing can be forthcoming to make one rationally revise one's partial belief, then one's VPB is also a VPB*.

Two features (at least!) of both (E) and the more basic account of indeterminacy, (C), need amplification. First, being a borderline case is a matter of degree, in that one thing can be more or less of a borderline case of such-and-such than another thing. Harry is a borderline case of being bald, but Lester, who is even closer to the mid-point between being determinately bald and determinately not bald, is more of a borderline case. This is distinct from the phenomenon of higher-order vagueness—being a borderline case of a borderline case, a borderline case of a borderline case of a borderline case, and so on. At the same time, the notions of SPB and VPB are, like virtually every other notion, vague, and in some cases it may be indeterminate whether someone flat-out believes p or v-believes p to a very high degree, and VPB shades into SPB in that VPBs are always *partial* beliefs: there isn't really (as opposed to merely notionally) any such thing as v-believing a proposition to degree 0 or to degree 1; one can only s-believe a proposition to degree 0 or to degree 1 (see 5.8). Nevertheless, I shall keep (C) and (E) as they are, now that we appreciate the idealizations implicit in them.

The second feature needing amplification is why I count a proposition as indeterminate if *just one person* can v*-believe it. Shouldn't I rather claim that *anyone* in ideal epistemic circumstances with respect to the proposition *would* v*-believe it? The reason I have it as I do is that I'm being cautious about a certain phenomenon characteristic of vagueness. It would seem that it is of the nature of vagueness that different people in the same ideal epistemic circumstances can differ, sometimes even radically, in their judgements about a thing's being a borderline case of a property (if we focus just on that mode of indeterminacy). Indeed, it is even the case that the same person, in the same ideal circumstances, would make different judgements on different occasions. It is a certainty that if we were to let Tom's hair grow back and repeat the experiment, Sally's qualified judgements on the second run wouldn't exactly match those of the first run. It would further seem that from a God's-eye perspective, the proposition being judged should qualify as being indeterminate. This is why the condition is formulated in terms of some one person's being able to have a VPB*.

Actually, what I just said needs qualification, and there's one kind of case that should be given explicit attention.[40] The qualification is that some, perhaps many, cases in which it appears that one person v*-believes a proposition to one degree while another person v*-believes the same proposition to a different degree are actually cases in which their VPB*s are not really about the same proposition. For example, imagine a person, Al, who says that a man who shaves or pulls out his hair doesn't count as bald, even when the man's scalp contains not a single hair visible to the unaided eye. According to Al, baldness requires *loss* of hair, and shaving your scalp or pulling out your hair doesn't count as losing your hair. Now, when in ideal epistemic circumstances Sally v*-believes to degree .5 Tom to be bald, Al, in the same ideal circumstances, says that Tom is definitely not bald. Here I think the correct thing to say is that Sally and Al are operating with somewhat different concepts of baldness, and that they are both correct.

But now—turning to the kind of case deserving explicit attention—consider the following story. On Sunday the Tom Cruise experiment is carried out and the point where Sally goes from believing to degree 1 that Tom isn't bald to believing that to an ever so slightly smaller degree is when the 2,393rd hair is plucked. It then happens that Sally is given a drug that causes her to forget Sunday's experiment, Tom's hair is miraculously restored, and the experiment performed again under identical conditions on Monday. This time the transition point occurs when the 2,387th hair is plucked. It may seem that I'm committed to saying that on Sunday Tom was to some extent a borderline case of baldness immediately after the 2,387th plucking when, at that point, Sally fully believed that Tom wasn't bald, because, as Sally proves on Monday, it is possible for someone to v-believe that Tom is bald at that point in the plucking. This may seem to be a problem. When on Sunday Sally believes to degree 1 that Tom isn't bald immediately after the 2,387th plucking, there seems nothing irrational or mistaken about her belief, but if Tom is in fact a borderline case of baldness (albeit to a minute extent), then it might

---

[40] Here and in the next paragraph I'm responding to the helpful comments in Marqueze (2000).

seem that I must after all hold that Sally isn't fully justified in believing to degree 1 that he isn't bald.

Two points. First, even if Tom is to some minute extent a border-line case of baldness, that wouldn't entail that one was irrational in believing that Tom was definitely bald. Such a belief can be rational even though one wouldn't have such a confident belief if one had in mind the larger epistemic picture. Secondly, I'm *not* committed to saying that Tom is definitely a borderline case of baldness by virtue of Sally's second judgement, because I'm not committed to saying that either of Sally's judgements were formed under ideal epistemic con-ditions. In setting up the example, I said that circumstances for mak-ing baldness judgements were ideal, and indeed they are—subject to a qualification. With no vague concept is there a definite point on one side of which lies the region of definite, or determinate, application, and on the other side of which lies the concept's penumbra. This is the region that generates higher-order vagueness, and no belief about Tom's baldness that Sally might form in this region can be a belief formed in ideal epistemic circumstances for judging baldness. This is because the concept of baldness is such that what *sort* of belief (an SPB or a VPB) gets produced in this region is to a large extent deter-mined by random vagaries of the situation, such as one's current mood or the associations one happens to be making at the time. The sort of 'epistemically ideal circumstances' I need for my purposes must make for a more settled disposition about the kind of partial belief apt to be produced in those circumstances. Of course, this (so to say) penumbral penumbral region is very vague and has therefore no definite starting or ending point. This is just to say what should come as no surprise, namely, that the notion of ideal epistemic circumstances is very vague. At the same time, the concept of such circumstances, like any other vague concept, can be put to work, because some epistemic conditions will be definitely ideal and others will be definitely not ideal.

5.7 COMPLEX VPBS AND THE INTERACTION OF VPBS AND SPBS

The fullest exposition of vagueness-related partial belief awaits answers to two related questions: What principles normatively govern logically complex VPBs? and What principles normatively govern the interaction of VPBs and SPBs? In other words, what principles normatively govern the formation of partial beliefs in any proposition?[41] I should confess at the outset that what I'm about to say is not entirely untentative.

SPB and VPB are distinct kinds of partial belief, each normatively governed by different principles. But SPBs and VPBs can interact, and there are principles that govern their modes of interaction. It is useful, however, to begin with the principles that govern each kind of partial belief at certain limits. In the case of SPB, this is when $SPB(p) + SPB(\sim p) = 1$ (and $VPB(p) + VPB(\sim p) = 0$); and in the case of VPB, this is when $VPB(p) + VPB(\sim p) = 1$ (and $SPB(p) + SPB(\sim p) = 0$). The case in which $SPB(p) + SPB(\sim p) = 1$ represents one's certainty that p is determinate, either determinately true or determinately false, and the case in which $VPB(p) + VPB(\sim p) = 1$ represents one's certainty that p is indeterminate, neither determinately true nor determinately false. As we'll see, SPB and VPB may interact in a way such that both $SPB(p) + SPB(\sim p)$ and $VPB(p) + VPB(\sim p)$ are positive but less than 1. It is only in the limit when $SPB(p)$ and $SPB(\sim p)$ add to 1 that SPB may (under suitable idealization) be identified with subjective probability. This is why when I introduced SPB in 5.4, I said that SPB was the kind of partial belief which *subject to a certain qualification* can under suitable idealization be identified with subjective probability. The identification would be complete if there were no VPBs, but the identification needs qualification when SPBs interact with VPBs.

We know how logically complex SPBs are normatively governed when $SPB(p)$ and $SPB(\sim p)$ add to 1—namely, by the standard axioms of probability theory. But we haven't yet considered how VPBs are normatively governed when in the limit $VPB(p)$ and $VPB(\sim p)$ add to 1. It will be heuristically useful to begin with this case before considering the principles that normatively govern the interaction of the two kinds of partial belief. Here I would like to suggest that, while the Łukasiewiczian might not have given an adequate degree-theoretic account of *truth*, what she says may be used to characterize VPBs

---

[41] A principle *normatively governs* the formation of partial belief just in case the principle is satisfied in the formation of partial belief *under suitable idealization*. What counts as a suitable idealization, over and above perfect rationality, will depend on the kind of partial belief in question.

when $VPB(p) + VPB(\sim p) = 1$. I'll ignore conditionals for now because of the unique problems they present (conditionals will be dealt with in Chapter 7), and, to keep the discussion simple, I'll also ignore the rules for $\forall$ and $\exists$, since they derive in a familiar way from [&] and [v], respectively. The proposal then is that, in the limit in question:

[$\sim$] $VPB(\sim p) = 1 - VPB(p)$
[&] $VPB(p \& q) = Min[VPB(p), VPB(q)]$
[v] $VPB(p \vee q) = Max[VPB(p), VPB(q)]$.

Two things to be said for [$\sim$] are, first, that it seems intuitively right (when Sally v-believes to degree .5 that Tom is bald she seems, *ipso facto*, to v-believe to degree .5 that he's not bald) and, secondly, it captures the all-important fact that our reaction to a borderline case is ambivalence.

Perhaps the most salient feature of VPB is the intuitiveness of the claim that Sally would v-believe to degree .5 that Tom is bald and thin when she v-believes each conjunct to degree .5, even though she regards the conjoined propositions as unrelated. This is captured by [&]. What will give one pause is that it follows that Sally will also v-believe to degree .5 that Tom is bald and not bald when she v-believes each conjunct to degree .5. But is this really unacceptable? First, v-believing a proposition to degree .5 is consistent with knowing that no proposition of its form can be determinately true. Secondly, a not unnatural reaction to the question 'Is Tom bald?', when Tom is a borderline case of baldness, is to say, albeit with appropriate ambivalence, 'Well, he sort of is and sort of isn't.' Thirdly, the truth-theoretic Łukasiewiczian version of [&] is not unmotivated, and there is something degree-of-truthish about v-believing a proposition, for if one v-believes that Harry is bald to a greater degree than one v-believes that Tom is bald, then one s-believes that Harry is balder than Tom (I'll have a little more to say on this below). The truth-theoretic version of [&] isn't unmotivated because if, as it were, God were to assure you that it was a *fact* that *both* the proposition that Tom was bald *and* the proposition that he wasn't bald were true to degree .5, then how could you rationally think that the conjunction of those two propositions was itself true to a degree other than .5? Fourthly, I've already suggested that one can v*-believe instances of excluded middle.[42] Suppose, then, one

---

[42] See also the further discussion of this in 5.8.

v-believes to degree .5 that Tom is bald or not bald. Then, by [~], one also v-believes to degree .5 that Tom is not (bald or not bald); but to v-believe that Tom is not (bald or not bald) is to v-believe that he's neither bald nor not not bald, which in turn is evidently to v-believe that he's not bald and bald.

Finally, [v] is arguably the most plausible rule, since it has a transparent motivation when the disjuncts are compatible, and I've suggested that the rule is plausible for instances of excluded middle.

I turn now to the question of how VPBs and SPBs interact. The basic law governing their interaction is that the ideally rational agent's partial beliefs in a proposition and its negation always add to 1. That is,

$$VPB(p) + VPB(\sim p) + SPB(p) + SPB(\sim p) = 1$$

always holds for every proposition in which the agent has any kind of partial belief.[43]

As already noted,

$$SPB(p) + SPB(\sim p) = 1$$

represents the agent's taking p to be either determinately true or determinately false, while

$$VPB(p) + VPB(\sim p) = 1$$

represents the agent's taking p to be indeterminate, that is, neither determinately true nor determinately false.

There are certain asymmetries between SPB and VPB. First, one can s-believe p to a degree greater than 0 and less than 1 while s-believing $\sim p$ to degree 0, but if one v-believes p to a degree greater than 0 and less than 1, then one will also v-believe $\sim p$ to a degree greater than 0 and less than 1. For one can think that p might be determinately true even though one thinks there is no chance that p is determinately false—one may be confident that Harry is either determinately bald or else a borderline case of a bald man; but to think that Harry is a borderline case of a bald man is *ipso facto* also to think he's a borderline case of a not-bald man. This is because for a proposition to be indeterminate (as all borderline propositions are) is for it to be neither determinately true nor determinately false.

---

[43] I owe the idea for this generalization to Hartry Field.

Secondly, whereas one may well s-believe p to degree 0 or 1, there is a sense in which one can't *really* v-believe p to degree 0 or 1; 0 and 1 are merely notional degrees as regards VPBs, since v-believing p to degree 1 collapses into s-believing p to degree 1, and v-believing p to degree 0 is allowed only when $SPB(p) + SPB(\sim p) = 1$.

Let's see how this plays out in three cases: (*a*) the case in which one both s- and v-believes the same non-logically complex proposition;[44] (*b*) the case in which one both s- and v-believes $(p \& / v q)$ when $SPB(p) + SPB(\sim p) = 1$ and $VPB(q) + VPB(\sim q) = 1$; and (*c*) the case in which one both s- and v-believes $(p \& / v q)$ when $SPB(p/\sim p)$, $SPB(q/\sim q)$, $VPB(p/\sim p)$ and $VPB(q/\sim q)$ are all positive.

(*a*) *One s- and v-believes the same non-logically complex proposition.* It will help to work with a highly artificial case. Sally s-believes to degree 1 that the hair situation on Tom's scalp is either H or else H'. If she were certain that H obtained, she would s-believe to degree 1 that Tom was bald; that is, intuitively put, H's obtaining would, she is certain, secure that Tom was determinately bald. Let's suppose that Sally s-believes to degree .7 that H obtains. If, however, Sally were certain that H' obtained, then she would v-believe to degree .8 that Tom was bald and to degree .2 that he wasn't bald. Consequently, since she s-believes to degree .3 that H' obtains, she v-believes that Tom is bald to degree .24 and to degree .06 that he isn't bald. In this situation, Sally in effect has no SPB that Tom is not bald, for, so to say, she's confident that he's either determinately bald or else a borderline case of a bald man, but it helps to represent this formally by saying that Sally s-believes to degree 0 that Tom is not bald. If Sally were in ideal epistemic circumstances for judging Tom's baldness, and assuming she's right about H and H' being the only two hair-situation possibilities, then she would either s-believe to degree 1 that Tom was bald and to degree 0 that he wasn't bald or else v*-believe to degree .8 that he was bald and to degree .2 that he wasn't bald. As things are, the situation is fully described by saying that Sally s-believes to degree .7 that Tom is bald, s-believes to degree 0 that he's not bald, v-believes to degree .24 that he's bald, and v-believes to degree .06 that he's not bald.

(*b*) *One both s- and v-believes $(p \& / v q)$ when $SPB(p) + SPB(\sim p) = 1$ and $VPB(q) + VPB(\sim q) = 1$.* An example of such a mixed complex belief would be Sally's partial belief that (Tom is bald (B) and she left

---

[44] I somehow managed to overlook this case in Schiffer (2000*b*), and because of that egregious oversight what I there said about case (*b*) was wrong.

her glasses in her office (G)), when she takes B and G to be independent and where for her $VPB(B) = .6$, $VPB(\sim B) = .4$, $SPB(G) = .3$, and $SPB(\sim G) = .7$. Here it seems reasonable to say that $SPB(B \& G) =$ 0 and $SPB(\sim(B \& G)) = .7$, since for Sally there is no chance the conjunction can be determinately true but there is a 70 per cent chance that it is determinately false. But what should $VPB(B \& G)$ and $VPB(\sim(B \& G))$ be for her? $VPB(\sim(B \& G))$ should be .12: Sally reckons there's a 30 per cent chance that $\sim G$ is determinately false, and given certain knowledge that $\sim G$ was false, $VPB(\sim(B \& G)) = VPB(\sim B) = .4$, which means we should take $VPB(\sim(B \& G))$ to be the product of $SPB(G)$ and $VPB(\sim B)$, which is .12. Since $SPB(\sim(B \& G))$ and $VPB(\sim(B \& G))$ add to .82, $VPB(B \& G)$ must be .18. The positive rationale for this is that, given certain knowledge that G was true, $VPB(B \& G) = VPB(B) = .6$; so we should calculate $VPB(B \& G)$ as the product of $SPB(G)$ and $VPB(B)$, which is .18. Analogously, $SPB(B \vee G)$ $= .3$; $SPB(\sim(B \vee G)) = 0$; $VPB(B \vee G) = .42$; and $VPB(\sim(B \vee G)) = .28$.

(c) One both s- and v-believes $(p \& / \vee q)$ when $SPB(p/\sim p)$, $SPB(q/\sim q)$, $VPB(p/\sim p)$, and $VPB(q/\sim q)$ are all positive. Here $SPB(p \& / \vee q)$ and $SPB(\sim(p \& / \vee q))$ are calculated in the standard probabilistic way for SPB, and $VPB(p \& / \vee q)$ and $VPB(\sim(p \& / \vee q))$ are calculated by the Łukasiewiczian rules [&/∨], except, of course, that neither $SPB(p \& / \vee q)$ and $SPB(\sim(p \& / \vee q))$ nor $VPB(p \& / \vee q)$ and $VPB(\sim(p \& / \vee q))$ will add to 1 (since all four must add to 1). It will help to have even an abstractly described example, but one whose structure is fairly simple. Let's suppose the following holds for ideally rational Sally:

- p and q are independent by every intuitive measure.
- $SPB(p) = .4$; $SPB(\sim p) = .4$; $VPB(p) = .1$; and $VPB(\sim p) = .1$
- $SPB(q) = .4$; $SPB(\sim q) = .4$; $VPB(q) = .1$; and $VPB(\sim q) = .1$.

As we should expect, $SPB(p \& q) = .16$ and $SPB(\sim(p \& q))$, as we should also expect, $= SPB(\sim p \vee \sim q) = SPB(\sim p) + SPB(\sim q) - SPB(\sim p \& \sim q) = .4 + .4 - .16 = .64$. Thus, $VPB(p \& q)$ and $VPB(\sim(p \& q))$ must add to .2, but how should the degrees of belief be distributed between these two partial beliefs? Well, $VPB(p \& q) = Min[VPB(p), VPB(q)] = .1$ and $VPB(\sim(p \& q)) = VPB(\sim p \vee \sim q) = Max[VPB(\sim p), VPB(\sim q)] = .1$.

We could go on with this, but something tells me that a sceptic about VPB won't have her scepticism emerge in the further arithmetical details.

5.8 VAGUENESS-RELATED PARTIAL
BELIEF AND THE SORITES PARADOX

How does the foregoing account of vagueness and borderline cases apply to the sorites? That paradox is manifested in the inference SI from 5.2:

(1) A person with $50 million is rich.
(2) $\forall n$(a person with $\$n$ is rich $\rightarrow$ a person with $\$n - 1\cent$ is also rich).
(3) $\therefore$ A person with only $37\cent$ is rich.

Since premiss (1) is obviously true, the conclusion is obviously false, and the validity of SI turns just on modus ponens and universal instantiation, one is apt to suppose that, at the least, the sorites premiss, (2), is somehow unacceptable. But we also noticed (in 5.2) that what makes this premiss apt to seem acceptable is the argument for it, SPA:

(i) $\sim\exists n$(the proposition that [a person with $\$n$ is rich & a person with $\$n - 1\cent$ isn't rich] is true).
(ii) $\sim\exists n$(the proposition that [a person with $\$n$ is rich & a person with $\$n - 1\cent$ isn't rich] is true) $\rightarrow \forall n$(a person with $\$n$ is rich $\rightarrow$ a person with $\$n - 1\cent$ is also rich).
(iii) $\therefore \forall n$(a person with $\$n$ is rich $\rightarrow$ a person with $\$n - 1\cent$ is also rich).

SPA, we noticed, creates its own paradox, since it is valid by modus ponens, has an apparently unacceptable conclusion, but also has two premisses that are apt to appear true, at least when considered on their own. Where must I stand on SI and SPA?

My account of indeterminacy commits me to holding that the sorites premiss in SI is indeed unacceptable—not because it is determinately false or because it is determinately neither true nor false, but rather because it is indeterminate.[45] This is best made clear by considering the long version of SI which forgoes universal instantiation and relies instead on millions of applications of modus ponens. A good many of these premisses will be determinately true; some

---

[45] Here I correct Schiffer (2000b).

will be determinately indeterminate (both the amount of money mentioned in its antecedent and that amount less 1¢ will be smack in the middle of the penumbra of the vague concept *rich*); none will be determinately false, for there is no amount of money such that it is determinately true that having that amount suffices for being rich but determinately false that having 1¢ less also makes you rich; and none will be determinately neither true nor false, for my account of VPB commits me to its being indeterminate whether borderline propositions are true or false.

Similarly, as regards SPA, I'm committed to holding that premiss (i) is indeterminate.[46] Once again, I take it to be obvious that (i) isn't determinately false: there is no numeral α such that the proposition expressed by $\ulcorner R(\alpha) \,\&\, {\sim}R(\alpha - 1)\urcorner$ is determinately true. Yet, also once again, I can't take (i) to be determinately true. There are two ways in which it might be determinately true: if (*a*) every proposition expressed by an instance of '$R(\alpha) \,\&\, {\sim}R(\alpha - 1)$' were determinately false, or if (*b*) some of those propositions were determinately neither true nor false. But (*a*) would imply the truth of the sorites premiss, and (*b*) is ruled out, for me, by my VPB-based account of indeterminacy.

My response to SPA might seem reasonable, given that its conclusion is indeterminate: one might expect a valid inference with an indeterminate conclusion to have a premiss that is either determinately false or indeterminate. My response to the sorites itself, however, may seem less felicitous. For not only must I hold that it is indeterminate whether the sorites premiss is false (and thus indeterminate whether it is true), but, since I must hold that it is indeterminate whether SI has true premisses and a false conclusion, I must also hold that it is indeterminate whether the inference is valid according to our common-sense notion of validity which classical logic seeks to formalize. An inference is valid by that notion of validity if it is impossible for its premisses to be true and its conclusion false, but I'm committed to holding that, though SI's conclusion is false, it is indeterminate whether its premisses are true. Nor can I very happily say that our common-sense conception of validity merely requires that if the premisses are determinately true, then so is the

---

[46] Perhaps my account also commits me holding that (ii) is indeterminate as well, but if it does, I must still hold that the disjunction of (i) and (ii) is indeterminate.

conclusion. For given that entailment is contrapositive (if p entails q, then $\sim q$ entails $\sim p$), one might expect the inference

$$R(\$50\,\mathrm{m})$$
$$\sim R(37\text{¢})$$
$$\therefore \sim \forall n(R(\$n) \rightarrow R(\$n - 1\text{¢}))$$

to be determinately valid if SI is. But if I'm right, it has determinately true premises and an indeterminate conclusion. I don't, however, think we should regard the displayed contraposed version of SI as invalid. Validity is a *semantic* notion, but indeterminacy, by my lights, is a *psychological* notion, so we are right to suppose that the pre-theoretic notion of validity that classical logic hopes to make precise is that an inference is valid just in case there is no possible world in which its premises are true and its conclusion isn't. In this sense, I'm committed to holding that it is indeterminate whether the displayed inference is valid.

Since what I've just said about SI also applies, *mutatis mutandis*, to its long version that relies only on modus ponens, I'm committed to holding that it is indeterminate whether modus ponens is a valid inference rule. There can of course be no determinate *counter-example* to modus ponens, but if I'm right, modus ponens can take us from premises that are indeterminately true to a false conclusion. Shouldn't we therefore junk the theory of indeterminacy that brought us to this result?

I don't think so. We are just being confronted with the way in which the sorites can't have a happy-face solution. The sorites, as manifested in SI, consists of three apparently mutually incompatible propositions each one of which is apt to appear plausible when viewed on its own: $R(\$50\,\mathrm{m})$, $\sim R(37\text{¢})$, and $\forall n(R(\$n) \rightarrow R(\$n - 1\text{¢}))$. I hold that the first two propositions are determinately true, the third indeterminate. It follows that I must say that it is indeterminate whether all the members of the paradox set are true, indeterminate, therefore, whether the members of the set are mutually incompatible. This result would belong to a happy-face solution to the sorites if I could give a satisfactory explanation that would explain away our paradox-inducing intuitions, but I can't. At the same time, I think a satisfactory explanation can be given of why a satisfactory explanation can't be given, and that explanation constitutes my unhappy-face solution to the sorites.

It is constitutive of vagueness that when confronted with a border-line proposition we have some inclination to accept it as true and some inclination to accept it as false. Our being conflicted in this way is of the essence of VPB. VPB is the psychological state induced by the conceptual conflict. What generates the conflict in the first place is the status that the truth-and-falsity schemas for propositions—

> The proposition that S is true iff S
> The proposition that S is false iff not S

—and the law of excluded middle (every proposition of the form S or not S is true) have in our conceptual repertoire. The underived conceptual roles of our notions of truth and disjunction dispose us to accept instances of excluded middle and the truth schemas, and these underived conceptual roles conspire with the underived conceptual role of each vague concept to cause a proposition to go into one's VPB box when a vague concept deployed in the proposition manifests the unsettled nature characteristic of its borderline applications. These are features of *underived* conceptual roles, and there is no conceptual court of appeals to sort things out.

Be that as it may. I take the more interesting question to be whether the paradoxes of indeterminacy have a *weak* or a *strong* unhappy-face solution. This is to ask whether we can have a paradox-free conceptual revision, thereby yielding a mildly unhappy-face solution, or whether there can be no such revision, thereby yielding a very unhappy-face solution. It all comes down to whether there is a suitable logic we might adopt—together, perhaps, with ancillary adjustments in our concepts of truth and falsity and/or our psychological responses to borderline cases.

Even while ignoring the semantic paradoxes, I don't think we can get out of conceptual quandary simply by resolutely adhering to classical logic, deeming it to be the determinately correct theory of the deductive consequence relation. Maybe this would be OK if we could somehow replace all our vague concepts with absolutely precise ones,[47] but that is clearly out of the question given how limited we are as information-processing devices. For suppose we stipulated classical logic. We should then have to decide whether it is to be accompanied

---

[47] Or maybe not: for problems regarding the semantic paradoxes and classical logic, see Field (forthcoming).

by a bivalent or a supervaluationist semantics. If we took the bivalent option, then we should have no use for vagueness-related partial belief (VPB). Confronted with borderline Harry, we would have to suppose that it was either true that Harry was bald or else true that he wasn't bald, in which case we should s-believe that Harry is bald to some suitable positive degree $n > 0 < 1$ and s-believe that he's not bald to degree $1 - n$. Actually, it's doubtful we could pull off the resolution, since it's doubtful we could maintain the certain belief that it was either a fact that Harry was bald or else a fact that he wasn't. Suppose, however, that we could take a pill that would enable us to have the appropriate convictions. We still wouldn't have achieved a paradox-free conceptual revision, for we would still be stuck with all the puzzles engendered by the epistemic theory of vagueness: How to explain why we can't know the truth about Harry's baldness, given that it is either true that he's bald or else true that he's not bald? How to account for how our use of 'bald' succeeds in having the word refer to an absolutely precise property (e.g. the property of having fewer than 3,241 hairs on one's scalp)?

Suppose we resolved to conjoin classical logic with a non-bivalent semantics, such as a supervaluationist semantics, whereby the proposition that borderline Harry was bald or not bald was determinately true, even though neither disjunct was true. I don't think this would give us the relief from quandary we seek. First, as Hartry Field has shown, while 'liar sentences' show that the naive theory of truth which accepts the unrestricted schema

'S' is true iff S

is inconsistent in classical logic, any attempt to restore consistency by weakening the naive theory 'requires massive revisions in ordinary principles about truth...that would be very hard to live with'.[48] Secondly, we would still be left struggling with the puzzle of how it could be true that someone in the car was asleep when Al and Betty were the only ones in the car and it was neither true that Al was asleep nor that Betty was, and of how it could be true that Al was or was not asleep when it was neither true that he was nor true that he wasn't. Thirdly, the revision would demand the impossible of us. Vagueness-related partial belief isn't some extra thing built on top of our ordinary concepts (being bald, being red, etc.). V-believing that borderline

----

[48] Field (forthcoming).

Harry is bald is how we *have* to respond to Harry given the concept of baldness we actually have; it belongs to the underived conceptual role of our concept of baldness that we are somewhat inclined to judge him bald and somewhat inclined to judge him not bald. These inclinations *just are* VPBs. But v-believing a borderline proposition would be an inappropriate response if we replaced our notion of truth with the supervaluationist's supertruth (truth-in-all-admissible-precisifications). If truth were supertruth, then the appropriate response to a borderline proposition would be to s-believe to degree 1 both that the proposition wasn't true and that it wasn't false. This could hardly sit beside partially believing that the proposition was true and partially believing that it was false.

If there's to be a weak unhappy-face solution to the sorites, then it would seem that it must entail a rejection of excluded middle. Hartry Field has proposed that in order to deal both with the semantic paradoxes and with vagueness and indeterminacy we should weaken classical logic by restricting the law of excluded middle.[49] We should reject problematic instances of excluded middle such as the proposition that borderline Harry is or isn't bald. But how, Field asks, should we understand 'rejection'? We don't want rejection to be denial, for that would mean that when we reject $p \vee {\sim}p$ we were accepting ${\sim}(p \vee {\sim}p)$, which on any reasonable logic would entail the contradiction ${\sim}p$ & ${\sim}{\sim}p$. Nor do we want rejection simply to be refusal to accept, for that won't allow us to distinguish taking a proposition to be indeterminate from thinking that it is likely to be indeterminate. Happily, Field agrees with me that rejecting $p \vee {\sim}p$ should be explained in terms of non-classical degrees of belief whereby one may believe $p \vee {\sim}p$ to a degree less than 1 without taking it to be false (unhappily—see note 37—he disagrees about the SPB–VPB distinction). To see how this might play out in a way that is agreeable to my account of indeterminacy, let's reconsider the Łukasiewiczian continuum-valued semantics briefly touched on in 5.2 (pp. 191–3).

The fuzzy logic accompanying this fuzzy semantics can take validity to be preservation of the designated value 1, whereby an inference is valid just in case its conclusion has value 1 if the conjunction of its premises has value 1, or it can take validity to be preservation of minimum value, so that the value of the conclusion is never less than that

---

[49] Field (forthcoming).

of the conjunction of its premises, and there are other less attractive options. On the first account of validity, SI—

$R(\$50\,m)$
$\forall n(R(\$n) \rightarrow R(\$n - 1\cent))$
$\therefore R(37\cent)$

—is valid, but on the second it is invalid. On both accounts the inference that contraposes the conclusion and sorites premiss—

$R(\$50\,m)$
$\sim R(37\cent)$
$\therefore \sim\forall n(R(\$n) \rightarrow R(\$n - 1\cent))$

—is invalid. Now, when I first considered the Łukasiewiczian semantics, I construed its semantic values as degrees of truth, thereby making it a 'third possibility' view of indeterminacy, and thus subject to various problems, not to mention making VPB otiose. But Field's construal of the non-classical logic he uses implies a way around this.[50]

Let's not understand the semantic values of fuzzy logic as degrees of truth, since construing them in that way precludes an adequate conceptual revision in more than one way. Let's not give any explicit construal of them, but let them earn their meaning implicitly, via their role in our total theory, which ties our understanding of them to the degrees of partial belief appropriate to them. The details would need to be worked out,[51] but the crucial idea would be that:

- When one assigns p value $1/0$ (and thus assigns $\sim p$ value $0/1$), one s-believes p to degree $1/0$. In this case VPB(p) and VPB($\sim p$) add to 0. This represents taking p to be determinately true/false.
- When one assigns p value n, for $n > 0 < 1$ (and thus assigns $\sim p$ value $1 - n$), then one v-believes p to degree n and v-believes $\sim p$ to degree $1 - n$. In this case SPB(p) and SPB($\sim p$) add to 0. This represents taking p to be indeterminate to degree n.

On this way of construing semantic values, we can allow the semantic value of 'True$(p \lor \sim p)$' to be greater than 0 and less than 1 for borderline

[50] Field (forthcoming).
[51] As we'll see in Ch. 7, our representation of ordinary-language conditionals can't be given by the rule [⊃] $(T(p \supset q) = 1$ if $T(p) \leq T(q)$, $1 - [T(p) - T(q)]$ otherwise). I won't here try to work out how they should be represented in a suitable non-classical logic. There is of course no problem with the material conditional, given the equivalence of '$p \rightarrow q$' and '$\sim p \lor q$'.

p, as opposed to the value 0, which it would have if 'True(p)' meant that p had value 1. This is crucial for avoiding a 'third possibility' account of indeterminacy.

Would adopting a fuzzy logic in the foregoing way give us a paradox-free conceptual revision, thereby constituting a weak unhappy-face solution to the sorites? The question is confused. Given our refusal to understand the values of the continuum-valued logic as degrees of truth and the subsequent way our understanding of those values was implicitly based on the partial beliefs appropriate to them, the Łukasiewiczian continuum-valued logic isn't in competition with classical logic. It doesn't in any sense replace a logic that isn't determinately correct with one we can deem to be determinately correct, and it doesn't need to be 'adopted'. In whatever sense it can be 'deemed correct' and we can 'have' it, it is already correct and we already have it. The sense in which it may be determinately correct is entirely consistent with the sense in which it may be indeterminate whether classical logic is correct. In fact, given the recommended construal of it, the fuzzy logic is, in a sense, nothing more than a theory that spells out the ways in which classical logic is indeterminate. To see the point, consider a theorist who first claims that it is indeterminate whether classical logic gives a correct account of the consequence relation, and that therefore there is no non-classical logic that is determinately correct, but who next claims that he can nevertheless give a correct 'logic of belief', a formal system that shows what partial belief one may have in the conclusion of an inference given one's partial beliefs in the premisses and whose rules of inference secured that inferences made in accordance with them secured the value 1 for the conclusion, if the premisses all have value 1. This 'logic' would be non-classical in that, for example, it did not require one to s-believe

$$\sim\forall n(R(\$n) \to R(\$n - 1\cent))$$

to degree 1 when one s-believed each of

$R(\$50\,\mathrm{m})$
$\sim R(37\cent)$

to degree 1, *but this theory's being determinately correct on the intended interpretation would be entirely consistent with the claim that it was indeterminate whether classical logic was correct.* What's important isn't what we privilege to call logic, but whether our understanding of a formal system constitutes a genuine alternative to classical logic as a theory of the consequence relation, in its intended sense of 'consequence'. Of course, there is one important sense in which the non-classical fuzzy logic would fill a logical need created by the indeterminacy of classical logic. Since, as we've seen, classical logic can take us from determinately true premises to an indeterminate conclusion, we do have a need to know what inference rules will preserve determinate truth, and the Łukasiewiczian continuum-valued logic, or some not too dissimilar non-classical logic, may do that. Its inference rules will in effect tell us which classical rules of inference preserve determinate truth, and this is something we certainly want to know.

Does what I'm saying constitute a strong or a weak unhappy-face solution to the sorites paradox? At the least, the question has lost most of its interest, if my account of the full story is correct. It is not a weak unhappy-face solution in that it doesn't offer any conceptual *revision*, and thus, a fortiori, doesn't offer the paradox-free conceptual revision definitive of a weak unhappy-face solution. But so what, if we may know which claims of classical logic are determinately correct and which ones aren't, and if we have inference rules at our disposal to tell us which classical inference rules preserve determinate truth?

I sometimes hear the objection that I'm 'giving up' or 'suspending' classical logic and that that's a bad thing to do. The complaint is confused. In the first place, classical logic isn't an *activity* or *practice*; it is best construed as a *theory* of the consequence relation and of logical truth. There is no reason to suppose that every pronouncement of this theory is determinately true. What theory about anything has everything exactly right? Classical logic holds that 'Borderline Harry is bald or not bald' is a consequence of the empty set of premises and thus a logical truth. I say that it is indeterminate whether it's true that Harry is bald or not bald; indeterminate, therefore, whether every instance of excluded middle is true. The issue isn't about what we should *do*; it is about whether a certain theory is *true*, and it is not preposterous to hold that certain instances of excluded middle—namely, those whose disjuncts are indeterminate—are not determinately true. In the second place, we are not put in dire straits by accepting the claim that some of classical logic's claims aren't determinately true, because our inferential practices don't seem to be affected in any very bad way. Classical logic is for the most part a perfectly good logic even for vague language, since to say that a claim is *vague* isn't to claim that it is *indeterminate* (the sentence 'Jennifer Lopez is a woman' is vague but determinately true), and the vast majority of vague claims aren't indeterminate. And there is reason to think that something like a Łukasiewiczian continuum-valued logic can provide us with reliable inference rules for the preservation of determinate truth. Truth be told, now that we've reached this point, I'm not sure I haven't offered a sort of happy-face solution to the sorites.

5.9   TWO REMAINING QUESTIONS

The first of these is: Are VPBs really *beliefs*? There can be little doubt that in making one of her qualified assertions that Tom is bald midway through his being plucked, Sally is expressing *some* relation to the proposition that Tom is bald. Let's dub this relation, whatever its nature, 'V'. Given the way V-ing is related to making a qualified assertion that such-and-such, and given that one can't make a qualified assertion that such-and-such without being prepared to make the same qualified assertion that it is true that such-and-such, we know that to V a proposition is to V that it is true. So, V-ing is a propositional attitude, and it's a propositional attitude that comes in degrees. But are V states partial *beliefs*? The reason for doubting that they are is that being an SPB—i.e. being the sort of partial belief which under idealization satisfies the axioms of probability theory—is apt to seem definitive of the contribution beliefs make in the production of behaviour, and something that can't be used to explain behaviour in the way beliefs standardly do has no business being called a belief. 'VPB' may be read as just another name for V states, whether or not they are partial beliefs, and we can see the dilemma for them in the following way.

You have one concern: to find your heart medicine as soon as possible. You s-believe to degree .67 that it's at place P and you s-believe to degree .33 that it's at place P'. The two places are equidistant from you, and you have easy access to both. There are no competing desires. Clearly, you will first look for your medicine at place P. But now suppose that instead of s-believing to those degrees, you V to those degrees, where your V-ing is based on your taking the stuff in question to be a borderline case of your heart medicine. It is no longer clear what you would do. What good, you may wonder, would a borderline case of your medicine do?

My initial intuitive basis for claiming that VPBs are a species of partial belief was the way they are implicated in the production of qualified assertions, evidently a hallmark of partial belief. Still, VPBs would be a very Pickwickian species of partial belief if the only behaviour they explained were qualified assertions of borderline propositions. But so what? Then I've explained vagueness and indeterminacy in terms of Pickwickian partial belief, or, if even that sounds tendentious, then I've explained them in terms of a new kind of propositional attitude, one that comes in degrees and that precludes standard partial beliefs. Nevertheless, I can do better than that; I do think VPBs are a species of partial belief that explains behaviour. For VPBs behave *as if* they were SPBs about the degree to which their propositional contents were true. The 'as if' is crucial, however: there is no reducing *x v-believes p to degree n* to *x believes that p is true to degree n*. First, the believer need have no concept of degrees of truth. Secondly, two people, or the same person at different times, may be equally correct in v-believing a proposition to different degrees, but this wouldn't be possible if v-believing a proposition to a certain degree reduced to believing that the proposition was true to that degree. For consider again our thought experiment in which the Tom Cruise experiment is miraculously performed from start to finish on two occasions, and that at a certain point in the plucking on the first run, Sally v-believes to degree .48 that Tom is bald, while at the same point in the plucking on the second run she v-believes that he's bald to degree .5. If this were equivalent to Sally's first believing that Tom was bald to degree .48 and then believing that he's bald to degree .5, then it couldn't be that both beliefs were true, nor, therefore, that she was equally correct on both occasions. Thirdly, if the reduction obtained, the applicable degree-theoretic notion of truth would be Łukasiewiczian, and we already know that the 'third possibility' view of indeterminacy it entails is unacceptable. What recommends the 'as if' gloss is considerations like the following.

Pretend that we had a coherent, Łukasiewiczian degree-theoretic notion of truth and that Sally believed that the proposition that Tom was bald was true to degree .5. This would be a straightforward SPB of Sally's and would explain her behaviour if it interacted in appropriate ways with desires whose propositional contents themselves concerned degrees of truth. For example, if it's her policy not to take aspirin unless she's having a sensation that was definitely a pain, then we could explain her not taking aspirin by citing the fact that she believed that the proposition that her sensation was a pain was true only to degree .4. My point is that we can achieve what is in effect the same explanation by citing the fact that she v-believes to degree .4 that her sensation is a pain.

The second remaining question is whether vagueness and indeterminacy belong to the world or merely to our thought and talk about the world. This question is itself pretty vague, but I think I can cover its relevant precisifications with the following claims. First, there certainly are vague properties: there is one for each utterance of a vague predicate. This is a corollary of my account of pleonastic properties, as well as of my account of pleonastic propositions. Secondly, there certainly are vague objects, in that there are objects with indeterminate boundaries. For example, there are numerous molecules such that it is indeterminate whether they belong to my body, and New England is a vague object, since it is indeterminate where precisely it begins and ends. It's not that 'Stephen Schiffer' and 'New England' sort-of-refer to myriad things; 'Stephen Schiffer' determinately refers to me, though it is indeterminate whether certain molecules belong to me, and 'New England' determinately refers to a geographical region, albeit one with vague boundaries. Thirdly, there being vague objects and properties in the sense just claimed is compatible with the further claim that all such vague objects and properties supervene on absolutely precise objects and properties, perhaps even objects and properties so finely and precisely individuated that we're incapable of having any useful kind of thought or talk about them. Nothing in what I have to say precludes this, although it seems unlikely given the current state of quantum physics.

What about Gareth Evans's famous argument to show that there can't be vague objects, objects that have fuzzy boundaries?[52] That argument may be reconstructed as follows.[53]

If there were vague objects, then there would be objects a and b such that

(i) It is indeterminate whether $a = b$.

Now, (i) ascribes to b the property of being such that it is indeterminate whether it is identical to a. Yet this isn't a property a has, since

(ii) It is not indeterminate whether $a = a$.

So, by Leibniz's law, if (i) were true, it would entail that $a \neq b$. But (i) can't be true if it entails that $a \neq b$. Therefore there can be no vague objects.

[52] Evans (1985a).   [53] Cf. Lewis (1988).

One problem with this argument is that even if it shows that identity can't be indeterminate, it doesn't thereby show that there are no vague objects; a separate argument would be needed to show that the existence of vague objects entails indeterminate identity. Such an argument may be hard to come by, since it would seem to be consistent with the hypothesis that every identity statement which contains determinately referring names is determinately true or determinately false that the names occurring in them refer to objects with fuzzy boundaries, so that '$a = b$' will be true only when 'a' and 'b' refer to objects with precisely the same fuzzy boundaries.

Another problem with the Evans argument is that it is doubtful it does show that identity statements involving determinately referring names can't be indeterminate. Given how compelling the case is for indeterminate identity, we should at best regard the Evans argument as presenting us with a puzzle whose resolution is unclear.

At time t I buy a bicycle and name it 'Al'. At t', exactly one year later, you see me riding a bicycle and name it 'Beth'. We may assume that 'Al' determinately refers to the bicycle I bought at t and that 'Beth' determinately refers to the bicycle you named at t'. We have the ingredients for the puzzle to which I just alluded.

On the one hand, it seems intuitive that

(A) It is indeterminate whether Al = Beth

would be true if between t and t' I replaced some but not all of Al's parts (the seat, the handlebars...), so that we feel unable to answer the question whether Al = Beth, but also know that there is nothing to be learned that would provide a determinate answer. In my view, the case for thinking (A) can be true finds considerable support in the further realization that if the proposition that Al = Beth must be determinately true or determinately false, then there must be a *precise point* in any series of changes inflicted on Al at which Al determinately ceases to exist, given that the changes eventually result in Al's not existing. Al determinately exists; I make certain changes and Al continues determinately to exist; then I make one more change (say, I replace the old seat with a new one), and at precisely that point Al determinately ceases to exist and the bicycle then in my possession is determinately not identical to Al. For so many now familiar reasons, this is pretty hard to swallow.

But on the other hand, we have the following Evans-type argument. If (A) were true, then Beth would have the property expressed by the open sentence

(B) It is indeterminate whether Al $= x$.

But that is not a property Al has. Since it's not indeterminate whether Al $=$ Al, Al has the incompatible property expressed by the open sentence

(C) It is not indeterminate whether Al $= x$.

Thus, we may conclude via Leibniz's law that if (A) were true, then Al $\neq$ Beth. But (A) can't be true if it entails that Al $\neq$ Beth.

On my view, it is not difficult to say where the argument just stated goes wrong. It is in the assumption that (B) and (C) are genuine open sentences expressing conditions that any given thing does or doesn't satisfy. On my view, the determinately operator is covertly *intentional*, so that the joint truth of

It is indeterminate whether Al $=$ Beth

and

It is not indeterminate whether Al $=$ Al

is no more problematic than the joint truth of

Fiona is uncertain whether Al $=$ Beth

and

Fiona isn't uncertain whether Al $=$ Al.

The argument to show that Al $\neq$ Beth presupposes that the sentence form (B) expresses a property that an object, in and of itself, may or may not have. Without this assumption we do not get any violation of Leibniz's law. But the assumption is false if, as I was at pains to show in Chapter 2, 'the proposition that a is F' and 'the proposition that b is F' may refer to distinct object-dependent propositions about the thing that is the referent of both 'a' and 'b'. For in that case, given my propositional-attitude account of indeterminacy, we cannot construe (B) as an open sentence like 'x is a dog' which an object may or may not satisfy in and of itself. We can speak of an object o as 'satisfying' (B) only in the sense that there is a rigid designator of o, n, such that, by virtue of containing n, the whether-clause in

It is indeterminate whether $a = n$

refers to an object-dependent proposition about o.

But what if we contrive to bring 'Al' and 'Beth' outside the intentional context, so that we have for consideration the following argument?

(1) ⟨Al, Beth⟩ is such that it is indeterminate whether *it* instantiates the identity relation.

(2) ⟨Al, Al⟩ is such that it is not indeterminate whether *it* instantiates the identity relation.

(3) $\forall \Phi, x,y(\Phi x \ \& \sim \Phi y \rightarrow x \neq y)$

(4) ∴ Al ≠ Beth.

The intentionality of the determinately operator has still not been escaped.

Let's put names aside momentarily and imagine an agent, Carl, reasoning as follows. 'Owing to the various replacements it suffered, the t-bike—i.e. the bike in my possession at time t—is v^*-believed to degree .5 by me not to exist at t'. But the t'-bike—i.e. the bike in my possession at t'—is not v^*-believed to any positive degree by me not to exist at t'; on the contrary, I s-believe it to exist at t' to degree 1. Therefore, by Leibniz's law, the t-bike ≠ the t'-bike.' This is not good reasoning on Carl's part. He is entitled to conclude that an application of Leibniz's law shows that the t-bike ≠ the t'-bike only if he is entitled to think that the t-bike has a psychological property the t'-bike does not have—namely, the property of being v^*-believed to degree .5 by Carl not to exist at t'. But since Carl v^*-believes to degree .5 that the t-bike = the t'-bike, he can't rationally *accept* that there is this property difference; all he can rationally do is v^*-believe to degree .5 that the property difference obtains.

Returning now to the last displayed argument that purports to show that Al ≠ Beth, we can appreciate that we are not in a position to think that it is sound, if my account of indeterminacy is correct. *De re* propositional attitudes must always be explained in terms of *de dicto* propositional attitudes in that in order to PA x to be F one must PA an object-dependent proposition about x that ascribes being F to it. This is really just to say that one cannot simply PA a thing to be such-and-such but must rather always PA it to be such-and-such in one way or another. Determinacy and indeterminacy are in the first instance properties of propositions: p is indeterminate when it is possible for someone to v^*-believe p, and if p is not indeterminate, then p is either determinately true or determinately false. Still, we may invoke *de re* readings of these operators. In this sense, to say that x is such that it is indeterminate that it is F is to say that x is such that it can be v*-believed to be F; and x is v*-believed by one to be F just in case (if you'll excuse the sloppy use of quotes) there is a rigid designator of x, 'τ', such that one v*-believes the proposition that τ is F. If we start with the account of indeterminacy *de re* just given, then there is an ambiguity in the claim that x is such that it is determinate that it is F. That can mean either that x is F and that it is not the case that x is such that it is indeterminate that it is F, or that there is a rigid designator of x, 'τ', such that the proposition that τ is F is both true and impossible to v*-believe. Thus, premiss (2) is indeterminate on the first reading, since one can v*-believe that Al = Beth, and while it is determinately true on the second reading, it yields no violation of Leibniz's law (since on this reading a thing can be such that it is both determinately and indeterminately such-and-such), thus rendering the argument invalid on this reading. Either way, as I said, we are not in a position to accept that the displayed argument is sound: on one reading of premiss (2) it is indeterminate whether the argument is sound, and on the other reading of that premiss the argument is unsound by virtue of being invalid.

The next two chapters explore consequences of my treatment of indeterminacy for two other philosophical problems: moral discourse in the next chapter, and conditionals in the chapter after that.

6

Moral Realism and Indeterminacy

6.1 INTRODUCTION

Moral discourse has always presented a puzzle for the theory of meaning and philosophical logic, and I take myself to be following the advice of Bertrand Russell when he recommended testing philosophical theories by their capacity to deal with puzzles, 'since these serve much the same purpose as is served by experiments in physical science'.[1] The theory to be tested is the theory of pleonastic propositions and, especially, its attendant account of indeterminacy. The puzzle on which the theory is to be tested is that puzzle about moral discourse whose resolution has been thought by many philosophers to require a non-cognitivist, and thus non-factualist, solution. The unhappy-face solution my application delivers is cognitivist, as one would expect given the theory of pleonastic propositions, but with a concession to non-factualism which some readers will find repugnant but which I can't help thinking may be true—namely, that there are no determinate moral truths.

The next section, 6.2, lays out the problem moral judgements provide and offers a partial resolution of it. That resolution is continued into 6.3, where two related arguments are given to show that there are no determinately true moral propositions. Those arguments incur a couple of explanatory debts, and in 6.4 I make claims about the nature of moral concepts which I hope will discharge those debts. Alas, however, my theory also implies a certain error theory about common-sense moral discourse, and this generates still more explanatory debts, which I explain and try to handle in 6.5. Finally, in 6.6, I briefly consider whether indeterminacy infects evaluative propositions in domains other than moral discourse, and here special attention is given to evaluative epistemological judgements.

---

[1] Russell (1956b: 47).

6.2 THE PROBLEM OF MORAL JUDGEMENTS

The problem—or at least *a* problem in this complex area—is that, on the one hand, there are reasons for thinking that there are moral propositions, while, on the other hand, there are reasons for thinking that there aren't. Let's see how this plays out.

Half the problem of moral judgements is that there are reasons for thinking there are moral propositions.

First, from, for example,

> Eating animals is wrong

we may infer its pleonastic equivalent

> It is true that eating animals is wrong,

which contains the that-clause 'that eating animals is wrong' whose referent is evidently the proposition that eating animals is wrong. Thus, not only do moral sentences generate their own proposition-yielding something-from-nothing transformations, but those transformations, by the pleonastic equivalences they induce, also evidently determine *truth conditions* for moral propositions via the general truth schema for propositions

> It is true that S iff S,

an instance of which is

> It is true that eating animals is wrong iff eating animals is wrong.

Secondly, these something-from-nothing transformations aren't the only place we find that-clauses whose apparent referents are moral propositions. Propositional-attitude and speech-act reports such as

> Sally believes that eating animals is wrong
> Sally told me that eating animals is wrong.

may evidently be determinately true and don't appear to differ in any relevant respect from such reports as

> Sally believes that eating animals is a source of protein
> Sally told me that eating animals is a source of protein.

Thirdly, moral sentences embed in sentences that evidently have truth-values, such as the apparently true disjunction

Either abortion isn't wrong or the Pope isn't infallible,

and this evidently requires that moral sentences in the indicative mood express the moral propositions they appear to express.

Fourthly, it is an obvious consequence of the theory of pleonastic propositions that there are moral propositions in exactly the same sense that there are any other kinds of propositions, so whatever reasons there are for accepting that theory are *ipso facto* reasons for thinking there are moral propositions.

The other half of the problem of moral judgements is that there are reasons for thinking there are no moral propositions. The best of these reasons have traditionally been encapsulated in two arguments, which I'll call the *Argument from Internalism* and the *Argument from Irresolubility*.

The Argument from Internalism. Here is one among several ways of stating this familiar argument:

(1) Necessarily, one who accepts the judgement that she morally ought not to X has some conation against her Xing.

(2) If there are moral propositions, then for a person to accept that she morally ought not to X is for her to believe the proposition that she morally ought not to X is true.

(3) But such a belief is consistent with a person's not having any conation against her Xing.

(4) ∴ There are no moral propositions.

Every premiss of this valid argument has been contested, but to see that it presents a *problem* we need only appreciate the plausibility of each of its premisses. Indeed, we can see that it presents a problem just by appreciating that there is a whole school of moral philosophers, those who are called *non-cognitivists*, who believe that the argument is sound and therefore accept its conclusion. These philosophers include David Hume (suitably interpreted), classical emotivists like C. L. Stevenson and A. J. Ayer, prescriptivists like R. M. Hare, and, with some qualification, quasi-realists like Simon Blackburn and expressivists like Allan Gibbard.[2]

---

[2] Hume (1739/1911, 1751/1957); Stevenson (1944); Ayer (1936); Hare (1952, 1963); Blackburn (1984); and Gibbard (1990).

Support for premiss (1) is based on two considerations. First, we typically make moral judgements in order to influence behaviour, and the inculcation of moral concepts in children is clearly intended to affect their behaviour. In some sense, it seems to belong to the point, or *raison d'être*, of our moral concepts that they guide behaviour. As Hume observed, 'the end of all moral speculations is to teach us our duty, and, by proper representations of the deformity of vice and beauty of virtue, beget correspondent habits, and engage us to avoid the one, and embrace the other'.[3] Secondly, for someone to proclaim that, while *X*ing was morally wrong, he neither had any inclination not to *X* nor any concern about anyone else's *X*ing has the intuitive feel of being some sort of conceptual impropriety.

Premiss (2) is obviously correct, if moral propositions are propositions in the same sense of 'proposition' as any other kind of propositions, and that they are is implicit in the reasons for thinking there are moral propositions in the first place. There is a more familiar way of making this point. The two sentences

(*a*) Eating animals is a source of protein
(*b*) Eating animals is wrong

appear to be semantically on a par, and the *cognitivist* is the theorist who says they really are on a par. The *non-cognitivist* agrees that (*a*) and (*b*) *appear* to be on a par but adds that in this case appearances are misleading. Normative sentences like (*b*) are masqueraders; the kind of meaning they actually have is different from the kind they appear to have—namely, the kind of meaning (*a*) in fact has. Now, whatever kind of meaning sentences like (*a*) have, it is what defines cognitivism. So what kind of meaning do sentences like (*a*) have? The basis of my answer to this question was given in Chapter 3: the meaning of any sentence is determined by two things: the kind of speech act the literal speaker must perform in uttering the sentence on its own, and the kind of propositional content those speech acts must have. If we assume, as I have been assuming, that stating and believing are relations to propositions, then, as regards (*a*), the literal speaker who utters it on its own must be *stating (saying/asserting) that eating animals is a source of protein*, where the proposition *that eating animals is a source of protein* is both truth-evaluable and

---

[3] Hume (1751/1957: 5).

something one might believe. It is truth-evaluable in that it is true iff eating animals is a source of protein, and false iff eating animals isn't a source of protein. By the criterion this implies, cognitivism is true if the meaning of (*b*) is determined by its being the case that the literal speaker uttering it on its own must be *stating (saying/asserting) that eating animals is wrong*, where the proposition *that eating animals is wrong* is both truth-evaluable and something one might believe (and believe in exactly the sense in which one believes that eating animals is a source of protein). The doctrine of pleonastic propositions clearly entails cognitivism, but even without that doctrine's being presupposed, the case for cognitivism is apt to seem compelling. There seem to be no relevant ambiguities in the schemas

It is true that S iff S
A believes that S
In uttering 'S', A was stating that S,

and it is pretty hard to see how one could convincingly argue that

It is true that eating animals is wrong iff eating animals is wrong.

Al believes that eating animals is wrong.

In uttering 'Eating animals is wrong', Al was stating that eating animals is wrong

are less bona fide substitution instances than

It is true that eating animals is a source of protein iff eating animals is a source of protein.

Al believes that eating animals is a source of protein.

In uttering 'Eating animals is a source of protein', Al was stating that eating animals is a source of protein.

At the same time, we'll later see that the cognitivism that obtains may be something less than full-blooded.

Premiss (3) derives its plausibility from the cogency of a familiar Humean worry. If there are moral propositions, as the cognitivist claims, then to believe that acts of a certain kind are wrong is just to believe that acts of that kind have a certain objective property, and, the worry goes, such a belief would be consistent with one's feeling any way at all about whether anything has that property. A belief that a certain fact obtains, Hume held, may *cause* a certain conation, but having the belief can never *entail* that conation.[4]

So much for a quick look at the plausibility of the Argument from Internalism. It is clear that a lot more needs to be said for each of its premisses for one to find the argument compelling, as opposed merely to having a certain degree of plausibility. For one who rejects the argument's conclusion, the interest of the argument lies in seeing how to solve the problem it presents. I am not persuaded by the combined weight of the three premisses to reject either the pleonastic conception of propositions nor its obvious application to moral judgements. Since I reject the conclusion of this valid argument, I'm committed to rejecting at least one of its premisses. I can't reject premiss (2), for the doctrine of pleonastic propositions leaves no room for an invidious comparison between moral propositions and any other propositions as regards their status as propositions. And premiss (1) seems right to me, or at least, more cautiously, I can see no reason to think it is determinately false. That leaves premiss (3), which I do reject. The challenge for me is to show how its falsity coheres with the conclusion's falsity. I think this can be done, but, as we'll see in 6.4, not in a way that speaks well for moral realism—the theory that there are determinate moral truths.

The Argument from Irresolubility. Sceptics about moral realism nearly always appeal to some form of this argument. David Hume was making such an appeal when he wrote: 'But when I reflect, that... yet men still dispute concerning the foundation of their moral duties: When I reflect on this I say, I fall back into diffidence and skepticism, and suspect, that an hypothesis, so obvious, had it been a true one, would, long ere now, have been received by the unanimous suffrage and consent of mankind'.[5] When this line of thought is made to yield a scepticism about the existence of moral propositions, the line of reasoning may be reconstructed as the following argument:

(1) If there are moral propositions, then it is always possible for two people to disagree about the truth-value of any moral proposition, even when they agree about all relevant non-normative issues, have equal mastery of moral concepts, and

---

[4] Cf. John Mackie's 'argument from queerness' (1977: 38–42).

[5] Hume (1751/1957: 98).

are equally intelligent, rational, imaginative, and attentive (please feel free to insert whatever I left out).[6]

(2) If there are moral propositions and such disagreement is always possible, then there are no *true* moral propositions.

(3) But if there were moral propositions, then surely *some* of them would be true.

(4) ∴ There are no moral propositions.

Subject to a certain qualification, I think premiss (1) is true, and since I accept its antecedent, I accept its consequent, subject to the qualification to which I just alluded, and therefore reject (4). I'll make the qualification explicit in 6.5; it can safely be ignored for now. The question for me, then, is: What is to be said for premisses (2) and (3) and why are those arguments unsound? But I don't want to go directly to those questions, because I don't think that what is important per se about the Argument from Irresolubility is the pervasive possibility of rationally irresoluble moral dispute. I believe that pervasive *possibility* is really just a symptom of a certain underlying *impossibility*, and that this impossibility provides the sound core of the Argument from Irresolubility. The impossibility to which I allude is the impossibility of moral knowledge. But we don't need to argue that no moral knowledge is possible to get a significant result about moral realism; merely showing that there can be no a priori knowledge of moral principles will be enough to show that there are no determinately true moral propositions.

6.3 THE INDETERMINACY OF MORAL PROPOSITIONS

The argument I have in mind begins with the following master argument (MA), whose interest lies in the arguments for its

[6] Crispin Wright would express the consequent of (1) by saying that moral discourse fails to exhibit *Cognitive Command*, where 'a discourse exhibits Cognitive Command if and only if it is *a priori* that difference of opinion arising within it can be satisfactorily explained only in terms of "divergent input", that is, the disputants' working on the basis of different information (and hence guilty of ignorance or error, depending on the status of that information), or "unsuitable conditions" (resulting in inattention or distraction and so in inferential error, or oversight of data and so on), or "malfunction" (for example prejudicial assessment of data, upwards or downwards, or dogma, or failings in other categories already listed)' (1992: 92–3).

premisses:

   (MA)(1) If there are determinately true moral propositions, then there are moral principles that are knowable a priori.

   (2) There are no such moral principles.

   (3) ∴ There are no determinately true moral propositions.

A few clarifications. First, for the purposes of MA, my use of 'determinately' doesn't presuppose the account of determinate truth I offered in the preceding chapter and may be regarded as pre-theoretic. Secondly, by a 'moral proposition' I mean a proposition, such as the proposition that eating animals is morally wrong, that can be the content of a substantive moral judgement. This would exclude trivial truisms such as the proposition that one morally ought not to do what is morally wrong. Thirdly, a priori knowledge is, at least to a first approximation, knowledge whose knowledge-making grounds include no empirical proposition believed to be evidence for what one knows. One reason this is a first approximation is as follows. Suppose I'm doing conceptual analysis and, after some labour, conclude that, necessarily, a speaker means p iff she intends to get her audience to believe p by means of the audience's recognition of her intention to get him to believe p. Suppose, too, that my philosophical exercise has been so well conducted that it actually results in my *knowing* the proposition to which it brought me. As most philosophers use 'a priori knowledge', my knowledge of the necessary truth about speaker-meaning would count as a priori. At the same time, these philosophers wouldn't deny that part of my justification for believing what I know is the *empirical* proposition that I have been unable to think of any counter-examples. I merely note this qualification to the standard gloss on a priori knowledge and won't try to achieve a more adequate gloss. Suffice it to say that I intend my use of 'a priori knowledge' to be on all fours with the use of most philosophers who believe the expression has application. Thirdly, the conclusion of the argument is that there are no determinately true moral propositions, but, were it not for a small qualification, the conclusion could also be that all moral propositions are indeterminate—neither determinately true nor determinately false. The small qualification is that a certain uninteresting class of moral propositions are determinately false—namely, those moral propositions whose negations are not moral propositions, such as the proposition that a certain earthquake was morally wrong, it being false because only the actions of intentional agents can be morally wrong, so that the determinately true proposition that the earthquake wasn't morally wrong isn't a moral proposition in that it doesn't entail that the earthquake was morally right. As regards those infinitely many moral propositions whose negations are also moral propositions, MA tells us that every one of those moral propositions is indeterminate.

Returning to MA, we see that it is plainly valid, thus reducing the issue it raises to that of the truth of its two premisses.

Re premiss (1): If there are determinately true moral propositions, then there are moral principles that are knowable a priori. If there are moral truths, then there are moral properties that are instantiated. For example, if it is true that my stepping on your blue suede shoes was morally wrong, then my act instantiates the property of being morally wrong. I assume—and assume no one would deny—that, for any x and any moral property M, if x has M, then there is some non-normative property Φ, however complex, such that x has Φ and having Φ minimally metaphysically entails having M—that is, having Φ metaphysically entails having M and nothing contained in Φ (so to say) is inessential to its metaphysically entailing having M. In the event, the proposition that whatever has Φ has M is a necessarily true moral principle. It follows that if there are determinately true moral propositions, then there are necessarily true moral principles. Such moral principles would themselves be determinately true. I take it to be obvious and not in need of argument that if there are such moral principles, then at least some of them are knowable, indeed known. What reader will claim she has moral knowledge but deny that, for example, she knows that it is wrong to torture children just for the fun of it? Now, if there are necessarily true moral principles that are knowable, then at least some of them are knowable a priori. This, too, I simply take to be obvious. I don't deny that some metaphysically necessary propositions can be known only a posteriori. This seems to be true, for example, of the necessarily true proposition that water is constituted of H_2O molecules. But I doubt that what explains the a posteriori status of these necessary propositions can apply to every necessarily true knowable moral principle. We couldn't with a straight face speculate that we know that prima facie it is morally wrong to inflict pain because someone made the empirical discovery that the property of inflicting pain was the hidden property that accounted for the superficial features of acts on the basis of which we ascribed the property of being morally wrong, or because it was discovered that the property of inflicting pain was the property that played such-and-such role in the moral theory that fixed the reference of moral terms. Just ask yourself why *you* believe that prima facie it is morally wrong to inflict pain and you'll find the a priori status of your belief written on its surface.

Re premiss (2): No moral principles are knowable a priori. There are two related reasons for accepting this premiss. The two reasons are related in that the first reason—which is apt to be perceived as somewhat tendentious when first presented on its own—sets up, and thus serves as a nice introduction to, the second reason, and the truth of the second reason explains the truth of the first reason. Because of this explanatory asymmetry, the second reason is the deeper reason for thinking that premiss (2) is true.

The first reason may be put in the following way. If one person knows *p* a priori, then, platitudinously, so will any other person in the relevantly same epistemic situation with respect to *p*, which means that if one person knows *p* a priori and another doesn't, then this other person is epistemically lacking in some way with respect to *p* that the first person isn't. Perhaps the non-knower lacks complete mastery of one or more of the concepts needed to know *p*, or perhaps she hasn't reasoned as well as the first person, or been as imaginative, etc. But now, as sceptics of moral realism have long claimed, whatever moral principle one believes a priori, it would seem to be possible that there is someone else who doesn't believe that principle but who does not differ in any relevant way as regards one's epistemic situation vis-à-vis the principle. The two of you agree about all relevant non-normative issues, have equal mastery of moral concepts, and are equally intelligent, sane, rational, imaginative, and attentive, and have attended to and reasoned about the principle equally well (and so on). You take yourself to know a priori that a woman has the right to abort a 3-week-old foetus if having a child would interfere with her career. But there are people just as intelligent and imaginative as you, with equal command of all relevant concepts and equal access to all relevant non-moral facts, who reason as well as you, and have reasoned on this issue as well as you, but who don't believe that a woman has the right to abort a 3-week-old foetus just because bringing the foetus to term would interfere with the woman's career. There need be nothing you can do to get the other to share your belief, where the reason for this has nothing to do with that person's being prevented or disabled from believing the truth in some way that doesn't beg the question.

Perhaps, it might be countered, we can imagine a stand-off over the principle about abortion, but what about the principle that it is morally wrong to torture children for the mere fun of it? Actually, it is not all that hard to think of people with not entirely outrageous moral views who wouldn't accept the principle in question. Consider someone who implicitly accepts what Derek Parfit calls the *Self-interest Theory* and has as her single ultimate moral principle that one ought to pursue those outcomes that would make one's life go as well as possible.[7] Such a person might be a sincere moral egoist in the cast of Ayn Rand who thinks that the only moral obligation anyone has is to achieve his or her potential and to satisfy whatever desires will give him or her the most accomplished, lucrative, and enjoyable life. This moralist might concede that only a monster would want to torture anyone but nevertheless stick to her guns about what is morally wrong (she can even allow that, while one can't assert without qualification that it is always wrong to torture children for the mere fun of it, in many cases such behaviour would be wrong because of the way it interferes with other, more important ends one has). This seems entirely conceivable to me, and if the example is adequately described, there need be no flaw of reason or concept possession or imagination to explain this person's not believing the principle; the conceptual strain is in imagining someone with such an unusual psychology. Yet if anyone has a priori knowledge of any moral principle, we could hardly find a better example of such knowledge than the a priori knowledge that it is morally wrong to torture children for the mere fun of it!

As I indicated above, I take the foregoing reason for accepting premiss (2) of MA to be relatively superficial. Although I think it can stand (somewhat shakily) on its own, it is best viewed as a prolegomenon to a deeper reason, a reason for accepting premiss (2) which accounts for why the first reason obtains. The deeper reason has to do with difficulties in explaining *how* one might have a priori knowledge of a moral principle, and may be elaborated in the following way.

If one has a priori knowledge of a moral principle, then there must be a correct explanation of how one has that knowledge, of what it is

---

[7] Parfit (1984).

by virtue of which one's mental state constitutes a priori knowledge of the principle. I can think of five ways one might try to account for one's having a priori knowledge of a given moral principle, and none of them holds much promise.

First, it might seem that one possible explanation of one's a priori knowledge of a moral principle is that one knows it on the basis of one's having deduced it from more ultimate moral principles one knows a priori. Clearly, this couldn't account for all of one's a priori knowledge of moral principles, since the explanation presupposes a priori knowledge of a moral principle that one doesn't know on the basis of having deduced it from some other moral principle one knows a priori. But even apart from this point, it is not a promising account of *any* plausible candidate for a priori moral knowledge. It is not that one can't know a moral principle on the basis of knowing a more ultimate moral principle (or principles); it is just that if there are such cases, then the less ultimate principle will be derived from the more ultimate principle (or principles) together with some empirical proposition, thereby precluding one's knowledge of the less ultimate principle from being a priori.[8]

Secondly, it might seem that one's a priori knowledge of a given moral principle is *concept-based* where, intuitively put, one's knowing *p* is concept-based provided that part of the explanation of one's knowing *p* is that no one could have the concepts involved in thinking *p* unless one believed *p*. For example, Smith knows a priori that every widow was once married. If asked how he knows, Smith might not be able to say anything very helpful, because his belief that every widow was once married isn't based on other beliefs he has; if asked why he believes the proposition, he might say that it is obvious, or that he can't imagine how it could be false. But whatever Smith might say, we might explain his a priori knowledge (at least in large part) by saying that Smith has the concept of a widow, and no one can be in full possession of that concept and not believe the conceptual truth that every widow was once married. Now, we evidently have concept-based a priori knowledge of the proposition that it is morally wrong to do what one morally ought not to do, but is it plausible that one has concept-based a priori knowledge of any substantive moral

---

[8] Perhaps a trivial exception is when one comes to know an unobvious restriction of a moral principle one knows a priori by deductive reasoning, as a dull thinker might come to realize that it is morally wrong to torture all children born out of wedlock for the mere fun of it since it is morally wrong to torture any child for the mere fun of it.

principle? I think not. Substantive moral principles link moral concepts with non-normative concepts, but our moral concepts float free of the non-normative concepts with which they are linked in substantive moral principles in that it is never the case that a person who possesses both concepts can't believe one applies unless she believes the other also applies. It is always possible for one to believe that something falls under a moral concept without also believing that it falls under a particular non-normative concept with which it may be linked in some plausible moral principle. There is no substantive moral principle such that it is impossible for anyone to find its negation conceivable. This, of course, is precisely the intuition that lies behind G. E. Moore's 'Naturalistic Fallacy' and his claim that 'propositions about the good are all of them synthetic and never analytic';[9] it is an intuition that isn't usually contested by either side in the debate between moral realists and their sceptics. For any non-normative concept Φ, it is always possible for some rational person who has command of the concept of moral wrongness not to believe that Φ acts are morally wrong, however her intuitions about the concept of moral wrongness are suitably tweaked, and likewise, *mutatis mutandis*, for every other moral concept. This wouldn't be so if one could have concept-based a priori knowledge of substantive moral principles.

(There is an ancillary point to be made in this connection. The discussion of a couple of paragraphs back showed how a rational person with full command of moral concepts might nevertheless not accept the principle that it is morally wrong to torture children for the mere fun of it. This illustrates the point just made about concept-based a priori moral knowledge, for if that's not a conceptual truth, then it is highly unlikely that any other moral principle can make a better claim to being a conceptual truth. Christopher Peacocke in effect claims that we have concept-based a priori knowledge of the principle that prima facie it is morally wrong to inflict avoidable pain,[10] but that hardly trumps the prohibition about torturing children. Suppose, however, I'm wrong and that Peacocke's example, or the one about torturing children, is an example of a substantive moral principle that is also a conceptual truth. Even so, my scepticism would be

[9] Moore (1903: 7). This sentence is quoted in Wedgwood (2001: 26 n. 35).
[10] Peacocke (forthcoming).

scarcely touched were I to concede that certain moral principles, such as the ones just cited, couldn't be denied by anyone in full possession of the concept of moral wrongness. For there would be so few such principles that any moral system having them as their only axioms would be useless as a guide to what to do. We don't need morality to keep us from torturing children for the fun of it. But what *useful* moral principle is there of which we might have concept-based a priori knowledge? If the only moral truths we could know were ones backed by principles for which it is possible to have concept-based underived a priori knowledge, then morality would be useless in helping us decide what to do.)

A third way of explaining a priori knowledge of a moral principle is suggested by a certain 'reflective-equilibrium' way of gaining a priori knowledge. This would be the way philosophical analysis typically yields a priori knowledge, when it succeeds in yielding knowledge. A philosopher starts his inquiry not knowing the answer to a certain question. After much hard work, he concludes that the answer he seeks is p, where p is a necessary truth, if true at all. Earlier I imagined a philosopher arriving in this way, rather improbably, at the a priori knowledge that, necessarily, a speaker means p iff she intends to get her audience to believe p by means of his recognition of her intention to get him to believe p. The philosopher's knowledge won't be based on a more ultimate principle about speaker meaning. The philosopher's justification for believing his new theory will be a story about how nicely it accounts for the known facts about speaker meaning, integrates in an illuminating way with other semantic notions, and, crucially, is resistant to the attempt to find counter-examples. No doubt something very much like this also applies to certain kinds of mathematical and logical inquiry. Might one have a priori knowledge of a moral principle that was of this sort? I doubt it. First of all, if one could know an ultimate moral principle that wasn't stated in terms of problematic expressions like 'prima facie' or '*ceteris paribus*', it would arguably be of this sort, unless it was like the principle that it is wrong to torture children merely for the fun of it. But it is hardly how one knows, if one does know, that principle or the principle that it is prima facie morally wrong to inflict avoidable pain. So even if the analytical exercise of reason could result in knowledge of some moral principles, it wouldn't explain all such knowledge one might take oneself to have. Second of all—and this is the more important point—the following consideration seems to preclude one's gaining a priori knowledge of a moral principle via the analytical route in question. Crucial to the idea that any sort of conceptual analysis might justify one in believing a necessarily true proposition is the ability of that proposition to resist the search for counter-examples by others like one in relevant respects. Yet such immunity can't be guaranteed for moral principles if, as I argued, moral concepts float free of the substantial non-normative concepts with which they are joined in candidate moral principles. Perhaps *you* can't find a counter-example to the claim that acts of such-and-such kind are wrong, but the guy with whom you are locked in irresoluble dispute finds them all over the place. Just think of the situation of a person who can't find a counter-example to the claim that it is morally permissible for a healthy woman to abort a healthy 1-month-old foetus because it would interfere with her career.

Are there other ways of explaining a priori knowledge of a moral principle that are worth considering? One thing that comes to mind is something like G. E. Moore's 'moral intuition'. But if that doesn't fall under what has already been discussed, then I doubt it is worth discussing. Another possible suggestion is that we have certain underived a priori beliefs as a result of natural selection, which could account for those beliefs' constituting knowledge if we assume, as seems reasonable, that beliefs produced by natural selection enjoy a reliability that is knowledge-inducing.[11] But it seems to me that there are two things that make this suggestion problematic. First, I doubt that we've had moral concepts long enough for natural selection to make any moral beliefs a priori, and secondly, since there is actual or nomically possible disagreement among otherwise normal humans on just about every moral principle, it is bound to be difficult to explain why Mother Nature favours some but not others.

Finally, there is this to notice about premiss (2) of MA. Whether or not being indeterminate entails not being true, it is a mere platitude that a proposition is knowable only if it is determinately true. Thus, although MA ventures to show that there are no determinately true moral propositions via a premiss which asserts that no moral principle is knowable a priori, the conclusion of the argument, if true, would in turn *explain* why it is that the premiss is true. This reflection reveals no circularity in my argumentation, for although there being

[11] Paul Horwich offered this suggestion.

no a priori knowable moral principles is explained by there being no determinate moral truths, the reasons initially offered for the claim that there are no a priori knowable moral principles in no way presupposed the conclusion the claim was being used to support. At the same time, to foreshadow a little, any argument for the indeterminacy of moral propositions that didn't presuppose premiss (2) of MA would itself be an independent argument for the truth of that premiss.

Anyway, I've claimed that MA is the sound core of the Argument from Irresolubility. If it is to be used in an argument to show there are no moral propositions, then that argument, a recasting of the Argument from Irresolubility, would be:

(1) There are no determinately true moral propositions (as shown by MA).
(2) But if there were moral propositions, then surely *some* of them would be determinately true.
(3) ∴ There are no moral propositions.

If I'm right so far, (2) must be false. Certainly the case for (2) isn't terribly compelling. It is merely the intuition that if there are consistent moral properties, such as the property of being morally wrong, then what on earth could explain why nothing determinately instantiates any of them? That is a good question, and one I must answer, but it is not much of an argument for (2).

Before taking on the good question, however, we should see that there is another argument to be offered for premiss (1) of the argument just displayed, the proposition that there are no determinately true moral propositions.[12]

Given my account of indeterminacy (see Chapter 5) the argument is straightforward:

(1) If there are no determinately true moral principles, then there are no determinately true moral propositions.
(2) For any moral principle P, someone can v*-believe P to any degree.
(3) If (2), then there are no determinately true moral principles.
(4) ∴ There are no determinately true moral propositions.

---

[12] Crispin Wright (2001) also argues that moral propositions are indeterminate, and his particular appeal to intuitionistic logic seems to imply his commitment to the indeterminacy of bivalence, with which I concur (see Ch. 5). Although my position and Wright's were developed independently, there are some striking parallels.

Premiss (1) was secured in 6.2 when we noted that if there are instantiated moral properties, then their instantiations supervene on those of non-normative properties, and this is enough to yield necessarily true generalizations of the form *Anything having non-normative property N has moral property M*, and such generalizations are moral principles.[13] The case for premiss (3) was made in the preceding chapter. That leaves premiss (2). Well, a priori moral beliefs, like all beliefs, come in degrees. Suppose that, for any candidate moral principle *P*, ideally rational Sally is undecided about the status of *P* as an ultimate moral principle—that is, as a moral principle she takes to be ungrounded in any other moral principle—and that she believes *P* a priori to degree .5; she's really torn, even though she takes herself to have access to all relevant non-normative and normative facts. I think it is clear that Sally's partial belief that *P* is a VPB, not an SPB. She won't think there's a fifty-fifty chance that *P* is true, and if she s-believes to degree .5 the independent proposition that it will rain tonight, then the degree to which she believes the conjunction that [*P* and it'll rain tonight] will be .5. If her partial moral belief were an SPB, she would believe the conjunction to degree .25. And if, as we may suppose, Sally is in ideal epistemic circumstances with respect to *P*, then she v*-believes *P* to degree .5—and likewise for any other positive degree between 0 and 1.

This argument from indeterminacy not only gives a new argument for the claim that there are no determinate moral truths; but also, as I earlier hinted (p. 253), offers still another reason to accept premiss (2) of MA—the claim that no moral principles are knowable a priori—a reason that also accounts for why the premiss is true. For if every moral principle whose negation is a moral principle is indeterminate according to my account of indeterminacy, then that explains why none of them is knowable a priori.

Let's take stock. What I called 'the problem of moral judgements' is the puzzle generated by there being arguments to show that there are moral propositions and arguments to show that there aren't. Hardly anyone nowadays (as opposed to forty or so years ago) doubts that in

---

[13] Nothing in my argument depends on our calling such necessarily true generalizations (if there are any) 'moral principles', since the argument merely depends on there being such generalizations.

some sense there are moral propositions and that there are truths such as

> It is true that eating animals is wrong iff eating animals is wrong.
>
> Al believes that eating animals is wrong.
>
> In uttering 'Eating animals is wrong', Al was stating that eating animals is wrong.

I have argued, in conformity with the pleonastic doctrine of propositions, that the sense in which there are moral propositions is the same sense in which there are any other propositions, and that, therefore, the sentences just displayed are instances of the unambiguous schemas

> It is true that S iff S
>
> A believes that S
>
> In uttering 'S', A was stating that S

in precisely the same way as

> It is true that eating animals is a source of protein iff eating animals is a source of protein.
>
> Al believes that eating animals is a source of protein.
>
> In uttering 'Eating animals is a source of protein', Al was stating that eating animals is a source of protein.

This, too, I think is not anything very many would wish to deny nowadays. So the arguments for moral propositions win out over the arguments against them. I also suggested what premises in the unsound arguments must be rejected, and those suggestions generate explanatory debts.

The explanatory debt generated by the Argument from Internalism is to explain how moral judgements can be conation-entailing given that moral judgements are statements, like any factual statement, of truth-evaluable moral propositions. The Argument from Irresolubility was recast as an epistemological argument predicated on the impossibility of having a priori knowledge of any moral principle, and this impossibility was explained by an independent argument, using the VPB-based account of indeterminacy, to show (nearly enough) that moral propositions are indeterminate. The considerable explanatory debt this argument generates is to explain why, though there are truth-evaluable moral propositions, not one of them can be determinately true. The two explanatory debts, as we'll now see, are intimately related.

6.4   TWO EXPLANATORY DEBTS: THE PECULIAR NATURE OF MORAL CONCEPTS

A little indirection will help. In Bob's conceptual scheme, the concept W is governed by the following two conditions.

(a) W, by its very nature, is a concept Bob applies to some things and withholds from others, but in order for Bob to believe that α is W, there must be some non-normative concept N such that Bob also believes both that α is N and that being N entails being W.

(b) It isn't required that N be any particular concept; N can be anything, provided certain conditions are met. These conditions pertain to what Bob *wants*; for example, Bob should want not to live in a world in which people do anything that is N.

Given this we should expect *two* kinds of indeterminacy to be manifested in Bob's beliefs involving W.

The first kind is simply the sort of indeterminacy manifested in borderline vague propositions. Thus, suppose that the value of 'N' Bob settles on entails the property of being a lie. Then the proposition that Jane's calling Bob a Republican was W may be indeterminate simply because Jane's utterance was a borderline case of a lie and thus, by Bob's lights, a borderline case of a W act.

The second kind of indeterminacy is that, for any given relevant non-normative concept N,[14] it may be indeterminate whether being N entails being W, where this isn't a matter of the *vagueness* of N or W. Indeed, independently of any account of indeterminacy it ought to be intuitively clear given the set-up that, for any N, the proposition that being N entails being W *must* be indeterminate. For suppose that the operative non-normative concept for Bob is N^*, whereas for Carla, whose concept W is also governed by (a) and (b), the operative

---

[14] 'Relevant' non-normative concepts are such that it is not impossible for anything to fall under them and such that it is not trivially true that they don't entail being W, as, for example, the concept of photosynthesis makes it trivially false that photosynthesis is W.

non-normative concept requires her to believe that being N^* does *not* entail being W. Given the conditions governing the role of W, it is patently absurd to suppose that either Bob or Carla has the determinately true belief in their dispute about whether being N^* entails being W. And this is just the verdict my VPB-based account of indeterminacy yields. For any non-normative concept N, Bob may, even under epistemically ideal conditions, believe to any degree that being N entails being W, and these beliefs will perforce be VPBs. Thus, for any non-normative concept N, someone can v^*-believe to any positive degree less than 1 that being N entails being W, and therefore the proposition that being N entails being W is indeterminate.

You won't be surprised to learn that it is my view that what goes for Bob's W isn't all that far removed from what goes for our moral concepts. There are differences, of course, but what makes it impossible for any substantive W proposition to be determinately true also makes it impossible for any substantive moral proposition to be determinately true. The differences are that:

(i) It belongs to our moral concepts that their application must supervene on the application of some non-normative concept, but, unlike Bob, an ordinary person needn't have complete non-normative sufficient conditions *explicitly* in mind when she applies a moral concept. If, for example, she judges an act to be wrong, she will believe that it has a certain defeasible, but undefeated, wrong-making property. What she typically won't be able to do with any great confidence is reel off the possible defeaters that don't obtain. (Still, if she's to be confident that no defeater obtains, then she must believe she can recognize a defeater when she sees one, and, if that's so, then she would evidently have some sort of tacit belief about the non-normative property on which she takes the moral property she's ascribing to supervene.)

(ii) I earlier implied that, while cognitivism (in the sense stipulated) was true, it wasn't true in an entirely full-blooded sense. I was alluding to what must be an important concession to the non-cognitivist— namely, that one's conative attitudes enter into the determinants of the non-normative notions on which the application of one's moral concepts will be taken to supervene. Since these conative attitudes are essential to one's having moral concepts, it further follows that the meaning of 'wrong' in one's *lingua mentis* (as it were) is unlike that of predicates which express non-normative concepts in that the former supervenes partly on *conative* facts.[15] This is the principal ingredient that distinguishes moral concepts from 'naturalistic' concepts that enjoy determinate application and that accounts for their not having determinate applications of the kind in question. At the same time, the conative requirements on our actual moral concepts are considerably vaguer than the conative requirement on Bob's *W*. The concept of having a certain moral concept, such as the concept of moral wrongness, is extremely vague, and it is even a cheat to speak of *the* concept of, say, moral wrongness. As with any concept, there will be significant individual differences. The paradigm possessor of a moral concept has a strong conative component in the underived conceptual role of her concept, but the vagueness inherent in the concept of possessing the concept no doubt allows for R. M. Hare's inverted-commas guy who makes moral judgements not caring who does what.[16] Still, the conative component is what gives cohesiveness to the concept, and is why we speak of substantial disagreements on moral issues, rather than supposing that people who accept different underived moral principles are employing different concepts, so that ostensibly irresoluble disputes about ultimate moral principles are really just verbal disputes, like a debate about whether whales are fish when one party's use makes it true that they are and the other party's use makes it false.[17]

Yet the resemblances that remain with Bob's use of *W* give to our moral concepts a conceptual role that explains the truth of premiss (2)—that for any moral principle *P*, someone can v*-believe *P* to any degree—in the indeterminacy argument of 6.3. Given the peculiar conceptual role common to all our moral concepts, it will always be possible for someone in ideal epistemic circumstances to believe a moral principle to any degree between 0 and 1, and such a belief will perforce be a VPB*. And given my account of indeterminacy, it follows that no moral principle is determinately true.

If the foregoing is right, we see why moral propositions are indeterminate, how internalism is compatible with cognitivism, but also how the conative element in moral concepts plays its role in making moral propositions indeterminate.

---

[15] The idea that the conative component in what fixes the meaning of a moral predicate yields a less than full-blooded cognitivism was suggested by a reading of Kit Fine (2001).

[16] See e.g. Hare (1952, 1963).   [17] See Schiffer (1990, esp. 609–10).

6.5 AN ERROR THEORY AND OTHER
EXPLANATORY DEBTS

When I first presented premiss (1) of the unreconstructed Argument from Irresolubility—the proposition that

> If there are moral propositions, then it is always possible for two people to disagree about the truth-value of any moral proposition, even when they agree about all relevant non-normative issues, have equal mastery of moral concepts, and are equally intelligent, rational, imaginative, and attentive (please feel free to insert whatever I left out)

—I said that it was subject to a qualification. My account of the indeterminacy of moral propositions implies an important disagreement with this premiss. My position is that if one person fully believes a moral proposition, then it is always possible in principle for there to be another person who doesn't believe the moral proposition but is nevertheless, as regards epistemic justification and knowledge, on a par with the believer. That is the truth contained in the displayed premiss; but the premiss goes further in holding that rationally irresoluble dispute about moral propositions is always in principle possible, and the opposite is implied by my position. For if, as I claim, the moral proposition is neither determinately true nor determinately false, then the two disputants may, at least in theory, be brought to believe just that—provided they have enough free time and philosophical ability (and, unlike you, my readers, are unencumbered by commitments to incompatible philosophical positions).

That philosophy is needed to get moral disputants to resolve their dispute by mutually coming to see that the moral proposition they are disputing is indeterminate ameliorates the 'error theory' to which my view commits me.[18] The extent to which moral realism—the theory that there are determinate moral truths—is the theory of common sense is debatable, as anyone knows who has ever taught an introductory course in philosophy, but no doubt very many people

---

[18] John Mackie's (1977) famous error theory is different from mine in that on his view we're in error in supposing there are moral properties for anything even indeterminately to instantiate. That said, there are of course considerable similarities between my views and Mackie's.

make moral judgements and in doing so take themselves to be stating things that are true. But if what they are really stating is things that are indeterminate, why don't they realize this? The answer resides in the very nature of moral concepts, and we can appreciate this by contrasting the indeterminacy of borderline propositions with the kind of indeterminacy manifested in moral propositions.

We need no 'error theory' for vagueness. Consider a vague concept such as one's concept of red. It belongs to the very nature of this concept that we confidently apply it in some cases, confidently withhold it in other cases, and display the VPB-based ambivalence in those cases we regard as borderline. No error theory is needed because it is an intrinsic feature of one's concept of red that in certain cases—the borderline ones—the proposition that such-and-such is red goes willy-nilly into one's VPB box. Now consider the concept of moral wrongness of Bob, who believes in determinate moral truths. It belongs to the very nature of this concept that Bob confidently applies it in some cases, confidently withholds it in other cases, and displays the VPB-based ambivalence in those cases he regards as borderline. There is nothing whatever in the concept as such to enable Bob to discern the indeterminacy of every one of his applications. That indeterminacy is generated by the way Bob's conative states help to determine the criteria that guide his applications of the concept, but Bob would have to do some philosophical theorizing if he's to conclude that nothing determinately falls under any of his moral concepts.

That, in effect, is why my solution to the problem of moral judgements is an unhappy-face solution. There is a serious glitch in our moral concepts. They are meant to be applied, but the way in which the criteria—the moral principles, if you will—guiding those applications are determined precludes the moral judgements we make from being determinately true.

What are the implications of this error theory for our practices involving the exercise of moral concepts?

Well, so what if we didn't have moral concepts? That wouldn't preclude anyone from having ultimate and underived desires about the kind of world he or she wants to live in. There is something puzzling about moral concepts anyway, at least as regards rational adults who are capable of thinking for themselves. What is puzzling is how moral properties can make a rational difference to what we do. Consider cruelty to children. Like you, I'm very much against this. Why? I just am, and the idea that it is because I recognize that acts of cruelty to children have the property of being morally wrong strikes me as ludicrous. My finding cruelty to children abhorrent has nothing to do with my recognizing that such acts have some irreducible property of moral wrongness, and I find it utterly mysterious why it should. Be that as it may, however; my point is that even without moral concepts we would have what are tantamount to moral views: underived desires about how we want our world to be, which include underived desires about how we want people to treat one another.

What would happen to moral language if *everyone* became convinced that there were no determinately true moral propositions? Clearly, no one could sincerely make unqualified moral judgements, because those judgements couldn't express propositions we s-believed to a very high degree. At the same time, I think an invisible-hand mechanism would lead us to introduce concepts that were in many ways like the moral concepts we actually have. For we would find that there was considerable agreement between ourselves and certain recognizable others about the kind of world we wished to inhabit, and if these others included people with whom we had to plan joint ventures and otherwise coordinate behaviour, then we would want quick and easy ways to mark the kinds of actions we mutually approved or disapproved. Perhaps we would introduce an indexical word 'shmwrong' such that when A said to B that it would be shmwrong for so-and-so to do such-and-such she was expressing a belief whose cash-value was that A and B would want so-and-so not to do such-and-such if they were agreed about all relevant facts. We would have no use for these notions when dealing with those whose basic and underived attitudes were relevantly different from ours. Come to think of it, what I have just described is my own continuing use of moral terms. My use is instrumental, but it gets across what I need to get across, and which I couldn't begin to get across if I had to express the truth in what I was saying without use of those terms.[19]

---

[19] Perhaps what I'm saying here can be used to give an innocent reading to what John Mackie intended when he wrote: 'Morality is not to be discovered but to be made: we have to decide what moral views to adopt, what moral stands to take....the object [of this exercise] is to decide what to do, what to support and what to condemn, what principles of conduct to accept and foster as guiding or controlling our own choices and perhaps those of other people as well' (Mackie 1977: 106).

6.6   INDETERMINACY AND OTHER EVALUATIVE DISCOURSE

Moral propositions, I claim, are indeterminate. What about the propositions expressed by other kinds of evaluative discourse? Yes for some, no for others; it is all a matter of whether the shoe fits, although it is not always easy to tell whether it does.

Many evaluative judgements are 'instrumental' or 'hypothetical', and these can be determinately true: 'That's a good electric tooth-brush', 'If you want to get to midtown the quickest and easiest way during rush hour, then you ought to take the subway', 'Shaquille O'Neal is a good NBA centre', 'She's the best safe-cracker in the gang', 'Eating a well-balanced diet is good for you'.

But the reasons for taking moral propositions to be indeterminate also apply, *mutatis mutandis*, to many evaluative aesthetic judgements: the proposition that Jackson Pollock was a great painter is indeterminate: someone can v^*-believe it to degree .5. Sometimes aesthetic propositions which are indeterminate may appear to be determinately true or determinately false because those making them have certain criteria in mind, and nothing precludes propositions about what does, or doesn't, satisfy those criteria from being determinately true or determinately false. An example might be the claim, made by someone knowledgeable about opera, that Mozart's *The Marriage of Figaro* is a better opera than Rossini's *The Barber of Seville*. At the same time, it does strike me as somewhat ludicrous to deny that the proposition that Pavarotti in his prime was a 'good' tenor is determinately true. That is probably because being a tenor hero of Italian opera is enough like, say, being an NBA centre to encapsulate ends capable of sustaining instrumental evaluative judgements.

I think the most interesting question concerns evaluative epistemo-logical judgements, such as the claim that a certain fact is *good evidence* that a certain proposition is true, and therefore provides a *good reason* to believe that proposition. It is certainly clear that some of these propositions are determinately true while others are determinately false. The proposition that a certain lab result is good evidence that a person is HIV positive may well be determinately true, and the proposition that the fact that I ate an enchilada last week is good evidence that the Hudson River will flood New York next week is determinately false. So one bottom-line thing this tells us is that the reasons for claiming there are no determinately true moral propositions don't apply to evaluative epistemological propositions. But might the fact that these normative judgements aren't indeterminate provide the basis for an argument, perhaps by some sort of parity of reasoning, to show that moral judgements aren't indeterminate either?

I'm inclined to reject that question because it is formulated in a way that presupposes that evaluative epistemological judgements are *normative*, and it is not clear to me that they are. Consider the following dialogue.

A: You have a very good reason to believe *S*.

B: How so?

A: Because you know *P*, *Q*, and *R*, and *S* follows from them.

B: Yeah, I know *P*, *Q*, and *R*, and now that you mention it, I see that *S* follows from them, and that I therefore have a good reason to believe *S*. Still, I don't feel like believing *S* and I'm not going to.

Now, let's notice the following about this bizarre dialogue. First, it is about as analytic as anything can be that one has a good reason to believe a proposition if one knows other propositions that entail it. Secondly, that is because of the analytic connection between one thing's being a reason for believing another thing and the probability that the second is true given that the first is true. In the example before us the connection is one of logical entailment, and it is so very clear that B has a good—indeed the best possible—reason to believe *S*, because the probability of *S* given *P*, *Q*, and $R = 1$, but the same general point applies when we say that the fact that the streets are wet constitutes good evidence that—and a fortiori a good reason to believe that—it rained during the night: the fact that the streets are wet constitutes a good reason for believing that it rained because the probability that it rained given that the streets are wet is pretty high. In response, someone might claim that the probability invoked here is a version of subjective probability, to be unpacked in terms of what a rational agent ought to believe given relevant information. Now, it is far from clear that a notion of 'subjective' probability is what is needed here, as opposed to a notion of 'objective' probability explicable in terms of relative frequencies and logical relations, but this may not even matter if facts underlying objective probability re-emerge in the explanation of why the rational believer believes that it is very likely that the proposition in question is true given the evidence at hand. In the example above, B believes that the probability of *S* given *P*, *Q*, and *R* is 1 because he knows that *P*, *Q*, and *R* entail *S*, and one who sees that the streets are wet believes that it is very likely that it rained, given the wet condition of the streets, because of relevant law-like statistical generalizations and known causal connections.

Thirdly, and most importantly, the weirdness of B's saying he's not going to believe S, despite his acknowledging that he has a good reason to believe it by virtue of its following from things he knows, is crucially different from the weirdness of saying that one steals from one's employer even though one recognizes that that is morally wrong. In the stealing case, there is nothing conceptually puzzling about knowingly stealing from one's employer. What is conceptually askew is deliberately and without conflict doing what one sincerely claims to be morally wrong, and this because that seems to be precluded by what is required to possess the concept of moral wrongness. In B's case, however, *we don't even have to bring in the notion of good reasons to find his behaviour incomprehensible.* He seems to be making a claim that can't possibly be true of a normal believer, namely, that he doesn't believe S even though he knows, and has actively in mind, both that (P and Q and R) and that that conjunction entails S. That rightly strikes us as impossible, since it seems ruled out by the functional role a state must have if it is to be a belief. It is a conceptual truth that, absent perhaps certainly extremely unusual medical conditions, one who knows $(p \,\&\, (p \Rightarrow q))$ also believes q. The apparent normative force of knowing that one proposition is a good reason for believing another derives from the conceptual impossibility of believing the non-evaluative fact which entails that the one proposition is a good reason for believing the other without having that belief relevantly affect one's degree of belief in the other proposition. Of course, this observation is compatible with the further observation that two people might reasonably disagree about what belief-forming practices are best because they disagree about what ends such practices should serve, and such a 'should' might well be normative, perhaps even bordering on the moral, and to the extent that that is so, I submit that those normative claims will be indeterminate.

At any rate, I see nothing yet in evaluative epistemological discourse to make me doubt my claims about moral discourse, but I admit that I've barely scratched the surface of a complex and important area of investigation.

7

Conditionals and Indeterminacy

7.1 INTRODUCTION

The preceding chapter explored the application of the doctrine of pleonastic propositions and its attendant account of indeterminacy to moral discourse. This chapter explores their application to conditionals—sentences of the form 'If...then...' and their stylistic variants (e.g. 'She won't come if her ex-husband is invited'). Once again, this application has surprising results.

Philosophers typically divide conditionals into two groups and give separate accounts of each. The two groups are so-called *indicative* conditionals, such as 'If Oswald didn't kill Kennedy, then someone else did', and so-called *counterfactual* or *subjunctive* conditionals, such as 'If Oswald hadn't killed Kennedy, then someone else would have'.[1] Whether, or to what extent, it is defensible to give separate accounts of these two kinds of conditionals is another matter. In any case, the distinction between them is a useful structuring device,[2] in that it helps to make a tangle of complex issues more manageable than it would be if one tried to deal with all conditionals at once. Accordingly, this chapter has the following structure.

The next section, 7.2, offers an initial exploration of the issues raised by indicative conditionals, and 7.3 offers a partial resolution of them, which includes an account of the truth conditions of indicative-conditional propositions. In 7.4 I raise a paradox induced by a conflict between, on the one hand, the kind of truth conditions indicative-conditional propositions have and, on the other hand, the way we form beliefs in those propositions. I also there offer a resolution that

---

[1] Adams (1970).

[2] The indicative–subjunctive distinction is a useful structuring device whatever the correct account of that distinction may be. There is a large literature on what that correct account is, but that interesting issue isn't one with which I'll be concerned.

vindicates the primary claim motivating non-cognitivism about indicative conditionals, the view that there are no indicative-conditional propositions. Section 7.5 turns to counterfactuals and argues that a lot of what was said in 7.3–4 about indicative-conditional propositions applies as well to counterfactual-conditional propositions. The final section, 7.6, gives a summary.

7.2   THE PROBLEM OF INDICATIVE CONDITIONALS

Indicative conditionals are a philosophical topic because there is, or is thought to be, a philosophical *problem* of indicative conditionals. The problem is like the one with moral discourse. On the one hand, there are reasons for thinking that there are indicative-conditional propositions, while, on the other hand, there are reasons for thinking that there aren't. Let's see how this plays out.

Half the problem of indicative conditionals is that there are reasons for thinking there are indicative-conditional propositions.

First, from, for example,

Harold is in Oxford if he's not in London

we may infer its pleonastic equivalent

It's true that Harold is in Oxford if he's not in London,

which contains the that-clause 'that Harold is in Oxford if he's not in London' whose referent is evidently the proposition that Harold is in Oxford if he's not in London. Thus, not only do indicative conditionals generate their own proposition-yielding something-from-nothing transformations, but those transformations, by the pleonastic equivalences they induce, also evidently determine *truth conditions* for indicative-conditional propositions via the schema

It is true that if A, then C iff if A, then C,

which schema is itself, of course, merely an instance of the general truth schema for propositions

It is true that S iff S.

Secondly, these something-from-nothing transformations aren't the only place we find that-clauses whose apparent referents are indicative-conditional propositions. Propositional-attitude and speech-act reports such as

Sally believes that Harold is in Oxford if he's not in London
Sally told me that Harold is in Oxford if he's not in London

may evidently be determinately true and don't appear to differ in any relevant respect from such reports as

Sally believes that Harold is in Oxford
Sally told me that Harold is in Oxford.

Thirdly, some indicative conditionals, e.g.

If my head is cut off, I will die
If I'm alive, then I'm alive,

are evidently determinately true, while others, e.g.

If I have hair on the top of my head, then I have hair on the bottom of my feet,

are determinately false.

Fourthly, our classical notion of validity requires indicative conditionals to be truth-evaluable. For example, I'll presently consider an argument to show there are no indicative-conditional propositions whose first premiss is

If there are indicative-conditional propositions, then they have reductive truth conditions.

How, one might wonder, can this argument, whose conclusion is that there are no indicative-conditional propositions, be sound if its just-displayed first premiss isn't true?

Fifthly, indicative conditionals embed in sentences that evidently have determinate truth-values, such as at least some possible utterances of

I don't plan to go to the conference, but I'll let you know if I change my mind.

Finally, it is an obvious consequence of the theory of pleonastic propositions that there are indicative-conditional propositions, so whatever reasons there are for accepting that theory are *ipso facto* reasons for thinking there are indicative-conditional propositions.

The other half of the problem of indicative conditionals is that there are reasons for thinking there are no indicative-conditional propositions. These reasons are encapsulated in three arguments, which I'll call the *Truth-Conditions Argument*, the *Probability Argument*, and *Gibbard's Sly Pete Argument*.

The Truth-Conditions Argument. This may be stated thus:

(i) If there are indicative-conditional propositions, then they have reductive truth conditions.

(ii) If there are indicative-conditional propositions, they have no such truth conditions.

(iii) ∴ There are no indicative-conditional propositions.

First a word about what the premisses of this valid argument mean, before asking whether they are true. If there are indicative-conditional propositions, then, as already noted, the truth schema for propositions

It is true that *S* iff *S*,

applies to them, thereby yielding true substitution instances of the form

It is true that if *A*, then *C* iff if *A*, then *C*.

In the event, indicative-conditional propositions would have at least the *non*-reductive truth conditions the schema provides. *Reductive* truth conditions would give a non-trivial set of separately necessary and jointly sufficient conditions. For example, if, as some claim, the indicative conditional is the material conditional, then indicative conditionals would have the reductive truth conditions displayed in

It is true that if *A*, then *C* iff it is false that *A* or it is true that *C*.

Anyway, now that we know what the premisses of the argument mean, what's to be said for their truth?

The reason for accepting premiss (ii) is a straightforward argument by elimination. Suppose there are indicative-conditional propositions and that they are truth-functional, i.e. that the truth-value of $A \rightarrow C$ (as I'll represent the indicative-conditional proposition that if *A*, then *C*) is a function of the truth-values of the propositions *A* and *C*. Then indicative-conditional propositions are truth-conditionally equivalent to material-conditional propositions and have the reductive truth conditions just displayed. This is a consequence of the fact that, on the assumption that indicative conditionals have truth conditions, then (*a*) an indicative conditional is false if its antecedent is true and its consequent is false and (*b*) there are true indicative conditionals with every other combination of truth-values for its antecedent and consequent—e.g.:

> If you study hard, you will pass the course [T, T]
>
> If Monica marries Bill, he will have a spouse [F, T]
>
> If I'm beheaded before lunch today, then I won't eat lunch today [F, F].

But it is not plausible that indicative conditionals are truth-functional, for they can evidently be false at combinations other than [T, F]. For example,

> (1) I won't be injured if I jump off the Empire State Building

will certainly strike most speakers of English as false. Philosophers who try to defend the view that indicative conditionals are material conditionals, such as Paul Grice and Frank Jackson,[3] will argue that the sentence's seeming false is due not to its being false but to its being unassertible. But as Dorothy Edgington has persuasively countered,[4] if that were the correct diagnosis, then (1) should be like, say,

> I don't have four noses

in that, while it can't be asserted, it is believed: everyone who knows me *believes* that I don't have four noses. Yet it seems plainly false that anyone—or at least anyone without a philosophical axe to grind— believes that I won't be injured if I jump off the top of the Empire State Building (I feel confident in saying it is not something *I* believe).

Might indicative-conditional propositions have reductive *non-*truth-functional truth conditions? There are two reasons for thinking the answer is no. The first reason goes as follows. If indicative-conditional propositions have reductive non-truth-functional truth conditions, then those truth conditions will most likely be along the lines of those given by philosophers, such as Robert Stalnaker, who aspire to a univocal account of all conditionals, counterfactual as well as indicative. As he first presented it,[5] Stalnaker's project was to

---

[3] Grice (1989*a*) and Jackson (1987).   [4] Edgington (1986, 1995).
[5] Stalnaker (1968).

find truth conditions for conditionals which would explain why we evaluate them in the way we do—namely, in the way explained by F. P. Ramsey,[6] wherein we evaluate conditionals according to this approximate guide: 'First, add the antecedent (hypothetically) to your stock of beliefs; second, make whatever adjustments are required to maintain consistency (without modifying the hypothetical belief in the antecedent); finally, consider whether or not the consequent is true.'[7] When it is an indicative conditional that is being evaluated and the evaluator is uncertain about the antecedent, then she simply adds the antecedent to what she already believes and in that light assesses the consequent. Notoriously, more complex adjustments are required when the evaluator believes the antecedent to be false.[8] In any case, the idea is that the proposition expressed by an utterance of 'If A, then C' is one that will be true just in case C is true in that A-world (i.e. possible world in which A is true) which is most like the actual world in such-and-such contextually determined respects.[9] If A is true, then the closest A-world is the actual world. But what if A is false? Herein lies a problem: (a) If the claim that w is the most similar A-world is merely equivalent in cognitive value to the claim that w would be actual if A were true, then the proffered account of conditionals is circular; it analyses conditionals in terms of conditionals. If there is to be a real account here, it must succeed in analysing the relevant similarity relation in non-conditional terms. (b) One may reasonably doubt whether this can be done, and Stalnaker himself doesn't think it can be done.[10] It is true that David Lewis

---

[6] Ramsey (1931).   [7] Ramsey (1931: 33).

[8] Actually, it's not true—even though it's what is commonly said—that when the evaluator is uncertain about the antecedent, she simply adds the antecedent to what she already believes and makes her assessment. For if one were to come to believe A to degree 1, then that would change the degrees to which one believed other things. For example, you're now uncertain whether the wife or the butler is the murderer—you believe each proposition to degree .5. When you now hypothetically believe to degree 1 that the butler did it, then you will at the same time hypothetically believe to degree 0 that the wife did it.

[9] Proponents of this approach must allow for its being indeterminate which A-world, if any, is closest in the intuitively operative respects of similarity. There is more than one way indeterminacy can be let in. On Stalnaker's account, conditional propositions are always bivalent and perfectly determinate. It's only the utterance of a conditional sentence that can be indeterminate, and its indeterminacy will consist in its indeterminately expressing two or more conditional propositions. An utterance of a conditional sentence is true just in case each of the propositions it indeterminately expresses is true, false just in case each is false, and neither true nor false otherwise. In this way, bivalence is maintained for conditional propositions but relinquished for utterances, with no threat to classical logic or semantics.

[10] See e.g. Stalnaker (1975).

and some others following him have tried to specify elaborate conditions involving miracles, bumps, and forks for some cases (no one seems to think conditions can be laid down for all cases).[11] But these conditions are disputable, and disputed.[12] They are also specified in terms of the metaphor of possible worlds, and to be made respectable, by my lights (see 2.6), would have to be restated in literal language without mention of possible worlds, and this may not be possible, at least not without the loss of plausibility such a switch to a periphrastic literal restatement is liable to incur. Furthermore, the proposals made by Lewis and others have no authority other than that they might agree with someone's intuitions about the sorts of cases the proposed conditions are meant to cover. What would explain why satisfaction of *those* conditions is sufficient for the truth of the conditionals that satisfy them?

A second reason for doubting that indicative-conditional propositions have reductive non-truth-functional truth conditions is an argument of Dorothy Edgington's.[13] The first step in the argument is (#) that a rational person who is certain that p or q—i.e. for whom $\Pr(p \text{ or } q) = 1$—but isn't certain either that p or that q will be certain that if not-p, then q. This seems right. Suppose God pops down and tells you, 'Your daughter will either grow up to be a rocket scientist or else she'll grow up to be dishwasher in a Des Moines diner [R or D, for short]—but I'm not going to tell you anything more.' Since you can be certain of whatever God tells you, you would be irrational not to be certain that your daughter will become a dishwasher in a Des Moines diner if she doesn't become a rocket scientist. But (#) would be false if indicative-conditional propositions had non-truth-functional truth conditions. For if they did, then the truth conditions for $\sim R \to D$ would be stronger than those for $\sim R \supset D$ (where '$\supset$' is the material conditional): it would take more for $\sim R \to D$ to be true than that R was true [$= \sim R$ was false] or that D was true; some further condition X would have to be satisfied. But then one who was merely certain that R or D could doubt whether X was satisfied, and could therefore doubt that $\sim R \to D$.

So much, for now, for premiss (ii) (the discussion of counterfactuals in 7.5 will also have some bearing on the plausibility of possible-worlds

---

[11] Lewis (1986a) and e.g. Bennett (2003).

[12] See Dorothy Edgington's objection discussed in the next paragraph.

[13] Edgington (1995).

accounts of indicative conditionals). Why should we think that premiss (i) is true, that there are no indicative-conditional propositions unless they have reductive truth conditions? I think it is because it's felt that if indicative conditionals had non-reductive truth conditions, then they would be 'barely true'—they would be true, but wouldn't owe their truth to the truth of some non-conditional proposition—and that it is not possible for there to be indicative-conditional propositions that are barely true.[14]

I agree that no indicative conditional can be barely true—at least, none can be barely *determinately* true (recall that on my view it is indeterminate whether indeterminate propositions have a truth-value). But the conjunction of that truth and the assumption that there are determinately true indicative-conditional propositions doesn't imply that indicative-conditional propositions have reductive truth conditions. The conjunction leaves open the possibility that whenever an indicative-conditional proposition is determinately true, its truth always supervenes on that of some non-conditional fact, even though there is no correct reductive completion of

It is true that if *A*, then *C* iff...

This would be the case if an indicative-conditional proposition can be *indeterminate* without its being indeterminate whether some reductive sufficient condition for its truth obtains. The account of indicative-conditional propositions I'll eventually offer won't allow for an indicative-conditional proposition to be 'barely determinately true', but it will allow for one to be 'barely indeterminate'—that is, to be indeterminate without its owing its being indeterminate to its being indeterminate whether some reductive sufficient condition obtains. My present point is merely that we haven't been given any compelling reason to accept premiss (i) of the Truth-Conditions Argument. I turn now to the second motivation for denying that there are indicative-conditional propositions, the Probability Argument.

The Probability Argument. This argument assumes the standard definition of conditional probability[15]—that is, the probability of *q* given *p*—namely:

(2) $\Pr(q/p) = \Pr(q \& p)/\Pr(p)$, if $\Pr(p) > o$

<hr />

[14] See Dummett (1976: 94).

[15] Karl Popper (1959) offers an axiom system in which conditional probability isn't undefined when $\Pr(p) = o$.

($\Pr(q/p)$ is undefined when $\Pr(p) = 0$)—and may be put thus (where 'subjective probability' refers to that subjective probability function which satisfies the laws of probability):

   (i) If there are indicative-conditional propositions, then the subjective probability of every such proposition = the conditional subjective probability of its consequent given its antecedent, provided the antecedent has a positive subjective probability.

  (ii) If there are indicative-conditional propositions, then it is not the case that every such proposition whose antecedent has a positive subjective probability is such that its subjective probability = the conditional subjective probability of its consequent given its antecedent.

 (iii) ∴ There are no indicative-conditional propositions.

I'll start with premiss (ii), the argument for which derives from a well-known paper of David Lewis's.[16] Let E = the proposition that a certain tossed fair die comes up even, and let S = the proposition that six comes up. Perfectly rational Ralph, who is present at the toss, will therefore have the following subjective probabilities:

- $\Pr(E) = 1/2$
- $\Pr(S) = 1/6$
- $\Pr(S/E) = 1/3$.

Now suppose, by way of reductio, that there are indicative-conditional propositions and that for any such proposition, $A \to C$,

  (3) $\Pr(A \to C) = \Pr(C/A)$, provided $\Pr(A) > 0$.

We therefore also have for Ralph

  (4) $\Pr(E \to S) = \Pr(S/E)$.

As Lewis shows, from the definition of conditional probability, (2), whose variables range over all propositions, and the assumption that (3) holds for all indicative conditionals, we may further derive that

$$\Pr(A \to C/B) = \Pr(C/A \,\&\, B), \text{ if } \Pr(A \,\&\, B) > 0.$$

But now a substitution instance of this is

$$\Pr(E \to S/{\sim}S) = \Pr(S/E \,\&\, {\sim}S), \text{ if } \Pr(E \,\&\, {\sim}S) > 0$$

---

[16] Lewis (1986c).

and since $Pr(E \& \sim S) > 0$, we get

$$Pr(E \to S/\sim S) = Pr(S/E \& \sim S)$$

and hence

$$Pr(E \to S/\sim S) = Pr(S/E \& \sim S) = 0.$$

At the same time,

$$Pr(E \to S/S) = Pr(S/E \& S) = 1.$$

A consequence of (2), the definition of conditional probability, is the principle of total probability:

$$Pr(p) = Pr(q) \times Pr(p/q) + Pr(\sim q) \times Pr(p/\sim q), \text{ when } 0 < Pr(q) < 1.$$

Letting $p = E \to S$, $q = S$, and given (4), we thus obtain

$$Pr(S/E) = Pr(S) \times 1 + Pr(\sim S) \times 0 = Pr(S).$$

But $Pr(S/E) \neq Pr(S)$: $Pr(S) = 1/6$, whereas $Pr(S/E) = 1/3$. Our initial assumptions entail a contradiction, so at least one of those assumptions isn't true. There are only two options worth taking seriously: either our assumption that there are indicative-conditional propositions is false, or else, while there are such propositions, it is false that they all satisfy (3). Yet the claim that, if there are indicative-conditional propositions, then they *do* satisfy (3) is precisely the claim of premiss (i). So let's see what can be said for that premiss.

The reason for accepting premiss (i) is sometimes put by saying that the assertability of an indicative-conditional sentence goes by the conditional subjective probability of the consequent given the antecedent. But this way of putting it isn't quite right for two reasons. First, on its standard definition, the conditional subjective probability of the consequent given the antecedent is undefined when the subjective probability of the antecedent isn't positive, but the assertability of an indicative-conditional sentence needn't be 'undefined' when the subjective probability of the antecedent isn't positive. The 'assertability' of 'If I am Jesus Christ, then I am Jesus Christ' is 1, even though its antecedent has for me a subjective probability of 0. Secondly, as various writers have noted, *assertability* isn't the right notion to be invoked here anyway, since the assertability of a sentence is partly determined by factors, such as relevance, other than the degree to which one believes what the sentence says.

There is, however, a better way of stating the apparent truth in the 'assertability' motivation for premiss (i). Whether or not there are indicative-conditional propositions, we can speak of the degree to which a person believes that if A, then C. We may therefore say that, when A has a positive subjective probability for a person, then the degree to which she believes that if A, then C = her conditional subjective probability of C, given A. If we now assume that the that-clause in 'x believes to degree n that if A, then C' refers to an indicative-conditional proposition, then we can conclude that the degree to which one believes $A \rightarrow C$, when one's subjective probability that A is positive, = one's conditional subjective probability of C given A. Would this give us premiss (i)? Not necessarily: it may be that although the degree to which one believes $A \rightarrow C$ = the degree to which one believes C given A (when one believes A to some positive degree), the degree to which one believes $A \rightarrow C$ *can't be construed as the degree of one's subjective probability of $A \rightarrow C$*, because the kind of partial belief one has isn't normatively governed by the laws of probability, and thus can't be construed as a 'subjective probability'. Thus, $A \rightarrow C$ may be such that while we can say that the degree to which one believes $A \rightarrow C$ = $\Pr(C/A)$, we *can't* say that one's *subjective probability* that $A \rightarrow C$ = $\Pr(C/A)$. For suppose $A \rightarrow C$ is such that it is indeterminate when A is false. It may be recalled from Chapter 5 that my VPBs aren't normatively governed by the laws of probability, so that on my VPB-based account of indeterminacy we can't coherently speak of the conditional *subjective probability of $A \rightarrow C$*, given $\sim A$—i.e. $\Pr(A \rightarrow C/\sim A)$ wouldn't be defined for one. But if $\Pr(A \rightarrow C)$ were defined for one, then $\Pr(A \rightarrow C/\sim A)$ would also be defined for one when $\Pr(\sim A)$ was positive. Presently I'll propose that $A \rightarrow C$ is indeterminate when A is false and in no way entails either C or $\sim C$ (the point of the 'in no way' prefix is revealed below). At the same time, we'll find an important wrinkle in the way our partial beliefs in indicative-conditional propositions are determined, a wrinkle that underlies the profound basis for holding that the real business of indicative-conditional *sentences* isn't to assert indicative-conditional *propositions*.

Gibbard's Sly Pete Argument. This argument is based on the following famous example of Allan Gibbard's:

Sly Pete and Mr. Thomas Stone are playing poker aboard a Mississippi River boat. Both Pete and Stone are good poker players, and Pete, in addition, is unscrupulous. Stone has bet up to the limit for the hand, and it is now up to Pete to call or fold...My henchman Zack sees Stone's hand, which is quite good, and signals its content to Pete. My henchman Jack sees both hands, and sees that Pete's hand is rather low, so that Stone's is the winning hand. At this point, the room is cleared. A few minutes later, Zack slips me a note which says 'If Pete called, he won,' and Jack slips me a note which says 'If Pete called, he lost.' I know that these notes both come from my trusted henchmen, but do not know which of them sent which note. I conclude that Pete folded.[17]

The argument may be put thus:

(i)   The indicative conditional isn't the material conditional.
(ii) If there are indicative-conditional propositions, then (*) both Zack's utterance of 'If Pete called, he won' and Jack's utterance of 'If Pete called, he lost' are true.
(iii) But if (*), then the indicative conditional is the material conditional.
(iv) ∴ There are no indicative-conditional propositions.

We may take premiss (i) as having been established. Gibbard puts the case for premiss (ii) thus:

In the first place, both sentences are assertable, given what their respective utterers know. Zack knows that Pete knew Stone's hand. He can thus appropriately assert 'If Pete called, he won.' Jack knows that Pete held the losing hand, and thus can appropriately assert 'If Pete called, he lost.' From this, we can see that neither is asserting anything false. For one sincerely asserts something false only when one is mistaken about something germane. In this case neither Zack nor Jack has any relevant false beliefs. The relevant facts are these: (a) Pete had the losing hand, (b) he knew Stone's hand as well as his own, (c) he was disposed to fold on knowing that he had the losing hand, and (d) he folded. Zack knows (b) and (c), and he suspects (a) and therefore (d). Jack knows (a) and (c), and knowing Pete as he does, may well suspect (b) and therefore (d). Neither has any relevant false beliefs, and indeed both may well suspect the whole relevant truth. Neither, then, could sincerely be asserting anything false. Each is sincere, and each, if he is asserting a proposition at all, is asserting a true proposition.[18]

The case for premiss (iii) goes as follows. If the two utterances express propositions, then it is reasonable to assume that the propositions are the same except for the won–lost difference; that is, Zack expressed the proposition that if Pete called, then he won, and Jack expressed the proposition that if Pete called, then he lost. Further, it is obvious that a necessary condition for either proposition's being true

---

[17] Gibbard (1981: 226).   [18] Gibbard (1981: 231).

is that its antecedent is false, for otherwise each proposition would have a true antecedent and a false consequent. Now, either the falsity of their antecedents is sufficient for the truth of the propositions, in which case the indicative conditional is the material conditional (for a conditional with a true antecedent and true consequent must be true, if it has a truth-value), or else the satisfaction of some further condition is also required. But what further condition? The further condition can't be that the consequent is false, as is made plain by a sentence like 'If I eat this apple, then I will grow a second nose'. Might it be (5)?

(5) $A \rightarrow C$ is true if there is a true proposition S—which may be a large conjunction of propositions—that doesn't itself entail C but is such that $S \& A$ is both consistent and entails C.

This thought isn't altogether implausible, but I don't think it can work for the following reason. Although

(6) If Oswald didn't kill Kennedy, then someone else did

is clearly something one intuitively finds acceptable, the same can't be said for

(7) If Oswald didn't kill Kennedy and Kennedy was hidden in a bunker on 22 November 1963, then someone else killed Kennedy.

Even though the conjunction of the antecedent and the true proposition that Kennedy was killed on 22 November 1963 entails the consequent, few would accept (7); they would protest that (7) can't be right, because if Oswald didn't kill Kennedy and Kennedy was hidden in a bunker that day, then a Kennedy impostor, and not Kennedy, was killed. Not only does an example like this show that the proposed additional condition (5) can't suffice for the truth of an indicative-conditional proposition whose antecedent is false; it also shows that when A is false but possible, we don't think $A \rightarrow C$ and $A \rightarrow \sim C$ can both be true (which, of course, is one of the reasons we don't think the indicative conditional is the material conditional). Another, more familiar thought, is that not only must A be consistent with S, it must also be, as Nelson Goodman put it,[19] *cotenable* with S: it must not be the case that S would not be true if A were true. Unfortunately, in addition

[19] Goodman (1947).

to Goodman's complaint that this merely explains the truth of one conditional in terms of another, it also has the more immediate problem of not distinguishing between (6) and (7): the proposition that Oswald didn't kill Kennedy is no more cotenable with the proposition that Kennedy was assassinated than is the antecedent of (7), since the counterfactual

> If Oswald hadn't killed Kennedy, then someone else would have

doesn't seem correct.

How forceful is Gibbard's Sly Pete Argument? A theorist like Robert Stalnaker will want to challenge the assumption that the two utterances assert propositions that are the same but for their different consequents.[20] I, however, would challenge the presupposition of the argument for premiss (ii), that the two propositions are true if they aren't false. Perhaps the two propositions in question are rendered *indeterminate* by the falsity of their antecedents, in which case, if my account of indeterminacy is correct, it is indeterminate whether either proposition even has a truth-value. I'll have more on this presently.

The upshot of this section is that we haven't yet been given a compelling reason to deny that there are indicative-conditional propositions.

7.3   INDETERMINACY AND INDICATIVE-CONDITIONAL PROPOSITIONS

The problem with the Truth-Conditions Argument is its first premiss:

> If there are indicative-conditional propositions, then they have reductive truth conditions.

The important truth motivating this premiss is that no indicative conditional can be 'barely determinately true': whenever one is determinately true, it is made so by some non-indicative-conditional fact (and likewise, *mutatis mutandis*, as regards being 'barely determinately false'). But this kernel of truth doesn't imply the displayed

---

[20] Stalnaker (1984).

premiss, for it may be that sometimes when a conditional is indeterminate, its being indeterminate isn't due to its being indeterminate whether a reductive sufficient condition is satisfied. In the event, as I pointed out in the preceding section, there may be reductive sufficient conditions and reductive necessary conditions but no set of reductive conditions that are separately necessary and jointly sufficient for the truth of indicative-conditional propositions. That this is so is a feature of the account of indicative-conditional propositions I'm about to propose.

The problem with the Probability Argument is also its first premiss:

> If there are indicative-conditional propositions, then the subjective probability of any such conditional = the conditional subjective probability of its consequent given its antecedent, provided the antecedent has a positive subjective probability.

The important truth motivating this premiss is that the degree to which one believes an indicative-conditional proposition = the degree of one's conditional subjective probability of its consequent given its antecedent, when the antecedent has a positive subjective probability. But this kernel of truth doesn't entail the displayed premiss. For it may be that the indicative-conditional can have no subjective probability when the negation of its antecedent has a positive subjective probability. This is accommodated in the account of indicative-conditional propositions I'm about to propose, for on that account the appropriate belief to have, for one who knows the antecedent is false, is a VPB, and VPBs aren't normatively governed by the laws of probability.

The problem with Gibbard's Sly Pete Argument is its second premiss:

> If there are indicative-conditional propositions, then both Zack's utterance of 'If Pete called, he won' and Jack's utterance of 'If Pete called, he lost' are true.

The argument for this premiss presupposes that bivalence holds for indicative-conditional propositions, but the expressed propositions may be *indeterminate* and, on my account of indeterminacy, if they are indeterminate, then it is indeterminate whether bivalence holds for them. That these propositions are indeterminate is a feature of the account of indicative-conditional propositions I'll now begin to lay out.

I hold the following:

(*a*) There are indicative-conditional propositions. The doctrine of pleonastic propositions applied to indicative-conditional sentences yields indicative-conditional propositions. There is no relevant semantic difference between, on the one hand,

> I won't eat lunch today; so, it's true that I won't eat lunch today,
> I believe that I won't eat lunch today,

and, on the other hand,

> If I'm beheaded this morning, then I won't eat lunch today; so, it's true that if I'm beheaded this morning, then I won't eat lunch today.
>
> I believe that if I'm beheaded this morning, then I won't eat lunch today.

(*b*) Another consequence of the doctrine of pleonastic propositions as applied to indicative-conditional propositions is that, subject to possible qualification pertaining to semantic paradox, every instance of the truth schema

> The proposition that if *A*, then *C* is true iff if *A*, then *C*

is true.

(*c*) But indicative-conditional propositions don't have *reductive* truth conditions.

(*d*) Still, some indicative-conditional propositions are determinately true and others are determinately false, and when such a proposition is determinately true/false, its being so is entailed by the determinate truth of some non-indicative-conditional proposition. I'll elaborate on this after the next point.

(*e*) There are two ways for an indicative-conditional proposition to be indeterminate. (i) An indicative-conditional proposition will be indeterminate when it is indeterminate whether a reductive sufficient condition for its determinate truth obtains. This may be either because there is a non-indicative-conditional proposition whose truth would entail the truth of the conditional but which is itself indeterminate or because it is indeterminate whether a certain non-indicative-conditional fact entails the conditional proposition. (ii) An indicative-conditional proposition may be indeterminate even though it is not indeterminate by virtue of (i), and this, as we'll eventually see, happens whenever ... —well, I'll get to that pretty soon.

Many of the indicative conditionals we're apt to express fall into this category. Let's consider an example.

At the firm's weekly partners' meeting, Mr Bigshot announces

(8) I will resign if the firm makes Snodgrass a partner,

thereby asserting the proposition that if the firm makes Snodgrass a partner, then he will resign ($P \rightarrow R$, for short). Ralph is a member of the firm present at the meeting, and immediately after Bigshot's utterance of (8), $\Pr(R/P) = .5$ represents Ralph's conditional subjective probability that R, given P. As it happens, the firm doesn't make Snodgrass a partner and Bigshot doesn't resign. Ralph knows this, and so at that point $\Pr(R/P)$ is undefined for him and for anyone else in his epistemic position. P and R are both false, but what about $P \rightarrow R$? Let's suppose that Mr Bigshot is pretty ordinary. There are no medical facts, or anything else out of the ordinary, that make it impossible for him to do, or fail to do, relevant actions. I submit that in the kind of case being imagined, there are no facts that would settle the issue, and that an ideally placed epistemic agent with access to all relevant non-conditional facts would v-believe $P \rightarrow R$. I think this is confirmed by the way we actually deal with such conditionals when we debate them knowing their antecedents are false. We resort to counterfactuals, in this case to counterfactuals about what Mr Bigshot would have done had the firm made Snodgrass a partner—but, and here's the rub, in considering such counterfactuals what we do is imagine ourselves in relevant scenarios in which we're uncertain about the antecedent and contemplate what $\Pr(C/A)$ would be for us in such a scenario.[21] Whatever we think that is, that is the degree to which one v-believes $A \rightarrow C$. There is a puzzle about the way we form our partial beliefs about indicative conditionals, and I'll get to it presently. My present point is that indicative-conditional propositions with false antecedents are typically indeterminate. This is the verdict of my account of indeterminacy, and I submit that conditional propositions like $P \rightarrow R$ in the Mr Bigshot example are intuitively indeterminate, so that *any* account of indeterminacy ought to deliver that verdict.

(f) I return to the point made in (d), that some indicative-conditional propositions are determinately true and others are determinately false, and that when such a proposition is determinately true/false, its being so is entailed by the determinate truth of some non-indicative-conditional fact. Under what conditions is an

---

[21] Cf. Edgington (1995).

indicative-conditional proposition determinately true, and under what conditions is one determinately false? I think it is *reasonably* safe to say both that

> (9) $A \rightarrow C$ is determinately true *if* (*a*) both A and C are determinately true[22] or (*b*) it is determinately the case that A metaphysically or physically entails C

and that

> (10) $A \rightarrow C$ is determinately false *if* (*a*) A is determinately true and C is determinately false or (*b*) it is determinately the case that A metaphysically or physically entails $\sim C$ (but not C).[23]

As I understand metaphysical entailment, it is that strong kind of entailment of which conceptual entailment, logical entailment, and mathematical entailment are species. Thus, the first two of the following examples are determinately true according to (9), while the second two are determinately false according to (10):

> If Hillary Clinton is a widow, then she was married to someone who died.

> If bedbugs are immortal, then bedbugs are immortal.

> If Hillary Clinton is a widow, then she was never married.

> If 2 is an even number, then so is 17.

'Physical entailment' is not an ideal label for what I have in mind—it may not be definable, and it's pretty vague; but I hope the following examples give a good enough idea of what I intend, the first two of which are intended to be determinately true according to (9), the second two determinately false according to (10).

> If I'm beheaded this morning, then I'll be dead before this afternoon.

> If this pure sample of water is heated to 100 °C at sea level, it will boil.

---

[22] An example such as 'Mary quit smoking ten years ago if I wasn't born in North Carolina' may seem to challenge this, but I'm content to say that, while it would be very misleading to assert, since Mary's quitting smoking ten years ago had nothing to do with my not having been born in North Carolina, it's nevertheless determinately true.

[23] The parenthetical qualification 'but not C' is to accommodate the case where A entails $\sim C$ by virtue of being impossible, thereby entailing C, as well as $\sim C$. No qualification is needed for (9), because it seems harmless to count $A \rightarrow C$ as true when A is impossible.

If nothing is done to increase the kinetic energy of this cold water, it will boil within seconds.

If you eat ten carrots, then you will be able to run faster than the speed of light.

Now, I could try to be more precise here about what should be included under the vague rubric 'physical entailment', but I see no need to be. The issue isn't of much interest, since however the notion is precisified, the really important fact will be that the indicative-conditional propositions with false antecedents which are of interest to us are all indeterminate.

Are the sufficient conditions given in (9) and (10) also *necessary* conditions? Consider again (6) ('If Oswald didn't kill Kennedy, then someone else did'), which seems to be taken by everyone to express a true proposition ($O \rightarrow E$, for short), if there are indicative-conditional propositions. If (6) is determinately true, then (9) fails to state a necessary condition, for O in no way entails E, and we certainly can't assume that O and E are true. But it is not clear to me (6) is true. To be sure,

(11) If Oswald didn't kill Kennedy—and given that Kennedy was assassinated—then someone other than Oswald killed Kennedy

is determinately true, and anyone prepared to assert (6) would certainly believe (11). My reservation about $O \rightarrow E$ is primarily based on the worry that if it were determinately true, then a condition considered earlier,

(5) $A \rightarrow C$ is true if there is a true proposition S that doesn't entail C but is such that $S \& A$ is both consistent and entails C,

would have to be correct, and I argued above that it wasn't correct. Of course, I haven't shown that nothing other than (5) could account for the determinate truth of (6), but nothing else very plausible occurs to me. There are also some supporting considerations for regarding $O \rightarrow E$ as indeterminate. First, the fact that (11) is determinately true does help to explain our intuition that (6) is true, since when we entertain (6) we instinctively do so on the fixed assumption that Kennedy was assassinated. Secondly, and related to this, our certainty that Kennedy was assassinated explains why one whose subjective probability that Oswald didn't kill Kennedy is positive has a conditional subjective probability that someone else killed Kennedy, given that Oswald didn't, that equals 1 (or very close to 1). Besides, consider again the example (7) used earlier:

If Oswald didn't kill Kennedy and Kennedy was hidden in a bunker on 22 November 1963, then someone else killed Kennedy.

What this example reveals is that in considering an indicative-conditional proposition with a false antecedent whose conjunction with known facts entails the consequent, it can be relevant to ask whether the known facts are cotenable with the false antecedent. In other words, would the known facts have been facts if the false antecedent had been true? Looked at in this light, it may be reasonable, in assessing $O \to E$ when one is certain that O is false, to wonder whether Kennedy would have been assassinated had Oswald not killed Kennedy, and of course we would then get an entirely different result. I think there is an explanation of what is going on here that supports the view that (6) is indeterminate. It is that when we assess $A \to C$ knowing A is false, we assess the counterfactual $A \,\square\!\!\to C$ (the proposition that if A had been/were true, then C would have been/would be true), but when we assess $A \,\square\!\!\to C$ we do so by contemplating contextually relevant scenarios in which we're uncertain whether A is true and asking what $\Pr(C/A)$ would be for us in that scenario. Further, there is no such thing as *the* scenario from which to evaluate a counterfactual; that will depend on contextually determined interests. I think what is going on in the famous Oswald–Kennedy pair

> If Oswald didn't kill Kennedy, then someone else did $[O \to E]$
>
> If Oswald hadn't killed Kennedy, then someone else would have $[O \,\square\!\!\to E]$

is this: when $\Pr(O) = 0$ and we assess $O \to E$, the scenario made contextually relevant for the assessment of $O \,\square\!\!\to E$ is one in which it is given that Kennedy was assassinated, but when we assess $O \,\square\!\!\to E$ on its own, the contextually relevant scenario is one in which it is not given that Kennedy was assassinated. So I'm inclined to conclude that (6), $O \to E$, is indeterminate.

But (6) isn't the only example to challenge the idea that (9) provides a necessary, as well as a sufficient, condition for the determinate truth of $A \to C$. A challenge is also provided by an example such as

> (12) If I got a huge raise in salary, I don't yet know it $[H \to K$, for short],

where H is false but where $\Pr(K/H) = 1$ owing to one's being certain that K is true (so one is certain that one doesn't know about getting a huge raise both if one got one and if one didn't). Since $\Pr(K/H) = 1$, one believes $H \to K$ to degree 1, and thus one may well be tempted to suppose that $H \rightarrow K$ is determinately true. This, I think, would be a mistake (although, as we'll soon see, there is indeed a puzzle here to be resolved). Although, being uncertain about H, you now believe $H \rightarrow K$ to degree 1, you are also not in ideal epistemic circumstances with respect to $H \rightarrow K$; if you were, you would know with complete certainty that H was false, which would mean that for you $\Pr(H) = 0$, and hence that $\Pr(K/H)$ was undefined for you. At that point, when you believed H to degree 0, you would assess the indicative-conditional proposition $H \rightarrow K$ by assessing the counterfactual-conditional proposition that if you had gotten a huge raise in salary, then you wouldn't now know about it, and this is something you're apt to disbelieve to a fairly high degree. So I don't have a problem in holding that (12) is indeterminate, given that its antecedent is false. (The salmonella example in 7.4 further elaborates the case for taking a proposition such as (12) to be indeterminate.)

There are also challenges to the idea that (10) provides a necessary, as well as a sufficient, condition for the determinate falsity of $A \rightarrow C$, but what was just said applies, *mutatis mutandis*, here, too. Thus, I'm inclined to have the following final position on the truth conditions for indicative-conditional propositions:

> $A \rightarrow C$ is determinately true iff (*a*) both A and C are determinately true or (*b*) it is determinately the case that A metaphysically or physically entails C, and determinately false iff (*a*) A is determinately true and C is determinately false or (*b*) it is determinately the case that A metaphysically or physically entails $\sim C$ (but not C).

$A \rightarrow C$ is of course indeterminate when it is not determinately true or determinately false, but what is most of interest is that it is indeterminate when A is both false and neither metaphysically nor physically entails either C or $\sim C$.

7.4   THE PARADOX OF INDICATIVE CONDITIONALS AND THE TRUTH IN NON-COGNITIVISM ABOUT THEM

Assume my VPB-based theory of indeterminacy and let A be a proposition that is determinately true if X is true, indeterminate if Y

is true, and determinately false if Z is true. Suppose, too, that one would s-believe A to degree 1 if one were certain that X was true, v-believe both A and $\sim A$ to degree .5 if one were certain that Y was true, and s-believe $\sim A$ to degree 1 if one were certain that Z was true. Further, one s-believes to degree .2 both that X is true and that Z is true, and to degree .6 that Y is true. In the event one should v-believe both A and $\sim A$ to degree .3 and s-believe both A and $\sim A$ to degree .2. Now here's the puzzle, for me, about indicative-conditional propositions, stated with respect to example (8), Mr Bigshot's utterance of 'I will resign if the firm makes Snodgrass a partner'. Consider an ideally rational agent, Ann, who agrees with the truth conditions for indicative-conditional propositions displayed at the close of the preceding section, so that $P \rightarrow R$, the proposition expressed by (8), is indeterminate iff P is false, determinately true iff $(P \& R)$ is determinately true, and determinately false iff $(P \& \sim R)$ is determinately true. Suppose that Ann's subjective probability function is such that

- $\Pr(\sim P) = .5$
- $\Pr(P \& R) = .25$
- $\Pr(P \& \sim R) = .25$
- $\Pr(R/P) = .5$.

Then it would seem that my theory predicts that Ann will s-believe $P \rightarrow R$ to degree .25, s-believe $\sim(P \rightarrow R)$ to degree .25, and v-believe both $P \rightarrow R$ and $\sim(P \rightarrow R)$ to positive degrees which sum to .5. But that's not what we find, if Ann is like everyone else: because for her $\Pr(R/P) = .5$, she'll believe $P \rightarrow R$ to degree .5.

What to do? It is apt to seem that my choice is either to declare speakers mistaken in their beliefs about indicative-conditional propositions or else to give up some theory in my conjunction of theories that leads to the mistaken prediction about Ann—my account of pleonastic propositions, which entails that there are indicative-conditional propositions, my account of indeterminacy, or my account of the truth conditions for indicative-conditional propositions. Actually, I believe the truth to lie in between, so to say.

I think the non-cognitivist about indicative conditionals, such as Dorothy Edgington, is right to claim that typically an indicative conditional is of interest to us only when we're uncertain about its antecedent, that when we then utter the indicative-conditional sentence our primary concern is to express our belief that the consequent is likely to be true given the truth of the antecedent, and that there is no indicative-conditional proposition whose truth conditions are such that to believe that those conditions obtain, when one is uncertain of the antecedent, is just to believe that the consequent is likely to be true, given the truth of the antecedent. But I don't think this warrants the conclusion that indicative-conditional sentences don't express indicative-conditional propositions. We have a paradox here, and like most philosophical paradoxes, it has an unhappy-face solution.

The paradox is that each of (i)–(iv) seems plausible when considered on its own, but the conjunction of them is inconsistent:

  (i) One is epistemically entitled to assertively utter 'If A, then C' iff one justifiably believes the proposition $A \rightarrow C$ to a very high degree.

  (ii) One is epistemically entitled to assertively utter 'If A, then C' (when one isn't certain that $\sim A$) iff one justifiably believes to a very high degree that C, given A.

  (iii) If (i) and (ii), then (ii) is implied by the truth conditions for $A \rightarrow C$.

  (iv) But (ii) isn't implied by the truth conditions for $A \rightarrow C$.

Now (i) is very plausible; it expresses the platitude that 'assertability goes by subjective probability'.[24] It is very plausible that there are indicative-conditional propositions, and it's a truism that one is epistemically entitled to utter a sentence assertively iff one believes to a very high degree the proposition thus asserted. To say that one is 'epistemically entitled' to assertively utter a sentence is to say that the belief requirements for an assertion are met, even though other requirements may not be. For example, I'm epistemically entitled to utter 'I am more than six months old', but it's hard to imagine a context in which other conditions for assertability, such as relevance and informativeness, would be met. As for (ii), it is arguably the one thing on which all writers on indicative conditionals agree; it expresses the platitude that in the case of indicative conditionals, 'assertability goes ... by the conditional subjective probability of the consequent, given the antecedent'.[25] As for (iii), the idea is that if the assertability of 'If A, then C' goes both by the probability of the truth of the proposition $A \rightarrow C$ and by the conditional subjective probability of C, given A,

---

[24] David Lewis (1986c: 133).   [25] Lewis (1986c: 133).

then that must be because $\Pr(A \to C)$ is high just in case $\Pr(C/A)$ is high (when $\Pr(A)$ is positive), and if that is so, it must be because the truth conditions for $A \to C$ are such that the proposition is likely to be true when C is very likely to be true, given that A is true. And (iii) is obviously true, given that $A \to C$ is determinately true only when either A and C are both true or A in some way entails C.

A happy-face solution of this paradox would do two things. First, it would tell us which of (i)–(iv) wasn't the truth it appeared to be, and secondly, it would tell us this in a way that removed from the culprit its patina of plausibility. Like most philosophical paradoxes, this one doesn't have an entirely happy-face solution. It's not hard (for me) to identify the odd guy out: it is (iii). What precludes a completely happy-face solution is that the explanation of what is going on here, as in every case of an unhappy-face solution, involves an essentially ineradicable glitch in our conceptual practices. Our concept of a proposition leaves us no option but to say that there are indicative-conditional propositions, and our concept of the indicative-conditional relation—that relation that must hold between propositions A and C in order for it to be true that $A \to C$—bestows on the proposition $A \to C$ the truth conditions already proposed: it is determinately true when, and only when, either A and C are determinately true or A determinately metaphysically or physically entails C, determinately false when, and only when, either A is determinately true and C is determinately false or A determinately metaphysically or physically entails $\sim C$ (but not C). At the same time, we evidently have a need to express conditional belief even when we don't have a need to express belief in a conditional, and somewhere along the way, the indicative conditional got co-opted for that purpose. But the practice of using indicative-conditional sentences to express conditional beliefs gets conflated with the practice of uttering sentences to assert, and thereby to express belief in, the propositions they express. Infelicities result. For example, you know with certainty that you are not now ill, so your conditional subjective probability that you're not ill, given that you ate salmonella-infected poultry = 1, and consequently you assertively utter with complete confidence, 'If I ate salmonella-infected poultry, it didn't make me ill'. In uttering this you take yourself to be asserting that if you ate salmonella-infected poultry, then it didn't make you ill (the proposition $S \to I$, for short) and to be asserting something you believe to degree 1. But wait! Perfectly rational Ralph knows nothing about your current state of health and believes to a very high degree that you got ill, given that you ate salmonella-infected poultry, and so he disbelieves $S \rightarrow I$. Ralph then learns with certainty that you didn't eat salmonella-infected poultry and that you weren't ill. Will he change his mind about the proposition $S \rightarrow I$? Of course not. Should he change his mind? Of course not. So you have to admit that although you believe $S \rightarrow I$ to degree 1, you're not entitled to belief that $S \rightarrow I$ is true! As I said, an unhappy-face solution.[26]

Does the present paradox admit of a *weak* or a *strong* unhappy-face solution? A paradox has a weak unhappy-face solution if a paradox-free conceptual revision of the trouble-making concepts is possible that does the work we expected the trouble-making concepts to do. To say that a paradox has a strong unhappy-face solution is to say that no such conceptual revision is possible. I think the present paradox of indicative conditionals has a weak unhappy-face solution, and it makes an important concession to non-cognitivists like Dorothy Edgington. Although we need to have and to express conditional beliefs about what's likely or unlikely given the truth of this, that, or the other thing, and although the material conditional is extremely useful, if not actually indispensable, in deductive reasoning, we don't seem to have any great need for indicative-conditional propositions. We can't in good faith assert propositions we take to be indeterminate, so if this is taken to heart, and what I said about the truth conditions of indicative-conditional propositions is correct, then

---

[26] If I can claim that our practice of uttering indicative conditionals isn't dictated by the truth conditions I've claimed for the propositions they express, then—Hartry Field has asked—why can't the theorist who identifies the indicative conditional with the material conditional dismiss the evidence against her theory by appeal to the same practice of uttering indicative conditionals to express conditional belief? There is, however, a crucial asymmetry between the claim that indicative-conditional propositions have material-conditional truth conditions and the claim that they have the ones I've proposed. Our intuition that it is not the case that 'If I sneeze within the next two seconds, there will never be another murder' is made true by the falsity of its antecedent is, I dare say, unconflicted and indefeasible. If propositions of a certain kind have truth conditions that are out of whack with our practice of uttering sentences that express those propositions, then there ought to be places where a *conflict* in our intuitions is revealed. For the truth conditions I've proposed, that conflict is revealed in examples like my salmonella example; but I see no place where a conflict is revealed when it's proposed that indicative-conditional propositions are really material-conditional propositions.

utterances of indicative-conditional sentences that were controlled just by the truth conditions of the indicative-conditional propositions they express would be warranted only when the speaker believed that it was either the case that A and C or that A metaphysically or physically entailed C. It is not at all clear what need we have for a connective $\Downarrow$ such that

'$S \Downarrow S''$' is true iff (a) 'S and S''' is true or (b) 'S metaphysically or physically entails S''' is true.

Of course, even if I'm right about this, the use of indicative-conditional sentences will continue without alteration—not only because the readers of analytical philosophy are small in number, but also because our current use doesn't do any harm.

7.5 COUNTERFACTUAL-CONDITIONAL PROPOSITIONS

David Lewis proposed the following truth conditions for counterfactual-conditional propositions:

(13) $A \,\square\!\!\rightarrow C$ is true iff some A-&-C world is more similar overall to the actual world than is any A-&-not-C world.[27]

Lewis admits that this account 'does little to predict the truth values of particular counterfactuals in particular contexts', and that, accordingly, it 'must be fleshed out with an account of the appropriate similarity relation, and this will differ from context to context'.[28] He does suggest how it should be fleshed out for at least one important class of counterfactuals, making it clear in the process that he didn't mean similarity by 'similar'.[29]

But talk of possible worlds, I argued earlier (see 2.6), can at best be a useful heuristic device for saying something that can be said without appeal to possible worlds. So the first thing I must ask about (13) is how it should be restated without mention of possible worlds. One

---

[27] Read '$A \,\square\!\!\rightarrow C$' as 'If it were/had been the case that A, then it would be/would have been the case that C'. [28] Lewis (1986c: 41).

[29] Lewis (1986c: 47–8).

thought, doubtless in need of refinement, would be that:

(14) $A \square \rightarrow C$ is true iff there is a maximally consistent set of propositions S such that (a) S contains A and C and (b) S bears relation... to the set of true propositions

where the gap is to be filled by the specification in non-counterfactual terms of some appropriate relation between sets of propositions. I don't think this can be done. First, as Stalnaker recognized,[30] talk of the A-&-C world that is 'closest' or 'most similar' to the actual world has no cash-value beyond that of 'the A-&-C world that would be actual if A were true'. Accounts like (13) seem substantive because we have intuitions about what the facts would have been like had A been true, but, as I'll suggest, we can account for these intuitions without supposing that (14) enjoys a reductive completion. Secondly, there is a more general problem, brought to light by Dorothy Edgington,[31] although I'll put it in my own terms. Consider the counterfactual

(15) If this fair coin had been tossed, it would have landed heads up.

The problem for the Lewisian reductionist is that there is no way for him to account for the fact that one is justified in believing (15) to degree .5. The antecedent is much too underspecified to allow the counterfactual to be deemed either true or false. An account of counterfactuals that would hope to give reductive truth conditions for $A \square \rightarrow C$ says that it is true just in case C is entailed by the conjunction of A, laws of nature, and relevant particular facts obtaining at some relevant time of assessment. But it is clear there can be no such conjunction for the antecedent of (15), since to get a relevant conjunction which includes that proposition and entails the consequent, one would have to have an enormously detailed description of physical facts about the precise weight and shape of the coin, the precise dynamics of the toss, the ambient air and gravity conditions, and so on. Thus, for the reductionist, one's believing (15) to degree .5 can't be construed as one's believing to degree .5 that (15) is *true*. Might the reductionist say that (15) is indeterminate, and that in believing (15) to degree .5 = one's v-believing it to degree .5? I don't see how. Even if it is assumed that the universe is deterministic (big assumption!), the reductionist would evidently have to say that (15) is indeterminate

---

[30] Stalnaker (1975).   [31] Edgington (1995).

because it is indeterminate which possible world is 'closest' to the actual world. But then to be justified in v-believing (15) to degree .5 one would presumably have to be justified in believing that the consequent was true in 50 per cent of the relevant antecedent worlds, and it is pretty hard to see how one could be justified in believing that.

Leona, a 47-year-old philosophy professor, announces, 'If I had become a lawyer instead of a philosopher, I'd be a wealthy woman today', and thereby asserts the proposition

(16) $L \square \rightarrow W$

(i.e. the proposition that if she had become a lawyer instead of a philosopher, then she would be a wealthy woman today). We may suppose Leona had an excellent undergraduate record, could have gone to a top law school, and has many of the qualities one associates with successful lawyers. Thus, Leona and others may well believe (16) to some non-negligible degree. At the same time, it seems to me extremely plausible that an agent in circumstances that were ideal for evaluating (16) could v*-believe it, thus rendering it indeterminate by my lights, and that by *any* reasonable lights (16) is indeterminate. Look at it this way: even if you help yourself to knowledge of all the non-conditional facts there are, what on earth would settle the truth-value of (16)?

At the same time, we may well believe (16) to some degree or other. If my account of indeterminacy is correct and (16) is, as I submit, indeterminate, then the ideally rational believer's partial belief in (16) will be a VPB. How are such beliefs formed? Here, as I said in 7.3, I agree with Dorothy Edgington and others that what we do when we form beliefs in counterfactual propositions like (16) is imagine ourselves in a scenario in which we are uncertain about the antecedent but help ourselves to this, that, or the other assumption, and ask what $Pr(C/A)$ would be for us in that situation.[32] Adding to that, I would also say that no such scenario can count as *the* scenario from whose point of view the counterfactual enjoys its correct evaluation. Thus, in evaluating (16), we needn't cast ourselves imaginatively back to a time when Leona was an undergraduate. We could assess the counterfactual from the point of view of one who doesn't know what Leona did after getting her BA degree but knows what senior lawyers at top firms make, knows relevant facts about Leona's intelligence,

---

[32] Edgington (1995).

verbal skills, personality, appearance, and so forth. Of course, relative to a scenario of evaluation, some partial beliefs may be more reasonable than others, but nothing can count as *the* correct degree of belief to have in a proposition like (16) in the scenario, although, to be sure, certain degrees would be unreasonable and others more reasonable than others. In no scenario can one reasonably hope to have such a partial belief *settled* one way or the other (although, of course, one may gain further information that would alter the degree to which one believes it), unless it is *stipulated* that it is a scenario in which the antecedent and consequent are true.

I am, of course, assuming that the reasons for holding that there are indicative-conditional propositions also hold for counterfactual-conditional propositions. After all, Leona believes, and asserted, *that if she'd become a lawyer instead of a philosopher, she'd be a wealthy woman today*, and her utterance

> If I had become a lawyer instead of a philosopher, I'd be a wealthy woman today

is pleonastically equivalent to

> It's true that if I had become a lawyer instead of a philosopher, I'd be a wealthy woman today.

It is also true that no counterfactual-conditional proposition can be 'barely determinately true' or 'barely determinately false', but, as before, this doesn't imply that those propositions must have reductive truth conditions. They don't; they have only the truth conditions they get from being instances of the general truth schema for propositions

> The proposition that S is true iff S.

Still, some counterfactuals are determinately true, and others are determinately false, though not nearly as many as philosophers who write on counterfactuals seem to suppose. I'll explain.

I think what was said about the truth conditions for indicative-conditional propositions can be said about the truth conditions for counterfactual-conditional propositions. In other words, as regards their truth conditions, there is a univocal account for all conditional propositions—namely, the following:

A conditional proposition of any kind is determinately true when, and only when, one of two conditions obtains. The first is that the antecedent determinately metaphysically or physically entails its consequent. We saw how this works for indicative conditionals, and it works in the same way for counterfactuals. Thus the following counterfactuals are determinately true:

> If you had been thinking of the number 2, then you would have been thinking of an even number.
>
> If the surface of the ball were entirely red, then it wouldn't also now be entirely green.
>
> If Mary were a widow, then she would have been married to someone who died.
>
> If roses were green and violets were black, then roses would be green.
>
> If I had been beheaded this morning, then I would have been dead before this afternoon.
>
> If this pure sample of water were heated to 100 °C at sea level, it would boil.

The second condition whose obtaining is sufficient for the determinate truth of a counterfactual-conditional proposition is that both its antecedent and its consequent are determinately true. Those conditionals called 'counterfactuals' don't necessarily have false antecedents, as is well known. Thus, in hypothesizing about a case a detective might say 'If the murderer had wanted to cast suspicion on the daughter, this is just the sort of thing he or she would've done', where this point might end up being part of an argument to show that the murderer had in fact wanted to cast suspicion on the daughter.

A conditional proposition of any kind is determinately false when, and only when, one of two conditions obtains. The first is that the conditional has a determinately true antecedent and a determinately false consequent. The second is when the antecedent determinately metaphysically or physically entails the negation of the consequent (but not the consequent). Thus, the following counterfactuals are determinately false:

> If I had been beheaded this morning, then I would still be alive this afternoon.
>
> If Mary were a widow, then she would never have been married.

A conditional proposition that isn't determinately true or determinately false is indeterminate, and, as with indicative-conditional propositions, a counterfactual-conditional proposition can be indeterminate even when it doesn't owe its indeterminacy to its being indeterminate whether some non-conditional fact obtains which metaphysically or physically entails the counterfactual. The proposition (16), that if Leona had become a lawyer instead of a philosopher, she'd be a wealthy woman today, is indeterminate in this way. It is possible for someone in ideal epistemic circumstances with respect to (16) to v-believe it, and not because he v-believes some other proposition on which the truth of (16) would supervene or v-believes that a certain non-conditional fact entails (16).

My view, then, is that virtually all the counterfactuals likely to interest us are indeterminate. Not all philosophers agree, as witness this from Jonathan Bennett:

> The dam burst at 8.47 p.m., and within two minutes the waters had swept through the valley, killing 19 occupants of cars on the valley road. Reflecting on the gratifying fact that the dam-burst did little other serious harm, when it might have been expected to kill thousands, someone remarks 'If there had been no cars on the road at that time, no lives would have been lost'. In the case I have in mind...the asserted conditional—call it No-cars $\Box\!\!\rightarrow$ No-deaths—[is] true.[33]

I, on the other hand, can see no good basis for judging No-cars $\Box\!\!\rightarrow$ No-deaths to be true in the absence of some non-conditional fact that makes it true, and it is doubtful there is any such fact. But what if some clever philosopher can lay down a bunch of conditions that agrees with the sorts of intuitions we have in cases like the one at hand, conditions having to do with what worlds are to count as closest and are stated in terms of miracles, bumps, and forks? I've already expressed my scepticism (see 7.3). First, no such conditions should be taken seriously until they are translated into literal language, language that avoids the metaphor of possible worlds and its ilk. Such translations might not exist. Secondly, although I won't go into actual proposals, I submit that when we look at those proposals, even when stated in their original, untranslated form, we find that they have no authority other than that they agree with someone's intuitions about the sorts of cases the conditions are meant to cover, and that there is nothing at all to explain why satisfaction of just those conditions is sufficient for the truth of a counterfactual.

---

[33] Bennett (2003).

Thirdly, we evaluate $A \square \rightarrow C$ by going to some contextually relevant scenario and contemplating what $\Pr(C/A)$ would be were the scenario actual. In the cases of interest, where A is false and entails neither C nor $\sim C$, $\Pr(C/A)$ may be high but it will never (for the ideally rational agent) be 1. But if there is even a little room for $A\text{-}\&\text{-}\sim C$, then how can one be certain that $A \square \rightarrow C$ is determinately true? The ideal epistemic agent will believe $A \square \rightarrow C$ to the degree to which she supposes $\Pr(C/A)$ would be for her in a certain contextually relevant scenario, but the partial belief thus formed will at best be a VPB*, not a SPB, thus rendering the counterfactual proposition indeterminate, at least by my theory. Fourthly, there is no such thing as *the* correct scenario from which to evaluate a counterfactual, although in context some are more relevant than others. For example, in a discussion of Bennett's No-cars $\square \rightarrow$ No-deaths, Al says its true, since only motorists were killed, but Betty disagrees, arguing that if there had been no cars on the road, then the neighbourhood kids might have taken advantage of the empty road for rollerblading and skateboarding. Who's right? The question, I submit, has no correct answer because there's no such thing as *the* correct scenario from which to evaluate a counterfactual. The temptation to think that No-cars $\square \rightarrow$ No-deaths is true is simply due to the fact that $\Pr(\text{No-deaths}/\text{No-cars})$ is reasonably high in one particular contextually relevant scenario which one imagines using to calculate what $\Pr(\text{No-deaths}/\text{No-cars})$ would be in that scenario, which value will fix, relative to that scenario, the degree to which one believes No-cars $\square \rightarrow$ No-deaths. But though the ideal epistemic agent may end up believing No-cars $\square \rightarrow$ No-deaths to a high degree, her partial belief will be a VPB—she will, that is, end up v*-believing the proposition to a high degree, thus rendering it indeterminate.

What I said about Bennett's example applies generally, even to backward-looking counterfactuals. Some people are taking turns betting on fair tosses of a fair coin. To avoid certain irrelevant complications, let's suppose that the outcomes of fair coin tosses are objectively chance events. Anyway, right before Lil's turn, her husband, Phil, tells her to bet heads. But Lil, who has grown resentful over the years of Phil's controlling nature, simply ignores him. Still before the toss, Phil sulkily adds,

(17) If you were to be on heads you would win.

Do we at this point think that Phil's assertion of (17) is proved true just by the fact that the coin is tossed and lands heads up? That's not my intuition. I think (17) is indeterminate; an ideally rational agent with access to all relevant facts could v-believe (17) to degree .5. But let's continue the story. Lil bets tails, loses, and grudgingly says,

(18) If I had bet heads, I would've won.

Now, unlike Phil's utterance of (17), Lil's utterance of (18) is apt to strike one as saying something true—after all, by hypothesis the result of the toss was undetermined, and thus whatever Lil bet, her bet was causally irrelevant to the outcome of the toss. So, should we say that, contrary to first appearances, Phil did say something true? I don't think so. I think this example illustrates that there is no one scenario for evaluating a counterfactual that is *the* correct scenario in which to evaluate it. We tend to evaluate counterfactual-conditional propositions by contemplating what $Pr(C/A)$ would be for us in a contextually relevant scenario. The scenario we were using in evaluating (17) was one in which we didn't know the outcome of the toss. That was the scenario that was contextually most appropriate at that stage in my saga of Phil and Lil. But later in the story, when we evaluated Lil's utterance of (18), which for all that matters expressed the same proposition as Phil's utterance of (17), the scenario we used to evaluate the utterance was one in which we were certain that the coin lands heads up, since that was the most contextually appropriate scenario at that stage of the story. So, I continue to hold that the proposition expressed in both (17) and (18) is indeterminate.

Since counterfactual-conditional propositions have the same truth conditions as indicative-conditional propositions, the paradox of indicative conditionals discussed in 7.4 is equally a paradox of counterfactuals: the way we form beliefs in counterfactuals isn't a way dictated by their truth conditions. We certainly need the hypothetical conditional beliefs we express in uttering counterfactual sentences ('hypothetical' because our concern is with conditional beliefs formed in non-actual scenarios), but I would again take a dim view of our need for counterfactual-conditional *propositions*. The paradox has the same weak unhappy-face solution whether we're considering indicative or counterfactual conditionals.[34]

---

[34] I see no unsettling implications of this for either causal decision theory or the role of counterfactuals in causal explanation (see the next chapter).

7.6 SUMMARY

According to the doctrine of pleonastic propositions, there are indicative-conditional and counterfactual/subjunctive-conditional propositions in exactly the same sense as there are any other kinds of propositions. As such, conditional propositions provide their own substitution instances of the propositional truth schema

The proposition that S is true iff S.

Although there are those who deny that there are conditional propositions, they offer no compelling reason to doubt the doctrine of pleonastic propositions.

No kind of conditional proposition has reductive truth conditions, but some conditional propositions are determinately true, others are determinately false, and every conditional proposition that is determinately true/false owes its determinate truth/falsity to the satisfaction of a non-conditional sufficient condition for its being determinately true/false. More specifically, we can say that every conditional proposition is determinately true just in case either its antecedent and consequent are determinately true or its antecedent determinately metaphysically or physically entails its consequent, determinately false just in case either its antecedent is determinately true and its consequent is determinately false or its antecedent determinately metaphysically or physically entails the negation of its consequent (but not its consequent). This leaves as indeterminate all conditionals, whether indicative or counterfactual, whose false antecedents don't metaphysically or physically entail their consequents. Indeterminate conditional propositions are indeterminate because it is possible for someone to v^*-believe them. As with the indeterminacy of moral propositions, many indeterminate conditional propositions provide a unique kind of indeterminacy, one that has nothing to do with the indeterminacy of borderline propositions.

Although both kinds of conditionals have the same conditions for determinate truth/falsity, there are important differences between the indicative-conditional proposition $A \rightarrow C$ and the counterfactual-conditional proposition $A \square \rightarrow C$, even when both are indeterminate. One will typically be interested in $A \rightarrow C$ only when one is uncertain about A, and then one believes $A \rightarrow C$ to the degree that one believes C, given A—never mind that this epistemic policy isn't dictated by the truth conditions of $A \rightarrow C$. When one is motivated to assess $A \rightarrow C$

even though one is certain that A is false, one does so by assessing $A \mathbin{\square\!\!\rightarrow} C$, but, at the same time, one assesses $A \mathbin{\square\!\!\rightarrow} C$ by contemplating what $\Pr(C/A)$ would be for one in a contextually relevant scenario in which one is uncertain whether A—never mind that this epistemic policy isn't dictated by the truth conditions of $A \mathbin{\square\!\!\rightarrow} C$.

The fact that the way one forms beliefs in conditional propositions, whether indicative or counterfactual, isn't dictated by their truth conditions generates a paradox, stated in 7.4 for indicative-conditional propositions but applying also, *mutatis mutandis*, to counterfactual-conditional propositions. This paradox, like virtually every other philosophical paradox, has no happy-face solution, owing to glitches in our conceptual practices. The paradox does, however, admit of a weak unhappy-face solution, which takes a dim view of the need, strictly speaking, for either kind of conditional propositions. Whatever needs to be said can be said using conditional subjective probability, entailment (of one stripe or another), or the material conditional. Needless to say, believing what I say in this chapter won't prevent me from saying to my son that I would have caught the fly ball if the sun hadn't been in my eyes.

8

Why Pleonastic Propositions?
Content in Information and Explanation

8.1 INTRODUCTION

I've argued that propositional attitudes and propositional speech acts
are what they seem to be, relations to propositions, and I've put forward an account of the nature of those propositions. My label
'pleonastic propositions' is a mnemonic for propositions as having
that nature. The prominence of proposition-involving semantic and
psychological concepts in our thought and speech makes it clear that
pleonastic propositions play an extremely important role in our conceptual economy. This chapter is about what pleonastic propositions
do for us, how we would be worse off if we didn't make use of them.

There are a few questions here. What important roles do pleonastic propositions play for us? What features of them allow them to play
those roles? Might other things—say, non-pleonastic propositions or
linguistic entities of some kind—play those roles as well as pleonastic propositions do? I think the two most important roles pleonastic
propositions play are, first, that they help us both to exploit the
propositional attitudes of others as sources of information about
the extra-cranial world and to exploit the extra-cranial world as a
source of information about the propositional attitudes of others,
and, secondly, that they help us to explain the behaviour of ourselves
and others. The two roles, as we'll see, are closely linked, especially in
the way the second relies on the first.

In 8.2 I explore the role of pleonastic propositions in the exploitation of those head–world reliability correlations which enable us to
know about the world on the basis of what people think about it, and
conversely, and I consider whether things other than pleonastic
propositions could perform as well in this way. My answer won't
surprise you, but my reasons for it might. The remaining sections are

about the role of content (i.e. pleonastic propositions) in propositional-attitude explanations: 8.3 considers reasons that have been
offered over the years for why content can't play a causal-explanatory
role; 8.4 considers proposals about what content might be doing in
propositional-attitude because-statements if it doesn't play a causal-
explanatory role; and 8.5 tries to reveal and explain the fundamental
raison d'être of those because-statements.

8.2   CONTENT IN INFORMATION

Remarkable! Someone utters the sounds 'It's snowing' and in hearing
those sounds I instantaneously acquire the knowledge that it's
snowing. The full story of what is going on here may not be entirely
clear, but two things do seem pretty clear. First, the ability to convey
information in this way is at least one important function of natural
language, if not *the* most important, and secondly, the utterance
provides me with knowledge that it's snowing by way of providing
me with knowledge that the speaker believes that it's snowing.
Utterances reveal what the speaker believes, and a person's believing
p is often very good evidence that p is true. Conversely, just as I can
sometimes infer p from the fact that so-and-so believes p, so, too, I
can sometimes infer that so-and-so believes p from the fact that p is
true. This direction is important in predicting what someone will do:
external facts enable me to know what a person believes and wants,
and that knowledge enables me to predict what she will do.

   In all of this we are exploiting what may be called *head–world
reliability correlations*. Given the nature of our environment and the
way we are built as information processors, there are head–world
correlations that make facts of certain kinds reliable indicators that
people of certain kinds believe those facts, and there are head–world
correlations that make the fact that certain kinds of people believe
propositions of a certain kind reliable indicators of the truth of those
propositions. We have some knowledge of these head–world reliability correlations, and we can use that knowledge to gain knowledge of
the world on the basis of what others believe, and to gain knowledge
about what others believe—and thereby of what they want—on the
basis of our knowledge about the world. It would be difficult to exag-
gerate the importance these two kinds of exploitations have in our

lives. Try subtracting from all that you know all that you wouldn't know if you couldn't use others as sources of information—if there were no one to tell you anything, no schools, no books, no radio or television, no newspapers or journals, no internet! Try imagining your interactions with others, including your ability to anticipate what they will do, if you could have no knowledge of what they think or want!

The important head–world reliability correlations that are describable by appeal to propositions are underlain by head–world reliability correlations that are describable without appeal to propositions. These predominantly pertain to how external events cause those brain states that subserve, or are, belief states, and how those brain states, via their effects on bodily movements, cause external events. But we don't really have access to these brain states, and even if we did, it would be next to impossible to exploit the barometric properties of those brain states if we could have knowledge of them only as brain states. In order systematically to exploit head–world reliability correlations we need a system that both indexes relevant brain states and correlates them with external states of affairs. The propositions in the ranges of our propositional-attitude relations provide such a system of indices.

Three features of propositions allow them to play their role in information acquisition. First, they afford an indirect way of classifying those brain states that subserve beliefs by indexing them in ways that explicitly correlate them with external states-of-affairs types (e.g. the proposition that snow is white correlates with the state of affairs of snow's being white). Secondly, the belief properties which embed those propositions—the property of believing that such-and-such, or, equivalently, of being a belief that such-and-such—indirectly type the brain states that subserve them in terms of functional roles that are crucial to capturing reliability generalizations. For example, to know that a normal person believes that there is a red object before her is to know that she is in a brain state of a type that will be tokened when lighting conditions are good and her eyes are open and facing the red object. Thirdly, the fact that belief properties have the functional implications just mentioned allows us to group them together under very general commonalities to yield further important reliability generalizations. For example, we know that the beliefs normal people have about what their names are and about what they are perceiving in their immediate environment are pretty reliable, that is, pretty likely to be true.

I am skirting some interesting epistemological questions. One interesting question is about the nature of knowledge by testimony, knowing that such-and-such on the basis of someone's telling you that such-and-such. Does one infer from the fact that the speaker uttered the sentence 'It's snowing' that she believes that it's snowing and then infer from that that it's snowing, or is all or part of knowledge by testimony in some way non-inferential?[1] It is clear that we can sometimes know that such-and-such because we rightly take the fact that so-and-so believes that such-and-such to be very good *evidence* that such-and-such, but it is not clear that this is what is going on in knowledge by testimony, nor is it clear that it is not what is going on. In any case, I think it is reasonably safe to say that when we come to know p on the basis of having been told p, it is crucial both that we believe that the speaker believes p and that the explanation of the speaker's believing p essentially includes the fact that p is true. Thus, when Sally informs Abe that it's snowing by uttering 'It's snowing', Abe acquires the knowledge that Sally believes that it's snowing, and this knowledge is crucial to Abe's coming to know that it's snowing, and this in part because part of the explanation of the fact that Sally believes that it's snowing is that it is snowing.[2] The rest of the story— the extent to which Abe's knowledge is inferential—is a matter for debate, but we have before us enough to raise the relevant questions

---

[1] See e.g. Burge (1993); McDowell (1998a); Cody (1990); Fricker (1995, 2003); and Schiffer (2001b).

[2] Is it really safe to say that knowing the speaker believes p is crucial to knowing p on the basis of her telling you p? Tyler Burge has objected that while in gaining knowledge by testimony we rely on a presumption of reliability, we 'need not engage in reasoning about the person's qualifications to be rational in accepting what he or she says, in the absence of grounds for doubt' (1993: 469). This is evidently the sort of consideration also at work behind Robert Audi's claim that knowledge by testimony is 'typically not inferential. Certainly when trusted friends speak to us on matters we have no reason to think are beyond their competence, we normally "just believe" what they tell us' (1998: 132). This is highly unpersuasive. If believing what someone says straight away, or not needing to engage in reasoning about a person's qualifications, were a reason for taking knowledge by testimony not to rely on one's knowing the speaker believes what she's saying, we could easily be shown not to have most of the evidential knowledge we have. What 'reasoning' is one actively and consciously engaged in when one immediately concludes from the sight of a wet sidewalk that it recently rained, or when one immediately believes that one's Vermeer has been stolen upon seeing that one's alarm system has been disabled and that one's back door is wide open? Whether knowing p is based on knowing q isn't about the actual movement of thought, the considerations one actually ponders; it's about the structure of beliefs that sustain one's conclusion.

about the role of pleonastic propositions in gaining knowledge of the world by way of coming to know the beliefs others have about it.

The foregoing assumes that the propositions in propositional attitudes are pleonastic propositions, and that therefore they provide the systematic indexing crucial to the exploitation of head–world reliability correlations. Might other kinds of propositions have served as well, if they were the propositions in propositional attitudes? I don't think so. Obviously, some kinds of propositions are better than others for exploiting head–world reliability correlations. Propositions enable us to exploit those correlations in part by indexing functional roles of the neurophysiological states that subserve beliefs, in that believing that such-and-such requires being in a token of a neuro-physiological state type that has a certain functional role associated with the proposition that such-and-such. Suppose we have two such neurophysiological states that are functionally alike in some ways relevant to the exploitation of head–world reliability correlations but differ in other ways that are also relevant. Then, all other things being equal, a system of propositional indices that assigns two propositions to these states in a way that captures their relevant functional difference will be better than a system that assigns just one proposition to both states which captures their functional commonality. In this light, we can appreciate that, all other things being equal, Russellian proposi-tions are better for indexing functional roles than are propositions construed as sets of possible worlds, and Fregean propositions are better than Russellian propositions. But pleonastic propositions, which can be as fine-grained as one likes, given the way they are indivi-duated in terms of what it would take to believe them (see 2.4), are best of all in this regard.

But do we need propositions of any kind in order maximally to exploit head–world reliability correlations? Suppose I introduce a sentential attitude, believing*, which holds between believers and sentences of my idiolect, such that

(1) x believes* S iff x is in a belief state whose content $=$ the content S has for me.

Thus, an example of a belief* report would be

Harold believes* 'frogs are immortal'

and this would be true just in case Harold is in a belief state whose content matches that of my sentence 'frogs are immortal'. Why wouldn't the sentential attitude believing* serve me as well as the propositional attitude believing as regards my exploiting the head–world reliability correlations of others? There are at least two problems. First, the relevant notions of content we actually have essentially involve propositions, so we are owed a reading of (1) that uses a proposition-free account of sameness of content. Secondly, 'S' in (1) can't range over sentence *types*, since that would give unacceptable results for belief* reports involving indexical sentences, such as

(2) Mary believes* 'he is foolish'.

One unacceptable result is due to the fact that on no understanding of content will the content of the sentence *type* 'he is foolish' exhaust the content of any belief state (it won't give the belief state enough content to enable it to have a truth-value). But if 'S' in (1) is taken to range over sentence tokens, we get a couple of new problems. First, when 'S' in (1) is taken to range over sentence tokens, believing* thereby becomes a relation between a believer and *my sentence tokens*, which implies that a person's beliefs will far outnumber her beliefs*. This is a bad feature for any account which hopes to rival the ability of propositions to exploit head–world reliability correlations; it would prevent me from making a substantial statement about Lester in saying 'All of Lester's beliefs about thermodynamics are true' if I've never ascribed to Lester a belief about thermodynamics, and the ability to make such generalizations is obviously very important if we're to exploit others as sources of information. If the sententialist's believing* is to do as well as believing, she'd better make sure it is possible for someone to believe* something that I've never expressed. Secondly, the sentence token to which the occurrence of the singular term 'he is foolish' in (2) refers must evidently be the one contained in it. But since 'he is foolish' is being *mentioned* and not *used* in (2), the occurrence of 'he' can't be referring to anyone there. But an utterance such as (2) would be of no use to us if it couldn't be used to ascribe a belief about some particular referent of 'he'.

At this point the sententialist might make a selective borrowing from Donald Davidson's paratactic account of propositional-attitude sentences,[3] so that the semantics of 'believes*' requires a belief* report to have the paratactic form

x believes* f(the next token of 'S', x). S,

[3] Davidson (1984*a*).

where f is a function that maps an utterance token of mine and a person onto the sentence in the person's Mentalese whose 'content' matches that of my utterance token.[4] Replacements for the schematic letter 'S' will be unasserted but will occur with the kind of sense and reference they would have if they were asserted. In a belief* report these sentences are uttered on their own, but only to provide a content in terms of which we say what the subject of the belief* report believes*. For example, in the belief* report

Mary believes* f(the next token of 'He is foolish', Mary).
He is foolish,

my utterance of 'He is foolish' is unasserted (since I needn't share the belief* I'm ascribing to Mary) but 'He is foolish' is nevertheless uttered in such a way that the uttered token of 'He' refers to someone and the uttered token of the sentence has a truth-value.

The function f, however, remains to be defined. As already noted, the definition can't say

$f(S, x) = m$ iff S is a sentence token of mine and m is that sentence in x's Mentalese that has the same content as S

since our actual notion of content is one that essentially involves propositions, and the whole point of the present exercise is to see if there can be a sententialist replacement for propositions that does as well as them with respect to the exploitation of head–world reliability correlations. This means that we have to complete the definition

$f(S, x) = m$ iff S is a sentence token of mine and m is that sentence in x's Mentalese that is related in way ... to S

in a way that doesn't overtly or covertly involve propositions. Evidently, the most promising strategy would be along the lines of

$f(S, x) = m$ iff S is a sentence token of mine and m is that sentence in x's Mentalese that has causal and functional features Q in common with the sentence in my Mentalese that is correlated in way C with S.

---

[4] Perhaps it's implausible that there is just one sentence of x's Mentalese which matches my token of 'S' in content. Very well, then the theorist should say that a belief* report has the form '$\exists\sigma(x$ believes* σ & R(the next token of 'S', σ) 'S.', where R is a relation that holds between public-language sentence tokens and Mentalese sentences. However, for expository convenience I'll continue to state the present proposal in terms of a function, since this doesn't affect my objections to the proposal.

The task then would be to say what Q and C are, and this may not be so easy to do. As regards C, a natural first thought is that it correlates my public token S with the Mentalese sentence of mine that is causally implicated in blah-blah way in my utterance of S. But this won't work. It may be a quirky fact about me that I wouldn't utter

> Mary believes* f(the next utterance of 'Zebras fly', Mary). Zebras fly,

unless, intuitively speaking, 'Zebras fly' meant what 'Carrots are conscious' now means for me.[5] This wouldn't be good for using the truths expressed by belief* reports to gain knowledge about the world. The moral, I think, is that an adequate specification of C wouldn't stay at the level of whole sentences but would involve correlations of the primitive words and structures of my spoken language with those of my Mentalese. But given how little can be assumed about languages of thought as regards indexical or demonstrative thought, it is far from clear (to me) how this would go. Anyhow, let's assume it can be done. What about Q? Q can't consist of *all* the causal and functional properties of my Mentalese correlate of S. It would have to be some subset of those properties. But what subset, and what is there to determine just that subset? I have no clear sense of how to answer these questions, but let's assume they can be answered.

Even if we could say what Q and C were, we still wouldn't have enough. The sententialist yet remains in need of a system for indexing belief states which correlates them with external states of affairs, and we need to be told how that is to be achieved. We are helping ourselves to the idea that we think in an internal system of mental representation, but so far the formulae of this system are just uninterpreted sentences, and to say that we need an indexing system for beliefs which correlates them with external states of affairs is equivalent to saying that we need such an indexing system for a person's *lingua mentis*. Moreover, given the present set-up, we don't even have such an indexing system for our own public-language utterances. If the sententialist is to rival the propositionalist's ability to exploit others as sources of information, she will need to be able to say things that are tantamount to saying that Jane is an expert on Italian opera. If I know that Jane is an expert on Italian opera, then I know that if she believes a proposition about Italian opera, then it is almost certain to be true.

---

[5] Cf. my objection to Stich's account of belief ascription in Schiffer (1987a: 77).

Then, when Jane utters 'Donizetti was kapellmeister to the Austrian court', I know enough to believe that Donizetti was kapellmeister to the Austrian court. So far, the sententialist, equipped merely with his Q and C, isn't able to match the propositionalist in this regard. To do so, he will need systematic ways of correlating Mentalese sentences and public-language utterances with external states of affairs. He will need, in effect, a non-propositionalist notion of truth for mental states and for utterances, and this is where the real point of propositions will reveal itself. What we're about to see is that *indexicality* reveals the real point of propositions, the reason the work they can do can't be duplicated by a sententialist alternative.

For the sententialist, access to the mental states of others or oneself must be via public-language utterance tokens, in the way revealed in the best sententialist form for ascribing beliefs, the paratactic form

x believes* f(the next token of 'S', x). S.

The sententialist, therefore, will be able to ascribe truth to belief states if, but only if, she can first have a truth predicate for public-language utterances. If the sententialist has a truth predicate for public-language utterances, she can then say that x's Mentalese sentence m is true if there could be a true public-language utterance such that m stands in the equivalence relation Q to that Mentalese sentence of the speaker's which would be related in way C to the true utterance. Thus, the challenge to the sententialist is to complete the right-hand side of the schema

An utterance of 'S' is true iff...

in a way that takes no direct or indirect recourse to propositions.

The problem concerning indexicality to which I alluded two paragraphs back is simply that there is no way for the sententialist to get a correct completion for, say,

(3) Ralph's utterance of 'She is a violinist' is true iff...

unless he already has a truth predicate applicable to public-language utterances, thus rendering the attempt self-defeatingly circular. For there is no way the sententialist can get a completion of (3) that was adequate to our information-exploiting needs without directly or indirectly invoking the speaker's intentions*. But intending* is a sentential relation, and the only way an ascription of it can get us to something non-linguistic, as it would have to in an adequate completion of (3), would be if we *already* had the truth predicate the sentialist is trying to introduce. This can be spelled out in the following way.

We wouldn't infer from Ralph's utterance of 'She is a violinist' that, say, Betty is a violinist unless we thought that in uttering 'she' Ralph was referring to Betty. An account of truth for utterances that doesn't see indexical reference as dependent on speaker's reference can't possibly provide an adequate basis for exploiting the speaker as a source of information about the states of affairs constituting the truth conditions of his utterances. But the sentialist can't appeal to referring, since that relation essentially involves propositional attitudes, most notably intending; he must instead invoke referring*, a relation defined in terms of the sentential attitude intending*. Now, there is no way for referring* to relate one to a non-linguistic entity unless one can forge a connection between the speaker's referential intentions* and the objects to which he is referring*, and this will require having a truth predicate applicable to the Mentalese sentences in the range of the intending* relation. But, as we saw above, such a truth predicate must be introduced in terms of a truth predicate applicable to the public-language utterances we uses to attribute beliefs* and intentions*. Irreducible indexicality is the bane of sentialism and the reason propositions are needed for the maximal exploitation of head–world reliability correlations.

It may seem that there are two possible things for the sentialist to say in reply. The first appeals to notions related to what Hartry Field has called a 'purely disquotational' notion of truth.[6] It might be said that the problem I raised for the sentialist is a problem for the sentialist for whom truth is a use-*dependent* notion, a notion whose application to expressions depends in part on how those expressions are used. But a purely disquotational notion of truth is a use-*in*dependent notion, a notion whose application has nothing to do with how expressions are used. Perhaps, it might be suggested, the problem of indexicality won't arise for the theorist who hopes to have her exploitation of head–world reliability correlations based on a use-independent, purely disquotational notion of truth. Let's first state the idea for sentence types. We begin with a 'purely disquotational' notion of truth, $true_{pdme}$, such that it applies only to sentences

---

[6] Field (2001*b*).

of my idiolect and (subject to possible qualifications pertaining to semantic paradox) such that every instance of the schema

'S' is true$_{pdme}$ iff S

is an analytical truth in which the left-hand side has the same cognitive value as

'S' exists and S.[7]

We then use truth$_{pdme}$ to define a notion of truth, 'true$_{others}$', applicable to the Mentalese sentences of others, in the way indicated above; that is, another's Mentalese sentence σ is true$_{others}$ provided that it stands in the equivalence relation Q to a mentalese sentence of mine related in way C to a true$_{pdme}$ sentence of mine. (Although the definition of 'true$_{others}$' invokes the 'use' features Q and C, the disquotationalist needn't disapprove, since those features afford no basis for explicating an interlinguistic inflationary notion of truth.) In this way, my utterance of

> Mary believes* f(the next utterance of 'Zebras fly', Mary).
> Zebras fly

ascribes a true$_{others}$ belief* to Mary just in case my sentence 'Zebras fly' is true$_{pdme}$. This might do just fine as a way of exploiting head–world reliability correlations—as long as we ignore indexicality.

But how does the idea get adjusted to accommodate indexicality?[8] How, just for a start, is the pure disquotationalist to define truth$_{pdme}$ for her own indexical sentences? How, for example, does the definition of 'true$_{pdme}$' get adjusted to provide a completion of (4)?

(4) An utterance by me of 'She is a violinist' is true$_{pdme}$ iff...

I assume the disquotationalist would seek to accommodate indexicality in the following sort of way.[9]

First, along with a purely disquotational notion of truth applicable to closed sentences, we can also have a purely disquotational notion of *truth of* applicable to open sentences. Thus, we introduce a notion, true-of$_{pdme}$, such that it applies only to open sentences of my idiolect and (paradox still aside) every instance of the schema

'$S(x_1,...,x_n)$' is true-of$_{pdme}$ $\langle a_1,...,a_n \rangle$ iff $S(a_1,...,a_n)$

---

[7] Field (2001b).

[8] An adjustment is also needed for ambiguity (see Field 2001b: 134–5), but the accommodation of indexicals is more problematic, so I'll focus just on it.

[9] What follows was inspired by Field (2001b: 134–7).

is an analytical truth in which the left-hand side has the same cognitive value as

'$S(x_1,...,x_n)$' exists and $S(a_1,...,a_n)$.

For example, to know that 'x is bald' is true-of$_{pdme}$ Harry is, bracketing the existence of 'x is bald', just to know that Harry is bald. Now, letting $S(i_1,...,i_n)$ be a sentence and $i_1,...,i_n$ the indexical or demonstrative terms in it,[10] we can begin to revise the truth$_{pdme}$ schema for sentences of my idiolect by first stipulating that:

An utterance by me of '$S(i_1,...,i_n)$' is true$_{pdme}$ iff $\exists a_1,...,$ $a_n(R(\langle a_1,...,a_n \rangle, \langle i_1,...,i_n \rangle)$ & '$S(x_1,...,x_n)$' is true-of$_{pdme}$ $\langle a_1,...,a_n \rangle)$.

The task now is to replace 'R', and to do so without overt or covert appeal to any proposition-involving intentional notions, such as my referential intentions, and, with that done, then to reconstrue 'true$_{others}$' so as to bring it in line with the new understanding of 'true$_{pdme}$'. There might be a way of doing this if we could assume that the Mentalese sentence 'expressed' by an utterance of an indexical sentence was itself non-indexical, thereby returning an indexical-free sentence of my public language with its easy-to-accommodate truth$_{pdme}$ condition; but it is well known that many utterances are irreducibly indexical in a way that precludes this. Hartry Field has in effect suggested that 'R' be replaced thus:[11]

(5) An utterance by me of '$S(i_1,...,i_n)$' is true$_{pdme}$ iff $\exists a_1,...,$ a_n(I 'regard $\langle a_1,...,a_n \rangle$ as appropriate to associate with $\langle i_1,...,i_n \rangle$') & '$S(x_1,...,x_n)$' is true-of$_{pdme}$ $\langle a_1,...,a_n \rangle)$.

Regarding, however, is a *propositional* attitude, so it should be replaced with the sentential attitude regarding*. Yet regarding* can't be appealed to in this context unless we already know how to understand 'true$_{pdme}$' when it applies to the indexical sentences that are the spoken correlates of the Mentalese sentences we regard*. There is also another problem. Suppose I say

(6) She won't be there,

where my utterance of 'she' refers to Mary and my utterance of 'there' refers to a certain meeting. Clearly, the only objects *I* will regard as

---

[10] A more complete treatment must allow for implicit indexicals, such as that in 'It's raining' requiring reference to a place at which it's raining.   [11] Field (2001*b*: 136).

appropriate to associate with my utterances of 'she' and 'there' are Mary and the intended meeting, and this is crucial to capturing the reliability of my utterance: the fact that I uttered (6) is, we may suppose, extremely good evidence that Mary won't attend the meeting, but if anyone assigns someone other than Mary to my utterance of 'she' and something other than the meeting to my utterance of 'there', then any inference from the fact that I uttered (6) will be at the peril of the one making the inference! If a theorist is to stay with some refinement of (5), what will be needed is a *general principle*, statable in wholly non-intentional terms, for correlating objects with indexicals and demonstratives that will tell me to assign Mary and a certain meeting to my utterances of 'she' and 'there'. I have no idea how this would go. The moral is the same as before. A system for maximally exploiting head–world reliability correlations needs a *context-independent* system of indices. This is provided by propositions (of just about any stripe), but it is not provided by sentences, given the unavailability of enough context-independent sentences. The omnipresence of irreducibly indexical utterances precludes sentences from doing as well as propositions in enabling us to exploit head–world reliability correlations to gain knowledge both of the world and of the mental states of others.

This brings me to the second thing it might seem the sententialist can say in response to the indexicality problem. It might seem the sententialist can claim to be able to introduce a system of indices that gets around the problem of indexicality by using n-tuples that are partly linguistic and partly non-linguistic. For example, we might take the index for the belief expressed by Ralph's utterance of

(7) She is a surgeon

to be

(8) ⟨Louise, 'is a surgeon'⟩.

This would also allow us to do away with the paratactic construal of belief* reports, since the sentence

Ralph believes* ⟨Louise, 'is a surgeon'⟩

could stand on its own. It doesn't matter that believing is not in fact a relation to such things; the present question is whether a system of quasi-sentential attitudes, whose objects were n-tuples on the order of (8), could do as well as propositional attitudes, with their pleonastic propositional indices, by way of enabling us to exploit head–world reliability correlations. I don't think so. For one thing, (8) isn't fine-grained enough; it suffers from the same liability as Russellian propositions: it will give the same index to belief states of a person one of which is good evidence for the truth of the belief, the other not. For example, we may suppose that the belief expressed by Ralph when he uttered (8) is extremely good evidence that Louise is a surgeon. But suppose Ralph glimpses a woman in the distance, whom he fails to recognize as Louise, and, mistaking her pale green pant suit for a surgical outfit, produces another utterance of (7), where, since Louise was again the referent of the utterance of 'she', the index for the belief expressed is again (8). This time the belief expressed by the utterance of (7) is very poor evidence that the belief is true. Belief states of a person which differ in this way need to have distinct indices if we're to take good advantage of the believer's reliability. For another thing, an inflationist sententialist concerned to capture head–world reliability correlations as well as pleonastic propositions do will want to correlate predicates with the properties they express, so (8) would in effect give way to something like

(9) ⟨Louise, ⟨'is a surgeon', the property of being a surgeon⟩⟩.

The theorist will want 'is a surgeon' in the index along with the property of being a surgeon in order to capture relevant functional differences that might go uncaptured if the property of being a surgeon were the sole index component, since distinct predicates that intuitively differ in meaning in reliability-relevant ways may both express the property of being a surgeon (there is not much point, however, in having ⟨'she', Louise⟩ in place of just Louise, since that would still give the same poor result for the two utterances of (7) just imagined). Indices like (8) are already familiar; they resemble Mark Richard's 'Russellian annotated matrices' and the 'interpreted logical forms' of Richard Larson, Peter Ludlow, and Gabriel Segal.[12] By my lights, however, the present proposal for quasi-sentential indices is a version of propositionalism, since one can define truth conditions for such indices in the same way one can for Russellian propositions. The real question is whether the linguistic parts of these indices, which are now playing the role of concepts in a sort of sentential Fregeanism, are adequate for the job. I don't think they are; the problem of indexicality looms again. What

[12] Richard (1990); Larson and Ludlow (1993); and Larson and Segal (1995).

linguistic entity is to be correlated with Louise? It can't be 'she', as we saw. But what else? A non-indexical definite description?

Perhaps there is a good argument to show that we can exploit head–world reliability correlations just as well without pleonastic propositions as with them, but if so, I don't know what it is.

8.3 CONTENT IN EXPLANATION: DOUBTS ABOUT CONTENT'S CAUSAL-EXPLANATORY ROLE

Common-sense propositional-attitude explanations, as put forth in propositional-attitude because-statements, are ubiquitous. They are offered in explanation of intentional mental states, as in:

> Sally wants to go to the mall because she thinks her friends will be there.

> I inferred that you must really hate New York because I heard you say you'd prefer to live in New Jersey.

They are offered in explanation of intentional actions, as in:

> Al is looking for the maternity ward because he heard that is where the babes are.

> Ava raised her hand in that way because she wanted the waiter to bring the bill.

And they are offered in explanation of non-intentional facts, as in:

> Henrietta is stretched out on the floor like that because she wants to find her collection of Frank Sinatra's cigarette butts and thinks it may be under the bed.

> Henry's face suddenly became red because he just then realized that Jerry Fodor overheard him say that Britney Spears was a better singer than any soprano the Met could produce; the redness of his face was a blush.

I will take it to be an extremely plausible, though defeasible, assumption that some of these because-statements offer correct explanations (or explanation-sketches—this qualification will be implicit throughout, except when made explicit), and that the propositional-attitude notions that occur in those because-statements do so non-superfluously—at

least not superfluously in the way that, say, being green occurs superfluously when I explain that the window broke because someone
threw that green brick against it. The interesting questions are these:

- Do the propositional-attitude properties mentioned in common-sense propositional-attitude because-*statements* occur ineliminably in the *explanations* those because-statements provide?
- Whether the answer is yes or no, what is the nature of the explanations provided by the because-statements? (Answering this
  question will require saying how those explanations mesh with
  underlying non-intentional explanations.)
- If the answer is yes, what explanatory role do propositional-
  attitude notions play in those explanations?
- If the answer is no, what job are propositional-attitude notions
  doing in propositional-attitude because-statements.

These questions are pretty vague. There is a risk of verbal disagreements passing as substantial disagreements, owing to differences in
what different people are willing to call explanations. Still, a good way
to get at what the substantive issues are is to discern and assess the
reasons philosophers have given for their claims about the explanatory role of propositional-attitude properties.

If there is a view to be defeated, it is that propositional-attitude
properties play a *causal-explanatory* role in that (i) propositional-
attitude because-statements offer *causal* explanations of the facts they
purport to explain, and (ii) the propositional-attitude properties
occur ineliminably in those explanations. This continues to be pretty
vague; there is some relevant vagueness to the question whether a
because-statement is offering any *causal* explanation, and there is a
whole lot of vagueness to the question of how to determine the causal
explanation offered by a because-statement once we're confident that
it is offering *a* causal explanation, and thus there is a whole lot of
vagueness to the question of how to determine whether the implied
causal explanation ineliminably contains the propositional-attitude
property mentioned in the because-statement. In any event, it will
help us to examine both the reasons philosophers have offered for
denying that propositional-attitude properties play a causal-explanatory
role and, after that, the alternative accounts these philosophers offer
of what propositional-attitude properties are doing in because-
statements if they're not occurring in causal explanations those statements offer. I begin with a survey of some of the reasons philosophers

have offered for doubting that propositional-attitude properties play a causal-explanatory role.

The reasons-aren't-causes objection. In the 1950s, beginning shortly after Wittgenstein's death, there were several books and articles by American and British philosophers many of whom considered themselves to be developing lines of thought that were either implicit in the later Wittgenstein or at least ones to which one would naturally be led when philosophizing in the style of his *Philosophical Investigations*. Some of these philosophers—e.g. Gilbert Ryle, Stuart Hampshire, A. I. Melden, R. S. Peters, and Peter Winch[13]—held positions which committed them to the following two claims, whose conjunction entails that propositional-attitude explanations aren't causal explanations, and that therefore content doesn't play a causal-explanatory role:

(1) Propositional-attitude explanations are causal explanations only if the propositional-attitudes mentioned in them are not merely the *reasons* for which the agent did what she did, but also the *causes* of her doing what she did.

(2) But reasons can't be causes because (i) as Hume taught us, causes must be contingently connected to their effects, whereas (ii) the reasons for which an agent performed an action are conceptually connected to the action in a way that precludes a contingent connection.

Now (1) is plausible. Just as the explanation one gives in saying

The match lit because it was scratched

wouldn't count as a correct causal explanation unless the match's lighting was caused by its having been scratched, so the explanation one gives in saying

Ava moved her hand in a certain way because she wanted to get the bill and believed that the best way to get it was to move her hand in that way

wouldn't count as a correct causal explanation unless Ava's belief and desire caused her hand movement. The Humean claim made in (2(i)) in its most plausible formulation is that the causation relation is one that

[13] Ryle (1949); Hampshire (1959); Melden (1961); Peters (1958); and Winch (1958). These and others are cited in Davidson (1980*a*).

holds contingently: the fact that c caused e is never a logical or conceptual or metaphysical necessity; there is always a sense in which c might have occurred without causing e. This most plausible formulation is likely to seem pretty plausible, so the crux of the neo-Wittgensteinian line is its claim that the relation expressed by 'x was the reason for which y did z' is 'conceptual' in a way that precludes reasons from being causes. This is where the neo-Wittgensteinian line falls apart. Two claims were made about the 'conceptual connection'. First, they said that the reason contains a 'reference' to the action, in the way that Henrietta's wanting to get drunk contains a reference to her getting drunk. Secondly, they said that when one tries to complete a propositional-attitude explanation sketch, one gets something that looks pretty close to being analytic, such as what you get when you move from

She went into the kitchen because she wanted a beer

to what they would call its completion, something like

If a person desires result R, believes that the best way to get R is to do Y, has no stronger competing desires, knows how to do Y, is not physically or psychologically prevented from doing Y, and doesn't change her mind, then, *ceteris paribus*, she will do Y. Mary desired to drink a beer, believed that the best way to accomplish that was to go into the kitchen and get one from the fridge, knew how to get into the kitchen, was in no way prevented from doing that, didn't change her mind, and *cetera* were *paria*. So, Mary went into the kitchen.

One problem with this second conceptual-connection argument is that even if there were connections of the kind suggested, it would do nothing to show it is not the case that when you did something for a certain reason, you might have had that reason without doing what you did. As numerous philosophers have pointed out, if the cause and effect are described under descriptions that make it analytic that a thing falling under the cause description would be followed by a thing falling under the effect description, this wouldn't show that it wasn't a contingent fact that the cause caused the effect. For example, rain clouds would contingently cause rain even if it were analytic that rain clouds cause rain, for it would still be the case that those things that were in fact rain clouds might not have been; it is merely a contingent truth about those clouds that they have the property of being rain clouds. A second problem with the just stated conceptual-connection argument is that no such analytic generalization either occurs, or needs to occur, in anything that could properly be called a complete common-sense propositional-attitude explanation. If by nothing else, this is revealed by the slack-absorbing role of the *ceteris paribus* clause in the displayed generalization, which seems simply to be telling us that if all other antecedent conditions obtain and the action doesn't ensue, then *cetera* weren't *paria*, without giving us any indication of what these *cetera* are supposed to be. A third problem, to be mentioned below, is that it is doubtful that *any* kind of 'causal laws' are an essential component of genuine causal explanations.[14] And as for the first of the two alleged cause-precluding conceptual connections, it is simply false that reasons refer to the particular actions they appear to be causing: if I want to win the sweepstakes but don't win it, no one will accuse 'Schiffer wants to win the sweepstakes' as suffering from reference failure. The important point, however, is that while it is true that, say, 'Henrietta wants to get drunk' involves the concept of getting drunk, that gives no reason whatever to think that Henrietta might not have had that desire and not gotten drunk.

John McDowell, interpreting Donald Davidson, has more recently proposed a variation on the neo-Wittgensteinian 'reasons-aren't-causes' objection.[15] McDowell, like Davidson,[16] doesn't deny that reasons are causes; his point is that 'the role played by "the constitutive ideal of rationality" in shaping our thought about propositional attitudes'[17] precludes propositional-attitude properties from playing a causal-explanatory role and shows that propositional-attitude explanations constitute 'a kind of explanation that is *sui generis*'.[18] I briefly consider this *sui generis* kind of explanation in 8.3; the question for now is what is meant by 'the constitutive ideal of rationality' and how it is supposed to preclude propositional-attitude properties from playing a causal-explanatory role. What McDowell seems to have in mind is that propositional-attitude notions involve ideals that are only imperfectly realized in agents who are never ideally rational. For example, McDowell claims that

deductive rationality is a capacity, more or less perfectly instantiated in different rational individuals, to hold beliefs, when, and because, they follow deductively from other beliefs that one holds.... it need do no harm to picture a particular instantiation of deductive rationality as a more or less

---

[14] See Schiffer (1991).   [15] McDowell (1998*a*).   [16] Davidson (1980*a*).
[17] McDowell (1998*a*: 325).   [18] McDowell (1998*a*: 332).

approximate grasp of a normative structure, determining what follows from what and thus what ought to be believed, given other beliefs, for deductively connected reasons.[19]

What I don't understand is why this constitutive ideal of rationality should preclude propositional-attitude properties from playing a causal-explanatory role. Why can't a state that, so to say, aspires to some ideal nevertheless contain enough within itself to be causally efficacious in the production of behaviour? McDowell does argue that the way propositional-attitude explanation involves ideal rationality precludes propositional-attitude properties from *reducing* to non-intentional properties, but, even if he is right about that, a further step is needed to get from it to the inability of propositional-attitude properties to play a causal-explanatory role, and McDowell does nothing to provide that further step. Another worry I have is that there are propositional-attitude explanations where the constitutive ideal of rationality can't possibly be involved, and these explanations don't seem to differ relevantly, *qua* explanations, from the sort of propositional-attitude explanations McDowell has in mind. An example of the sort to which I'm alluding is one given above, where one explains that Henry blushed because he realized that Jerry Fodor overheard him say that Britney Spears was a better singer than any soprano the Met could produce.

The strong-reduction objection. Let's stipulate that the property of being F *strongly reduces* to the property of being G only if the property of being F = the property of being G. Then the present objection to the common-sense view of propositional-attitude explanation—at least as applied to propositional-attitude explanations of non-intentional facts (the continuation of the objection to encompass explanations of intentional facts merely adds complexity)—may be stated as the following two-part claim:

(1) A propositional-attitude property plays an essential role in a correct causal explanation of a non-intentional fact only if it strongly reduces to a non-intentional property that figures essentially in a correct non-intentional causal explanation of the same fact.

---

[19] McDowell (1998a: 326–7).

(2) No propositional-attitude property strongly reduces to any non-intentional property.

The usual argument for (2) is one that is also taken to apply to mental properties that aren't propositional-attitude properties; this is that such properties are *multiply realizable*, may, that is, be 'realized' by various non-intentional properties without being identical to the disjunction of them. This invites the counter-response of David Lewis, Jaegwon Kim, and others that what really enters into correct propositional-attitude explanations isn't, say, the property of believing that such-and-such, but rather a contextually relevant species-specific property such as, so to say, the property of human-believing that such-and-such, which property, they further claim, is arguably not subject to multiple realization and can be identified with a causal-explanatory non-intentional property and, ultimately, with a property statable in the language of fundamental physics. 'In this way,' Kim argues, 'multiple realized properties are sundered into their diverse realizers in different species and structures, and in different possible worlds.'[20]

In fact, however, there is a much more compelling case for (2) than any based on multiple realization. For even if multiple realization is the best reason for supposing that non-intentional properties like pain can't be identified with any non-mental property, there is a much better reason that applies only to propositional-attitude properties. The point is very simple: no property in an underlying non-intentional explanation will have what it takes even to be a candidate for strongly reducing a propositional-attitude property. For consider the property of believing that there are no unicorns. It is a *composite* property composed of *the belief relation* and *the proposition that there are no unicorns*. If it is to be identical to a physical property, then the belief relation must be identical to a *non-intentional* relation between believers and propositions. Given this, any non-intentional property that could strongly reduce the composite belief property would itself have to be a composite property one part of which was identical to the belief relation, the other part identical to the proposition that there are no unicorns.[21] But just try finding the non-intentional

---

[20] Kim (1998: 111). For Lewis, see e.g. (1983*b*).

[21] Being a relation to a proposition doesn't per se make a relation intentional, any more than being a relation to person makes a relation intentional just by virtue of the fact that thinking about that person involves an intentional relation. There is no more pressure on a physicalist to reduce propositions to physical entities than there is to reduce numbers to physical entities.

relation to the proposition that $1^2 + 1^2 = 4$ in the physical explanation that subserves the fact that little Johnny wrote '4' because he was trying to answer the question 'What is the sum of $1^2 + 1^2$?' and he believed that $1^2 + 1^2 = 4$.[22] If correct propositional-attitude explanations of non-intentional facts are causal explanations that essentially involve propositional-attitude properties, then the non-intentional explanations that underlie the propositional-attitude explanations won't be statable using composite non-intentional predicates that express relations to propositions. We can dismiss out of hand the idea that propositional-attitude properties strongly reduce to properties involved in non-intentional explanations. It further follows that propositional-attitude properties don't reduce to functional relations that require physical realizations; for such realizations would have to be physical relations to propositions. (This leaves open whether propositional-attitude relations can be identified with topic-neutral relations that aren't involved in underlying non-intentional causal explanations, such as the ones implied by Jerry Fodor's theory of asymmetric-dependence;[23] but it seems clear to me on independent grounds that no such identification can be made to work.[24])

We're therefore forced to conclude that if (1) is true, then propositional-attitude properties don't enter essentially into correct causal explanations of non-intentional facts. With so much riding on (1), what is to be said for it?

Some theorists accept (1) because they accept the *covering-law model of explanation*, which holds that explanations are deductive or probabilistic inferences at least one premiss of which is a law—a non-probabilistic law in the deductive case, a probabilistic law in the probabilistic case.[25] Explanations that take the form of deductive

[22] But why can't it be an a posteriori discovery that the property of believing that $1^2 + 1^2 = 4$ is identical to a certain monadic neurophysiological property? Well, it's puzzling how this could be 'discovered', since it's clear there can be no sortal concept under which we could identify the property of believing that $1^2 + 1^2 = 4$ and the property of being N, for suitable neurophysiological characterization N, and, so identified, discover there is just one property that is both a property of believing that $1^2 + 1^2 = 4$ and a monadic neurophysiological property N. But the more important obstacle to such an identity is that it evidently leaves the belief relation off on its own as an irreducibly intentional relation. Yet it is playing a causal-explanatory role if the property that contains it is.   [23] Fodor (1990c).

[24] See Schiffer (1987a, ch. 4), and the essays in Loewer and Rey (1991).

[25] The idea of a probabilistic covering-law *causal* explanation strikes me as a sort of philosophical oxymoron. A probabilistic explanation of p on the covering-law model has as its conclusion the claim that p was probable to such-and-such degree. For example, a probabilistic explanation of why a certain accident occurred might have as its premises

inferences are called *deductive-nomological* (DN) explanations. An example of a DN explanation of a singular fact would be:

> Water boils at 100 °C at sea level.
> This water was heated to 100 °C at sea level.
> Ergo, this water boiled.

When what is being explained is a theory, where that is taken to be a conjunction of laws, then the explanation takes the form of a deduction of that theory from premises one of which is a more basic theory and the other of which is a conjunction of 'bridge laws' linking the theoretical terms of the theory being explained to those of the explaining theory. These bridge laws effect a reduction of the theoretical properties of the derived theory to their counterparts in the theory from which the derived theory is derived. As Patricia Churchland puts it, 'intertheoretic reduction is an instance of DN explanation, where what is explained is not a single event but a law or set of laws'.[26] Those who hold this view also hold that all true nonbasic theories ultimately reduce to fundamental physics.

But what does 'reduction' come to in this context? The dominant answer among covering-law theorists seems to be what I've called *strong reduction*: the reduced properties must be *identical to* the properties with which they're correlated in the bridge laws. The rationale for this construal is succinctly put by Jaegwon Kim (where 'F^*' is the counterpart in the reducing theory of 'F' in the reduced theory):

> [Identities of the form *property F = property F^**] are essential to the ontological simplification that we seek in theory reduction, for they enable us to dispense with facts involving F and G as something in addition to facts involving F^* and G^*. They also allow us to give simple answers to potentially embarrassing questions of the form, 'But why does property F correlate this way [i.e. in the way of the biconditional '$(x)Fx \equiv (x)F^*x$'] with property F^*?' Our answer: 'Because F just is F^*.'[27]

---

certain probabilistic laws together with particular facts about the road conditions, the drunkenness of the driver, etc., and have as its conclusion that the accident was very probable. But how can that in any way explain why the accident occurred? The fact that the accident was made very probable by the truth of the premises is entirely consistent with its having been caused by something that has nothing to do with the premises. (The objection just aired is intended to apply only to probabilistic explanation on the covering-law model of explanation; it affords no objection to, for example, those who hope to explicate causation in probabilistic terms.)

[26] Patricia Churchland (1986: 294).   [27] Kim (1996: 215).

The sort of rationale Kim offers for why the covering-law theorist needs strong reduction can motivate strong reduction independently of the covering-law model; it is what lies behind Kim's advocacy of what he has called ' "the problem of causal/explanatory exclusion": For any single event, there can be no more than a single sufficient cause, or causal explanation, unless it is a case of causal overdetermination'.[28] To see the motivating idea, suppose that Ava steps off the kerb to cross the street, sees a car speeding towards her, and prudently steps back onto the kerb. Now, one thing is clear: there will be a correct explanation of Ava's stepping back in neurophysiological terms. In accordance with this, let's stipulate that at time t neurophysiological state token n was a cause of Ava's stepping back, that n has the neurophysiological property N (i.e. n is a token of state type N), and that N enters ineliminably into the neurophysiological explanation by virtue of the fact that it is the property of n responsible for n's being a cause of Ava's stepping back. So far so good. But we also appear to have another causal explanation of Ava's stepping back—namely, *that she stepped back because she didn't want to risk getting hit by a car and saw that she would be at risk of being hit by the car speeding towards her if she didn't step back*, which because-proposition I'll call PA. If PA is a correct causal explanation, then we may suppose that at time t there is a state token b that was a cause at t of Ava's stepping back, that b has the property of being a belief that a car was speeding towards her (B, for short), and that B enters ineliminably into the propositional-attitude explanation by virtue of the fact that it is the property of b responsible for b's being a cause of Ava's stepping back. Whether or not PA is a correct causal explanation, we may continue to suppose at least that Ava had b at t and that she wouldn't have stepped back when she did if she hadn't had b at t (i.e. if she hadn't then believed that a car was speeding towards her).

We are thus faced with the following options (they don't exhaust logical space but they're the only ones we need to consider):

(i) $b \neq n$ and $B \neq N$, and we have two correct causal explanations of Ava's stepping back. Both n and b were causes at t of Ava's stepping back, and both B and N belong ineliminably to distinct but equally correct causal explanations (which isn't to suggest that the two explanations would be on a par).

---

[28] Kim (1996: 150). Cf. Schiffer (1987a, ch. 6).

(ii) $b = n$ but $B \neq N$ (i.e. we have token–token but not type–type identity) and both B and N belong ineliminably to distinct but equally correct causal explanations.

(iii) $b \neq n$ and $B \neq N$, and, of the two purported explanations, only the one involving n and N is correct. The state token b merely *appears* to be a cause owing to the fact that it supervenes on facts involving n in such a way that n wouldn't have occurred if b hadn't occurred, and likewise, *mutatis mutandis*, for the apparent causal relevance of B.

(iv) $b = n$ but $B \neq N$, and there is really just one causal explanation, the one containing N: B appears causally relevant because n wouldn't have been a cause if it hadn't had B, but that is just because B supervenes on a property that entails N in such a way that if B hadn't been tokened, then N wouldn't have been tokened.

(v) $b = n$ and $B = N$, and the propositional-attitude explanation of Ava's stepping back strongly reduces to the neurophysiological explanation of it.

Faced with these options, it is not surprising that a theorist might opt for (v): (i) and (ii) violate Kim's principle of 'causal/explanatory exclusion', since if there were two such correct explanations, they wouldn't manifest the sort of causal overdetermination Kim had in mind (the sort that would occur if two lethal bullets struck Ava's brain at precisely the same moment), and (iii) and (iv) manifest the bogey of epiphenomenalism, making one wonder what the biological point of propositional attitudes is if they don't earn their explanatory keep.

Not surprising, perhaps, but also not warranted. By my lights the most certain thing in this tangle of issues is that the composite propositional-attitude property *believing that a car is speeding towards one* isn't identical to the neurophysiological property N (for, as noted, no such property will itself be a composite property containing a proposition and a neurophysiological relation between people and propositions(!)); so, as I see it, (v) is the first option to rule out. I also think that, for all that presently matters, we can straight away rule out (ii) and (iv) as being determinately true, since, as I've argued earlier (2.3 and 3.8), while the token–token identity thesis might be determinately false, it can't be determinately true unless some version of the type–type identity thesis is true (non-identity all the way down is the default position, if, as I believe, propositional-attitude properties can't be identified with properties that enjoy an intrinsic non-intentional characterization). If there is a contest for determinate truth, it is between (i) and (iii).

Well, the statement made by

(10) Ava stepped back because she didn't want to risk getting hit by a car and saw that she would be at risk of being hit by the car speeding towards her if she didn't step back

—the proposition I'm calling PA—certainly *seems* true, and as we use 'explanation' in ordinary speech, PA would certainly count as an explanation, indeed a causal explanation, of Ava's stepping back. Admittedly, ordinary speech is sloppy; we'd count 'The window shattered because someone threw that green brick at it' as an explanation, even though the fact that the brick was green, or even a brick, wasn't part of the *explanation* of why the window shattered. But there is nothing in (10) that stands to that statement in the way that being green stands to the because-statement that explains why the window shattered. Do those philosophers who reject (i) mean to deny that (10) is true, or do they allow that it is true but have in mind a notion of explanation that doesn't admit PA, the proposition *that Ava stepped back because she didn't want to risk getting hit by a car and saw that she would be at risk of being hit by the car speeding towards her if she didn't step back*? If PA isn't true, then why does it look so true and why are propositions like it so extremely useful (to put it mildly) to us? If it is conceded to be true, then what is the notion of explanation philosophers have in mind such that, according to that notion, PA can't be an explanation, even though it is true? Let's put off trying to answer these questions until after we've considered further reasons that have been offered for denying that propositional-attitude properties play a causal-explanatory role in correct explanations of non-intentional facts. Some of these further reasons will overlap with some of the considerations that have just been under discussion (my inventory of arguments against the idea that content plays a causal-explanatory role isn't neatly exclusive).

The wide-content objection. This once popular objection goes like this:

(1) If propositional-attitude properties played a causal-explanatory role in correct explanations of non-intentional facts,

then they would supervene on what is in the head—i.e. on the non-intentional features of one's neural states which would be shared by any of one's doppelgängers, regardless of the doppelgänger's external environment. As Stephen Stich put it:

any state or property properly invoked in a psychological explanation should supervene on the current, internal, physical state of the organism. Thus, a pair of Putnamian doppelgangers, being molecule for molecule replicas of one another, must share all the same explanatory psychological states and properties.[29]

Jerry Fodor expressed the same view, only wrapped in a dire warning:

Causal powers supervene on local microstructure. In the psychological case, they supervene on local neural structure. We abandon this principle at our peril; mind/brain supervenience... is our only plausible account of how mental states could have the causal powers that they do have.[30]

(2) Propositional-attitude properties typically don't supervene on what is in the head.

Fred Dretske's gloss of the problem, which might have been cited earlier, is representative of those who accept (1) and (2):

The prevailing wisdom among materialists is that even if we can give an otherwise creditable account of Intentionality, the properties that give a structure its intentional identity, the facts that underlie its content... will... turn out to be explanatorily irrelevant. Even if some events have a meaning, and even if... they have an impact on their material surroundings, the fact that they mean what they do won't help explain why they do what they do.

This doctrine about what Dennett calls the *impotence* of meaning should not be taken to imply that the objects having meaning are causally inert. It only means that it is not their intentional properties, their content or meaning, from which they derive their causal powers. Though a brick was made in Hoboken, it gets its power to break windows from its velocity and mass, not from its having been made in Hoboken. By the same token, although events in the brain, those we might want to identify with a particular thought *about* Hoboken, are *about* Hoboken, their power to stimulate glands and regulate muscle tension—and thus to control behavior—derive, not from what they mean, not from the fact that they are about Hoboken, but

---

[29] Stich (1978: 239).   [30] Fodor (1987: 44).

from their electrical and chemical properties.... This ... problem about the causal role of meaning ... arises from the fact that meaning ... supervenes on a set of facts that are different from the facts that explain why a structure (with that meaning) has the effects it has. Let *M* be the set of properties and relations in virtue of which event *E* means what it does. Let *C* be the set of properties and relations in virtue of which *E* causes what it does. *M* is not identical to *C*.... What gives sounds the meaning they have is not what confers on them the power to shatter glass and rattle eardrums; what makes ... a picture *of* ... my Uncle Harold is not what gives it the power to reflect light in the way it does.... The same can be said about those physical events, processes and structures in the brain that are supposed to *be* a person's thoughts, hopes, and desires. The fact that something in the head, a thought for instance, has truth conditions doesn't help explain the thought's effect on motor output. Thoughts, the things *with* content, make a difference ... but the fact that they are thoughts ... is not relevant to the difference they make.[31]

No one should question (2), the claim that content doesn't supervene on what is in the head, and hardly anyone nowadays would. For suppose that the things to which your Twin Earth doppelgänger applies the word 'dog' look and behave exactly like dogs but are actually of a different zoological species and thus aren't dogs. Nevertheless, it is not plausible that only one of you expresses a true belief when she says 'There is a big dog growling at me'. The belief your doppelgänger expresses has as much right to be true as the one you express, thus showing that in this case propositional-attitude properties don't supervene on what is in the head. But why accept (1); why take this to show that propositional-attitude properties don't play a causal-explanatory role?

One answer is more or less explicit in Dretske. He's saying two things: first, that propositional-attitude properties like believing that a car is coming aren't 'causal powers' of the states that have them, and, secondly, that it follows from their not being causal powers that they're also 'explanatorily irrelevant', which I take to mean that though we may cite such properties in giving psychological explanations, the reason we cite them isn't that they really occur in the explanations we're giving. Now, 'causal power' is a term of art and we're entitled to ask what it means. It is hard to say what it means; it is not defined, so we have to garner its meaning by figuring out when those who use it are willing or unwilling to apply it. Still, it does seem that

---

[31] Dretske (1990: 5–7).

the following is taken to be sufficient for a property Φ's *not* being a 'causal power' of c with respect to its causing e:

- in addition to having Φ, c also has a property Ψ that would count as a 'causal power' on any precisification of that vague notion;
- although c wouldn't have caused e if c hadn't had Φ, that is just because c's having Φ supervenes on c's having a certain property that includes Ψ in such a way that c wouldn't have had Ψ or any other same-level causal power if c hadn't had Φ;
- while there may well be a causal law involving Ψ, there is none (or none that is relevant) containing Φ.

Very well, let's agree to use 'causal power' in such a way that satisfaction of the foregoing conditions is sufficient for not being a causal power. Why should a propositional-attitude property's not being a causal power in that sense be taken to show that it's *explanatorily irrelevant*? An argument is needed to get us from 'Such-and-such isn't a causal power' to 'Such-and-such is explanatorily irrelevant'. What is it? While Dretske's considering that question, we should also ask him the following question:

> It is clear that by virtue of its meaning 'You make me feel like a virgin', the sequence of sounds produced by the soprano was neither a causal power with respect to its causing the glass to break nor relevant to the explanation of why the glass broke. This is clear because we would without any hesitation reject the explanation that the glass broke because the emitted sounds meant 'You make me feel like a virgin'. Even without any philosophical theorizing, that is just not an explanation anyone would countenance. The fact that the sounds had that meaning is as explanatorily irrelevant as the fact that the soprano who emitted them was wearing purple nail polish. Yet the situation is radically different as regards the explanation of Ava's stepping back to the kerb, when she stepped back to the kerb because she saw that a car was coming. Without any philosophical theorizing, we would without any hesitation accept the claim that she stepped because she believed that a car was coming, even though, as it is now revealed, the property of being a belief that a car is coming isn't a 'causal power' of the neural state that at the relevant time caused her stepping back. What explains *this*

difference between the property of meaning 'You make me feel like a virgin' and the property of believing that a car is coming?

We count (10) ('Ava stepped back because she didn't want to risk getting hit by a car and saw that she would be at risk of being hit by the car speeding towards her if she didn't step back') true, but we wouldn't count

(11) The glass broke because the sounds emitted by the soprano meant 'You make me feel like a virgin'

true. Something important is being left out when a philosopher like Dretske assimilates (10) to (11). Even though the propositional-attitude properties mentioned in (10), like the meaning property mentioned in (11), aren't, by the foregoing stipulation, 'causal powers', there is a very important difference between (10) and (11) which still needs to be articulated. What is that difference, whether or not PA, the proposition expressed by (10), is true and whether or not it should count as a 'causal explanation', in some not yet clarified sense of 'causal explanation'?

In fact, there is good reason to think that propositional-attitude properties are causally essential even though they contain too much extraneous stuff to supervene on underlying causally efficacious properties. For suppose Sally is walking down the street and suddenly lands on her keister. One person explains Sally's fall by saying that she stepped on a banana peel, and someone else explains it by saying that she stepped on a fairly frictionless (i.e. slippery) surface (for simplicity I'll drop the 'fairly'). It certainly seems wrong to say that the two statements give different but equally correct explanations. But if both statements give the same explanation, then, by virtue of the asymmetry between the property of being a banana peel and the property of being frictionless, we should conclude that, though there are good pragmatic reasons for citing the former property, it is not an *essential* part of the explanation the because-statement offers. Things get interesting, however, when we next ask whether the property of being frictionless is essential to its explanation. For suppose we now have a third explanation, offered by one physicist to another, which says that Sally fell because she stepped on a surface having blah-blah microphysical structure. There is an asymmetry between the property of being frictionless and the property of having blah-blah microphysical surface structure, but if we say that being frictionless isn't essential to the explanation it is used to give, then we'll for sure end up saying that the only explanatorily essential properties are those expressible in quantum physics. And that simply isn't how common sense individuates common-sense explanations.[32]

Is there a difference between the banana peel–frictionless asymmetry and the frictionless–blah-blah microphysical surface structure asymmetry that would account for our intuition that while being a banana peel isn't essential to the explanation it is used to give, there is a sense in which being frictionless is? I think so. The first asymmetry is that stepping on a banana peel is liable to cause a fall only because banana peels tend to be (relatively) frictionless, but stepping on something frictionless isn't liable to cause a fall because some frictionless things are banana peels. The second asymmetry is quite different: stepping on something frictionless is liable to cause a fall regardless of the surface's microphysical structure. Of course, being frictionless *supervenes* on having blah-blah microphysical structure (or on a property that includes that microphysical property). The point, however, is that being frictionless would be causally relevant in the way it is no matter what microphysical property subvened it.

When we turn back to a typical propositional-attitude property mentioned in a true because-statement (e.g. Ava's belief that a car is coming), we see that there is no other property in the offing that stands to it in the way being frictionless stands to being a banana peel, although, of course, lots of properties stand to it in the way having a certain microphysical surface structure stands to being frictionless. (And note that in this respect there is nothing any more special or explanatorily relevant about an underlying computational-cum-physical explanation of behaviour, even if it can be called 'psychological', than there is about an underlying purely physical explanation of the same behaviour.)

There are two further problems for the Dretskean line of thought. One is that it implicitly assumes that Ava's belief state token is identical to the neural state token that was a cause of her bodily movement; but this assumption is highly controversial (see 2.3

---

[32] But mightn't the physicist say that he's not giving a different explanation of the fall than the one that cites slipperiness? Yes, she might *say* that, but then she's best interpreted as saying she's not offering a different *competing* explanation.

and 3.8). In no way, however, should this non-identity make one conclude that beliefs can't be causes of non-intentional states—unless
one's also prepared to conclude that beliefs can't be effects of non-
intentional states, as when light reflected from an oncoming rock
enters your eyes and causes you to have the belief that a rock is coming towards your head (which belief in turn causes you to duck). Yet
the Dretskean line of thought supporting (1) would imply that Ava's
belief that a car was coming played no role either in causing her
bodily movement or in the explanation of her stepping back to the
kerb, unless that state token were identical to a neural state token.
That should strike one as considerably more counter-intuitive than
the claim that the property of being a belief that such-and-such isn't
playing a causal-explanatory role.

The second further problem is that although those sympathetic to
the Dretskean line say that content would be explanatorily relevant if
only it supervened on what is in the head—precisely what is suggested by the wording of (1) of the wide-content objection—that is in
fact not a view to which they're entitled. What is really implied by the
Dretskean argument for (1) is that it is entirely irrelevant whether or
not content supervenes on what is in the head. For if the argument
were sound, it would show that, whatever the supervenience situation
was, the only explanatorily relevant property would be that neuro-
physical property that was the causal power.

A second reason some have found for accepting (1) is motivated by
the following sort of thought experiment, this one by Brian Loar:

suppose that I do not know whether in Bert's linguistic community 'arthritis'
means arthritis or tharthritis, but that I know all the relevant individualist
facts about Bert [i.e. intentional facts that supervene on what is in Bert's
head]. I read in his diary: 'I fear I have arthritis, and so today I have made an
appointment with a specialist.' It is difficult to accept that we do not fully
understand the psychological explanation given here, despite our not being
in a position to produce the correct that-clause.[33]

Loar's point is that since you can know the explanation of Bert's
going to a specialist without knowing the propositional contents of
the beliefs and desires involved in it, content is irrelevant to propositional-attitude explanation and hence doesn't play a genuinely

[33] Loar (1987: 572).

causal-explanatory role. But we should be suspicious of Loar's example when we realize that he might just well have said the same thing about our reaction to Bert's diary entry 'I fear I have aldosteronism, and so today I have made an appointment with a specialist', when we have no idea what medical condition aldosteronism might be. A better response to such examples is that common-sense explanations are answers to contextually implicit why questions, and it is easy to imagine contexts in which the diary entry would tell us all we'd want to know about Bert's behaviour. You might as well conclude that a computer's hardware properties don't play a causal-explanatory role because you could be satisfied by being told that your computer isn't working properly because of a defect in its motherboard, even though you have only the foggiest idea of what a motherboard is.

A third reason for accepting (1) is offered by Daniel Dennett, but one can find it repeated by Fodor and others: 'If psychology is going to be science, it had better not posit *mysterious action-at-a-distance*, so a principle of the "supervenience" of the psychological on the physiological must be honored: the brains of organisms differ whenever their minds differ'.[34] The main problem with this (there are others) is that action-at-a-distance requires distant but unconnected *causes*, and an absence of action-at-a-distance is entirely consistent with causes having properties that relate them to distant things.

A fourth reason for accepting (1), which at one time was the reason most often given, went like this.[35] Suppose Ralph reaches for a glass of water, and suppose Twin-Ralph reaches for a glass of twater. What explains each person's arm movement, simply *qua* bodily movement? By hypothesis, the two movements are exactly the same, the only difference being that in Ralph's case it constitutes a reaching for water, while in Twin-Ralph's case it constitutes a reaching for twater. Since the two movements are exactly the same, they have the same explanation. But the only candidate explanation that is the same for both is the neurophysiological explanation of the arm movement. This line of argument, however, simply begs the question against one who claims that propositional-attitude explanations can provide causal explanations of bodily movements. This theorist doesn't deny that

---

[34] Dennett (1988: 385); my emphasis.
[35] Stich (1978); Fodor (1987); Devitt and Sterelny (1987).

the two propositional-attitude explanations—that Ralph wanted a glass of water, etc., and that Twin-Ralph wanted a glass of twater, etc.—supervene on facts that entail the same underlying neurophysiological explanation; her point is that the desire for water and its attendant beliefs and the desire for twater and its attendant beliefs can in a case like this cause the same bodily movement. Where is the principle that precludes this? If what is tacitly being relied on is Kim's principle of causal/explanatory exclusion, then this twin earth scenario doesn't represent a new reason for accepting premiss (1). The implicit principle can't be Mill's method of difference and agreement, since there is a relevant difference between the two cases, namely, Ralph's movement constitutes a reaching for water, whereas his twin's constitutes a reaching for twater.[36]

The abstractness objection. Philosophers sometimes worry about how mathematical entities can play a causal-explanatory role. After all, numbers, being abstract entities outside space-time, are not things with which anything can causally interact, so how can something's standing in a relation to a number causally explain anything? Since propositions are also abstract entities with which it is impossible for anything to causally interact, they are subject to the same worry. The worry is well expressed by David Braddon-Mitchell and Frank Jackson:

a problem of content arises from the role of content in explaining behaviour. The contents of belief and desire are causal-explanatory properties of them, as well as being the feature of them that allows beliefs to be true or false and desires to be satisfied or unsatisfied. Jones's running away is causally explained by the fact that she has a belief with the content that there is a tiger nearby, along with her having a desire with the content that she wishes to go on living. When we tell the story abut how a belief gets to have truth conditions, and further the particular truth conditions that it does have, we must ensure that the story centrally involves a property of the belief that can serve to explain behaviour. . . . We must, that is, respect and account for content's dual role in psychology. This point gives us another reason [for doubting that having a belief or desire involves standing in a] special relationship to a proposition conceived as something outside space-time: it is completely obscure how a relation to something outside space-time could play a role in causal explanation.[37]

---

[36] Cf. Jackson and Pettit (1988: 389).
[37] Braddon-Mitchell and Jackson (1996: 178).

At least propositions are not worse off than numbers, and it is pretty clear that numbers play *some* sort of explanatory role; after all, the read-out on the scale is '124' because the person standing on it weighs 124 pounds. True, we can't causally interact with the number 124, but how does it follow from that that the property of weighing 124 pounds can't play an explanatory role in causal explanations, especially since it is true that the scale wouldn't read '124' if the person on it didn't weigh 124 pounds? Of course, properties like weighing 124 pounds and believing that there is a tiger nearby get their counterfactual roles by virtue of supervening on more basic explanatory properties that are specifiable without reference to numbers or propositions, but that sort of thing can be said for the causal-explanatory role of any non-basic property. In any event, it is true that propositions and numbers are in the same boat, that they are doing some sort of non-superfluous work in because-statements, and that it remains to be said what that work is. In the next section I'll try to answer this question for propositions, but I must leave it to others to expatiate on the explanatory role of mathematical entities.

The no-law objection. This can be put in the following way.

(1) Propositional-attitude properties play a causal-explanatory role only if they figure in true causal laws.
(2) Propositional-attitude properties figure in no such laws.
(3) So, propositional-attitude properties don't play a causal-explanatory role.

Many who want to resist the conclusion—e.g. Jerry Fodor when he's not accepting the conclusion—deny (2) by claiming that while there are no true *strict*, or exceptionless, propositional-attitude laws, there are true *ceteris paribus* propositional-attitude causal laws. I doubt that there are such laws, and in my article '*Ceteris Paribus* Laws' I try to show why.[38] The same issue of *Mind* contains Jerry Fodor's 'You Can Fool Some of the People All the Time, Everything Else Being Equal: Hedged Laws and Psychological Explanations',[39] which replies to my paper. When the issue containing our papers appeared, Fodor said to me that the editors of *Mind* forgot to say who won. I'm going to assume that I did, so that the question now is what can be said for premiss (1). Why, that is, think that causal explanations require causal laws?

---

[38] Schiffer (1991).   [39] Fodor (1991).

One who thinks causal explanations require laws is most likely an adherent of the covering-law model of explanation and holds tenaciously to the view that if there were no *ceteris paribus* laws there would be no special-science laws, hence no special-science explanations, and hence no special sciences. But when we look at typical explanations in special sciences such as biology or geology, one's apt to wonder whether the covering-law model is the best model for the explanations taken to be correct in those sciences. Where are the geological laws in the preferred explanation in plate tectonics of how the Himalayas were formed? Where are the biological laws in the explanation of how the HIV penetrates host cells? What one finds are law-free stories about the *mechanisms* by which certain things happen. To be sure, laws may well be needed to account for how the mechanisms work, but these laws will be laws of more basic sciences, not laws of the special sciences offering the geological or biological explanations. And many correct common-sense explanations seem far removed from a nomological component, as in the following example which Terry Horgan attributes to Barry Loewer:

there are examples of causal transactions in which the cause and the effect have properties which evidently are not connected by even a [*ceteris paribus*] generalization, but which seem explanatorily relevant anyway. Suppose, for instance, that Barry's noticing a flower shop causes him to remember that tomorrow is his wife's birthday. The properties *being a noticing that there is a flower shop yonder* and *being a remembering that tomorrow is one's wife's birthday*, certainly appear explanatorily relevant to the causal transaction; yet generalizations like

> *Ceteris paribus*, a (married) man who notices that there is a flower shop yonder will remember that the following day is his wife's birthday seem just false.[40]

Anyhow, suppose I'm wrong about *ceteris paribus* laws. Wouldn't there then be relevant propositional-attitude *ceteris paribus* laws— e.g. if you want *E* to obtain, believe that *E* won't obtain unless you cause it to obtain, that you can bring about *E* by doing *A*, which you know you can do, have no conflicting desires, then, *ceteris paribus*, you'll do *A*? It is not clear, since the candidate just mentioned does look pretty analytic (albeit vacuously so), on any reasonable way of unpacking '*ceteris paribus*', and the sorts of *ceteris paribus* generalizations that are usually mentioned as laws are contingent. But if the

[40] Horgan (1989: 55).

apparent analyticity isn't a problem, then one who believes in *ceteris paribus* laws has a good way to deny premiss (2).

The eliminativist objection. This objection enjoys a simple statement: propositional-attitude properties can't play a causal-explanatory role because there are no propositional attitudes. There are at least two reasons philosophers have claimed for believing there are no propositional attitudes (it is their oxymoron, not mine). The first is associated with Paul and Patricia Churchland, though it has precursors in Paul Feyerabend and Richard Rorty.[41] As stated by the Churchlands, the idea is that the notion of a propositional attitude is implicitly defined by its role in common-sense psychology and, as so defined, it requires that our brains enjoy a certain functional organization. Since, they further claim, there is very good reason to suppose that our brains don't have that functional organization, there is very good reason to suppose there are no propositional attitudes and that, therefore, the theory that defines the notion of them is false. Propositional attitudes and propositional-attitude theory must go the way of phlogiston and phlogiston theory. The other reason for denying that propositional attitudes exist is that the truth of propositional-attitude reports—e.g. the claim that Ralph believes that the earth is flat—require abstract entities called 'propositions' to be the references of that-clauses, and propositions don't exist. This is reminiscent of Hartry Field's claim that arithmetical statements such as '1 + 1 = 2' can't be true since there are no numbers for numerical singular terms like '1' and '2' to refer to.[42] Just as Field tries to lighten the counter-intuitiveness of his theory by claiming that arithmetic statements are at least true in the 'fiction of arithmetic',[43] so one who takes this line may want to hold that propositional-attitude statements are true in the fiction of, I guess, the story of propositional attitudes. And just as Field needn't reject physical explanations that try to refer to numbers, so the fictionalist about propositions needn't deny that correct explanations are given by propositional-attitude explanations. It is just that those propositional attitudes don't enter essentially into those correct explanations.

To the Churchlands I say that, while I can't speak for them, *I* know that nothing could convince *me* that I don't have any beliefs. If I were to learn that, like a chocolate Easter bunny, I was hollow inside, that

---

[41] Patricia Churchland (1986); Paul Churchland (1981); Feyerabend (1963); and Rorty (1970)
[42] Field (1989).   [43] Field (1989).

would just tell me that you don't need a stuffed head to have beliefs. To those who deny the truth of propositional-attitude statements because they deny that propositions exist, I say (*inter alia*—see the discussion of fictionalism below) that their position is not well motivated because they don't have the good reasons they think they have for doubting that propositions exist. If their worry is how to account for knowledge or reliable beliefs about propositions, then they should appreciate that given the right conception of propositions, it is a conceptual truth which we know a priori that propositions exist (see Chapter 2).

The psychology-doesn't-need-them objection. In his well-known and influential paper 'Mental Representation',[44] Hartry Field wrote:

> If the task of psychology is to state (i) the laws by which an organism's beliefs and desires evolve as he is subjected to sensory stimulations, and (ii) the laws by which those beliefs and desires affect his bodily movements, then semantic characterizations of beliefs and desires are irrelevant to psychology: one can state the laws without saying anything at all about what the believed or desired sentences mean, or what their truth-conditions are or what their subject matter is.[45]

This was then taken by Field and others to show that content doesn't play a causal-explanatory role, doesn't, that is, occur essentially in whatever correct explanations are implied by our common-sense propositional-attitude because-statements.

The main problem I have with this objection is that I don't see how the truth of the quotation is supposed to show anything about whether content occurs essentially in correct propositional-attitude causal explanations. The proposition expressed by the quotation in no way *entails* that content doesn't play a causal-explanatory role. An additional premiss is needed. What is it? What is the necessary condition for content's playing such a role which the truth of the quotation shows can't be satisfied? It can't be a point about 'explanatory exclusion' per se. If, as many would claim, the result of replacing 'psychology' with 'neuroscience' in the quotation would again yield a truth, nobody would take that to show content doesn't occur essentially in correct causal explanations. So why should putting 'psychology' back make a difference? If the integrity of propositional-attitude explanations isn't threatened by the existence of more basic neurophysiological explanations, then why should they be threatened by the existence of more basic non-propositional-attitude psychological explanations?

8.4   CONTENT IN EXPLANATION: WITHDRAWAL POSITIONS

Suppose a theorist takes one or more of the foregoing objections to be valid. To where in conceptual space should she withdraw now that she denies that propositional-attitude properties don't occur essentially in any correct causal explanation given by a common-sense propositional-attitude explanation?

Extreme withdrawal. This is the position of the Churchlands and perhaps of no one else. It holds that we should react in the same way scientists who tried to explain combustion in terms of phlogiston reacted when they discovered there was no such thing as phlogiston: they simply realized that they were wrong in the explanations they gave and stopped giving them. No doubt the Churchlands would allow that we might continue with our propositional-attitude talk in some unserious instrumental vein, since that talk does at least have *some* predictive value. No further comment.

Withdrawal to ideal-involving sui generis *explanation.* This is the position proposed by John McDowell and alluded to in (8.3).[46] In so far as I understand it, it is a conception of propositional-attitude explanation to which any proponent of the reasons-aren't-causes objection (8.3) might be drawn. According to McDowell, merely to recognize the way in which the 'constitutive ideal of rationality' is involved in our propositional-attitude notions

is to appreciate that the concepts of the propositional attitudes have their proper home in explanations of a special sort: explanations in which things are made intelligible by being revealed to be, or to approximate to being, as they rationally ought to be. This is to be contrasted with a style of explanation in which one makes things intelligible by representing their coming into being as a particular instance of how things generally tend to happen.[47]

---

[46] McDowell (1998a).   [47] McDowell (1998a: 328).

In the *sui generis* kind of explanation into which propositional attitudes enter, the ideal of rationality plays a special explanatory role. Unfortunately, it is quite unclear to me what that explanatory role is. Propositional-attitude explanations purport to tell us *why* people do what they do; they are correct (in the absence of a very rare kind of overdetermination) only if the fact being explained wouldn't have obtained if the propositional-attitude facts cited in the explanation hadn't obtained; by McDowell's own admission, they cite psychological causes of behaviour; they say nothing explicitly about the extent to which the agent achieves some unstated ideal of rationality; and they may explain why an agent did what he did even though they reveal him to be irrational in the extreme ('He believes that it will rain because there is a bug on the wall, even though he can give no account of how a bug's being on the wall is evidence that it will rain'). Even if a propositional-attitude explanation reveals (though doesn't state) the extent to which an agent approximates ideal rationality, why should that debar the propositional-attitude notions occurring in the explanation from playing a causal-role explanatory role? Part of what may be motivating McDowell, as revealed in the bit just quoted, is his recognition that propositional-attitude explanations don't explain by subsuming agents under lawlike statistical generalizations. But such subsumption, I've suggested, isn't an essential feature of causal explanations, however that vague notion is precisified.

Withdrawal to science. Embarrassed by the stridency and counter-intuitiveness of their earliest pronouncements about content, which seemed to imply that our *common-sense* propositional-attitude explanations were on a par with appeals to phlogiston in explanations of combustion, theorists like Stich and Fodor retreated to claims about what is needed for *scientific*, as opposed to common-sense, psychological explanations of behaviour. OK, but where does that leave the idea that content plays an essential role in correct *common-sense* causal explanations? If that is still denied, what is the relevance of the claim about scientific explanation? Is the idea supposed to be that our common-sense explanations are crude efforts in the direction of scientific explanations, not yet available to anyone, which won't involve propositional attitudes? Why on earth think that? If it is no longer being denied, then the retreat is irrelevant to our present concerns.

Withdrawal to fictionalism. This response begins with the claim that while common-sense propositional-attitude explanations are never true (since there are no propositions), they are 'true in the fiction of propositional-attitude theory', and although not literally true, our propositional-attitude because-statements are of such importance to us because of their instrumental value in predicting and controlling behaviour and in exploiting head–world reliability correlations to gain information about the extra-cranial world. I suppose that if we can account for the role of propositions in explanation and in exploiting head–world reliability correlations, then the fictionalist can use that account to explain how propositional-attitude state-ments can have their instrumental value, even though there are no propositions. That is certainly a mark in favour of fictionalism about propositions. The very big problem with it is that it is unmotivated; there is no good reason to deny that propositions exist and there is no problem in accounting for our knowledge and reliable beliefs about them: these are conceptual truths we know a priori (see Chapter 2). A second, though smaller, problem is that it makes no sense to say that a propositional-attitude statement is 'true in the fiction of propositions' unless something can be identified as the story of propositions, as arithmetic can serve as the relevant story for the fictionalist about numbers. But it is quite unclear what this official doctrine about propositions is supposed to be, such that it can do all the fictionalist needs it to do.

Withdrawal to 'narrow content'. There was a time, about ten to fifteen years ago, when most of those who advanced the 'wide-con-tent objection' went on to claim that what psychology needed was a notion of *narrow* content, a notion of content which, unlike the wide content ascribed by that-clauses, did supervene on what is in the head. With the exception of David Chalmers's version of two-dimen-sional semantics,[48] this view seems no longer to be in favour, and for good reason, I would say. Some of the things being called narrow content, such as computational roles, had no business being called *content*, so that the claim of these theorists was just the claim, in dis-guise, that the only correct psychological explanations of behaviour were non-intentional. Fodor suggested an intentional notion but it was hard to make both precise and plausible, and it wasn't clear that it really could be narrow. Other characterizations of narrow content were quickly seen to be flawed (for example, it is sometimes said that the 'narrow content' of 'water' is the description 'unique clear liquid

---

[48] Chalmers (1996, forthcoming).

we find in our lakes, etc.'; but beliefs involving these descriptions no more supervene on what is in the head than do beliefs about water[49]). The main objection I would make, however, is that, as already implied above in the discussion of the 'wide-content objection', the usual arguments advanced to show that wide content didn't play a causal-explanatory role would, if sound, also show that no notion of narrow content could play a causal-explanatory role. For the moral of the argument is that the only 'causal power' is the one that enters into the more basic neurophysiological explanation. This effectively cuts the legs out from under those who accept the argument against 'wide' content's playing a causal-explanatory role and go on to claim that what is needed is a notion of 'narrow' content. What they ought to conclude is that no kind of content can play a causal-explanatory role. For what those arguments really imply is that the only properties of a cause which genuinely play a causal-explanatory role are those of its properties that are the causal powers by virtue of which the cause caused its effect.[50] Any other property of the cause would be epiphenomenal if it wasn't a causal power, regardless of whether it happened to supervene on a causal power.

Withdrawal to functional explanation. Perhaps content plays an explanatory role even though it doesn't play a *causal*-explanatory role. For a long time, mostly in the 1970s, the dominant view was that mental concepts were *functional* concepts and that, therefore, psychological explanations were functional explanations. Suppose you ask why a certain boiler turned on and someone explains that it was caused by an event in the boiler that had some unknown physical property Φ that was related to such-and-such inputs to the boiler and such-and-such other boiler states and conditions in such a way that an event's having Φ would be a necessary part of a causally sufficient condition for the boiler's turning on. You would have been given a kind of causal explanation, but the second-order functional property used in the explanation—the property of having some physical property Φ such that...—seems intuitively not to be playing anything worth calling a *causal*-explanatory role. According to the functionalist, propositional-attitude explanations are functional explanations.

---

[49] See also the critical discussion of Chalmers in 3.8.

[50] This probably isn't true of Loar's (1987) argument for narrow content, which is primarily based on the kinds of examples of his considered in 8.3 and not so much concerned with wide content's failure to supervene on what is in the head.

A functional *role* is a property of (e.g. neurophysiological) state *types* which details how tokens of those types are related to tokens of other state types, to sensory and other inputs and to behavioural and other outputs (and, crucially to its bearing on present issues, does so without any recourse to any intentional notions).[51] A functional *property* is a property of state *tokens*; it is the property of being a token of a state type that has such-and-such functional role.[52] Thus, suppose neurophysiological state token n was the cause at time t of Ava's stepping back, and suppose that n was a cause of Ava's stepping back by virtue of being a token of neurophysiological state type N. Now, N will have functional role FR, which is such that any token of a state type having FR will, when certain conditions obtain, cause a movement of a type to which Ava's belongs. Because N has functional role FR, any *token* of N *ipso facto* has the functional property of being a token of a type that has FR. The functionalist claims that the explanations afforded by propositional-attitude because-statements are functional explanations. The explanation provided by (10) is that Ava's stepping back was caused by state tokens having such-and-such functional properties, those functional properties somehow or other provided by the propositional-attitude properties.

On classical versions of functionalism, the functional explanation afforded by a propositional-attitude because-statement exhausts the content of the statement. This is because on those versions of functionalism propositional-attitude properties are identical to functional properties.[53] But it is extremely implausible that propositional-attitude properties *are* functional properties.[54] At the same time, it is not implausible to suppose that propositional-attitude properties *entail* functional properties; so it remains open that propositional-attitude because-statements entail functional explanations, even

[51] Any kind of input–out system admits of functional explanation, but I'm limiting my discussion to functionalism concerning human information processing. What applies to state types and tokens applies as well, *mutatis mutandis*, to event, process, etc. states and tokens.

[52] See Schiffer (1987a, ch. 2).

[53] On David Lewis's version of functionalism (1983a,b), mental properties aren't themselves functional properties but are the unique realizers of the functional properties determined by the functional roles expressed by mental terms. Multiple realization is a problem for this version of functionalism, but the results as regards functional explanation are otherwise no different from those of the more plausible version of functionalism.

[54] See e.g. Schiffer (1987a, ch. 2) and Block (1980a).

though those functional explanations don't exhaust the content of the statements that entail them. Still, the view is problematic. You ask, 'Why's Bob filing for divorce?' and I explain:

(12) He's filing for divorce because he wants to become a rabbi and believes that rabbis have to be single.

Suppose that wanting to become a rabbi entails being in a state that has functional property F^w and that believing that rabbis have to be single entails being in a state with functional property F^b. These functional properties can be completely characterized in wholly non-intentional, non-propositional terms; they could be characterized using the uninterpreted formulae of some programming language. Help yourself to what F^w and F^b might be. No matter; the following will still be true. If all you know about Bob is that he's in an internal state that has F^w and an internal state that has F^b, then you will have absolutely no explanation of why Bob does anything. From your knowledge that he's in these two functional states you couldn't predict so much as a finger movement. What you would have couldn't by any stretch of the imagination be called even a partial explanation or explanation sketch. What would you need to begin to get an explanation, not of Bob's filing for divorce, but merely of the bodily movements that constituted his filing (for those sorts of non-intentional facts are the most you could hope to explain using a non-intentional explanans)? Well, you would need at least a complete functional theory of Bob, a complete account, in non-intentional terms, of the information-processing programs he was running plus a complete functional state description of him at some relevant time prior to his filing for divorce plus a complete state description of the physical world, or at least that part of it that bears on Bob's bodily movements, plus a complete physics. The reason you would need all the physical stuff—a physical state description and compete physical theory—is that the complete functional theory of Bob plus a complete functional description of him at a given time will enable you to predict only what basic bodily movements Bob will undergo at that time or immediately thereafter. You would then have to use all the physical stuff to predict sensory inputs, so you could get an updated functional state description of Bob for the time immediately following the aforementioned bodily movements, so that you could then predict other basic bodily movements, and so on. Proceeding in this way, it would take you about a million years, at least, to get to the hand movements that actually constituted his filing for divorce, and even then you wouldn't yet have any way of knowing what intentional actions those movements constituted. Moreover, even if, *per impossibile*, there were such an explanation, it would be of no interest or use to you. It wouldn't be the kind of thing you wanted to be told when you asked why Bob filed for divorce. Would it help if we threw in head–world reliability correlations, so that we could exploit the fact that being in certain functional states was very good evidence that Bob would do this, that, or the other thing in the future? Not really, since the functional properties we could reasonably take to be implied by the propositional-attitude properties mentioned in (12) wouldn't be unique to those properties but would be shared by propositional-attitude properties with quite different contents, so that it is unlikely that the fact that Bob was in states having F^w and F^b would enable us to predict anything of any interest.

But what if what is going on is something like the following? When I explain Bob's filing for divorce by saying he wants to be a rabbi and believes that rabbis have to be single, what I'm in effect doing is saying that:

(13) Bob filed for divorce because he was in tokens of neural state types that had functional and indicator-relation properties similar to the those of the neural state tokens that I would be in if I wanted to be a rabbi and believed that rabbis had to be single.[55]

This only makes matters worse. First, how could this possibly account for the *interest* of the propositional-attitude explanation, since that explanation is of considerable interest—if we accepted it, we would feel we knew why Bob filed for divorce—but your merely knowing that Bob's in states that are like mine in unknown functional and

---

[55] This is suggested by Hartry Field's suggestion that 'when I explain Al's raising his gun by saying he believes there is a rabbit nearby, what I am in effect doing is explaining [the fact that Al raised his gun] in terms of his believing* a representation that plays a role in his psychology rather similar to the role that "That are rabbits nearby"...plays in mine' (2001d: 78). In fairness to Field, this proposal was meant to be conjoined with an account of propositional-attitude reports according to which to say that Al believes that there are rabbits nearby is (nearly enough) to say Al is in a belief state whose content is the same as that of my utterance, in the belief report, of 'there are rabbits nearby'.

indicator ways would hardly have answered your question about why Bob filed for divorce. Secondly, how did *indicator relations* get into the causal picture, given the nature of the objections to content that motivated the search for alternative accounts of content's explanatory role? The main problem with propositional-attitude properties was supposed to be that they contain causally extraneous matter, yet head–world indicator relations, while of relevance to the *predictive value* of Bob's mental states, are subject to the same objections about causal efficaciousness as propositional-attitude properties. Thirdly, the proposal doesn't get the truth conditions of propositional-attitude because-statements right. For any number of reasons, (12) might be true while (13) was false, or false while (13) was true.

If propositional-attitude because-statements were of interest to us because of the functional explanations—or partial explanations or explanation sketches—they afforded, they would be of no interest to us at all and we would never utter propositional-attitude because-statements. Whatever the point of these statements is, it is not to provide functional explanations.

Withdrawal to other kinds of 'program explanations'. Functional explanations are what Frank Jackson and Philip Pettit have called 'program explanations', but they aren't the only kinds of program explanations.[56] Program explanations cite features that causally program without causing. Jackson and Pettit give the following example:

> We may explain the conductor's annoyance at a concert by the fact that someone coughed. What will have actually caused the conductor's annoyance will be the coughing of some particular person, Fred, say; but when we say that it was someone's coughing that explains why the conductor was annoyed, we are thinking of someone's coughing as Fred's coughing or Mary's coughing or Harry's coughing or . . ., and saying that any one of these disjuncts would have caused the conductor's annoyance—it did not have to be Fred.[57]

Their general characterization of program explanation is this:

> Suppose state A caused state B. Variations on A, say, A', A'', . . . would have caused variations on B, say B', B'', . . ., respectively. It may be that if the A^i share a property P, the B^i would share a property Q; keep P constant

[56] Jackson and Pettit (1988, 1990).   [57] Jackson and Pettit (1988: 394).

among the actual and possible causes, and Q remains constant among the actual and possible effects.[58]

But I wonder if this captures what they really have in mind. For I suspect that *any* non-basic causal explanation—any explanation in chemistry, biology, geology, etc.—will be a program explanation by this criterion.

In any event, two questions must be answerable if propositional-attitude explanations are program explanations: (*a*) For what causes do propositional-attitude explanations program? (*b*) How do they program for those causes? I suppose the best answer for (*a*) is neurophysiological causes. But what is the best answer for (*b*), if it is not a functionalist answer already rejected? We know how someone's coughing programs for Fred's coughing: there is just one event that is a coughing by Fred and a coughing by someone, and that event has the property of being a coughing by someone because it has the property of being a coughing by Fred, since being a coughing by Fred entails being a coughing by someone. Obviously, nothing like that is going on in, say, the propositional-attitude explanation of Ava's stepping back to the kerb (see the discussion centring on (10) in (8.3). In the conductor example we don't even *seem* to have two distinct causes at the same time, Fred's coughing and someone's coughing, but the problem in the Ava example was that at a certain time we had the neurophysiological cause, n, of Ava's stepping back, and we also seemed to have the distinct psychological cause, b, her coming to believe that a car was speeding towards her. We certainly can't assume that $b = n$, and even if we could, it would be false that N, the property of n causally responsible for its being a cause of Ava's stepping back, in any way entailed B, the property of being a belief that a car was speeding towards one. If B were a functional property, we could say that N realized B, i.e. that it was the property that had the functional role in terms of which B was defined, but we know B isn't a functional property. The suggestion that propositional-attitude explanations are program explanations seems to have no cash-value over and above the suggestion that they are functional explanations.[59]

[58] Jackson and Pettit (1988: 393–4).

[59] In fact, Jackson and Pettit were concerned to show that propositional-attitude explanations might afford a functional explanation in terms of broad functional roles (functional roles that took into account distal causes of inputs) as opposed to functional explanations couched just in terms of narrow functional roles (functional roles bounded by sensory input on the input side and motor responses on the output side). But my objections to functionalism are indifferent to the broad–narrow distinction.

Withdrawal to teleological explanation. Several philosophers—e.g. Fred Dretske, Colin McGinn, and Ruth Millikan—hold that content plays some sort of *teleological* role, although they don't all opt for quite the same teleological role.[60] Fred Dretske, for example, has claimed that propositional-attitude properties explain not why propositional attitudes cause the actions they cause, but rather why we have those internal causes in the first place. But it is hard to see how anything like this can be going on when we explain that Johnny wrote '4'on his exam paper because he believed that $1^2 + 1^2 = 4$, or that Ralph was looking for a virgin so that he could catch a unicorn. Something teleological no doubt enters into the explanation of how creatures came to have propositional attitudes, but it is hard to see how propositional-attitude explanations of particular actions can appropriately be called teleological.

8.5 CONTENT IN EXPLANATION: THE BOTTOM LINE

The largest part of what makes the issue of content's causal-explanatory role so murky has nothing per se to do with content. It has to do with our notion of causal explanation per se, what it is and what its requirements are. These are important issues, of course, but the bottom line is that the explanatory role of propositional-attitude notions is their use in correct because-statements, and it is possible to account for the *value*, or point, of propositional-attitude because-statements simply by appeal to features of them no one would dispute. The propositions expressed by propositional-attitude because-statements play such an important role for us—whether or not we decide to call them causal explanations, or even explanations—because, quite simply, they have both *counterfactual* and *predictive* value, in the following sense:

Counterfactual value. If someone did something because she had such-and-such propositional attitudes, then, all other things being equal, *she would not have done what she did if she hadn't had those propositional attitudes.*

[60] Dretske (1988); McGinn (1989); Millikan (1984).

Predictive value. We have *epistemic access* to the propositional attitudes of others, and *we can often predict what they will do on the basis of knowing what they believe and want.*

These two values combine to enable us in myriad instances to know what others will or won't do, and to enable us to influence the behaviour of others by affecting their beliefs or desires. One would really have to be imaginative to over-emphasize the importance of this in our lives. Both the counterfactual and predictive values of propositional attitudes in some way supervene on more basic non-intentional facts. But we don't have access to those facts, and their complexity and that of relevant probabilistic generalizations involving them would prohibit our making a use of those facts for prediction and control of behaviour that comes anywhere near that afforded by propositional-attitude facts. That is the bottom line about propositional-attitude 'explanations', whatever else we decide about them.

Further questions of course remain, on top of the bottom line.

Are propositional-attitude 'explanations' really *explanations*? If so, are they really *causal* explanations? The answer to both questions is clearly yes, if we go by our common-sense understanding of those notions; and if we're going by some other understanding, it will have to be one that is stipulated. So they can't really be the philosophically interesting questions. The interesting ones must include, but probably aren't exhausted by, the following overlapping questions:

(i) What explains the fact that propositional-attitude because-statements have their counterfactual value (their predictive value was explained in 8.2)?

(ii) How will the answer to (i) require propositional-attitude facts and explanations to be related to underlying non-intentional facts and explanations?

(iii) Will the answer to (i) require that there be propositional-attitude 'laws'—e.g. causal *ceteris paribus* laws?

(iv) How are propositional-attitude explanations like, or unlike, paradigm non-basic, or special-science, causal explanations such as those in biology?

(v) If the argument of this book is correct, the propositions in propositional-attitude explanations are pleonastic propositions. Could other things, comprising different kinds of propositional attitudes or comprising sentential attitudes of one kind or another, be fashioned that would serve our explanatory needs as well as pleonastic propositions?

As regards (i) and (ii), I think that the most reasonable thing to hold at this stage in the history of our subject is that propositional-attitude facts can't be identified with physical or topic-neutral facts, but that they do supervene on physical facts and that it is this supervenience that explains the counterfactual value of propositional-attitude because-statements. Ava stepped back because she saw that a car was speeding towards her, and this implies that, absent an extremely rare kind of overdetermination, she wouldn't have stepped back when she did if she hadn't seen that a car was speeding towards her. This is because if she hadn't seen that a car was speeding towards her, then she wouldn't have been in a certain neurophysiological state that was a cause of her stepping back. And this in turn is because her seeing that a car was speeding towards her supervened on a very large physical state, perhaps one stretching back into the past and taking in very complex relations to all sorts of distal things that included the neurophysiological state, and that neurophysiological state is a part of the large subvening state that wouldn't have obtained if the propositional-attitude state hadn't obtained. There remains the question about the modal sense in which propositional-attitude facts supervene on physical facts and the question about what accounts for this supervenience, but I have said what I'm able to say about those issues in 4.4.

As regards (iii), I hold three things. First, if propositional-attitudes require propositional-attitude causal laws, those laws will be *ceteris paribus* laws. Secondly, as I've argued elsewhere,[61] there is no explanatorily relevant sense in which there are any *ceteris paribus* laws: non-basic, or special-science, explanations don't use them and don't need them.[62] Thirdly, even if that weren't so, there wouldn't be relevant propositional-attitude *ceteris paribus* laws. As indicated above,[63] the best-candidate generalizations seem to be conceptual truths, not contingent causal laws. These, however, are big issues, and since I still believe what I've already published, I won't rehash them here.

As regards (iv), we could probably answer this pretty easily if we had a complete account of special-science explanations. My bet is that nothing here would give us reason to say that propositional-attitude explanations aren't causal explanations, especially since there isn't any good reason to think that causal-explanatory special-science notions must be related to underlying physical notions in any

---

[61] Schiffer (1991).   [62] Cf. Earman and Roberts (1999).
[63] 8.3; see also Schiffer (1991).

stronger sense than supervenience. For example, when we explain the decrease in the number of Mary's T4 cells in terms of her being infected with the HIV virion, that explanation isn't impugned by the fact that only some of the chemical properties definitive of HIV are essential to the decrease.[64] And while it is true that causal-explanatory propositional-attitude properties typically don't supervene on what is in the head, and thus can't be identified with any relevant 'causal powers' that are in the head, it is also plausible that many special-science explanatory notions are analogously 'wide'. For example, the property of being a gene doesn't supervene on the microstructural properties of DNA sequences, for, as Ron McClamrock points out, in order to be a gene something must contribute to the phenotype in ways that will typically depend on relations to other genetic materials and to the nature of the coding mechanisms that act on the DNA sequences. 'So the properties of a particular gene considered as that kind of DNA sequence are supervenient on its local microstructure, but its properties considered as that kind of *gene* are not.'[65] But these are very big issues and can't be dealt with here.

Finally, (v) has already been answered. The predictive value of propositional-attitude facts is absolutely crucial to their role in explanation. Propositional-attitude because-statements wouldn't have anything like the value they have for us if we didn't have the access we have to the propositional attitudes of others or if we couldn't use that access to predict what others will do. This predictive value falls under the evidentiary value of propositional-attitude facts generally, and this was explained in 8.2. Nothing other than pleonastic propositions could do their explanatory work as well as they do because nothing other than them could serve us as well in the systematic exploitation of head–world reliability correlations.

So we need pleonastic propositions, and in this book I've tried to give a theory both of what they are in themselves and of their place in nature, language, and thought.

---

[64] Cf. Schiffer (1991).   [65] McClamrock (1995: 29).

REFERENCES

ADAMS, E. (1970), 'Subjunctive and Indicative Conditionals', *Foundations of Language*, 6: 89–94.

ALMOG, J., PERRY, J., and WETTSTEIN, H. (eds.) (1989), *Themes from Kaplan* (Oxford University Press).

ARMSTRONG, D. (1989), *Universals: An Opinionated Introduction* (Westview Press).

AUSTIN, J. L. (1962), *How to Do Things with Words* (Oxford University Press).

AYER, A. J. (1936), *Language, Truth and Logic* (Victor Gollancz).

BACH, K. (1997), 'Do Belief Reports Report Beliefs?', *Pacific Philosophical Quarterly*, 78: 215–41.

BARBER, A. (ed.) (2003), *Epistemology of Language* (Oxford University Press).

BARNETT, D. (forthcoming), 'Vagueness, Knowledge, and Rationality'.

BEALER, G. (2002), 'Modal Epistemology and the Rationalist Renaissance', in T. Gendler and J. Hawthorne (eds.), *Conceivability and Possibility* (Oxford University Press).

BEALL, J. (ed.) (forthcoming), *Liars and Heaps* (Oxford University Press).

BENACERRAF, P. (1965), 'What Numbers Could Not Be', *Philosophical Review*, 74: 47–73.

BENNETT, J. (2003), *A Textbook on Conditionals* (Oxford University Press).

BLACKBURN, S. (1984), *Spreading the Word: Groundings in the Philosophy of Language* (Oxford University Press).

BLOCK, N. (1980a), 'Troubles with Functionalism', in Block (1980b).

——(1980b), *Readings in Philosophy of Psychology*, vol. i (Harvard University Press).

——and STALNAKER, R. (1999), 'Conceptual Analysis, Dualism, and the Explanatory Gap', *Philosophical Review*, 108: 1–46.

BOGHOSSIAN, P. (1991), 'Naturalizing Content', in Loewer and Rey (1991).

——and PEACOCKE, C. (eds.) (2000), *New Essays on the A Priori* (Oxford University Press).

BRADDON-MITCHELL, D., and JACKSON, F. (1996), *Philosophy of Mind and Cognition* (Blackwell).

BURGE, T. (1979), 'Individualism and the Mental', *Midwest Studies in Philosophy*, 4: 73–121.

——(1980), 'The Content of Propositional Attitudes', Central Division APA talk, abstract published in *Noûs*, 14: 53–8.

——(1982a), 'Other Bodies', in Woodfield (1982).

BURGE T. (1982*b*), 'Two Thought Experiments Reviewed', *Notre Dame Journal of Formal Logic*, 23: 284–93.

—— (1993), 'Content Preservation', *Philosophical Review*, 102: 457–88.

BYRNE, A. (forthcoming), 'Chalmers on Epistemic Content'.

—— and PRYOR, J. (forthcoming), 'Bad Intensions'.

CAMPBELL, J., O'ROURKE, M., and SHIER, D. (eds.) (2001), *Essays on Meaning and Truth* (Seven Bridges Press).

CHALMERS, D. (1996), *The Conscious Mind: In Search of a Fundamental Theory* (Oxford University Press).

—— (2002*a*), 'The Components of Content', in Chalmers (2002*b*).

—— (ed.) (2002*b*), *Philosophy of Mind: Classical and Contemporary Readings* (Oxford University Press).

—— (forthcoming), 'The Foundations of Two-Dimensional Semantics'.

—— and JACKSON, F. (2001), 'Conceptual Analysis and Reductive Explanation', *Philosophical Review*, 110: 315–61.

CHIHARA, C. (1979), 'The Semantic Paradoxes: A Diagnostic Investigation', *Philosophical Review*, 88: 590–618.

CHURCHLAND, PATRICIA (1986), *Neurophilosophy: Toward a Unified Science of the Mind/Brain* (MIT Press).

CHURCHLAND, PAUL (1981), 'Eliminative Materialism and Propositional Attitudes', *Journal of Philosophy*, 78: 67–89.

CODY, C. (1990), *Testimony: A Philosophical Study* (Oxford University Press).

COLE, P. (ed.) (1978), *Syntax and Pragmatics, ix: Pragmatics* (Academic Press).

CRIMMINS, M. (1992), *Talk About Beliefs* (MIT Press).

—— and PERRY, J. (1989), 'The Prince and the Phone Booth: Reporting Puzzling Beliefs', *Journal of Philosophy*, 86: 685–711.

DAVIDSON, D. (1980*a*), 'Actions, Reasons, and Causes', in Davidson (1980*c*).

—— (1980*b*), 'Mental Events', in Davidson (1980*c*).

—— (1980*c*), *Essays on Actions and Events* (Oxford University Press).

—— (1984*a*), 'On Saying That', in Davidson (1984*c*).

—— (1984*b*), 'Truth and Meaning', in Davidson (1984*c*).

—— (1984*c*), *Inquiries into Truth and Interpretation* (Oxford University Press).

—— (2001*a*), 'What is Present to the Mind', in Davidson (2001*b*).

—— (2001*b*), *Subjective, Intersubjective, Objective* (Oxford University Press).

DENNETT, D. (1988), 'Review of J. Fodor, *Psychosemantics*', *Journal of Philosophy*, 85: 384–9.

DEVITT, M., and STERELNY, K. (1987), *Language and Reality: An Introduction to the Philosophy of Language* (MIT Press).

DRETSKE, F. (1981), *Knowledge and the Flow of Information* (MIT Press).

—— (1988), *Explaining Behavior: Reasons in a World of Causes* (MIT Press).

—— (1990), 'Does Meaning Matter?', in Villanueva (1990).

DUMMETT, M. (1976), 'What is a Theory of Meaning? (II)', in Evans and McDowell (1976).

DUMMETT, M. (1981), *Frege, Philosophy of Language*, 2nd edn. (Duckworth).

EARMAN, J., and ROBERTS, J. (1999), '*Ceteris Paribus*, There is No Problem of Provisos', *Synthese*, 118: 439–78.

EDGINGTON, D. (1986), 'Do Conditionals Have Truth Conditions?', *Critica*, 18: 3–30.

—— (1995), 'On Conditionals', *Mind*, 104: 235–329.

—— (1996), 'Vagueness by Degrees', in Keefe and Smith (1996).

EVANS, G. (1982), *The Varieties of Reference* (Oxford University Press).

—— (1985*a*), 'Can there be Vague Objects?', in Evans (1985*b*).

—— (1985*b*), *Collected Papers* (Oxford University Press).

——and MCDOWELL, J. (eds.) (1976), *Truth and Meaning: Essays in Semantics* (Oxford University Press).

FEYERABEND, P. (1963), 'Materialism and the Mind–Body Problem', *Review of Metaphysics*, 17: 49–66.

FIELD, H. (1980), *Science without Numbers* (Princeton University Press).

—— (1989), *Realism, Mathematics and Modality* (Blackwell).

—— (2001*a*), 'Attributions of Meaning and Content', in Field (2001*c*).

—— (2001*b*), 'Deflationist Views of Meaning and Content', in Field (2001*c*).

—— (2001*c*), *Truth and the Absence of Fact* (Oxford University Press).

—— (2001*d*), 'Mental Representation', in Field (2001*c*).

—— (2001*e*), 'Indeterminacy, Degree of Belief, and Excluded Middle', in Field (2001*c*).

—— (forthcoming), 'The Semantic Paradoxes and the Paradoxes of Vagueness', in Beall (forthcoming).

FINE, K. (1975), 'Vagueness, Truth and Logic', *Synthese*, 30: 265–300.

—— (2001), 'The Question of Realism', *Philosophers' Imprint*, 1: 1–30.

FODOR, J. (1987), *Psychosemantics: The Problem of Meaning in the Philosophy of Mind* (MIT Press).

—— (1990*a*), 'Review of Stephen Schiffer's *Remnants of Meaning*', in Fodor (1990*b*).

—— (1990*b*), *A Theory of Content and Other Essays* (MIT Press).

—— (1990*c*), 'A Theory of Content, I: The Problem' and 'A Theory of Content, II: The Theory', in Fodor (1990*b*).

—— (1991), 'You Can Fool Some of the People All the Time, Everything Else Being Equal: Hedged Laws and Psychological Explanations', *Mind*, 100: 19–34.

—— (1998), *Concepts: Where Cognitive Science Went Wrong* (Oxford University Press).

FREGE, G. (1892), 'On Sense and Reference', *Zeitschrift für Philosophie und philosophische Kritik*, 100: 25–50.

FRICKER, L. (1995), 'Critical Notice of C. A. J. Coady: *Testimony: A Philosophical Study*', *Mind*, 104: 393–411.

—— (2003), 'Understanding and Knowledge of What is Said', in Barber (2003).

GIBBARD, A. (1981), 'Two Recent Theories of Conditionals', in Harper *et al.* (1981).

—— (1990), *Wise Choices, Apt Feelings: A Theory of Normative Judgment* (Harvard University Press).

GOODMAN, N. (1947), 'The Problem of Counterfactual Conditionals', *Journal of Philosophy*, 44: 113–28.

GRAFF, D. (2000), 'Shifting Sands: An Interest-Relative Theory of Vagueness', *Philosophical Topics*, 28: 45–81.

GRICE, H. P. (1989*a*), 'Logic and Conversation', in Grice (1989*b*).

—— (1989*b*), *Studies in the Ways of Words* (Harvard University Press).

GRIMM, R., and MERRILL, D. (eds.) (1987), *Contents of Thought: Proceedings of the 1985 Oberlin Colloquium in Philosophy* (University of Arizona Press).

HALE, B., and WRIGHT, C. (2000), 'Implicit Definition and the A Priori', in Boghossian and Peacocke (2000).

HAMPSHIRE, S. (1959), *Thought and Action* (Chatto & Windus).

HARE, R. M. (1952), *The Language of Morals* (Oxford University Press).

—— (1963), *Freedom and Reason* (Oxford University Press).

HARPER, W., STALNAKER, R., and PEARCE, C. (eds.) (1981), *Ifs* (Reidel).

HOLTON, R. (2000), Reviews of John McDowell, *Meaning, Knowledge, and Reality*, and *Mind, Value, and Reality*, *Times Literary Supplement*, 23 June 2000.

HORGAN, T. (1989), 'Mental Quausation', *Philosophical Perspectives*, 3: 47–76.

HORWICH, P. (1998), *Meaning* (Oxford University Press).

—— (2000*a*), 'Stephen Schiffer's Theory of Vagueness', *Philosophical Issues*, 10: 271–81.

—— (2000*b*), 'The Sharpness of Vague Terms', *Philosophical Topics*, 28: 83–92.

HUME, D. (1739/1911), *A Treatise of Human Nature* (J. M. Dent).

—— (1751/1957), *An Enquiry Concerning the Principles of Morals* (Liberal Arts Press).

JACKSON, F. (1987), *Conditionals* (Blackwell).

—— (1998), *From Metaphysics to Ethics: A Defence of Conceptual Analysis* (Oxford University Press).

—— and PETTIT, P. (1988), 'Functionalism and Broad Content', *Mind*, 97: 381–400.

—— —— (1990), 'Program Explanation: A General Perspective', *Analysis*, 50: 107–17.

JOHNSTON, M. (1988), 'The End of the Theory of Meaning', *Mind and Language*, 3: 23–42.

KAMP, J. (1975), 'Two Theories about Adjectives', in Keenan (1975).

KAPLAN, D. (1978), 'Dthat', in Cole (1978).

—— (1989), 'Demonstratives: An Essay on the Semantics, Logic, Metaphysics, and Epistemology of Demonstratives and Other Indexicals', in Almog *et al.* (1989).

KEEFE, R., and SMITH, P. (eds.) (1996), *Vagueness: A Reader* (MIT Press).

KEENAN, E. (ed.) (1975), *Formal Semantics of Natural Language* (Cambridge University Press).

KIM, J. (1996), *Philosophy of Mind* (Westview Press).

——(1998), *Mind in a Physical World: An Essay on the Mind–Body Problem and Mental Causation* (MIT Press).

KING, J. (forthcoming), 'Designating Propositions', *Philosophical Review*.

KRIPKE, S. (1973), John Locke Lectures.

——(1979), 'A Puzzle About Belief', in A. Margalit (ed.), *Meaning and Use* (Reidel).

——(1980), *Naming and Necessity* (Harvard University Press).

LARSON, R., and LUDLOW, P. (1993), 'Interpreted Logical Forms', *Synthese*, 95: 305–55.

——and SEGAL, G. (1995), *Knowledge of Meaning: An Introduction to Semantic Theory* (MIT Press).

LEWIS, D. (1983a), 'Mad Pain and Martian Pain', in Lewis (1983d).

——(1983b), 'An Argument for the Identity Theory', in Lewis (1983d).

——(1983c), 'Languages and Language', in Lewis (1983d).

——(1983d), *Philosophical Papers*, vol. i (Oxford University Press).

——(1986a), 'Counterfactual Dependence and Time's Arrow', in Lewis (1986b).

——(1986b), *Philosophical Papers*, vol. ii (Oxford University Press).

——(1986c), 'Probabilities of Conditionals and Conditional Probabilities', in Lewis (1986b).

——(1988), 'Vague Identity: Evans Misunderstood', *Analysis*, 48: 128–30.

——(1999a), 'Many, but Almost One', in Lewis (1999b).

——(1999b), *Papers in Metaphysics and Epistemology* (Cambridge University Press).

LINSKY, L. (ed.) (1952), *Semantics and the Philosophy of Language* (University of Illinois Press).

LOAR, B. (1987), 'Social Content and Psychological Content', in Grimm and Merrill (1987).

LOEWER, B., and REY, G. (eds.) (1991), *Meaning in Mind: Essays on the Work of Jerry Fodor* (Blackwell).

LUDLOW, P. (1995), 'Logical Form and the Hidden-Indexical Theory: A Reply to Schiffer', *Journal of Philosophy*, 92: 102–7.

——(1996), 'The Adicity of "Believes" and the Hidden Indexical Theory', *Analysis*, 56: 97–101.

LUKASIEWICZ, J., and TARSKI, A. (1956), 'Investigations into the Sentential Calculus', in Tarski (1956a).

MCCLAMROCK, R. (1995), *Existential Cognition: Computational Minds in the World* (University of Chicago Press).

MCDOWELL, J. (1998a), 'Functionalism and Anomalous Monism', in McDowell (1998b).

McDOWELL, J. (1998*b*), *Mind, Value, and Reality* (Harvard University Press).

—— (1998*c*), 'Meaning, Communication, and Knowledge', in McDowell (1998*d*).

—— (1998*d*), *Meaning, Knowledge, and Reality* (Harvard University Press).

McGEE, V., and McLAUGHLIN, B. (1994), 'Distinctions without a Difference', *Southern Journal of Philosophy*, 33, suppl., 203–51.

McGINN, C. (1989), *Mental Content* (Blackwell).

MACKIE, J. (1977), *Ethics: Inventing Right and Wrong* (Penguin Books).

MARQUEZE, J. R., 'Partial Belief and Borderline Cases', *Philosophical Issues*, 10: 289–301.

MATES, B. (1952), 'Synonymity', in Linsky (1952).

MELDEN, A. (1961), *Free Action* (Routledge & Kegan Paul).

MILLIKAN, R. (1984), *Language, Thought, and Other Biological Categories* (MIT Press).

MOLTMANN, F. (2002), 'Nominalizing Quantifiers', unpub. ms.

MOORE, G. E. (1903), *Principia Ethica* (Cambridge University Press).

PARFIT, D. (1984), *Reasons and Persons* (Oxford University Press).

PAUTZ, A. (forthcoming), 'An Argument against Fregean That-Clause Semantics'.

PEACOCKE, C. (1992), *A Study of Concepts* (MIT Press).

—— (forthcoming), 'Moral Rationalism'.

PETERS, R. (1958), *The Concept of Motivation* (Routledge & Kegan Paul).

POPPER, K. (1959), *The Logic of Scientific Discovery* (Basic Books).

PUTNAM, H. (1975*a*), 'The Meaning of "Meaning" ', in Putnam (1975*b*).

—— (1975*b*), *Mind, Language and Reality: Philosophical Papers*, vol. ii (Cambridge University Press).

—— (1983), 'Vagueness and Alternative Logic', *Erkenntnis*, 19: 297–314.

RAFFMAN, D. (1994), 'Vagueness without Paradox', *Philosophical Review*, 103: 41–74.

RAMSEY, F. (1931), *The Foundations of Mathematics* (Routledge & Kegan Paul).

READ, S., and WRIGHT, C. (1985), 'Hairier than Putnam Thought', *Analysis*, 45: 56–8.

RICHARD, M. (1990), *Propositional Attitudes: An Essay on Thoughts and How we Ascribe Them* (Cambridge University Press).

RORTY, R. (1970), 'In Defense of Eliminative Materialism', *Review of Metaphysics*, 24: 112–21.

RUSSELL, B. (1910*a*), 'Knowledge by Acquaintance and Knowledge by Description', in Russell (1910*b*).

—— (1910*b*), *Mysticism and Logic* (Unwin Books).

—— (1956*a*), *Bertrand Russell: Logic and Knowledge, Essays 1901–1950*, ed. R. Marsh (George Allen & Unwin).

—— (1956*b*), 'On Denoting', in Russell (1956*a*).

RYLE, G. (1949), *The Concept of Mind* (Barnes & Noble).

SAINSBURY, M. (1986), 'Degrees of Belief and Degrees of Truth', *Philosophical Papers*, 15: 97–106.

SALMON, N. (1986), *Frege's Puzzle* (MIT Press).

—— (1995), 'Being of Two Minds: Belief and Doubt', *Noûs*, 29: 1–20.

—— (2001), 'Mythical Objects', in Campbell *et al.* (2001).

SCHIFFER, S. (1972), *Meaning* (Oxford University Press); paperback edn. with new introd., 1988.

—— (1977), 'Naming and Knowing', *Midwest Studies in Philosophy*, 2: 28–41.

—— (1978), 'The Basis of Reference', *Erkenntnis*, 13: 171–206.

—— (1987*a*), *Remnants of Meaning* (MIT Press).

—— (1987*b*), 'The "Fido"–Fido Theory of Belief', *Philosophical Perspectives*, 1: 455–80.

—— (1990), 'Meaning and Value', *Journal of Philosophy*, 87: 602–14.

—— (1991), '*Ceteris Paribus* Laws', *Mind*, 100: 1–17.

—— (1992), 'Belief Ascriptions', *Journal of Philosophy*, 89: 499–521.

—— (1993), 'Compositional Supervenience Theories and Compositional Meaning Theories', *Analysis*, 53: 24–9.

—— (1994), 'A Paradox of Meaning', *Noûs*, 28: 279–324.

—— (1995*a*), 'Descriptions, Indexicals, and Belief Reports: Some Dilemmas (But Not the Ones you Expect)', *Mind*, 104: 107–31.

—— (1995*b*), 'Reply to Ray', *Noûs*, 29: 397–401.

—— (1995–6), 'Contextualist Solutions to Scepticism', *Proceedings of the Aristotelian Society for 1995/96*, 96: 317–33.

—— (1996), 'The Hidden-Indexical Theory's Logical-Form Problem: A Rejoinder', *Analysis*, 56: 92–7.

—— (1998), 'Two Issues of Vagueness', *The Monist*, 88: 193–214.

—— (1999), 'The Epistemic Theory of Vagueness', *Philosophical Perspectives*, 13: 481–503.

—— (2000*a*), 'Horwich on Meaning: Critical Study of Paul Horwich's *Meaning*', *Philosophical Quarterly*, 50: 527–36.

—— (2000*b*), 'Vagueness and Partial Belief', *Philosophical Issues*, 10: 220–57.

—— (2000*c*), 'Replies to Commentators on "Vagueness and Partial Belief"', *Philosophical Issues*, 10: 321–43.

—— (2001*a*), 'Meanings', in Campbell *et al.* (2001).

—— (2001*b*), 'Communication', in Smelser and Baltes (2001).

—— (2002), 'Amazing Knowledge', *Journal of Philosophy*, 99: 200–2.

—— (forthcoming), 'That-Clauses and the Semantics of Belief Reports', *Facta Philosophica*.

SEARLE, J. (1979), *Expression and Meaning* (Cambridge University Press).

—— (1989), 'Direct Reference and Propositional Attitudes', in J. Almog, J. Perry, and H. Wettstein (eds.), *Themes from Kaplan* (Oxford University Press).

SMELSER, N., and BALTES, P. (eds.) (2001), *The International Encyclopedia of the Social and Behavioral Sciences* (Elsevier Sciences).

SOAMES, S. (2002), *Beyond Rigidity: The Unfinished Agenda of Naming and Necessity* (Oxford University Press).

SORENSEN, R. (1988), *Blindspots* (Oxford University Press).

STALNAKER, R. (1968), 'A Theory of Conditionals', *Studies in Logical Theory*, American Philosophical Quarterly Monograph Series 2, 98–112.

—— (1975), 'Indicative Conditionals', *Philosophia*, 5: 269–86.

—— (1984), *Inquiry* (MIT Press).

—— (2001), 'On Considering a Possible World as Actual', *Proceedings of the Aristotelian Society*, suppl. vol. 65: 141–56.

STAMPE, D. (1977), 'Towards a Causal Theory of Linguistic Representation', *Midwest Studies in Philosophy*, 1: 42–63.

STANLEY, J., and WILLIAMSON, T. (2001), 'Knowing How', *Journal of Philosophy*, 98: 411–44.

STEVENSON, C. L. (1944), *Ethics and Language* (Yale University Press).

STEWART, D. (1970), 'Of Abstraction', excerpt from *Elements of the Philosophy of the Human Mind*, vol. ii, in van Iten (1970).

STICH, S. (1978), 'Autonomous Psychology and the Belief–Desire Thesis', *The Monist*, 61: 201–27.

TARSKI, A. (1956a), *Logic, Semantics, Metamathematics* (Oxford University Press).

—— (1956b), 'A Semantic Conception of Truth', in Tarski (1956a).

VAN FRAASSEN, B. (1966), 'Singular Terms, Truth-Value Gaps, and Free Logic', *Journal of Philosophy*, 63: 481–95.

VAN ITEN, R. (ed.) (1970), *The Problem of Universals* (Appleton Century Crofts).

VILLANUEVA, E. (ed.) (1990), *Information, Semantics and Epistemology* (Blackwell).

WEDGWOOD, R. (2001), 'Conceptual-Role Semantics for Moral Terms', *Philosophical Review*, 110: 1–30.

WILLIAMSON, T. (1994), *Vagueness* (Routledge).

—— (1999), 'Schiffer on the Epistemic Theory of Vagueness', *Philosophical Perspectives*, 13: 505–17.

WINCH, P. (1958), *The Idea of a Social Science* (Routledge & Kegan Paul).

WITTGENSTEIN, L. (1953), *Philosophical Investigations* (Blackwell).

WOODFIELD, A. (ed.) (1982), *Thought and Object: Essays on Intentionality* (Oxford University Press).

WRIGHT, C. (1983), *Frege's Conception of Numbers as Objects* (Aberdeen University Press).

—— (1992), *Truth and Objectivity* (Harvard University Press).

—— (2001), 'On Being in a Quandary: Relativism, Vagueness, Logical Revisionism', *Mind*, 110 (Jan.), 45–98.

INDEX